Facets of an Academic's Life

Michael Wertheimer

Facets of an
Academic's Life

A Memoir

 Springer

Michael Wertheimer
Department of Psychology and
Neuroscience
University of Colorado Boulder
Boulder, CO, USA

ISBN 978-3-658-28769-6   ISBN 978-3-658-28770-2   (eBook)
https://doi.org/10.1007/978-3-658-28770-2

This Springer imprint is published by the registered company Springer Fachmedien Wiesbaden GmbH part of Springer Nature.
The registered company address is: Abraham-Lincoln-Str. 46, 65189 Wiesbaden, Germany

Michael Wertheimer

Preface

I have been blessed, awesomely so, by an amazingly rich, varied, and fulfilling life for which I am immensely grateful. But who, if anyone, might be interested in reading an account of the life of a more than ninety year old retired professor? Several different readers of earlier drafts of this manuscript suggested that various phases or aspects of my life might be of modest interest to quite different audiences: those interested in experiences of an immigrant from Europe to the United States, or in the career of a twentieth-century academic, mountaineering in Colorado, involvement in various professional associations, extensive national and international travels, and perhaps even fascination with multilingualism.

Accordingly, the narrative presented here is relatively brief, and a few appendices provide details about such things as a childhood "newspaper" I published for a short time, my travels, my scholarly efforts, my roles in a variety of professional organizations, and my experiences after retirement. The reader is urged to skip those pages that provide information about aspects of my life in which the reader isn't really interested.

Anyone who prefers to start looking at this memoir by getting a kind of overview of the author's entire life is encouraged to start by reading Chapter 11, "Who Am I?".

Early drafts of this manuscript were entitled "Musings about a Memoir," "A Psychologist's Saga," or "Notes for an Autobiography." One alternative title, "Opa's Opus," was based on the German "Opa," roughly equivalent to a kind of informal but respectful English "Grandpa"; my role as currently the oldest surviving member of my large and supportive family and clan is indeed a core part of my identity. Other titles have come to mind, but none have seemed truly appropriate, although the present one feels sort of okay.

Several grandkids, kids, colleagues, and friends did suggest over the years that I should write something about my life. It's true that I have written quite a few books, articles for technical journals, and other pieces, but almost all of them have been about psychology. As a youngster, like almost all my contemporaries, I tried my hand at composing poetry and generating short essays but, including a few actually published in summer camp newsletters or even a college "literary magazine," few if any of them are all that memorable. Besides, they were all just fiction or imagination.

So this task was a new one for me: not something semi-technical about psychology or its history, nor something just made up for the fun of it: I should try to record facts about my life. Facts. Or at least my best effort to remember events, people, places in my life without their being only figments of my fallible memory. Human memory being what it is, it is unlikely that everything one "remembers" is actually factually true; human memory is notorious for being creative: many recollections of past events are distortions of veridical truth—or even fabrications. But one should try to avoid recounting as fact anything about which there is reasonable doubt. A daunting task, but it appeared likely to be fun to try my hand at it nevertheless.

Every human life is unique. And given my belief, which I learned during my college years from the Quakers, that "there is that of God in everyone," every human life is inherently and intrinsically valuable. Maybe there is even "something of God" in me, but I know that, like doubtless every other human being, I have done many things which I now regret. Indeed, some of my misdeeds have brought me to episodes of despair. But there have also been many things that have happened to me, and even a few things that I have done, that I believe were good. In fact, I have been blessed with so much, far more, I'm sure, than most of the rest of humanity. And it is rather frightening to realize that there are now so many of us—some seven billion, and increasing exponentially—who are all trying to have the same privileges that have been my fortunate lot; the result is that we are polluting our home planet and rapidly using up non-renewable resources such as clean water, fossil fuels, and pure air. Unless the human race manages to learn how to live productively and sparingly with the boons that the earth provides, it is in danger of annihilating itself either by unbelievably efficient weaponry or by simply using up limited and essential resources necessary for sustaining not only human life but all other forms of life as well.

But now that my rich, full, sometimes frustrating but always privileged life is approaching its end, even though my generation appears to have become aware of the hazards awaiting our species unless it changes its profligate ways, it no longer seems to be a task essential to my own generation to save our planet and its resources for future generations. Yet that task is near at hand; my children, my children's children, and especially my great-grandchildren (of whom there are now twelve) will not be able to avoid confronting the risks to the human species in the way that my generation and its predecessors have. So, I do hope that human ingenuity, sacrifice, courage, and determination will succeed in dealing with this potentially enormous problem.

Such thoughts, though, stray from the present job. The task should be to tell my story (which, like every biography, is both unique and also in a sense universal) dispassionately, accurately, and factually. I will endeavor to tell the truth, and not limit the narrative to only the many good things I have experienced and have done. The regretted, the unpleasant, even the unconscionable should at least occasionally be recorded together with the positive. But there is no point in telling too much about the sleazy side of my life; yet I will try to be honest. If my effort ends up offending someone, let me apologize for that here and now. But I believe a reasonably straightforward account (in the sense of including much that I happen to remember, both the good and even a bit of the bad) will be more honest than a carefully edited and expurgated overly positive narrative.

What follows kept me occupied off and on for some seven years when other chores weren't screaming for higher priority. Much of it was first written not in Boulder, Colorado, where I've been living for over half a century, but in Phoenix, OR, or nearby Ashland, OR, while my wife Marilyn and I were visiting her brother Jack Schuman there. Jack, retired from teaching the history of art at Washington State University in Pullman, WA, is Marilyn's only living blood relative. He used to visit us for a couple of weeks in Boulder annually for many years (and we'd visit him annually for two weeks in Washington and later the Ashland, OR, region after he retired there), but during the last half decade or so he preferred not to travel away from Oregon any more, so we've been visiting him twice annually now for a couple of weeks at a time, lately in his cottage at a retirement community in northern Ashland. Much of the manuscript for this project was first drafted there while Jack and Marilyn were taking naps or were watching political shows on television of which I had experienced more than enough for my taste.

My word-processing "equipment," as it has been throughout my long career, consisted of pencil, paper, and eraser; those first drafts were put into electronic form by a granddaughter and great-granddaughter, and then my editing of that material was duly made electronic by my daughter. I am deeply grateful to all three of these generous and competent ladies. A fairly large number of friends and relatives looked over the draft after that and made useful suggestions, many of which were used to generate the version you have now. Remaining errors in it are, of course, my fault (even though inadvertent).

Table of Contents

List of Figures

1 Childhood in Germany

My paternal ancestry is already fairly well documented in the biography of my father, Max Wertheimer, published by Transaction Publishers of Rutgers University Press in 2005, and in other places, so I needn't elaborate on it too much here. But a few thoughts nonetheless:

I was early informed that there was a Baron von Wertheim in my ancestry, probably sometime in the 18th century, that Wertheim is a venerable town in what is now Germany, and that for some reason he decided to drop the "von" from the family name and changed it to "Wertheimer."

"Wertheimer" in German of course means someone from Wertheim, as "von Wertheim" also meant. And "Wertheim" meant and means something like "valued" or "valuable" home: the German "Wert" or "value" is a cognate of English "worth"; the German "Heim" is a cognate of the English word "home." I recall hearing that there used to be a family coat of arms, consisting of a string of pearls above a bucket or pail; the string of pearls symbolized value or worthiness (German "Wert" or, in the older spelling, "Werth") and the pail is a kind of pun on the German "Eimer," or bucket. Whether this coat of arms ever truly existed or whether my father or one of his ancestors made it up as a kind of joke will never be known.

My mother, Anni Caro, came of physicians' families on both sides. Her father, Rudolph Caro, was the son of a doctor and a doctor himself; he died young because he became mortally infected by a patient. Two of her mother's uncles were doctors, and her mother's brother, Ludwig Pick, was a pathologist known for his contributions to the understanding of Niemann-Pick disease and the rare Lubarsch-Pick syndrome (as well as a rabbi who in 1912 published a short book titled *Die Weltanschauung des Judentums*

1-1 My mother when I was little
(family archives)

© Springer Fachmedien Wiesbaden GmbH, part of Springer Nature 2020
M. Wertheimer, *Facets of an Academic's Life*,
https://doi.org/10.1007/978-3-658-28770-2_1

[The World View of Judaism] and, like one of my mother's two sisters, died in a Nazi concentration camp). My father and mother were a rather unlikely couple; she was some twenty years younger than he. They were married in Berlin, where she was a university student.

1-2 My mother and father at their 1923 wedding *(family archives)*

She told me that she fell in love with my father's Gestalt theory, about which she heard him lecture, and married him to make sure that he would have offspring.

Family lore has it that he had been in love with a sister of the renowned artist Käthe Kollwitz, Lisbeth Stern. Lisbeth at the time was married to a successful industrialist, Georg Stern. My father was actually for years a member of the Berlin household of Georg and Lisbeth Stern; the couple had four daughters, all of whom were also fond of my father. I have wondered about the nature of this "ménage à trois" since my childhood, when I first heard about it, but never did find out all that much about it. I do know that Georg wrote the music for an opera that he and my mother planned to write; it was never completed. I recall a brief passage from it; when or how I found out about it I don't recall ("Herodes sprach: 'Kommt 'rein zu mir; ich will Euch geben Wein und Bier. Ich will Euch geben Nahrung.'" ["Herod spoke: 'Come in to me; I want to give you wine and beer. I want to give you nourishment.'"]).

Lisbeth wrote and illustrated a wonderful simplified account of Genesis in the Bible, with carefully done and beautiful watercolor paintings of the biblical events, dedicated to "Wertheimer's children" (in German, of course), a handmade book from 1936 or 1937 that I still own. A copy of this book appears in Appendix A. On my fireplace mantelpiece, I also have a striking small clay sculpture of a destitute elderly woman sitting with a baby at her feet, also made by Lisbeth Stern. (There is a picture of this statuette on page 531.) Käthe Kollwitz at some point apparently claimed that her sister Lisbeth was at least as good an artist as she herself was.

1-3 Lisbeth Stern (then Schmidt), 1890 *(courtesy of Kollwitz estate © Käthe Kollwitz Museum Cologne)*

I also remember in detail a mournful, tragic old song, in minor and in dialect, which we were told was a favorite of Käthe Kollwitz, and which became a beloved part of the many songs sung by my family when I was a child:

Es soll sich kein Mensch mit der Liebe abgeben.
Sie brachte so manchen jungen Kerl ums Leben.
Nu hat mir mein Truschel die Treu ufgesaget;
Ik hab se verklaget.
    Tü te rü tü tü tü, Tü te rü tü tü tü.

Dat kommt wenn man d' Mädchen zum Tanze lasst gahne.
Da muss man ja immer in Sorgen erstahne:
Dass sie sich verlieben in andere Knechte;
Solch' Menschen sind schlechte.
    Tü te rü tü tü tü, Tü te rü tü tü tü.

Und bin ich gestorben, so lasst mich begrabe'.
Und lasst mir sechs hölzerne Bretter abschlage'.
Zwei feurige Herzen die sollt ihr druf mahle.
Ik kanns' ja bezahle.
    Tü te rü tü tü tü, Tü te rü tü tü tü.

Und lasst mir auch singen die Sterbegesänge.
Da liegt nun der Esel die Kreuz und die Länge.
Im Leben da hatt' er manch' Liebesaffäre;
Zu Dreck muss ei were.
    Tü te rü tü tü tü, Tü te rü tü tü tü.

Translation:

No person should give in to love.
It brought quite a few young fellows to end their lives.
Now my beloved has broken her betrothal;
I took her to court.
    Tü te rü tü tü tü, Tü te rü tü tü tü [nonsense syllables].

That's what happens if you let the girls go to the dance.
You always have to fall into worries—
That they will fall in love with other fellows;
Such people are bad.
    Tü te rü tü tü tü, Tü te rü tü tü tü.

And when I die, let me be buried.
And let six wooden boards be cut for me.
Two fiery hearts should you paint on them;
I can pay for it.
    Tü te rü tü tü tü, Tü te rü tü tü tü.

And let the dirges also be sung for me.
There the donkey lies all stretched out.
In life he had some love affairs;
To dirt he must return.
    Tü te rü tü tü tü, Tü te rü tü tü tü.

My daughter came up with the following translation, which isn't quite as literal but does fit the rhyming pattern and melody of the German version even better:

Now love is a thing one should never give in to;
It's ended some young men and all they have been through.
She said we would wed, now says I was on trial;
My complaint is on file.
    Tü te rü tü tü tü, Tü te rü tü tü tü.

That happens if you let girls go out to dances;
Your grief is begun and goodbye to your chances.
They'll fall for new guys and forget what you had;
Such people are ba-ad.
    Tü te rü tü tü tü, Tü te rü tü tü tü.

And when I have died, let me buriéd be.
And let them cut six wooden boards out for me.
Paint two fiery hearts on the sides of the boards flat;
My estate can afford that.
    Tü te rü tü tü tü, Tü te rü tü tü tü.

And let them sing dirges—I know they have practice:
Stretched out in that coffin there lies one more jackass.
In life he went through some affairs of the heart;
From this world he must part.
    Tü te rü tü tü tü, Tü te rü tü tü tü.

My mother and father were married in 1923, after my father had taken his be-
trothed to play string quartet with his friend the famous physicist Albert Einstein
and his wife. My mother reported that on that occasion Einstein's wife was wearing ribbons crossed over her nose which, it turned out, were there to hide an
insect bite, and that Einstein did not play the violin very well. My father played
viola and my mother second violin. She didn't report who was playing cello.

Their first child, named Rudolf after my mother's father, died a few weeks after he was born, of an infection in his navel. Their next son, Valentin Jakob
Thomas, was born May 12, 1925, and had a minor heart arrhythmia at birth (he
died suddenly at age 53 in 1978 after being a highly successful lawyer for the
Amalgamated Clothing Workers Union in New York). And then I was born on
March 20, 1927, in Berlin (the district of Karlshorst). My sister, Lise, was born
there too, on October 12, 1928.

*
**

Early childhood memories
tend to be sparse and often
somewhat inaccurate. Not surprisingly, I have no memories
of Berlin. The family moved to
Frankfurt in 1929 and I do have
a few rudimentary memories
from my four years there, from
1929 to 1933.

1-4 My father playing his viola *(family archives)*

1-5 Me, about 1929 *(family archives)*

But first a few comments about our names. As I just mentioned, Rudolf Wilhelm Walter Georg, the first born, was named after my mother's father. The middle names were probably for my father's father Wilhelm and for my father's then-deceased older brother Walter—and possibly Georg Stern.

According to family lore, Valentin was named after a town in Switzerland, St. Valentin, where he was presumably conceived. Jakob was the name of Max's mother's brother (Onkel Jakob), so that may be where Val's first middle name came from. Why he had a second middle name, I don't know, and I am unaware of any Thomas among any of our ancestors.

Lise was named Lisbeth Ruszena: the first name is clearly after my father's long-time first love, Lisbeth Stern, and the second is Czech, Rosa in English, the same as my father's mother's name. The sources of my own names are another story; I have no idea where either Michael or Matthew (Mathias, on my birth certificate) came from.

I have been fascinated by names since my earliest years. I am also aware of the many names that have been used for me during my own lifetime. I presume that it is true of most people that there are strict rules about who may use which names for whom under what particular circumstances; many taboos apply to the use of names. Use of a "wrong" name at any time can be a source of insult, embarrassment, confusion, and even offense. In my case, depending on various relationships and various changes in my life, I have been Michel, Mikey, Michelchen, Michael (with the German pronunciation that separates into three syllables), Michael (English, two syllables), Sie, Du (the German second person pronoun, formal and informal), Mr. Wertheimer, Dr. Wertheimer, Professor Wertheimer, Mike, Dr. Mike, Mr. Chairman, Mr. President, Papa, Pa, P, Sweetheart, Darling, Grandpa, Granddad, Opa, O-Opa, Uncle Mike, Hey you!, and several others that don't come to mind at the moment. To repeat, the rules for the use of particular versions of a name are exquisite and rigorous, and I could try to specify the circumstances under which each of these appellations has been appropriate during my lifetime, as well as those under which use of a particular variant would have been awkward or offensive. There's more on my names later, in Chapter 11.

1-6 My father and me, about 1929 *(family archives)*

But back to my very few memories of my childhood in Frankfurt. We lived in a rather large house (number 6, if my memory serves) on Klaus-Groth-Strasse, a fairly quiet side street; some blocks away was a major thoroughfare, the Eschersheimer Landstrasse, which we were taught to avoid because it had dangerous voluminous traffic. We had a modest yard with lawn, various bushes, and a rose garden. Val and I shared a room on the second floor, a fairly large bed-and-playroom painted in an off-white light cream color. We had separate beds and there were small cabinets with doors containing our toys. Among the toys I remember was a small metal car with rubber wheels in which I could ride, with a functioning steering wheel and pedals under the seat which could be used to propel the vehicle. I also remember a baby carriage in which Lise would lie on her back with her feet sticking straight up, with the soles of her feet parallel to the sky; this posture was a source of amusement and conversation in the family.

My father had a study on the third floor; in this room were numerous tables and shelves covered with piles of paper, as well as a harmonium (a reed organ pumped by pedals, with several stops that produced tones of different timbres)— but I hardly remember hearing him play it. The children were allowed to come visit him in this study, and ask for tasks to perform (chores that he would give us with paper and pencil, as "work"—"eibeiten," a distortion of the German word "arbeiten," to "work," comparable with what my father did in that room), after which we were encouraged to leave him alone again and go downstairs, so that he could resume his work, *his* "eibeiten." If he was very busy when we disturbed him there, we were encouraged to leave again and come back later. But usually he graciously found us some entertaining task to perform.

We had a pet cat whose name was Fuchsi, or "little fox." When I was three or four years old, I was given a caged yellow canary whom I named "Männlein," or "little man." It was my job to make sure he had water in a little porcelain tray at the bottom of the cage, as well as enough bird seed to keep him fed. I recall finding him dead one day at the bottom of his cage; I was told that the cat had done him in. I was very sad to have lost him, and soon he was replaced by another canary, who was again named "Männlein." I don't remember what happened to this second one.

Singing was part of family life from the beginning. It was an activity which we all enjoyed, with parents and children all joining in. Most of the songs were German folk songs from a then very popular songbook, the *Zupfgeigenhansl* or *Fiddle-Plucking Hans*; most of the songs in the book had indications of accompanying chords for guitar or piano. We would sing them in the evening after dinner with either my mother playing guitar or my father playing piano, sometimes with a fire in the living room fireplace (but this memory may be confused;

1-7 *Der Zupfgeigenhansl (family archives)*

1-8 "Bumsta" for my mother, about 1974; left to right: my brothers Peter and Val, me, Peter's daughter Monika, my mother Anni, my sister Lise, her daughter Rachel, and Val's daughter Ellen *(family archives)*

we may not have had a fireplace in the home until several years later, when we lived in New Rochelle, a suburb of New York City, where we also often sang songs after the evening meal).

Family rituals included birthday celebrations and Christmas. Part of every birthday celebration was a "Geburtstagstisch" or "birthday table" for the "birthday child" (so named whether child or adult): a small table with gifts, flowers, and candles (one for each year of the child's age) on some kind of birthday cake. One ritual was to "bumsta" (pronouncing the "u" like the "oo" in "book") the birthday child. The "child" was placed in the center of a ring composed of the other members of the family holding hands around the circle. Singing a nonsense ditty, "A la bumsta, bumsta bi; a la bumsta, bumsta bi; a la bumsta, bumsta bilibi, di bumsta, bumsta bi," the outer ring rotated in one direction while the "child" in the center, also singing, rotated in the other direction; the ditty was repeated, during which time the circle and center figure rotated in the other direction, all ending with the members of the outer circle hugging the "child" of honor. Also, when the birthday child first saw the birthday table and blew out the candles (including a "Lebenskerze" ["life candle"], a large center candle in addition to the smaller ones indicating the number of years), the rest of the family sang:

Heil sei der Tag an dem er [sie] uns erschienen,
Dideldum, dideldum, dideldum;
Es ist schon lange her; das freut uns umso mehr.
Wir könnten keinen besseren Michel [keine bessere Lise, etc.] finden,
Dideldum, dideldum, dideldum.
Es ist schon lange [emphasized] her; das freut uns umso mehr.

or

Hail to the day on which he [she] appeared to us,
Deedeldoom, deedeldoom, deedeldoom [nonsense syllables];
It is already long ago, which makes us all the happier.
We couldn't have found a better Mike [Lise, etc],
Deedeldoom, deedeldoom, deedeldoom.
It is already *long* ago, which makes us all the happier.

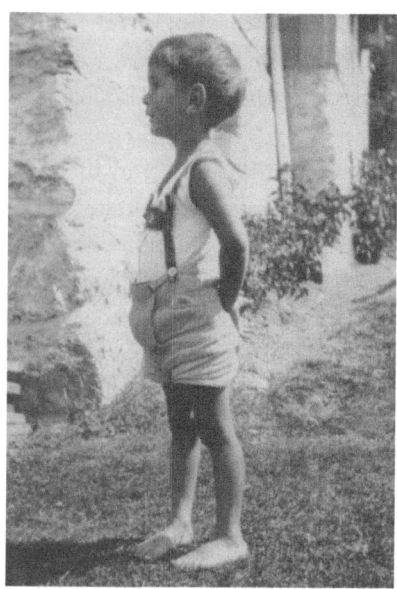

1-9 Me in Lederhosen, about 1930 *(family archives)*

This set of rituals continued throughout my life at birthday celebrations, and has been continued on into later generations.

For Christmas, we always had an evergreen tree with tinsel, glass balls of various sizes (small ones near the top of the tree, larger ones further down) that were bright solid red, green, blue, silver, or gold, and small metal clip-on candleholders with red or white wax candles, as well as a star for the top of the tree. We sang the traditional German carols. And on appropriate days once a week for the four weeks before the actual Christmas celebration, there were small "advent" celebrations. Marzipan, Lebkuchen, Pfeffernüsse, chocolate, nuts, and nonpareils (small circular pieces of chocolate raised in the center, strewn with tiny colored balls of hard sugar) were part of the Christmas rituals. And every member of the family (including servants and pets) had a small individual "Weihnachtstisch" or "Christmas table" with individual presents, some of which typically were hand made.

For Christmas, shortly before I was two years old, I was given an enormous stuffed teddy bear with somewhat mournful glass eyes. I named him "Gustav" (I don't know where that name came from) and he was a warm friend and solace for me for decades; he still exists now, some ninety years later, and was recently given to my daughter to keep as part of the paraphernalia in her fam-

1-10 Gustav *(family archives)*

ily archive. Gustav always listened with infinite patience whenever I complained to him about something, never uttered a discouraging word or any criticism, was always there for me, totally understanding and dependable.

Early on I was also given a much smaller stuffed bear, the flat back of whose head was used in a soothing ritual which involved my squeezing my nose and mouth on the soft fur on the back of his head, and saying "Mmm-meh" when I released the squeeze. Where this ritual came from and for how long I practiced it, I don't remember. I don't recall if this much smaller teddy bear ever had a name other than Mmm-meh, and I don't think he was considered any kind of relative to Gustav.

I remember two servants in Germany, Kätti Moser and Paula Schläger. My memories of Paula are dim; I think she did the dishes, the laundry, and the housecleaning and made the beds and was a relatively minor figure. Kätti was the chief servant; she probably did the cooking and helped take care of the children. She must have had a drinking problem, because I remember one event in which I saw my mother emptying a fairly large glass bottle of clear liquid into

1-11 Kätti with Val, or perhaps me
(family archives)

the toilet while Kätti stood lamenting next to her to no avail, clearly devastated at having the precious liquid (probably vodka or gin) get poured down the drain. Later, when the family decided to leave Germany for America, she wanted to come along, and I think my parents also wanted her to do so, but there must have been some visa problems or something else that prevented her from emigrating with us. She didn't come along, and I don't know what became of her.

Val taught me to read when I was about four years old. One reason I know that is that I recall getting a book at that age, a book of which I remembered the smell for a decade or so thereafter, even though I no longer can remember its smell at all. Indeed, I have been almost totally anosmic for most of my life. According to family lore, apparently I broke bits of plaster from the wall of my room and ate them. I don't actually remember doing so. Presumably some earlier occupant of that room had had scarlet fever. At any rate, I developed a rather severe case of scarlet fever at age four, and was bedridden for quite a while with it. Penicillin had not yet become a regular treatment for the disease, so in my case it ran its course without mitigation. I was given the book while sick and remember that I described its smell as "brown," pleasant, and rather distinctive; as I mentioned, that smell, or rather its memory, remained with me for a good decade or more afterwards, although my ability to smell almost anything disappeared from my life from then on. I could and still can sense coffee, gasoline, and a few other strong smells a little bit, but not much else. This anosmia hasn't troubled me, except that I have been totally unable to sense any perfumes and can't distinguish between plain hot water and any tea (other than by its slight bitterness). Indeed it had advantages when my own children were little, since I had no problem with changing and washing babies' diapers; I was unable to smell them. But one feature of my later life is a bit puzzling to me: I seem to have a reputation as a fairly good cook with my children and other members of the family. I do use spices, sparingly, in my cookery, and their contribution to food is at least largely attributed to aroma, but my use of spices (often after I become aware of their presumed appropriateness for various dishes by reading the labels of their containers) is, if anything, praised by those who eat foods I prepare. Yet I myself can't distinguish well among spices other than garlic, pepper, and several other rather strong ones. At any rate, my smell blindness has not interfered in any major way with my enjoyment of my life. Anosmia is obviously a far less debilitating blindness than visual blindness or deafness.

Probably just about every family develops a familect, or a use of language that is unique to that particular family. My family was no exception. In fact, we had a name for the use of familect terms; the familect was called "Nabadatz," and was almost certainly in use already while we were still in Germany, although its use continued after we emigrated to the United States. I only remember a few special words from it now, though I suspect there were quite a few others that I have forgotten. A "Kuller" was any round object that could roll; a "Laban" was any item that is long, thin, and light; a "Puripu" was a reflection of an image or the light thrown upon a wall by a prism hanging in a window in sunlight—and it

1-12 Val and my father, 1930 *(family archives)*

was also the name for a bit of dust. "Kabapsen" was the word for his coffee used by my father, who was called "Papsen" by us and by my mother when she referred to him while speaking with us. And my father used to tell us bedtime stories, including one character, Gelchen-Ku, a small round lady whose name sounded like a diminutive followed by "cow" but was actually derived from "Kugelchen," literally a diminutive sphere.

Occasionally, during the early years of their marriage, my father would bring a hot roll, a "Semmel," to my mother for breakfast; the family story was that a "Mohr" (which sounds the same as "Moor" in English) had brought it so fast that its friction with the air made it warm—and had also blackened the Moor's skin.

1-13 Painting of a family vacation, probably by Lisbeth Stern *(family archives)*

Family vacations occasionally took us to Switzerland or to northern Italy near the Lago Maggiore. I have a large water-color painting, probably by Lisbeth Stern, of us three children there in a mountainous landscape. There are black-and-white prints of family photographs of us on sand beaches, naked except for socks and shoes while on such vacations, or even at home in our back yard, but I don't have any actual memories of these trips. I do know that from my earliest childhood on I developed a love of mountains and of water; this love has stayed with me throughout my life.

I have a dim memory of watching my widowed grandfather Wilhelm's maid and valued house companion, Karolin, making apple strudel one day in Wilhelm's home in Prague by taking a small ball of dough, rolling it flat with a rolling pin on top of a small round table, and then pulling it out with her fingers into a very thin uniform sheet, which she stretched out and down on all sides of the table almost down to the floor. This memory must have come from an early year, when we visited my grandfather and Karolin in Prague. My grandfather, who died in 1930, had, according to some photographs of him, a magnificent white beard, but I don't have any actual memories of him.

Shortly before we left Europe, Val started being home schooled by my mother. She was also teaching Peter Kortner; I don't remember what our relation with the Kortners was, but I do know that Peter's father, Fritz (pictured on page 275), was a well known film star, and Peter's younger sister Manni, a large girl, was apparently a good friend of Lise, though I didn't get along very well with her myself.

Specific other snippets from that time include hunting in the neighborhood with Kätti or Paula for dog excrement to place as

1-14 My paternal grandfather, Wilhelm Wertheimer *(family archives)*

fertilizer at the base of rose bushes in our yard, searching in nearby woods for edible mushrooms with Paula, and being asked by some school official shortly before I was to begin going to school what it was I would like to be when I grew up—and answering "Postkutscher" or mailman (literally, mail-coach driver).

One other memory: A story in the brown book I got when I was sick with scarlet fever went something like this:

—Vati, ich habe eben hundert Häschen gesehen!	"Daddy, I just saw a hundred little rabbits!"
—Junge, du lügst.	"Boy, you're lying."
—Sicher waren es wenigstens sieben.	"For sure it was at least seven."
—Junge, du lügst.	"Boy, you're lying."
—Es war wenigstens ein Häschen.	"It was at least one little rabbit."
—Junge, du lügst.	"Boy, you're lying."
—Aber Vati, da raschelte doch 'was!	"But Daddy, somethin' rustled over there!"

Perhaps other memories from my first six years, in Germany, could be triggered by going through some old photographs and other mementos from that time, 1927 to 1933. But this is all that comes spontaneously to mind so far. It was a pleasant time for me, with loving parents, a warm and close older brother and younger sister, supportive and dependable servants, and long, interesting, and varied days.

2 Childhood in the United States

My rather idyllic childhood in Germany was disrupted by Adolf Hitler. Sometime early in January, 1933, my parents went to a neighbors' house several doors away to listen to a campaign radio speech by Hitler. We didn't have a radio in the house, but those neighbors did. Hitler was a candidate for election as Chancellor, and even though this particular talk was somewhat subdued because of a bad cold he had at the time, my parents were sufficiently concerned by the tone and message of his campaign speech that they decided on the way home from their neighbors' house to leave Germany the next day for Czechoslovakia to wait until this craziness was over; my father's father had owned some property in Prague. We escaped to Czechoslovakia to wait out the Hitler menace. The expectation was that we could stay there until after the election, and then go back to Frankfurt and resume our accustomed family life. But that, of course, is not how things worked out.

We left the next morning for Marianske Lasne, or Marienbad, where we rented rooms in a hotel called Die Goldene Harfe, or The Golden Harp. I don't have any specific memories of our sojourn there, which lasted until September, but I know that we had a number of visitors, including some relatives of Georg and Lisbeth Stern. It was probably during that time that I learned my one Czech phrase, one that has no vowels other than a vocalic "r": *Strč prst strs krk*, or "Stick your finger down your throat."

In April my father requested a leave of absence from the University of Frankfurt, where he had been teaching, but about the same time he learned that because of his Jewish ancestry he was, in effect, fired from his tenured professorship. Through various friends and colleagues he was given options for continuing his already very influential and successful academic career: a position in Oxford or Cambridge in England, in Jerusalem, or in New York. Why he chose to join the New School for Social Research in New York

2-1 Die Goldene Harfe *(from http://hamelika.webz.cz/h97-10.htm)*

© Springer Fachmedien Wiesbaden GmbH, part of Springer Nature 2020
M. Wertheimer, *Facets of an Academic's Life*,
https://doi.org/10.1007/978-3-658-28770-2_2

rather than either of the other universities I don't know, but I sure am grateful that he did. Early in September the five of us left Czechoslovakia for Cherbourg, France, where we were booked on the RMS *Majestic* to sail to New York. We went south and west through Switzerland and France in order to avoid Germany, and stopped for several days in Paris. I dimly recall my first taste of ice cream, which I probably had in Paris, pleasantly astounded by the sweet, cold, creamy, heavenly vanilla sensation. It may also have been in a hotel in Paris that I experienced what we called "Seifenpapier" or "soap paper": small thin pieces of paper that were covered with soap and that were presumably to be used only once when one was washing one's hands. I don't recall ever running across this particular commodity again any time during the rest of my life, but it made an impression on me at the time.

The *Majestic*, an immense vessel with a capacity of some 3000 passengers, was owned by the Cunard White Star Line; family lore had it (perhaps erroneously) that she was the largest ocean liner in the world at the time, and this was its final trans-Atlantic voyage. My memories of the trip are very dim. I do know that Rainer Schickele accompanied us on the trip; he was in effect a "Kindermädchen" or "children's maid," whose task it was to take care of the children during the crossing, which took about a week. Rainer became the father of a son who later was famous in the music world as "PDQ Bach." I remember my father sitting with a heavy sweater and a thick blanket on the deck in a folding deck chair, "working" as usual with pencil and paper, and I recall cups of delicious warm bouillon that were served on board. There was also shuffleboard available on the ship. Otherwise, the trip did not generate any other memories for this six-year-old child who felt quite safe in the bosom of his German-speaking family with his loving mother, father, older brother, and younger sister, together with the young man, Rainer, whom I hardly remember playing with us during the voyage.

I know we landed in New York, where we were met by a Miss Mayer (pictured on page 258), Clara Woolie Mayer, at the time an administrator and later Dean of the New School, who spoke some German with us and took us under her wing. We had a large amount of luggage, including big steamer trunks, which were deposited with us at Ellis Island. Somehow we ended up for a week or so in

2-2 Arrival in New York, September 1933. Left to right: Val, Anni, Lise, me, Max *(family archives)*

a Hotel Halle in Manhattan, and family lore holds that, when my mother went out to buy some cheese and bread, the family was astonished by what she brought back: that (American cheese) is *cheese*? This "Wattebrot" or "cotton bread" (probably white Wonder® bread) is *bread*? The family often later joked about the enormous difference between the tasty, firm German cheeses and "American cheese" and between the crusty, chewy, moist, dark German yeast breads and what was called bread in the United States.

My mother also shared with my niece Ellen a story about the first night in the hotel. As Ellen tells it: "Anni was with Max and others downstairs in the hotel, and had left my father [that is, my elder brother Val] in charge in the room the three children were in. There was a lot of homesickness, so my father, in his long white nightgown, found his way to the elevator, told the person operating the elevator 'Mama,' and pointed downwards. The elevator operator somehow took my father downstairs and helped him find Anni."

By late in September we were living in a fairly large rented house at 12 The Circle in New Rochelle, a suburb of New York. Several blocks away was a railroad station from which my father could catch a train of the New York, New Haven, and Hartford line that took him to downtown Manhattan, where the New School was located. We stayed in that rented house for ten years, and it became a real home. I can still picture it well in my mind.

12 The Circle

2-3 The Circle, seen from above *(imagery: Google 2019)*

The "Circle" contained a park some two or three city blocks wide and long, with a large grassy area as well as mature trees and a formal flower garden with hedges at its north end. Our house was across the street on the northeast side of this park, in a quiet residential area three blocks south of bustling North Avenue, which had lots of shops and the train station. We had a small front yard and a rather large back yard, with lawn, trees, a thriving bamboo patch in the northeast and a mature apple tree in the southeast corner, east of which there was for years a "victory garden," a vegetable patch that produced ample foodstuffs during the summer and fall. A large front porch and a small side porch with a nearby magnolia tree were among the many places we played outside, as well as in the park and the back yard.

The house had a big, dark cellar with a coal furnace and coal chute. Access to the cellar was via a steep staircase from the kitchen; there was also a staircase into the cellar from outside in the back yard, covered by two large green wooden doors at a 45-degree angle.

When one came into the house from the wrap-around front porch through a large, heavy, white-painted wood

2-4 12 The Circle, New Rochelle. This photo is probably by Val. *(family archives)*

door with an immense oval glass window in it, one entered a dark ample front hall with deep brown wood paneling and a big fireplace to the right. Beyond the fireplace was a door to the living room, and just past that an opening to the dining room. Directly opposite the front door was the door to a small room that later served as a bedroom. Immediately to the left of the front door was a kind of window seat with a wooden cover, above which was a stained-glass window with luxurious deep saturated reds, blues, and greens. Just past that a large formal staircase began, going up a few steps to a small landing near the stained-glass window, after which it continued up the entire left wall to another larger landing, whence it continued via a few more stairs to the second floor. Heavy lathed wood columns stained a deep dark brown supported a massive hand rail all the way up the staircase. Underneath the staircase was a large coat closet, access to which was provided by a dark brown paneled wooden door. The floor was covered by heavy carpets with deep dark red and black patterns. Altogether it was a quite large, dark, formal entrance hall.

The dining room and living room were paneled with dark stained woods, although parts of the walls were also covered with dark green cloth wallpaper. The large, square, heavy dining table was centered in the dining room underneath a big round stained-glass Tiffany lamp, with multiple light bulbs and a fringe of metal chains, that hung by a heavy chain from the ceiling. The wooden chairs in the dining room had massive carved backs and elaborate cushioned fabric seats which later were removed and replaced by plywood. At the far right the dining room had French door windows that provided access to a small outside porch. The porch was surrounded on all three sides by a high white wooden railing and was partly covered by a big magnolia tree. The dining room also had a large, dark wood sideboard and a small couch, which was placed in front of a fireplace on the left wall that was, as far as I remember, never used for a fire.

A huge floor-to-ceiling dark wood sliding double door with two panels, to the right of the dining room entrance, gave access to the living room; this arrangement permitted the doors to be used as theater curtains whenever we children produced "plays" for any adults who had the patience to watch them. The audience sat in the dining room, and the adjoining part of the living room served as the stage. When one entered the living room via these doors, there were dark wood bookcases with glass doors all along the left wall as well as several windows; there were also windows, looking west to the street, in the wall opposite the sliding doors. At the right was another fireplace, which doubtless shared a chimney with the front hall fireplace. The room had several comfortable easy chairs, an upright piano, and a few small tables. Many family events took place in this room, including songs in the evening, often with my mother playing the guitar or my father playing the piano, and with a cozy wood fire in the fireplace.

To the left of the French outside doors in the dining room was a swinging door that connected to a hallway with two sinks in it and floor-to-ceiling dark wood cabinets with glass doors, below which were big heavy drawers containing silverware and pots and pans; the cabinets held a plethora of glasses and dishes, most of them with an oriental blue-and-white decoration. This room was where the dishwashing took place in two large sinks, by hand. Directly opposite the door from the dining room another door in this room gave access to the steep, narrow back stairs ("the brown stairs") leading to the second floor. A high window between those two doors provided light. At the far left in this utility room,

2-5 Rosa Mae Anderson *(family archives)*

beyond the built-in cabinets and the two side-by-side sinks, an open doorway provided access to the large, bright kitchen.

The kitchen had a big table in the middle, and two gas stoves as well as ample cabinets and shelves and another sink. Just past the door from the utility room on the right was a door providing access to the stairway going down to the cellar, and beyond that was a large closet-style pantry with many shelves. On the east outside wall past this pantry was a large double door, the top half of which contained a window with red and green glass in it. This door opened onto an enclosed back porch that held a big ice box, and stairs went down to the left from this porch through a big door into the back yard. This kitchen was the domain of our beloved maid and cook, Rosa Mae Anderson, who was with us for many years. She was a short, overweight, affable and friendly African-American servant, who insisted on the rules of her place in the family. Her principles kept her from ever eating with the family in the dining room; she and her fellow servants always ate in the kitchen. More about Rosa in a little while.

On the second floor of the house was a large hallway at the top of the formal, wide front staircase. As one came up the stairs, the first room on the left had three large north windows in a dormer and was painted a light yellow; it was a bright and sunny room. Originally it was my mother's room, and later it became my younger brother Peter's room. On the right of the hallway were two large connecting rooms with windows looking southwest out the front side of the house at The Circle; these rooms were my father's bedroom and work room. He had a large bed with a big wooden headboard, several dressers, many surfaces with papers piled on them, and a "standing desk" or "Stehpult" at which he often worked after pacing about in his two rooms, as well as a variety of bric-a-brac. Across from the top of the stairs was another room which was Lise's, although my father also often worked in that room when Lise wasn't there. His work always consisted of thinking a while about something; jotting down some notes at

2-6 My father working in Lise's room *(family archives)*

the Stehpult or on some of the papers strewn about in various places in the rooms, including several shelves made of boards and cinderblocks; pacing about; thinking; jotting down something; pacing some more; and so on for hours on end.

A hallway leading toward the back of the house led to the left past the door to Lise's room. Between this hallway and the door to my mother's room was a steep staircase heading up to the third floor, where there were two more rooms, used by the servants. Underneath this staircase was a large closet, access to which was given by a white wooden door. Opposite this door was the door to the "white" bathroom, which had a large bathtub and green walls, with white wood trim; this was the bathroom my father used for shaving and other such rituals.

The hallway going back beyond the stairs to the third floor and past Lise's room continued all the way to the back of the house, where there was a window and the top of the steep back stairs that came up from the utility room between kitchen and dining room. As one went toward the back, on the right was the "brown bathroom," with stained wood paneling and off-white light tan walls and another bathtub; across from this room was another room which Val and I shared.

I present all these details about the house because, even though I left it more than seventy years ago, they are still vivid for me. I'm sure I'm not alone in having detailed memories of the place in which I grew up; doubtless many people have comparable impressions about their childhood homes. And a home it clearly was for me. It was safe, cozy, dependable, familiar, and a place I loved and took for granted. It provided a kind of quiet and reassuring fundament for the many everyday activities, events, and relationships that helped define who I was, what I could and couldn't do, and where I belonged. It obviously played a major role in my early development.

The people in the house changed in several ways during my decade there. During the first few months or so we had a succession of help, usually younger foreign females, none of whom lasted very long. I don't really remember any of them. But Rosa soon became a core part of the household; she was an essential part of the family for at least eight years. Then an African-American friend of hers, Lillian, moved in as well; she did many chores, from the laundry and cleaning the rooms to washing dishes, pots and pans, and silverware (and polishing the silverware as well). After some years, an African-American handyman named Albert Dixon was hired by my family. He did house repairs, made some not very stable wooden benches, put up a fence for a few rabbits that we at one time kept in the back yard (I remember they managed to burrow under the fence so they could come and go of their own free will), and performed other odd jobs such as shoveling coal—but my recollection is that he was not very valued because he was viewed as not being very competent or bright. He did move in, and ended up marrying Rosa; I don't know how productive or pleasant that marriage was for Rosa, who became Rosa Mae Dixon.

I remember Albert took me several times in the family car to a nearby bar, where he would buy me a root beer and some alcoholic drink for himself; I recall enjoying the fizzy carbonated drink, but occasionally would have an uncomfortably distended stomach from the root beer. Albert may have been an alcoholic; at any rate he died several years after marrying Rosa, long before we left 12 The Circle.

We frequently had guests for dinner at the house; many of them spoke German with my father and with us. Probably most of them were refugees from Europe, like ourselves. I remember a rather distinguished-

2-7 Albert Dixon *(family archives)*

looking older man who spoke a kind of Dutch with my father; I couldn't keep myself from laughing out loud about his pronunciation of "German." But clearly this was a major breach of etiquette; I was chided for being so discourteous to our guest.

My mother used to make up little rhyming ditties, sometimes leaving them on a piece of paper on the dining-room table for my father to discover when he came home late at night after presenting an evening lecture at The New School in New York. I recall one of them was "Immer bleibe es so hell (may it always remain so bright); 12 The Circle, New Rochelle." Another, written as part of the script for a puppet show that included a bear, was "Sonne brennt mir auf den Pelz; ich muss sagen, mir gefällt's"—"Sun is burning on my pelt; I must say, how good it felt." She had a pet name for my father, "Heimere," and they had a whistle for calling each other which I learned much later was a phrase from a well-known piece of classical music, a Beethoven string quartet:

Despite obvious problems including separate bedrooms and in many ways separate lives, my parents were clearly very fond of each other.

Val and I were enrolled respectively in second and first grade at a nearby public school, the Mayflower School, soon after we arrived in New Rochelle. I remember one of the first English words I learned was "goodbye," which puzzled me a bit, since it made me think of "Gut' Brei," or "good porridge." A second one, which became part of the early familect, was "gubbleyou," a contraction of a phrase I thought the children said when the teacher sneezed: "God bless you"; the sibilant had disappeared from the phrase.

My teacher, Miss Erich, managed to develop an ambience in my first-grade class for which I am still immensely grateful. How she did so, I don't know. I knew essentially no English at all when I entered the school, a problem which might have been expected to make all the other pupils bully, ridicule, or tease me any time I opened my mouth. But even though I quickly picked up the fact that the mode of communication in school was very different from the taken-for-granted, natural home language of German, I did not initially know any English expressions at all. She managed to get my fellow pupils not to tease me, but instead to give me advice, teach me, and encourage my initially halting attempts to speak English, and gently to correct me when I made errors. As a result, within a couple of months I had become

2-8 Mayflower elementary school, New Rochelle *(courtesy of the Westchester County Historical Society)*

reasonably fluent in English, and was even able to serve as an occasional six-year-old interpreter between my mother or father and various English-speaking adults such as service personnel or other workers. The fact that I had already, with Val's help, learned to read German fairly well I'm sure helped me also learn to read English. Indeed, my language facility improved so quickly that during the Christmas break of 1933 to 1934 I was skipped to second grade, even though I was still only six years old.

I remember little else of my years at elementary school, other than a female math teacher during fourth grade, who managed to hold the rapt attention of the class by always whispering rather than speaking out loud, and who insisted on excellent posture. There may be something apocryphal about this memory, which I distinctly recall: she had an ample bosom, and proudly displayed her superb posture by placing a round pencil horizontally under her chin at the top of her bosom and stood so straight with arched back that the pencil didn't roll down her chest when she let her chin let go of it.

There was a weekly school assembly at which the entire student body as well as the faculty sang songs. And the school had some kind of a band, in which I remember playing a snare drum. I think the band competed in some county or even state meets with other bands, but don't recall how well we did in those settings.

2-9 Left to right: me, Lise, and Val, mid-1930s *(family archives)*

Weather permitting, in the summer my mother would occasionally drive us kids to a nearby pleasant small sand beach at the west end of Long Island Sound, where we would play in the sand, swim in the salt water, and clamber on rocks above the beach. We would also take some picnic outings in the family car to local city and state parks, some with interesting small waterfalls.

I don't specifically remember any friends I had at Mayflower School, although I still have an autograph book from that time, with names that no longer conjure up images of the kids with those names. I do remember a young African-American boy with whom I used to play at home; I nicknamed him "Smokey" after a fire fighter in a comic strip in the newspaper whom I admired. It wasn't until years later that I became embarrassed when I realized that calling him "Smokey" might have been inadvertently offensive to a dark-skinned person.

I found school enjoyable, as did Val and Lise. One thing I recall learning in third grade was how to parse sentences, with a noun phrase on a line to the left followed by a verb phrase on the line to the right, and various modifying adjectives, adverbs, and subordinate clauses hanging down on slanted lines in appropriate places. Those grammar lessons, together with my having become truly bilingual (German at home with the family, English in all other settings including school), helped engender a love of language and languages that has blessed my entire lifetime.

After finishing sixth grade at the Mayflower School, I started seventh grade at the Albert Leonard Junior High School in New Rochelle, but don't remember anything specific about that public-school setting. Val and I attended Fieldston School in Bronxville for our high school. I started in what they called second form, and went on through the first semester of sixth form, the equivalent of the senior grade.

Probably at first Albert drove Val and me to Fieldston. It was fairly far away. Later Val was old enough to do the driving, and during the last few months, I, too, had my first driver's license (available at the time in New York State at age sixteen) and sometimes drove us to school in the car. We carpooled with a fellow student whose name I don't recall who lived in nearby Larchmont, and who also occasionally drove all three of us.

I have few memories specific to Fieldston, other than being hazed and bullied at one point by a much older and bigger boy, who pinned me on my back between his feet under a fence and spit at my face any time I moved to the right or left under the fence. I felt helpless and degraded; it was one of the most unpleasant experiences I ever had in school, and I simply didn't understand why he treated me in the cruel way he did. I didn't think I had done anything to offend him; apparently he did it simply because he was bigger and stronger than I.

One class at Fieldston was required of every student. A half hour every week was dedicated to it throughout my whole time there: it was called Ethics and was taught by highly-respected Dr. Algernon D. Black. It may well have had something to do with the fact that the school had been started by the Ethical Culture Movement; there was an affiliated elementary ethical cul-

2-10 In foreground: Eleanor Roosevelt and Dr. Algernon D. Black *("Encampment for Citizenship— Participants' snapshots," VCU Libraries Gallery, https://gallery.library.vcu.edu /items/show/81347)*

ture school in downtown Manhattan. In that ethics class discussion was encouraged; either Dr. Black or a student in the small class would refer to some current event in the news, or some other issue of interest, and everyone was encouraged to deliberate about the ethical implications and consequences of that particular matter. It engendered in me a lifelong interest in trying to figure out in any situation what alternative actions exist, and what their ethical implications are—and then to try to act in a way that would be truly ethical. Another class that had a lifelong impact was Latin-Greek, which I took during my last full year at Fieldston. Monday was Latin, Tuesday Greek, Wednesday Latin, Thursday Greek, etc. While I learned enough vocabulary from both classical languages to foster a lifelong fascination with etymology (the study of the origins of roots of words), the mutual interference between the two languages by successive alternating study of them caused the school to drop the course again after offering it for only one year. I was given the opportunity to study both some modern French and some Spanish at Fieldston, and further developed my knowledge of them later in college and even thereafter.

A course called "shop" was also offered, and I eagerly learned how to do

some metal work such as pounding out a metal ashtray and especially how to work with wood, including the use of the lathe. Following the instructions of the shop teacher, I made an adjustable floor lamp; it had a rather ingenious design (not my own), permitting the lamp to be raised to various levels by a double wood stand. The downward-slanting notches in the upper half of the stand permitted it to be hooked at a variety of vertical positions on a dowel attached to the lower stand. That lamp is still in use by my brother Peter (or Pete, as I often call him). I'm not sure how he got hold of it; he might have inherited it from my mother, to whom I probably gave it long ago.

The Ethical Culture School system also spon-

2-11 Adjustable lamp made by me
(family archives)

sored a summer camp (ECSC: Ethical Culture

School Camp) on Lake Otsego near Cooperstown in upstate New York, a camp which closed down many years ago. Campers of ages about 7 to 13 or 14 spent two summer months there, perhaps typically close to 100 campers, with more than a dozen counselors. There was a "girls' line" with cabins on one side of a hill above the northeast coast of the lake, and a "boys' line" of several cabins and some large tents on the other side of the hill. The huge "Main House" on top of the hill, where the whole first floor was devoted to dining rooms and kitchen, contained a second story with a nature room, a small "museum," a nurse's station and various other activity rooms, as well as the rooms of the camp director Willys P. Kent and his wife Roxie ("Uncle Willys" and "Aunt Roxie" to the campers). An enormous elm tree outside the Main House at the top of the hill held a big swing from a branch high above. There were clay tennis courts and various out-buildings: a "social hall" for shows, social or square dancing, singing

2-12 Campers at the Ethical Culture School Camp: square around me, Val at arrow in top row above that *(family archives)*

2-13 Pete at the tiller of the *Uncle George*; my feet in foreground *(family archives)*

and other events mostly in the evenings, a wood-working and metal-working shop, and some other utility buildings. Val and I, and later Lise and Peter too, were campers there for several summers, and I also became first a junior counselor and then a full-fledged counselor there. Those summers, which seemed endless at the time, were some of the happiest and most carefree times of my life.

A large number of varied activities were available for each camper, for whom a weekly schedule was set up with an ingenious system. For each camper, for each available hour of the day for each day of the week, different colored thumbtacks were inserted on a large wooden board, with each color indicating a different activity: swimming, sailing, rowing, canoeing, lifesaving, shop, art, nature study, jewelry, tennis, softball, etc., etc. In the earlier years, there were also gardening (in a large food patch in which were grown beans, peas, greens, potatoes, tomatoes, and various other items that were prepared for lunch or dinner in the dining room) and horseback riding. I remember falling off a big horse one summer, but (falsely) claiming that I had been thrown off by the horse.

I learned to sail at the camp, on Lake Otsego, and later taught sailing there as well. The camp owned two rather basic, simple, and old sailboats. One was a small wooden centerboard boat painted green that was propelled by a single fore-and-aft sail, and that could hold no more than three or four passengers at most. The other, my favorite, was the *Uncle George*, a much larger wide-beamed lapstrake boat, the hull of which was covered by several layers of canvas with thick paint, in a somewhat vain effort to keep the boat reasonably seaworthy (bailing out water while sailing it was a commonly required activity). This boat, too, had a centerboard and also a large heavy mast to which were attached a large sail with a boom at the bottom and a fairly heavy gaff at the top. This boat could hold up to ten or more campers at one time and would almost always win any race with the smaller green sailboat, whoever was at the helm of either one.

During my last season at the camp, it was decided that this larger boat was no longer safe, and I was ordered near the end of the season to get rid of it. I duly removed the centerboard, the rigging, the mast, and the rudder, and filled it with heavy stones. Then I paddled the hull by hand out into deep water, and proceeded to fill it with water with the bailing bucket that previously had always been used to remove water from the bilge. Soon the hull was full enough with water that I could continue filling it by causing water to flow in by pushing either the port or the starboard side under water. The poor hull dutifully started to sink. But before the boat touched bottom, it rolled over, dumped out the load of rocks, and upside down came back up to the surface. I took it back to shore and again filled it with heavy rocks, and paddled it out to deep water once more. I filled it with water again until it sank. It reacted as it had done before: it turned over, dumped out the rocks, and rose back up to the surface. Discouraged, I dragged the hull

2-14 The boat bookcase *(courtesy of Chuck Opperman)* and, upside down, the bottom of the boat's mast *(family archives)*

2-15 Bobbie, Val's bride, with Val, 1948 *(family archives)*

back to shore. Soon thereafter Nan, a fellow counselor and my fiancée at the time, persuaded one of the handymen who was an expert with a double-headed axe to cut off the bow for me and trash the rest of the hull. That bow, fitted out with several shelves, became a bookcase in my home for many years. It had an honored place in the basement of my home in Boulder for a half century. That boat held many precious memories for me. And the base of its mast is now resting on the patio of our retirement apartment.

Peter remembers those days with a fondness like mine. As he wrote to me in December 2017:

I remember so well the summers we spent in camp. You were a counselor, I was a young camper, maybe nine or ten. We were planning on going to New York on the train together for Val's wedding. An evening softball game had been scheduled for the day before our trip. I didn't play, but you did. Of course nobody kept score. You didn't do that at Ethical. But you did do your best anyway. You slammed a base hit far into center field. A solid double. But the outfielder fumbled the ball a bit, and you dashed on to third base. Then, for some reason, you decided to go for a home run. (What do you mean "for some reason," Peter? That was you all over.) You slid pretty dramatically into home plate…and broke your leg. To add insult to injury, I think you were called "out." Of course, we couldn't go to Val's wedding the next day.

I'm still a little embarrassed that I spent the rest of the day and some of the next sitting in the Counselors Room at camp crying about not going to Val's wedding. But if the truth be told, I was pretty proud to have another brother who had scored a home run…almost. Not just getting married.

But there is another much happier-ending story about camp. To tell the truth, you made me prouder of myself than ever before or since. And that involved sailing.

The camp had two sailboats. One was a small green wooden cat boat and the other was the Uncle George, which of course you know better than I. I used to go down to the waterfront in the mornings to bail the green boat which, by the time I got there, was always under water. The Uncle George was still more or less lakeworthy at that time. There was also a large wooden tub which Nick Vovcsko built for Dr. Silver [the medical attendant at the camp] and his crew of little kids. As you remember, that was the boat that Dr. Silver would drive around the lake under motor, chortling to the little kids he had aboard, "Now we're sailing." I used to love to actually sail circles around him in the green boat.

You taught me how to sail, both in the little green boat and the Uncle George. There was one time I was in the Uncle George with Dr. Silver in the boat with me. He told me I should spill wind because the mast was weak. Of course I ignored him. (If he had told me that it was you who told him about the mast, of course I would have spilled wind.) There was a strong puff, as I remember, down near the point, and the mast went over, right at the deck line. I remember you coming out to rescue us but you never blamed anyone, neither Dr. Silver nor me. I wonder whether Silver would be surprised to know that you still had the bow of the Uncle George in the cellar of your house in Colorado when you moved out. You generously offered it to me but I didn't know how to get it here.

As I said, you gave me some of the proudest moments of my life. You taught me to sail both the sinking green cat boat and the Uncle George. At that time, campers who wanted to go out in a sailboat had to have a counsclor on board, or Dr. Silver. But you changed that. One day you announced that there would be sailing exams and any experienced sailor who passed would be permitted to take a sailboat out without a counselor. Of course I took the test and I passed. In fact I was the first camper to pass. What really made me proud was when you went down to Cooperstown and got me a captain's hat. It was white with a shiny black brim and gold braid around the bottom. I wore that hat every day. Never, be it in law school, government work, writing or whatever, was I so proud as when I was wearing my captain's hat. And one great feature of it was that it came from you.

There is one detail I should add. You were always rigorously unbiased in your dealings with me. None of the other campers could have the impression that I won that cap because you were my brother. Of course I knew that. You were too honest for that…still are.

Of course there are many more mini-stories I could tell you. Like bouncing on the empty beds in the attic in New Rochelle (or were they Rosa's?). Or the time you rescued poor Papsen who was trying to work, by luring me away to wrap a penny in what must have been 100 sheets of newspaper.

Every afternoon after lunch was nap time at the camp, and several times a week this was followed by a letter writing time, to send news home. There was a small shop, where one could buy stamps, candy, toothpaste, and other items, which was staffed by campers so they could practice arithmetic and learn how to make change. Several times each summer there were also overnight camping canoe trips on the nearby Susquehanna River for older campers, one night for camping in pup tents for the younger participants and two and even three nights for the oldest campers.

The boys' line and the girls' line each had toilet lines down the hill behind them, and there were showers available as well. An ingenious system handled the sewage; small cantilevered devices automatically added small amounts of chlorine to the sewage as it flowed past into leach fields. These devices, as well as general maintenance, were handled by old Mr. Tripp and by Nick Vovcsko, a probably illiterate Pole with a slight foreign accent who could fix anything. Nick also was skilled on the harmonica, and taught me how to play.

I learned not only to play many folk songs on the harmonica at camp, but also how to swim, how to row, how to sail, how to canoe, how to play tennis (modestly), and other things such as water safety and "lifesaving." Uncle Willys generated new lyrics for many classical songs and melodies; almost every evening in the social hall, after dinner, he would play the piano while the campers sang these songs, the lyrics of which were projected onto a screen at the front of the hall—or engaged in social dancing or square dancing. Some evenings there were also skits performed by campers on the little stage in the social hall, and most summers there were also productions of greatly shortened Gilbert and Sullivan operettas.

Breakfast, lunch, and dinner (except for an occasional picnic on the big lawn outside the Main House) were served in the dining rooms, and announced by a large loud bell hung on the Main House porch. The meals were served at many long tables in the dining rooms, each with a coun-

2-16 The boys' line at ECSC *(family archives)*

2-17 The girls' line at ECSC *(family archives)*

2-18 Approaching the ECSC Main House *(family archives)*

selor and from four or five to six or seven campers. Platters with food were passed around each table, and each camper could take whatever was desired. I can't say that I remember much about the food, other than that it was plentiful, good, and much enjoyed by all. The mostly outdoor life produced healthy appetites.

Back at 12 The Circle, my father was gone one or two evenings a week for his classes and seminars at the New School. Soon, on most weekends, my mother was gone for a few days and nights. On Saturday afternoons, Val and I, sometimes with Lise as well, would go to a nearby movie theater for a double feature as well as a newsreel, previews of coming attractions, and an installment of a serial on Dick Tracy or Flash Gordon or some other superhero: these five-minute snippets typically spent the first half minute resolving a crisis that had been set up the previous week, and then developing a new crisis which would be resolved the following week. I think admission to the theater was a dime for each of us; we often went to a White Kitchen nearby after the films, where a copious ham-

burger complete with fixings such as pickles, lettuce, onion, relish, ketchup, and mustard was available for a nickel.

2-19 A small tray (originally a pie tin) which my mother painted for me *(family archives)*
The tray says, in rhyming German, "verkehrtes Segelgetriebe / aus wahrer Herzensliebe / für meinen Michel" or "crazy sail rigging / from true heart's love / for my Mikey"
The accompanying note simply says, still in German, "I love you."

One unpleasant memory concerned Val's thumb sucking, which for some reason bothered me tremendously. When we were trying to go to sleep in our separate beds in the back room we shared at 12 The Circle, I could hear his rhythmic slurping accompanied by a soft clicking as he continuously flipped the hem of a sheet or a handkerchief back and forth with the forefinger of one hand while he stretched the cloth edge with his other hand, and also made the slurping noises of sucking his thumb. Why those noises bothered me as much as they did, I don't know, but they drove me bonkers. I would repeatedly, to no avail, shout "Lutsch' nicht!," or "Don't suck!," but he always persisted nevertheless with this habit which obviously provided solace to him but torment to me. I believe his thumb sucking continued well into his teens. This experience doubtless also led to my being unable to tolerate thumb sucking in my own children; I even remember holding poor Karen, my first-born, in my left arm in such a way that her right arm was wedged firmly behind my back so that she could not release it to suck on her right thumb, and left my own right arm free to engage in various household chores such as cooking or cleaning up. This abhorrence of thumb sucking by anyone has continued to bedevil me down to the present. This revulsion about thumb-sucking has been a compulsive obsession that has plagued me ever since my childhood.

One other sound I hated was that of a shooting gun. Whether it was someone else's idea or my own I don't recall, but I remember going out on the front porch of 12 The Circle to shoot a cap pistol to try to cure my dislike. The first time it was pulling the trigger once with squinting eyes, the next time twice, and thereafter three loud reports, but I don't think that this treatment helped much. I discontinued it pretty soon. I still don't like gun shots—or any guns, for that matter. Even any form of toy gun was banned from my home when my children were young.

Late in my childhood I was attacked by appendicitis, and my appendix was duly removed. Unfortunately the incision became infected at one end, and as a result I have had a rather unsightly scar for the rest of my life on the lower right side of my stomach. The appendix was successfully removed, the infection was successfully treated, and the scar remains as just a reminder of a childhood illness that was long ago and had no consequences other than that scar.

As a 1942 Christmas gift, my father gave Val, Lise, and me each a small loose-leaf booklet filled with blank pages, to be used as a kind of diary. I don't think any of those booklets has survived to the present day. But on presumably the first page of the booklet was a little note from my father, with an uplifting—even inspiring—message, wishing for all kinds of good things in the recipient's life. Somehow the first page of the booklet I received did survive.

When I was eleven and twelve years old, for a while I presumptuously wrote and edited a monthly newsletter, grandiosely called *The Wertheimer Times*. It recounted mostly significant events in the lives of the

2-20 Note from my father, Christmas, 1942 *(family archives)*

family members and in the lives of various friends who were important to the family. A detailed account of this immodest endeavor is available in Appendix B of this narrative.

2-21 Masthead of Volume I, Issue 1 of *The Wertheimer Times (family archives)*

3   Early Teen Years

The transition from childhood to teenager and becoming an adolescent was smooth, rather uneventful, and gradual. I don't remember any major event that made me feel I was no longer a child.

Music, including making it ourselves, has always been a pleasant family activity since my early childhood. Val and I were given piano lessons from when we were quite young; he became proficient at it, but my piano teacher gave up on me early because she and my parents were unable to convince me to bother practicing. I now deeply regret that I didn't continue with piano lessons, nor learn how to read music fast enough to play it. Val also learned how to play the clarinet.

When I was about twelve or thirteen years old, Miss Mayer took me to a production of Shakespeare's "King Lear," which impressed me. It was a very sparse production by famed director Erwin Piscator, at the theater in the New School. When it came time for the scene in which, on stage, Gloucester's eyes are gouged out, Miss Mayer warned me about the gory event to be depicted next on stage, and took my hand—for which I was grateful, considering how realistically that horrible scene was presented.

Another experience that remains with me from about this same time is one which, I'm afraid, interfered with my ever being able to enjoy opera as much as I otherwise might have. I think I was probably about twelve or thirteen years old when I somehow had the opportunity to

3-1 Me on a bicyle, in my teens *(family archives)*

© Springer Fachmedien Wiesbaden GmbH, part of Springer Nature 2020
M. Wertheimer, *Facets of an Academic's Life*,
https://doi.org/10.1007/978-3-658-28770-2_3

attend a performance of "Tristan and Isolde" at the Metropolitan Opera House in Manhattan. I was standing at the very top of the balcony, from where I could see the stage far down below. The world-famous singers Lauritz Melchior and Helen Traubel were cast in the title roles, and the house was packed. While I did enjoy the music and elaborate staging, my main memory is of two large and very overweight people trying desperately and without success to get their arms around each other, while facing each other screaming at the top of their lungs. Not the best introduction to opera for a teenager. But my love of music, and making music, persisted in spite of this experience. I continued to sing, and to play a variety of instruments in a highly amateur fashion.

My younger brother Peter gave me both the harmonica I'm still using and another one several decades before that. He was born in late October of 1936, when I was nine and a half years old; I didn't discover until several years later that he is my half-brother, the son of my mother and my (later) step-father, John (Schani) Hornbostel. I finally realized that when my mother was gone for several days and nights from 12 The Circle over various weekends, she was spending that time with Schani. He was the son of my father's good friend and colleague, Erich von Hornbostel, a distinguished scholar who is often considered to be the

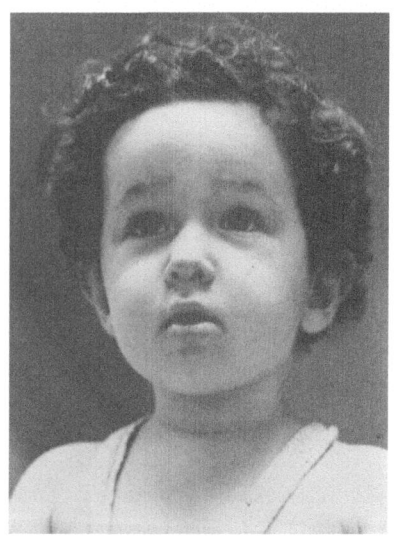

originator of the scholarly discipline of ethnomusicology. Erich and my father were contemporaries who had worked together at Carl Stumpf's Phonogram Archive at the University of Berlin near the end of the first decade of the twentieth century, doing both joint and separate projects in musicology (indeed the first publication of my father that included clear hints of what later was to become his famous Gestalt theory was a 1910 paper on the strict and logical structure of the music of the Vedda, a so-called "primitive" tribe in Ceylon, now called Sri Lanka).

3-2 Peter as a toddler *(family archives)*

Schani and my mother, I later learned, became lovers in the late 1920s or early 1930s; he was almost the same age as my mother. The complex relationships—the fact that my mother was still married to my father, that Schani and my mother had been lovers for years, that Peter was biologically Schani's son even though he was named Peter Anthony Wertheimer on his birth certificate—became intolerable in 1941. My mother flew to Reno, NV, to obtain a divorce from my father, and married Schani a week after the divorce was final. She moved with Schani into a small house in New Jersey; Peter's last name was officially changed to Hornbostel, and he was removed from our household at 12 The Circle.

Ironically, in the family archives there are letters from Reno from my mother to us children as well as to my father in which she continued to express her deep love for all of us, including my father, even though she had abandoned us all.

The effect of these developments on my father was devastating. He already, partly because of his heavy smoking of Chesterfield or Camel cigarettes, was not well, and the stress of this period in his life was debilitating. He only lasted two more years, dying almost instantaneously of a massive heart event in October 1943.

I remember my mother and father arguing about telling the children about the upcoming divorce. I could, from my room at the top of the back stairs, hear them vehemently discussing the matter in the utility room between the kitchen and the dining room. My father rarely displayed sheer fury; this was one occasion when he was clearly very angry. It seems they had agreed before that the two of them would jointly tell us children about the enormous changes the family was about to make, but that she had broken that agreement, and had told us about them without him. His fury led

3-3 Schani *(family archives)*

him to say in German
something like "I'm
going to smash all of
these dishes because of
what you have done,"
but fortunately that
threat was not carried
out.

Peter had become a
beloved component of
the 12 The Circle fami-
ly. I remember when he
was still very young I
used to spend an hour or
two early each morning
playing with him and
taking care of him in his
bright room at the head
of the front stairs while
my mother escaped to
the third floor to sleep
after she had fed him; I
did this in the early

3-4 Peter spraying Lise, 12 The Circle *(family archives)*   dawn hours before go-

ing to school. Rituals with him as a baby included elaborately serving him small
bits of food, on a tiny plate on top of a larger plate on top of a third still-larger
plate, which we both enjoyed, as well as my putting my mouth on his stomach
and making a rough noise there with my lips and breath, which would send him
into paroxysms of laughter. There are black-and-white photos of him playing
with a hose in the back yard of 12 The Circle, gleefully spraying his older siblings.

It turned out to be quite disruptive to the family to be broken up when he was
taken away to live with my mother and Schani. Indeed, Schani was extremely

possessive of my mother's time and attention and was intolerant of Peter's interference with his precious time with her, which made life very difficult for the
little boy. I seem to remember his occasionally being returned to the Wertheimer
household after the breakup; it was pleasant for my father, Val, Lise, and me (as
well as Rosa) to have him back with us, and I think he reveled in the freedom of
being "back home"—but I suspect the main motive behind these visits was
Schani's desire to be rid of Peter for a while so he could again have my mother
to himself without any interference from Peter.

Peter also later joined his siblings as a summer camper at the Ethical Culture
School Camp after he became old enough. By then I had already become a junior
counselor or a regular counselor at the camp.

In later years at the camp, I was also requested by its director, "Uncle
Willys," to come one week early and stay for a week after the campers left, to
help set up and take down camp equipment, including the somewhat elaborate
waterfront. Part of my duty during these weeks was constructing and later removing the piers that held up a large wooden dock system that was used as
mooring for the sailboats and rowboats of the camp's small fleet and that was
used to stretch ropes with floats to define three areas in which swimmers of different levels of skill (beginner, intermediate, and advanced) would be confined.
Long heavy steel poles were screwed vertically into submerged logs held down
on the bottom with weighty stones, and then numbered wooden logs with appro-

priate holes that fitted on the
steel poles were stacked like a
log house until each pier was tall
enough to reach above water
level to hold long planked
wooden docks in multiple six-
foot slabs. My ability to work
under water without having to
come up for a breath for a minute or longer was useful in
building those piles to hold the
pier—then to take it all apart

3-5 The waterfront at the ECSC *(family archives)*

again after the camping season was over. I remember mustached Uncle Willys standing in the water, with sunglasses and a big straw hat, supervising me in those activities. But my relationship with Uncle Willys, who also taught wood shop at the school, was complex, and I didn't really understand it very well until years later. His interest in me, I'm afraid, was part of his proclivity toward pedophilia; but I won't elaborate on that here.

I remember that the summer's pay for a counselor for the two months was something like a total of $200 plus room and board. At the time, this seemed generous to me; I recall adding that amount several times to my savings account at The People's Bank for Savings in New Rochelle. That account had been opened years before, probably with money saved from weekly allowances. The allowance was perhaps a quarter or so a week—I don't recall the amount, but it sufficed for the Saturday movies and hamburger as well as an occasional candy treat. I do recall being impressed by the fact that there actually were a few cents of interest added periodically to the account, and duly recorded in ink by a teller in my savings account booklet. That money just sitting in a bank account, doing nothing, would gradually grow all by itself seemed magical.

One summer while I was a counselor, I was in charge of a tent in the boys' line that held five campers. One of them was a small, dark, wiry, athletic African-American boy from Harlem. He carried a chip on his shoulder when he first came to the camp. (He appears in the photo of my campers and me, second from the left; he and I have our arms around each other.) I don't remember his name, but initially he handled interpersonal relationships in ways that he obviously had learned on the streets of Harlem. If he wanted something that belonged to someone else, he just took it and belligerently fought to maintain possession of it if he was chal-

3-6 Me as counselor, with the five boys in my tent, 1946; Clifford Alexander far right *(family archives)*

lenged. He sulked and looked mean and unhappy most of the time during the first week or so of camp. Understandably unpopular, he was never chosen in a pick-up game of softball or capture the flag or in other competitive settings. But after a few weeks he began to realize that the tough ways that worked on the Harlem streets didn't work all that well at the camp. He gradually became sensitive, empathetic, friendly and cooperative, and by the middle of the season he had become one of the most popular children in the camp. The camp directors—and I, his counselor—were overjoyed by the changes in him, which persisted until the end of the camp season. Several months later, I had the opportunity to visit him at his home in Harlem—and he had reverted to the sullen, belligerent, obstinate, and tough style with which he had at first arrived at camp. There had been no major personality change after all; he had simply learned that different modes of behavior seem to be called for in different settings: be tough on the mean streets of the inner city and be kind and gentle in the totally different cooperative warm camp setting.

The waterfront used by the camp was about a quarter of a mile down the hill from the Main House, the boys' and girls' lines, and the out-buildings. A gently sloping dirt road led down to it. Another physical feature of the camp grounds was that there were three clay tennis courts. The courts had to be brushed and then rolled to smooth them out after a rainstorm or after vigorous play, and the white tapes used to mark the courts had to be straightened and pins beaten through them into the ground. I didn't realize until later that not all tennis courts need this much attention. I did learn a quite modest skill at tennis there, and in later years I even ended up teaching tennis to campers of various ages.

In the spring of 1943, when I turned 16, I was again offered a job as counselor at the camp for the coming summer. But by then I had become aware that my father was a rather respected scholar. Many visitors to our house—both his students and various colleagues—displayed an awe or admiration for him and his work. It occurred to me that I would rather spend that coming summer writing his biography than going back to camp as a counselor. In my naïveté, I assumed that a few months in the summer would of course suffice to complete that chore. After all, by then I had read many books, and unrealistically assumed that it wouldn't take all that long to write one. When I proposed the project to my fa-

3-7 A classic formal portrait of my father *(family archives)*

ther, he was visibly touched and obviously appreciated my interest in him and his career. But he gently suggested that it would make more sense for me to go back to camp that summer with Lise and Pete. (Val was probably already preparing to become an undergraduate student at Columbia University.) So I did go back to the camp that summer—and by that October my father was dead. A month or two later there was a memorial for him at the New School. There were several rather lavish speeches given about him, and the occasion was also attended by the renowned physicist Albert Einstein. I had of course heard of him, and was awed when he shook my hand.

My father's death from a massive coronary event seems to have been mercifully quick. He was in the white bathroom upstairs in the afternoon, shaving in preparation for an evening lecture at the New School, and Lise was with him there while he was shaving. It had become customary for one or more of us children (including Peter, when he was still a member of our household; my father treated him just as much as his son as he treated Val and me) to keep him company when he shaved, because those were among the rare moments when we could interact with him without interfering with his work. He collapsed almost immediately, and I found out about it as soon as I got home from school. My mother was there too, and there was general household incredulity. I don't remember any other details of the occasion, but do recall that I was sent out to stay at the home of a schoolmate in Manhattan for several months to finish out the fall term at Fieldston. I never did graduate from Fieldston School, but went immediately to Swarthmore College early, for the spring semester of 1944, when I was still 16 years old. The arrangements for my going to Swarthmore were doubtless facilitated by my father's colleagues Hans Wallach and especially Wolfgang Köhler, both of whom were teaching there.

While I was still a student at Fieldston, one of my fellow students was Paul Robeson, Jr., the son of the famed singer, Paul Robeson. I remember being invited to the Robeson house for dinner one evening, and how welcomed and accepted I felt there. Paul Robeson Senior was just a warm, friendly, quiet host to his son's school companion; I didn't realize until much later what a prominent, deservedly famous singer he was.

While I was living those few months in an apartment in Manhattan with another school colleague (I'm afraid I don't remember either his name or his family's name), Val was a student at Columbia University, and Lise was in high school in New Jersey, living in the household with our mother, Schani, and Peter. I believe that these few years must have been especially difficult for Lise, since she, like Peter, was typically banished from the house during weekends so that Schani could be alone with our mother. I too had a room in each place Schani, my mother, Peter, and later Lise lived (in both Essex Fells and later Caldwell, New Jersey; I think they were for a year or two in each of those two towns before moving to Center Moriches, Long Island), and I would come there during school vacations. I don't believe that these were very happy times for any of us.

But to go back to retrieve a few more memories from the days at 12 The Circle, New Rochelle: My father was a very thoughtful and warm parent, even though he was old enough to be our grandfather. Some of his wonderful paternal interactions with his children are described in his biography, *Max Wertheimer and Gestalt Theory* by D. Brett King and myself issued in 2005 by Transaction Publishers, and re-issued in 2007 in a paperback format. But it feels worthwhile to reminisce a bit more here

3-8 Anni and Schani's house at 25 Beachfern Road, Center Moriches; my desk was just inside the window at the upper left. *(family archives)*

about those many wonderful experiences, as well as describing some of the games we children played.

From an early age, the children were encouraged to join in dinner conversations, even when we had distinguished guests (and I remember my father occasionally jokingly thanking guests for the especially fine dinner that was served to us all because we had a distinguished visitor for that meal). As the oldest, Val often joined in more than we other children; he was typically well informed about recent events. The discussions sometimes seemed to be somehow similar to Dr. Black's ethics classes at Fieldston, because often at issue was what would be the best thing to do in a given situation. We were all avid Democrats and fans of President Franklin Delano Roosevelt and First Lady Eleanor Roosevelt, and admired the United States for its dedication to justice for all, freedom, and democracy—and support for the downtrodden. If someone expressed an opinion on some issue, there typically was exploration of the reasons for that opinion, as well as discussion of alternate opinions and their pros and cons. You couldn't just express an opinion, but you also had to be able to defend it. And often the discussion would indeed lead to someone changing an opinion after joint deliberation. The discussions never involved confrontation and intimidation, but were always respectful, even if sometimes quite passionate and intense.

After dinner, especially when we were younger, my father would sometimes lie down on the couch in the dining room and entertain us with stories about a wise old man with a long gray beard, Enegobitz, who spent much of his time reading huge old dusty tomes, but would stop his reading and welcome the Wertheimer children when they came to visit him in his modest hut. He would prepare hot chocolate for them and listen with interest to their tales of events in school or with friends, and would always insist that they should come to visit him again soon when they had to leave and go home. For that matter, this character, Enegobitz, also became a major character in stories I told to my own children many years later. And this practice has continued into the next generation, with my children telling Enegobitz stories to their children and grandchildren.

He also entertained us with innocent skits involving his two thumbs—the left one Stefan Ponitz and the right one Anton Ponitz. These two would converse by my father holding his two thumbs up facing each other; whichever one was speaking would be wagging appropriately toward the other one. My father also taught us many songs (doubtless many from his own childhood), and also how to play chess. He typically insisted that any "bad" move by either side should be taken back and replaced by a better move, so that the entire chess game would be as "good" as possible.

One other game that was described in my father's famous posthumous book, *Productive Thinking*, concerned badminton as played by Val and me. Val was older than I and a much better player than I. He always won; so I soon refused to play with him because he always beat me. But my father (not we boys, as *Productive Thinking* claims) came up with an ingenious restructuring of the game: rather than seeing how many points either player could win by sending the shuttlecock across the net into a section of the opponent's court where the opponent was unable to hit it back, the aim of the game became trying to get the shuttlecock back and forth over the net as many times as possible without it hitting the ground. This version got Val and me to play for long periods with both of us enjoying it. Incidentally, as for chess, Val became so good at it that for a time he was First Board on the Columbia University chess team.

Val, Lise, and I also enjoyed playing Monopoly, a game that was popular when we were young. But while Val usually was very protective and supportive of his younger siblings, he would occasionally propose some deal to Lise during a Monopoly game that would obviously benefit him without being of much value to Lise. In those situations, I would earnestly counsel Lise to think carefully about Val's deal before accepting it.

Both Lise and I also enjoyed my braiding her long black hair; for a time when she was young she wore it in two thick braids hanging down below her shoulders.

3-9 Lise and me in a snow igloo, 1942
(family archives)

At some point during our time at 12 The Circle, Val and I made kites out of tissue paper and balsa wood, sometimes with rag tails as well. When wind conditions permitted, we would fly those kites on the huge lawn in the park of The Circle west of our house. Sometimes my father would see us from his study or bedroom windows where he was working upstairs, and come down (in slippers with an unbuttoned sweater over his shirt) to the grass. He would take the kite string, gently making the kite rise with expert movements of his hands, and compliment us on how well the kites were flying, and how well we had made them. He made us feel very proud.

I remember that, early during our stay at 12 The Circle, Val was permitted to go down into the cellar to paint some small new wooden tables that were to become Christmas and birthday tables, but I was told that I wouldn't be allowed to paint them because I was too young. I was deeply disappointed. But today I still have one of those tables, one that probably was painted white by Val more than eighty years ago; it has a prominent place on the patio of our apartment at the retirement community where we now live. Another memory is of a despicable act I performed, perhaps in response to intense sibling rivalry: I set on fire and launched from an upstairs window into the back yard a small rubberband-powered balsa wood and tissue paper airplane model Val had made; it was totally destroyed. I never did, unfortunately, apologize to him sufficiently for this awful deed.

After my mother had left in 1941, Val and I filled in for Rosa in the kitchen on her weekly day off. I remember that we often prepared spaghetti and meat sauce, which all of us at 12 The Circle enjoyed. Rosa's meals for years were very good, including a variety of meat dishes, vegetables and salads, as well as occasionally pies and cakes and special dishes for my father.

3-10 The "Christmas table" that I wasn't allowed to paint, but Val painted back in 1934 or 1935. It now needs paint. *(family archives)*

When our cat had disappeared from the house one time, we put a sign up on the street in front of our house, asking anyone who found her to return her to us, and that whoever would do so would receive a chocolate cake to show our appreciation. The cat was indeed returned, and Rosa baked a magnificent chocolate cake as a reward for the neighbor who had returned the cat. Rosa also prepared many dishes that my father requested, from stewed prunes for him to help his delicate digestive system to his morning "Kabapsen" (a cup of strong coffee, some zwieback, and a hardboiled egg for his breakfast), and to clabbered sour milk and "rote Grütze," a kind of red gelatin for dessert that he liked (and about which he often remarked, "bibbere nicht; ich fress' Dich nicht" or "don't shiver; I won't devour you," but would always end up eating it with pleasure).

Another food reminiscence concerns a simple chicken noodle soup which was sometimes part of the fare on overnight canoe camping trips at the summer Ethical Culture School Camp. It was enjoyed during those outdoor meals prepared with water, from a dry mixture, on a camp fire, but since it was cooked in a setting where there were pine trees that were shedding their needles, it was called not "chicken noodle soup" but "pine noodle soup."

My father tried out on us children at the dinner table or after dinner many stories and puzzles that he later used in his lectures or (rather sparse) publications. One favorite character was a modest old mullah, or wise man, who spent his life doing good things and solving problems for his fellow human beings. Some of these mullah stories are told in the biography of my father.

One mullah problem I still remember him once posing for us involved the old wise man walking in a desert tent town. The tents typically had a single large vertical pole in the middle of the tent that held up the center of the tent fabric. The mullah heard a not very desperate call for help from a woman in one of the tents. The mullah raised the flap of the tent that served as a front entry door and saw the woman standing in the middle of the tent near the center pole, preparing dough for bread. Directly in front of her was a small table on which she had been kneading the dough; the table was up against the center pole. On the opposite side of the pole from her was a bag of flour on the floor. She had reached around the pole, and had picked up in her cupped hands precisely the amount of flour she needed to add to the wad of dough on the table in front of her—but the pole was in the way, and she couldn't transfer the flour onto the dough without separating her hands and losing some of the flour back into the bag. That is why she was calling for help. The mullah's hands were not clean enough to let her drop the flour into his cupped hands from hers, and there was no other available receptacle into which she could have dropped the flour for the mullah to catch and carry around for her to the table on her side of the tent pole. But the mullah quickly came up with a simple solution to the problem. What was it? All the woman had to do was to retain the flour in her cupped hands and carefully walk 180 degrees around the pole to the other side where the bag of flour was located; her hands would then be directly above the wad of dough on the table, and she could release the flour directly onto the dough.

Another problem discussed at length in a chapter in my father's book, *Productive Thinking*, concerns finding the area of a parallelogram. To find the area of a rectangle, you need to know how many units wide it is (its width) as well as how many units it is tall (its height). Then you figure out how many columns of units it has, each composed of how many units; so, all you need to do to find its area is multiply the number of rows of units by the number of columns. A rectangle that is two units high by three units wide is thus composed of three columns of two units each, for example, so its area is two times three (or three times two, if you calculate how many columns of two units there are), or six units. But this strategy doesn't work on a parallelogram, because its units aren't squares but little parallelograms themselves. So the problem becomes how to transform a parallelogram into a rectangle of equal area. The usual strategy involves dropping vertical lines from the top left and right corners of the parallelogram down to its (extended) base, and proving the equality of the two triangles constructed in this way, a fairly elaborate geometric proof. But Lise solved the problem in a much simpler and more elegant way when she was only six or seven years old. She proved that the area of a parallelogram is its height times its width by asking for a pair of scissors to cut the paper parallelogram that had been handed to her. Cut the parallelogram anywhere vertically to its base, and you have two pieces which you can now place end to end so that the two angled ends perfectly match each other; and you now have a rectangle of exactly the same area, the area of which is simply the rectangle's height times its width—the same as the original parallelogram's base times its height.

We had occasional contacts with various other families while we were at 12 The Circle. One family, the Benno Elkans, prominently referred to in Appendix B: *The Wertheimer Times*, were angels who supplemented my father's finances for a number of years, and occasionally visited with us. There was the Kruskal family too, whom we occasionally saw; at least one of their sons became well known in statistics.

I recall that after my mother and father's divorce, Miss Mayer from the New School was a fairly frequent visitor at our house; she had helped the family in many ways ever since meeting us at the pier when our ship, the RMS *Majestic*, arrived in New York in September, 1933. I remember worrying that she might have thoughts about becoming my father's wife, but that didn't happen. I also remember visiting her quite a few years later, after she had retired; she previously had often been busily writing checks to support various other families and charities, but now, as a small shriveled version of the rather imposing woman she had been before, was no longer doing that.

We had many interactions with the family of the renowned mathematician

Richard Courant, which lived at the northern end of North Avenue, past the small lakes in front of the New Rochelle High School. Mrs. Courant was an avid musician who sometimes kept beat with a piece of classical music in her head when she was driving, by the way in which her foot on the accelerator would go pumping up and down. The oldest son in that family was Ernst, and the next was daughter Gertrud, known by us as "Dudu," who occasionally babysat for us children. (I remember doing some babysitting myself when I was twelve years old or a little older, for 25 cents an hour, but I don't recall for whom I did that

3-11 Mathematician Richard Courant, father of Dudu, Lori, and two sons *(courtesy of New York University)*

babysitting.) There were another younger brother Hans and a girl, Lori, who became one of Lise's good friends. I remember becoming aware of Lori's femininity and attractiveness, but never did anything based on that impression. Another girl whom I found very attractive was Val's friend Judith Brodsky; I recall a photograph of her in a bathing suit that piqued my budding interest. But that, too, led to no actions to fulfill my fantasies.

An occasional visitor at 12 The Circle was Rudolf Arnheim, who sometimes babysat for us and later became a prominent pioneering scholar in the field of the psychology of art, who was named to a professorship created for him in that specialty at Harvard University, and who lived to be more than a hundred years old. There was also Edwin ("Eddie") B. Newman, whom I remember attaching a bird house high in a tree at 12 The Circle; he later became chair of the department of psychology at Harvard. Among my father's doctoral students were Gwan-Yuen Li, his last PhD, and Abraham S. Luchins. Luchins came often and long to visit with my father, who sometimes, on getting ready to do something other than consult with Luchins on his dissertation, would unceremoniously say to him, "Disappear, Mister," and poor Luchins would obediently leave the house.

Another visitor who came for long periods, often staying overnight for several days at a time, was Solomon Asch, a professor of social psychology who was helping my father in the challenging task of dictating chapters for his book on productive thinking and coming up with expressions that make good sense in English while at the same time also managing to convey precisely the meaning my father intended. It was a frustrating task, and Asch consistently displayed endless tolerance and patience at it, even when my father would shout out loud in exasperation at their not managing to find just the right phrases. Sometimes, I remember, my father would utter an English adage he may have made up, after

3-12 Rudolf Arnheim, Lise, and me, about 1940 *(family archives)*

an especially frustrating session with Asch or on other occasions when things didn't seem to be going right: "cheer up: there is no hope"—always said with a kind of wistful smile.

My father was surprisingly competent and re-sourceful when it came to one rather dramatic household emergency. Early one morning, in the wee hours, I woke from a nightmare of some

3-13 Solomon Asch *(courtesy of Eric Asch)*

kind, and turned on the bare-bulbed lamp on my bedside table; for some reason, Val wasn't in our shared bedroom that night. I looked around the room, checking that none of the shadows were actually something menacing, and then noticed that the lamp had fallen over and the bare bulb was lying on top of the quilt on my bed; the quilt under it had started to glow and to smolder. I put the lamp back on my bedside table, but there was a glowing ring around the small blackened circle where the bare bulb had been lying on the quilt. Having seen my father routinely blow out matches he used to light his ubiquitous cigarettes, I blew on that glowing ring, hoping to blow it out. Instead, it burst into flame. Alarmed, I ran down the hall to my father's room, shouting "Feuer! Feuer!" ("Fire! Fire!"). I woke him up, trying to get him to come deal with the problem as quickly as possible. To my consternation, he took his time putting on heavy woolen socks as he usually did before placing his feet into his slippers. He must have thought that I was imagining things, and that there really was no hurry. Finally he did come back down the hall with me to Val's and my room. The entire surface of my bed was now in flames, several feet high. Without hesitating even a moment, my father folded the two ends of the quilt to its center, and carried the smolder-ing quilt across the hall into the brown bathroom, where he threw the quilt into the tub and turned on the water full force. The fire was soon completely out and there had been no other damage from the smoke or fire. I'm sure that if he hadn't acted so quickly and appropriately, the whole house might well have been afire before too much longer. As it happens, the quilt did end up with a big hole in it where its cover and the kapok filling had burned. It was repaired to some extent by someone, probably Lillian, sewing a patch of flower-patterned cloth over the burned part, and that quilt many years later was still doing service occasionally at our Colorado mountain cabin during cold nights. It is now in my daughter's household.

3-14 Verses sending me off to college, from Lise; "später" (in line 12) is German, meaning "later" *(family archives)*

4   College Years

I was still sixteen years old when I enrolled in January 1944 as a midyear freshman at Swarthmore College in Pennsylvania. Although I officially had a half
year yet to go before graduating from Fieldston School, my late father's close
colleague and friend Wolfgang Köhler, a professor at Swarthmore College, (and
perhaps Hans Wallach as well), somehow played a role in my being admitted to
Swarthmore as a regular student. I did graduate from college in June of 1947 at
age 20, having attended one summer term there (spending much of that summer
term studying while lying in a bathtub filled with cold water, because of the
extreme summer heat). Those years at Swarthmore were wonderful; I enjoyed
the experience there so much that I decided to try to prepare for an academic
career myself.

4-1 Main building of Swarthmore College: Parrish Hall *(from*
https://commons.wikimedia.org/wiki/File:Swarthmore_Parrish_Hall.jpg by Kungming2)

© Springer Fachmedien Wiesbaden GmbH, part of Springer Nature 2020
M. Wertheimer, *Facets of an Academic's Life*,
https://doi.org/10.1007/978-3-658-28770-2_4

4-2 Wolfgang Köhler *(Archives of the History of American Psychology, The Drs. Nicholas and Dorothy Cummings Center for the History of Psychology, The University of Akron.)*

What convinced me was the heady experience of my last two years there in the honors program. At that time, if one had done reasonably well during one's freshman and sophomore years, one could enroll in that honors program. While the record of my first two college years was not scintillating, it was good enough that (possibly again with Köhler's help) I was accepted into the honors program. It turned out to be an immensely challenging and enjoyable intellectual experience. Back then, for each of the last four semesters, you no longer enrolled in any further regular courses, but instead took only two honors seminars each semester; that was the full academic load. Four of the final eight seminars were to be in a major, and two in each of two minors. The seminars were typically taught in a professor's house, usually scheduled from 6:30 to 9:00 one evening each week, and the enrollment in a seminar could be as few as two students and hardly ever more than seven or eight. Almost each week in each seminar each student had to write and present a paper, and one of the students was, on a rotating basis, appointed to keep a record of the evening's discussion and to present a report on it for review and discussion the following week. While scheduled to end after 2½ or 3 hours, the seminars often lasted much longer, often past midnight.

One significant feature of the program was that the students were never graded by their professors. This produced a radical reorientation in the student-teacher relationship; rather than engaging in "apple polishing" to gain favor from the professor, the students used the professors' expertise to develop their own understanding of the subject matter. The students could pester their mentors for advice, suggestions about topics and relevant readings, corrections of their mistakes and any other demands on their expertise, all with impunity; ultimately, it didn't matter what the professor thought of the student, and the professor's task was simply to hone the student's understanding of the topic at hand as well as possible.

The last month or so of the last semester, though, was a major challenge. Outside examiners were brought in to evaluate each student's competence. Each student had to take a three-hour written and a one-hour oral exam on each of the eight seminar topics from the last two years of college. The eight examiners of each student met after the grueling written exams and the one-hour oral exams had been evaluated, and had the responsibility and power to decide whether that student graduated with highest honors, with high honors, with honors, or "in course" (without honors)—or would have to stay and complete further requirements before being allowed to graduate at all. We did have the opportunity to practice written exams on the four seminars we had had by the end of the junior year; these practice exams were typically read and reviewed by the relevant professors, who made helpful suggestions about how the essays could have been improved.

During my first four semesters at Swarthmore, I took various required liberal arts courses, as well as some elective courses in French and Spanish. One full-year course was in European history; my first-semester grade was one of the few C's I ever got; I hardly learned anything. During the second semester, I thought I began to understand a bit more, but my grade was a D+, the only such low grade I ever received in my whole life. (I have occasionally mused about the ironic fact that during the last three or four decades of my academic career I had managed to get a fairly good reputation as an historian of psychology and that the courses at Swarthmore in which I had gotten the lowest grades were on history.)

I had several memorable teachers at Swarthmore. Miss Philips taught a course on French literature which I enjoyed a great deal, and for which I wrote several term papers in French. From Hans Wallach (whose picture appears on page 89) I took an honors seminar on perception, and under his supervision I performed with a research assistant of his, Dorothy Dinnerstein, some of the first experiments I ever designed (on the determinants of contour belong-

4-3 Miss Philips, French professor at Swarthmore *(courtesy of the Friends Historical Library of Swarthmore College)*

4-4 Maurice Mandelbaum *(courtesy of the Friends Historical Library of Swarthmore College)*

4-5 Karl Reuning *(courtesy of the Friends Historical Library of Swarthmore College)*

4-6 Dr. Silz *(courtesy of the Friends Historical Library of Swarthmore College)*

ingness in perception), which were published some ten or so years later in the prestigious *American Journal of Psychology*. Wolfgang Köhler's honors seminar on "systematic psychology" was devoted primarily to the advantages of Gestalt theory and the errors of all other systems of psychology. Maurice Mandelbaum's honors seminar on the philosophy of esthetics made me aware of the enormous contribution of Gestalt theory to the understanding of beauty. Karl Reuning offered an inspiring honors seminar on linguistics. From Dr. Silz I took an honors

4-7 Robbie MacLeod *(courtesy of the Department of Psychology, Cornell University)*

seminar on Goethe with only two students in it: my native-German-speaking Austrian-born roommate Stefan Machlup and myself; Professor Silz's wife always prepared fresh-baked German coffee cake or cookies for the mid-seminar coffee break. And Robbie MacLeod insisted that every serious student should learn to master several foreign languages and taught an honors seminar on language and thought, which inspired me to become interested in this topic for the rest of my life, partly because of my early bilingualism and my interest in sentence parsing at Mayflower School.

One other one-semester course I remember was taught by the famed poet W.H. Auden, who was for one year a visiting professor at Swarthmore. He would come into class wearing slippers and a dilapidated sweater, dump some books out of his briefcase onto the table at the front of the classroom, pick one up apparently at random, open it haphazardly and start reading some poem. He would ask for impressions of it and provide his own comments as well. Assignments he would make for the class could require such things as generating a short poem with a very strict struc-ture and rhyming pattern, or other esoteric re-quirements. I also remember Auden inviting a group of us students to his rented apartment one evening and encouraging us to join him in downing small glasses of pure vodka.

4-8 Wystan Hugh Auden *(from https://www.flickr.com/photos/augu stusswift/524399404: W. H. Auden by NC Mallory)*

Activities at the college were not limited to classes and seminars. I hosted a weekly 15-minute radio program at the college's radio station WSRN, and some-times played (not very well) tympani or double bass in the college orchestra. I also learned to play bridge, and I was exposed to TV for the first time: a friend who was a member of a fraternity (I never was invited to join one) asked several of us non-members into his frat house, to show off a small black-and-white screen, perhaps three or so inches high by some five inches wide, in the front of a huge wooden cabinet box perhaps three feet wide by five feet high; I have no memory of the particular pro-gram. I also had the opportunity to hear an interesting lecture on anthropology by the famed Margaret Mead, as well as a concert of singing and guitar playing by the legendary African-American musician Leadbelly.

4-9 TV set much like the first one I ever saw *(courtesy of the Early Television Foundation and Museum)*

I earned some spending money by washing silver-ware in a pantry off the dining room and by serving as a "reference librarian" (with little or no knowledge or skill) in the college library. For a while I distributed mail early in the mornings to students, faculty, and staff into boxes at the college post office. I was (and am) very fond of soft-boiled eggs, which several of my fellow students didn't care for, and they would save up to a dozen or so for me every morning, to consume with great pleasure after completing my mail sorting duties and shelling the eggs into a large bowl.

A couple of my "poems," available on pages 446-449, were published in the college "litmag" or "literary magazine," the *Dodo*. Pianos were available in a number of places on campus; I often played impromptu improvised pieces, sometimes for female students I was dating. There was a record player near the top of a dormitory, Worth Hall, where one could choose and play whatever met one's fancy; I remember that several times I went there alone and played De Falla's *Fire Dance*, to which I would dance vigorously.

Someone suggested that I should attend "meeting" some time. Swarthmore had been founded by Quakers, and although there were few traces left of the Quaker heritage, there was a "meeting house" on campus where every Sunday, or "First Day" to the Quakers, a meeting "for worship" was held in the morning. Attenders sat in pews or on benches around the four sides of a single empty cen-

4-10 Friends Meeting Hall, Swarthmore College campus *(from https://commons.wikimedia.org/wiki/File:Swarthmore_Friends_Meeting_a.jpg by Smallbones)*

tral square, and most of the hour or so of "meeting" was spent in silence. If some member of the congregation was sufficiently moved to do so, that member would stand up and briefly and in simple words deliver the message that had inspired the "sharing," then sit down after the minute or two required for the message. Each such sharing was followed again by at least several minutes of silence, during which the members of the congregation meditated on the message. Some meetings were silent for the whole hour, some included three or four sometimes related and sometimes unrelated messages, and some might have had as many as six or seven. At the end, the clerk shook hands with those seated nearby, and the rest of the group shook hands with their neighbors as well. After that there usually was a period for sharing "joys and sorrows," events in individual members' lives or that of their families that they wished to share with others. Often after "sorrows" the clerk suggested that the group should "hold in the light" the afflicted person or persons, a form of silent prayer by the whole congregation. And that was about all that happened at most meetings. No sermons, no hymns, no music. Having been raised in an essentially agnostic (basically areligious, not theistic or atheistic) family, I found this form of shared group worship very congenial, as I did the Quaker or "Friends" belief that "there is that of God in everyone," and that one's task in life is to bring "that of God" out from oneself, as well as encouraging that goal in other people. I found this perspective and orientation to be compatible with whatever I may have learned about ethical culture at Fieldston School, and to the extent that I have been involved in any religious activities during the rest of my life, I have claimed that, if anything, I might be considered a Quaker, even though I have always just been an "attender," never formally requesting to become officially a "member" of a Quaker group. But I did officiate at my younger son's Quaker wedding.

There were many warm relationships with fellow students at Swarthmore, both male and female, but none of them have persisted to the present day, even if a few did last a long time. The longest lasting probably was with Stefan Machlup, who was a roommate for a while. He was one of a V-12 Navy group at the college, and went on to become a professor of physics at Case Western Reserve University in Cleveland, OH. Until shortly before his death a few years ago, he came to Colorado every winter for a week or so to ski with me and my family.

At Swarthmore, Stef was a physics major, who tried some rather peculiar ways to improve his use of time, including times for study. At one point, for at least a few months, he developed a routine of sleeping for three or four hours, studying or going to class for five or six hours, then sleeping for three or four, and so on, so that often he would be awake, studying during wee hours of the morning when everyone else was sleeping, or sleeping during the middle of a day when everyone else was wide awake.

I remember that he had a distinctive alarm clock which he would carefully place somewhere far across the room from his bed so that he would have to go some distance to turn it off, far enough away to dissuade him from returning to bed. At the appointed time, the clock would begin with a soft "ding," followed some ten seconds or so later with another "ding"; this would go on for about a minute. If it didn't get turned off before the end of the minute, it would break into a loud and insistent almost explosive screeching alarm, which would cause anyone near it to go to it and turn it off.

Stefan was the son of a prominent political economist, Fritz Machlup, an Austrian who was an ardent skier and became famous enough to be president of the prestigious AAAS, the American Association for the Advancement of Science, which only rarely elected someone who was not a physical scientist to its top post. Author of many influential monographs and textbooks, Fritz, and his Austrian wife Mitzi, later served as surrogate parents for me when I was a graduate student at The Johns Hopkins University, where he was a distinguished professor.

Stef had a somewhat tragic life. He devoted enormous amounts of energy and resources during his academic career at Case Western University to the teaching of physics, and spent decades in writing what he hoped would

4-11 Stefan Machlup as a student at Swarthmore *(courtesy of the Friends Historical Library of Swarthmore College)*

become a major textbook for teaching introductory physics in colleges, but when this magnum opus was published late in his career, it did not do at all well, and shortly went out of print. Stefan did serve as a consultant to many institutions of higher learning, with the support of his national association, advising them on the teaching of introductory physics, and made many personal visits to different institutions to evaluate and try to improve their instructional practices and resources. Although he did manage to publish a few research papers (and articles about the teaching of introductory physics), he was disappointed that he did not manage to make any significant theoretical or experimental contribution to his field. I think that although he did achieve tenure, he never rose above the rank of associate professor, much to his frustration.

Stefan had a brief, unhappy marriage to a girl who left him soon after the birth of their twin boys, Peter and Eric. Hoping to help his sons adjust to the difficult circumstances, he supported their undergoing psychotherapy when they were quite young with a lay psychoanalyst in Cleveland—whom he later married. This second marriage I believe worked better than his first one.

Music was an important component in Stef's life, and he frequently practiced on the cello. His hearing unfortunately became quite poor fairly early in his life, and he was seriously deaf during his last years. Nevertheless, he managed to remain reasonably cheerful down to the end; although he was a few months younger than I, he died several years ago.

During his later visits to Colorado my wife and I noticed that he and his wife were taking an enormous number of pills every day. We didn't know what those pills were for, but wondered whether all that medication and the possibly deleterious effects of the interaction of all those pills might not have played a role in his rather early demise.

Earlier, during better times, Stef would attempt to teach my children how to ski; his father Fritz had been a ski instructor in the Austrian Alps, and Stefan tried to keep this tradition going. I remember Stef taking me on a ski trip to Stowe, VT, possibly during my first semester at Swarthmore, probably over a week-long spring break. We stayed at a farm family's house, Countess Dale Farm, where Stef had stayed before. I recall the overnight train trip from the environs of Philadelphia to a small town in southern Vermont, White River Junc-

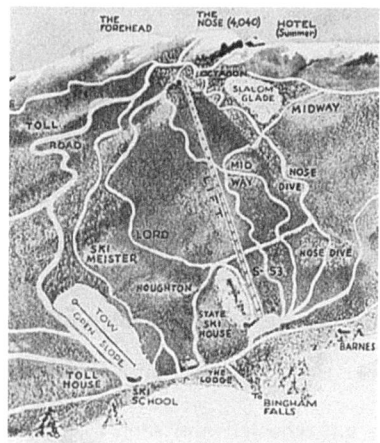

4-12 A historic poster of Stowe, including the Lord Trail *(from https://www.stowetoday.com/things_to_do/spotlight/a-stowe-legend-the-nose-dive/article_d129ca83-66bf-535d-a829-049f0a31f936.html)*

tion, where we changed trains at some time like two in the morning to take a local milk train to Stowe that got us there fairly early in the morning.

I had been introduced to skiing when I was some two or three years old, on tiny short skis perhaps a foot long with large curved tips and using a single pole, but hadn't skied thereafter as far as I remember until Stef took me to Stowe. The trails on Mount Mansfield ranged from the expert S-53 down to the beginner's trail that was a dirt one-lane vehicle road needed during the summer to drive to the summit of the mountain: the Toll Road. Stef started me on an intermediate trail, the Lord Trail. There was a chair lift to the top of Mt. Mansfield. When it was very cold, riders of the lift were given a large blanket in the center of which was a hole for one's head, to keep one relatively warm during the cold and windy trip up to the summit. I remember falling down over a dozen times during my first descent on that "intermediate" Lord Trail. The owner of Countess Dale Farm had some "horse liniment" good for injured joints, which he gave me to help take care of a bruised knee. It did help.

I remember one other event which probably occurred while I was still a student at Swarthmore. Skiing in my usual pretentious attire including a white shirt and a black tie with white polka dots on it, I entered a race at Mount Mans-

4-13 Cross-country skiing in my modest uniform *(family archives)*

4-14 Brad Fisk *(courtesy of the Friends Historical Library of Swarthmore College)*

field, and even though I managed to fall down during my rather recklessly fast descent, I won a pin of a bronze pair of skis by coming in third. I have no idea what became of that pin, but I do remember my classmate Brad Fisk cheering me on during that race.

Stef also encouraged me and my children to stop off in Cleveland and spend the night there in his house with him when for several summers I was driving with them to spend a month or more with my mother and Schani in Brookhaven, Long Island, NY. "Motel Machlup" was always a pleasant break during the almost two thousand mile drive from Colorado to the east. He was indeed a good friend.

4-15 Larry Weiskrantz as a student at Swarthmore *(courtesy of the Friends Historical Library of Swarthmore College)*

Another roommate at one point was Larry Weiskrantz, a quiet, brilliant student who later joined me as a graduate student in experimental psychology at Harvard and then had a distinguished career as a prominent psychologist at Oxford; the children and I visited him once many years later in England in his beautiful thatch-roofed home there, and he came to visit us in Boulder once during the early 1970s when I remember there was a huge snowstorm. I recently again resumed rewarding communication with him, but he passed on a little while ago.

There were also several members of the Yntema family, originally from Hol-

4-16 George Yntema *(courtesy of the Friends Historical Library of Swarthmore College)*

4-17 Douwe Yntema *(courtesy of the Friends Historical Library of Swarthmore College)*

4-19 Howard Sachar
*(courtesy of the Friends
Historical Library of
Swarthmore College)*

4-18 John Pessolano
*(courtesy of the Friends
Historical Library of
Swarthmore College)*

4-20 H. C. R. Landon in
later years *(from
https://www.geni.com/peo
ple/H-C-Robbins-
Landon/60000000264653
42165)*

land, who were students at Swarthmore when I was there: George, Douwe, and a sister whose name I have forgotten. Douwe had been an airplane pilot in the military before he returned to college to complete his undergraduate education; he too later was a fellow graduate student of experimental psychology at Harvard. When we graduated, he asked me to join him in renting a small two-seater propeller plane at a nearby airport for a half hour to celebrate our graduation; he let me take the controls for a while during that flight, which I greatly enjoyed. I had fewer interactions with his older brother, George, who did once visit us years later in Boulder.

Brad Fisk, who cheered me on in the race at Stowe, was another good friend with whom I exchanged Christmas cards for decades; he became the owner of a small ship yard on western Cape Cod, and visited us once years later, admiring the primitive mountain cabin we owned and in which he stayed with us overnight once. He too has passed away. Howard Sachar was another friend with whom I had occasional encounters many years later; he made quite a name for himself as an historian.

I also dimly remember John Pessolano, a kind of Italian don nicknamed "Pesso," who as an undergraduate had an admiring entourage, both male and female, who doted on him. One other memorable person was a roommate at one time: Howard Chandler Robbins Landon, or H.C.R. Landon, or "Robbie"; I remember him playing records of Haydn symphonies and accompanying them enthusiastically on a single tympani drum that he had tuned to two different notes at two ends. He later became the world's expert on Haydn, writing the definitive biography of that composer and overseeing the recording of performances of all of Haydn's many symphonies. He too has passed on.

John Rosselli was yet another roommate at one time. He was an expert cartoonist and spoke with a British accent. He later married an attractive fellow undergraduate, Nickie Timbres, returned to England, and had a distinguished career there as a journalist, working among other papers with the *Guardian*.

I don't recall how I met Amy Roosevelt, but we enjoyed a good friendship at Swarthmore. She got in touch again decades later, in Colorado. It was pleasant to see her. She invited Marilyn and me to play tennis with her and a partner unfamiliar to us; they were by far the better players, and trounced us soundly.

David Beardslee was a fellow psychology major who went on to a successful academic career in Michigan. For that matter, one of the first books in which I was involved was a joint project with Beardslee, a rather lengthy anthology of articles on perception. He and I selected the items for the anthology and condensed most of them. I translated and condensed several of my father's German articles for the book, as well as an excerpt from Albert Michotte's French writing on the perception of causality. The book ended up being published by Van Nostrand at Princeton, NJ, and turned out to be quite successful.

Ward Edwards (whose picture appears on page 106), another psychology major, became a fellow graduate student at Harvard; more about him in that part of the story. A few female psychology majors, who were enrolled in the same seminars I was—Jane Torrey, Rachel Hare, and others whose names I can't recall—also went on to successful academic careers later.

4-21 John Rosselli
(courtesy of the Friends Historical Library of Swarthmore College)

4-22 Amy Roosevelt
(courtesy of the Friends Historical Library of Swarthmore College)

4-23 David Beardslee
(Oakland University Archives and Special Collections)

4-24 Jane Torrey *(courtesy of the Friends Historical Library of Swarthmore College)*

Remembering all these illustrious fellow students makes me realize again what a privilege it was to be at Swarthmore at that time. Not only inspiring interactions with stellar faculty members, but also many discussions with other students, often impassioned and lasting until late at night, made the Swarthmore experience an enormously exciting and stimulating intellectual delight. We were encouraged to explore freely any intellectual issue or problem that took our fancy, read and write and argue about it to our hearts' content, and share our thoughts about it with eager colleagues. It was enormous fun.

I changed my major several times, from French literature, to linguistics, to philosophy, and finally to psychology, and graduated in 1947 with high honors in psychology and a Phi Beta Kappa key. I became committed to an academic career in which I could actually be paid (a modest amount, it's true) for spending my time exploring fascinating intellectual issues in an atmosphere of academic freedom with eager colleagues and students and with library and laboratory resources—and I might even occasionally help to make modest but possibly significant pro-gress in clarifying some fascinating issues or solving

4-25 Rachel Hare *(courtesy of the Friends Historical Library of Swarthmore College)*

some new problems, or old problems in new ways. I'm deeply grateful to my Swarthmore experience for having instilled and encouraged that love of open but rigorous inquiry in me; it became a continuing inspiring perspective for all the rest of my life, and not only in my career. It has been an immense source of satisfaction, pleasure, and fulfillment as well as, of course, a frequent source of frustration when a particularly recalcitrant issue refused to become clarified. But the positives have far outweighed the negatives over the years and decades.

The Swarthmore years were also the time when I became fully aware of the intense attractiveness of the feminine sex and the enormous pleasures that sexual activities with attractive and responsive girls could yield. I'm still puzzled by the mystery of sexual attraction; I never have been able to figure out why I find some females extremely attractive while others leave me cold. My reaction is often immediate and very strong: there simply is something about my first impression of females that automatically ignites an immediate attraction to some, while I couldn't possibly react that way to some others. The proportion of these reactions is very unbalanced; probably some 90% of women don't produce attraction in me at all, and no more than four or five percent immediately do so intensely. It is all a mystery. I'm sure there are enormous individual differences among males about what they find attractive in a female. In my case, females who are small, firm, and lithe, whose bodies look like that of a teenager irrespective of the female's actual age, who are demure, have a fetching smile and a positive outlook on life, tend to produce the impression that they are attractive and desirable, but I doubt that I can put into words what it is that makes them so distinctive for me. But this immediate reaction to females on first meeting or even seeing them has been with me from my early adolescence until well into my eighties. It is a source of pleasure—and of mystery.

One of the first girls whom I found so attractive at college was Enid, a shapely, blushing young lady whom I remember seeing in a revealing tight-fitting black full-body bathing suit while we were both swimming in the college pool. She and I dated briefly for a while, and engaged in impassioned petting, but it went no further than that. I found out very little about her, and have no idea what she was studying nor what became of her. I remember that during one particularly passionate kissing and petting session she confessed that she was having occasional intercourse with a sailor who, like Stefan, was part of a V-12 Navy group at the college. When with some concern I asked her whether her intimate encounters with him involved use of a condom, she replied that they did.

4-26 Enid *(from https://archive.org/details/serpentine1947penn/page/116, Special Collections, Francis Harvey Green Library, West Chester University, West Chester, PA)*

For that matter, I remember going to a drug store in downtown Swarthmore once to buy condoms in case I would ever have the opportunity to use one with a co-

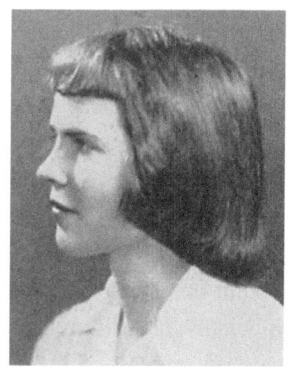

4-27 Janet Gay *(courtesy of the Friends Historical Library of Swarthmore College)*

ed; somehow I did manage to make that purchase from a young clerk even though I felt intensely embarrassed. But it didn't really occur to me until somewhat later that it was disconcerting that Enid was promiscuous enough to engage in impassioned petting activities that produced strong arousal in both of us while she was also engaging in intercourse with another male occasionally during the same period.

Another female student whom I found enticing but whom I never even dated was called Janet Gay. Her last name struck me as appropriate (the term "gay" had not yet taken on the meaning of "homosexual" at that time); she was a vivacious, active girl with a fetching smile. I was too timid to dare to ask her for a date, but I do remember having fantasies about interactions with her. Another girl with whom I occasionally played bridge also had a last name I found fit the impression I had of her; she was called Janet Hotson, and I thought the adjective "hot" was appropriate for her. (I never dared to ask her for a date either, but I remember seeing her again many decades later when I attended the 50th reunion of my graduating class, and to my surprise, even though there were previous acquaintances whom I could hardly recognize, I found her just as attractive at that time: still a lithe, ebullient lady with a body like a teenager's.)

I did once date Wolfgang Köhler's daughter Karin, who was several years younger than I, but probably because of my admiration for her father and my fear of his possible displeasure, I did not pursue that relationship.

Then there was Jocelyn, another slender girl whom I found attractive, and whom I did date several times; I even brought her for a weekend stay over to my mother's and Schani's house in Center Moriches on Long Island, but that romance did not

4-28 Elizabeth *(courtesy of the Friends Historical Library of Swarthmore College)*

flower either. Years later I also dated Elizabeth, the daughter of a famous nuclear physicist. I remember taking her on some drives in a car at speeds faster than the limit, which excited her and aroused her; and I even persuaded her to become a fellow counselor at the Ethical Cultural School Camp one summer, but soon tired of her because I found her to be too bulky and heavy. How selfish and inconsiderate of me! Not a very kind or compassionate reaction or bit of behavior on my part, I must confess, but as I mentioned a little while ago, I haven't managed to figure out my reactions to females. They remain an enigma. And I'm afraid that I have been thoughtlessly unkind to all too many women in my life, including my first wife.

My most passionate relationship at Swarthmore was with John Rosselli's cousin, Silvia, who was two years younger than I when she became my sister Lise's roommate. Lise had come to Swarthmore too as a student, one and a half years after I started college. I remember during Lise's first year there I became devastated during a course I was taking on the history of philosophy when I was reading René Descartes and encountered his proof of his own existence, "Cogito ergo sum," "I think, therefore I am." I followed his arguments about doubting everything because of the fallibility of all sensory information since all senses are prone to illusions. But his tortuous reasoning that brought back a belief in reality left me unconvinced. The Latin "cogito" or "I think" grammatically contains the first person singular, "I"—but grammatical content is not an epistemological proof. All that of which one can be convinced is that thinking is occurring, Latin "cogitans," but there is no connection from that thinking to an "I." This left me in consternation for several days, unable to keep from doubting everything including my own existence. Perhaps all human experience, as well as the sense of self and one's own existence, is nothing but an illusion. Lise managed to pull me out of this adolescent blue funk, urging me to join her in pleasant activities from singing and laughing to enjoying a fine meal in the college dining room.

But getting back to Silvia. She was tiny, slender, soft yet wiry; I soon had a nickname for her, Piccola or Pico, "little one" in Italian; she had been raised in Italy. I found her irresistible, and was obsessed by her for months. We spent many evenings together, and couldn't stay apart.

Many years later, just a few years ago, I was visiting my sister Lise in Durham, NC, where she was teaching at Duke University; Lise showed me an autobiography that Silvia had sent her. She had gone back to Italy, had married and had at least one son, and had had a successful and rewarding life. I had never forgotten my intense time with Silvia at Swarthmore, and was somewhat surprised to read in the book, which was in Italian (which I can hardly decipher), that Silvia briefly mentioned me in her life story. She claimed that she had had a "little seduction" of me when we were students. For decades I had assumed that it was I who had tried to seduce her; apparently from her perspective it was she who had tried to seduce

4-29 Silvia Rosselli and me *(family archives)*

me. Maybe that is why our relationship was so intense, and for me so memorable: we each thought we were responsible for seducing the other. I believe that it was a significant, memorable experience for each of us.

During my years at Swarthmore, I still spent several summers at the Ethical Culture School Camp. I remember a number of young females there whom I found attractive. A few young female counselors attracted me; there was one whom I enjoyed watching paddling in the front of a canoe while I was paddling in the back, whose name I don't remember. One young plump camper by the name of Ruth seemed to enjoy my attentions when we escaped during an evening under the social hall. Helen, whose elder brother was a counselor, was also a strikingly attractive young teenager. Two very young girls in bathing suits down at the swimming areas on the waterfront excited me too. Janie probably was no more than seven years old, wore only a swimming suit bottom and no top, and would gleefully shake her ample head of water-filled hair at older male counselors; and I remember Susan, probably no more than twelve years old, who wore a white semi-transparent bathing suit that revealed her already well-developed teenage body.

Connie, the daughter of the principal at Fieldston School, I found very attractive; she, too, often wore a red full-body bathing suit that revealed her very well-shaped young teenage body. She occasionally slipped from her cabin on the girls' line late in the evening to join me; we would fondle each other, with that activity clearly pleasurable for both of us. I wisely didn't pursue this relationship any further, even though at one point I remember talking with her about a longer lasting relation sometime after the magic summer months at camp were over.

Then there was Nancy Miller, the lithe, tiny, athletic, and extremely attractive little teenager who typically wore a skin-tight gray full-body bathing suit that exquisitely displayed her gorgeously formed, round, firm little body. She may have been only eleven or twelve years old, but I remember that she and I, for some reason or other, several times walked, just the two of us, down the dirt road to the waterfront, both barefooted. Her graceful almost dancing walk and her blush and smile revealed that she clearly was aware of my admiration of her body. She was a close friend of a small, dumpy girl with a very similar name, Nancy Mills, whom I didn't find attractive at all. I never did anything to express my intense attraction to Nancy Miller, but her image has remained with me for decades as the quintessentially attractive young female, the ideal. I have no idea what became of her, but her image remains indelibly etched in my memory.

5 Graduate School: Hopkins

Wolfgang Köhler thought that I had devoted more of my time as an undergraduate student to social sciences and humanities than I should have, and encouraged me to become more conversant with experimental psychology and the natural sciences. While I had been duly indoctrinated into Gestalt theory at Swarthmore (and during my childhood at home), he arranged for me to begin graduate work in experimental psychology at The Johns Hopkins University, where the ghost of the founder of behaviorism, John B. Watson, was still haunting the theoretical orientation of the psychology department.

Köhler also encouraged me to apply to the Belgian-American Education Foundation for a grant to spend a year or two to study with Albert Michotte at the University of Louvain; Michotte had done some beautiful experimental work on the perception of causation (how the apparent motion of one object colliding with another appears to impart the movement to the second one), experiments the results of which fit neatly into the body of Gestalt work on perception. I had read Michotte's work at the suggestion of both Köhler and Hans Wallach, and had found it inspiring. My command of French was good enough by then that I had little trouble in reading Michotte's monograph on the perception of causation, which at the time was available only in French, and my knowledge of French probably would have sufficed for me at the University of Louvain. I did obtain the necessary forms for applying for the grant, but for some reason never bothered to fill them out and submit them.

Instead, in the fall of 1947, I enrolled as a graduate student in psychology at Hopkins. I remember being badly confused by the fact that everything I had

5-1 Part of the Johns Hopkins University's Baltimore Homewood campus *(courtesy of Johns Hopkins University)*

© Springer Fachmedien Wiesbaden GmbH, part of Springer Nature 2020
M. Wertheimer, *Facets of an Academic's Life*,
https://doi.org/10.1007/978-3-658-28770-2_5

learned was right about psychology at Swarthmore was considered wrong at Hopkins, and that everything I had learned was wrong was here considered right. The spirit of behaviorist Watson was indeed still very much alive. The objectivist fetish considered everything subjective, such as the Gestalt interest in perception, as inappropriate for scientific study, and insisted that all wholes are basically nothing more than the associated concatenation of their elemental parts, a position that was anathema to Gestalt theory.

Another challenge was that right away, during my first semester at Hopkins, I was given a teaching assistantship. I had the responsibility of conducting fairly small recitation and discussion sessions for a large introductory lecture course on psychology. It was a daunting experience, since quite a few of the students were older than their inexperienced twenty-year-old TA. But it did provide me with some income, helping to defray the costs of tuition and a room in the attic of a house near the Hopkins campus which I was renting from an older retired couple.

The room I rented for the year and a half I spent in Baltimore cost me $30 a month. Included in that fee was 10 cents each morning for a breakfast of toast and coffee. But I remember many mornings at breakfast in that house when the lady of the house would surreptitiously slip me a fried egg when her husband wasn't looking, or her husband would slip me a slice or two of bacon when his wife wasn't looking. They were very generous to me. I recall that I found, hanging inside the door of the small closet of my room under the roof, a chart indicating the colors of ties that would be appropriate for different colors of suit jackets. And my room was directly above the couple's bedroom. The

5-2 Me in 1949 *(family archives)*

husband was quite deaf, and I remember his often snoring loudly during the night—and his wife first saying, not very loudly, "Stop it!" and then more vehemently, "Stop it!" and finally shouting, "STOP IT!," which would end his snoring, at least for a while.

One thing that struck me about my graduate career in psychology, in preparation for a career of teaching psychology at an institution of higher learning, is that at no time was I ever trained how to teach. Graduate instruction was purely on the content of the field, and on how to do publishable research and other scholarly work. I'm afraid that this is still typical at most graduate programs in most fields in the more prestigious graduate schools in the United States: future professors never learn anything about how to teach, even though there is a quite substantial research literature now available about effective teaching methods. Lecturing, typically known to be the least effective instructional technique, is still the one that is most frequently used.

One course in which I was enrolled beginning with the first semester was an undergraduate year-long one that was an introduction to the physical sciences. I must have taken that course to try to fill in my lack of previous exposure to the natural sciences that Köhler had deplored. It was divided into three successive parts, respectively on physics, on chemistry, and on geology. I didn't get much from the sections on physics or chemistry, and the identification of different kinds of rocks in the geology section left me cold—but I did enjoy the sections on meteorology and especially on vulcanology that were part of the geology sequence.

Another was a graduate-level laboratory course held in the prestigious Hopkins Medical School, on physiological psychology, a predecessor to what is now called behavioral neuroscience. The course required students to cut up and partly dissect sections of the musculature and nervous systems of live cats that had been brought into the laboratory. I was greatly disturbed by having to anesthetize and then cut apart these poor creatures who, at the beginning of the lab session, had walked around unsuspiciously, and had rubbed my ankles while purring. The experience traumatized me sufficiently that I never again did any experimental work with live animals.

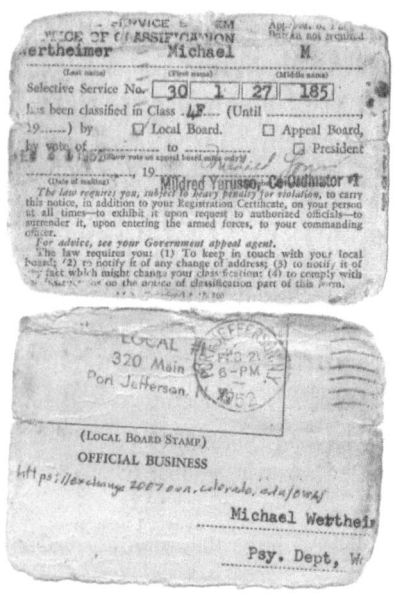

Early in my career at Hopkins, in addition to my teaching assistantship, I was given a research assistantship, which further helped defray the costs of my stay there. This assistantship also provided me useful experience with psychophysics, the experimental study of the relationship between physical aspects of stimulus conditions and the qualities and intensities of resulting sensations and perceptions. My task was to measure the visibility of blips on different designs of radar scope screens. Because of the potential military utility of the results of these experiments, the project was classified. Anyone involved with it had to undergo and pass a security check.

5-3 My draft card *(family archives)*

By then I had a draft card showing that I was classified as 4F, ineligible for military service, because of a physical problem (not a so-called "student deferment" because I was working on a project with potential military benefits) produced by several knee injuries. Back at the time I was drafted while still a student at Swarthmore, the use of safety bindings while skiing was not yet widespread. I had had a bad fall, twisting a knee while skiing with Stefan one season, as a result of which one knee had a circumference several inches greater than that of the other. After I had prepared myself for my expected induction into military service by returning borrowed clothes to their owners and had gotten rid of various pieces of furniture such as a hassock and an overstuffed chair to fellow students, the physician who examined me at the induction center noticed the swollen knee and ordered me to return a couple of months later for induction. But by the time I returned later to the draft board, I had managed to twist the other knee badly, so that now the previously uninjured knee had a substantially larger circumference than the previously injured one. The examining physician noticed the problem, and declared me 4F, claiming that if I did not have corrective surgery on both knees, I probably would not be able to walk in ten years. I didn't have the surgery and I was still skiing more than sixty years later, and haven't had any problem walking or running—or even rock or mountain climbing.

But my draft card (which I still carry in my wallet some seven decades later because the card says in small print, *"The law requires you, subject to heavy penalty for violation,* to carry this notice…on your person at all times") didn't suffice to establish my clearance to work on a sensitive classified military project, such as measuring the detectability of blips on various designs of radar scope screens. I couldn't supply a US birth certificate (I did have my German one, which didn't help), and I had no certificate attesting to my US citizenship. The chagrined authorities at Hopkins rushed me from Baltimore to Washington, DC, where I did obtain an official certificate of derivative citizenship, because my parents had indeed become US citizens late during the 1930s, so this potential threat to US security was removed, and I was permitted to continue with the research project by having been cleared to have access to confidential sensitive information.

My graduate professors included Alphonse Chapanis, from whom I took a rigorous course in statistics, and who was one of the pioneers in the field of human engineering, or research on "man-machine" relations, including such matters as training in expert trouble shooting, designing complex mechanisms in such a way that average human beings could learn to operate and use them while making a minimum of errors, and making complex displays of information such as in a fighter plane cockpit easy to read—for example, having all the pointers in an array of dials pointing in the same direction if everything is functioning as it should, so that a single pointer out of line would become immediately noticeable.

5-4 Alphonse Chapanis *(courtesy of the Archives of the History of American Psychology, The Drs, Nicholas and Dorothy Cummings Center for the History of Psychology, The University of Akron)*

Another professor, scarcely five or six years older than I, was Wendell R. "Tex" Garner, a psychophysicist. He supervised the experimental project I undertook for the master's degree, a study of binaural auditory localization. The two ears were separately stimulated by soft pure tones via earphones, varying the phase of the tones, their relative intensity, and their times of onset and offset to see how this affected the apparent locus of the sound source in the space around the head: directly in front, to one side, or at an angle between these two. The results of the experiment ended up published under both Garner's and my name in the prestigious *Journal of the Acoustic Society of America*.

One other empirical study I performed informally at Hopkins was the outgrowth of a rather obscure monograph on "speech physiognomy" by Heinz Werner I had read earlier at Swarthmore. One of Werner's claims was that the sound of spoken words often appears somehow to match the words' meaning, typically to a far greater extent than mere onomatopoeia. Köhler had also done an experiment years earlier, in which he asked participants to match two different nonsense line drawings, one a curved, bulbous shape and the other a spiky one with straight lines and sharp points, with either of the nonsense words "maluma" and "takete" (pronounced in German *ta-keh-teh*); the result had been almost universal matching of "maluma" with the curved shape and "takete" with the spiky one. I had asked various multilingual students at Swarthmore to provide me with words from their (foreign) language in which they felt that the sound somehow matched the meaning of the word but were not cognates of a word with similar meaning in English. On the basis of their input, and of my own intuitions based on acquaintance with German, French, Spanish, some Latin and some Greek, I pre-

pared a modest "test" in which, for each foreign word, two possible meanings were presented (one that was the actual meaning of the word and another which either meant the opposite or something entirely unrelated), and the participants had to guess which of the two was the correct meaning. I've forgotten how many words there were on this "test," but I think it may have been some thirty or forty or so. At any rate, if there was nothing to the idea that some words' sound actually in some way matches their meaning, then the result should be

5-5 Wendell "Tex" Garner
(courtesy of Franklin and Marshall College)

chance, that is, that participants would usually get no more than half of them "correct." But typically, if I remember right, most participants (who were haphazardly chosen friends and others) got more than three quarters of them right.

I gave this test to Tex Garner, too. He was convinced that my interest in Gestalt theory and other subjective nonsense, such as this business that words' meanings may in some way match their sound, was misplaced. When I scored the results of his test, I saw to my astonishment that he only got about a fifth of them "right," a result that definitely could not be attributed to chance. He must have had the same reaction to the words as my other partici-

5-6 Clifford T. Morgan *(from https://www.psychonomic.org/pag e/clifford_t_morgan)*

pants, and in his ornery way, in order to try to disprove my hypothesis, deliberately chosen the alternative meaning that did *not* match the sound of the word.

The department chair was Clifford T. Morgan, perhaps ten or so years older than I, who had just published a textbook on physiological psychology that quickly became very popular. He struck me as rather self-assured and imperious. I have no idea any more why I did so, but fairly early during my second year, sublimely naive and impetuous, I went into his office once and complained to him about his department's commitment to objectivism and behaviorism and its utter disdain for the Gestalt theory, which I knew from childhood on was brilliant and correct. I don't remember his responses—if, indeed, he made any—but I did decide to leave Hopkins after three semesters, after finishing the requirements for my master's degree. Tex Garner tried to dissuade me, arguing reasonably that if I stayed there for another two years or so I could complete my PhD degree by the age of 23, but I didn't follow his advice. Instead I left for Swarthmore College again, where, for one semester, I was to become a full-time research assistant to Solomon Asch.

Other memories of my time at Johns Hopkins are sparse. I remember there was a tall, broad-shouldered, muscular fellow graduate student in the experimental psychology program whose name was Mike Leyzorek. He, much taller

5-7 Fritz Machlup *(from the 1957 Hullabaloo; courtesy of the Ferdinand Hamburger Archives, Sheridan Libraries, Johns Hopkins University)*

than I, would greet me with "'Lo, Mike" and I greeted him with "Hi, Mike," and we both enjoyed the joke. I remember several pleasant evenings at the home of Fritz and Mitzi Machlup, Stef's parents; they not only invited me for dinner on several occasions, but also took me along on several ski trips to New England. I was impressed to learn that Mitzi claimed to have been the first woman to ski down the tremendously steep Head Wall of Tuckerman's Ravine on New Hampshire's highest mountain, Mt. Washington. I also remember her handing out delicious sandwiches during the drive north to go skiing.

Another rather sordid memory is of a not very attractive fellow female student whose name I can't recall, with whom I had a brief affair that wasn't satisfying to either of us. And then there was Betty. She was a secretary in the department who had recently been divorced, an extremely attractive, slender girl probably no older than in her middle twenties, and we had a number of dates, including playing badminton in a nearby gymnasium. I even took her for a weekend to my mother's and Schani's Long Island house in Center Moriches; she clearly was interested in a longer-term relationship with me. That affair did last a few months. Fortunately, though, nothing came of this relationship in the long run.

My time at Hopkins was devoted almost entirely to my studies, being a TA, and doing laboratory research, as well as a few social activities with the Machlups and my escapades with females: I never really got acquainted with the rest of the university or with the city of Baltimore. But one memorable event occurred when there was a (rare) heavy snowfall in Baltimore, and the local newspaper carried a brief story and photo of Fritz Machlup and me cross-country skiing on a local city street.

I'm not sure how or by whom it was arranged for me to return for a semester to Swarthmore. I must have been paid from a research grant obtained by Solomon E. Asch (pictured on page 57), who had helped my father prepare the manuscript for his influential book, *Productive Thinking*, and who by then insisted that I use the same nickname for him, "Shlaym," which his attractive, pleasant wife Florence used. Asch was doing experiments with students from Swarthmore and from nearby Haverford College that explored the effect of group pressure on perceptual reports, ingenious experiments that deservedly became classics in experimental social psychology.

The experimental setup was as follows. A group of six participants sat in a small room in separate chairs that faced a blackboard with a chalk tray that ran its full length. Displayed about two feet apart from each other on the chalk tray were pairs of vertical white cardboard sheets, about six inches wide by about two feet high. The one on the left displayed a single vertical black stripe perhaps an inch wide, and varied in height in successive pairings from as short as about six inches to as high as a foot and a half. On the right in each pair of displays was a comparable piece of cardboard with three vertical black lines also an inch wide, but varying in length, labeled below the lines as 1, 2, or 3. One pair might, for example, consist of a twelve-inch high black line on the left sheet of white cardboard, and the lines eleven, twelve, and thirteen inches high on the right-hand cardboard. The participants' task was to report which line on the right was the same height as the one on the left; ostensibly to save time, they were asked to report their judgment out loud to the experimenter, who would record them. For this particular pair, the six participants would, for example, duly all say "2" in succession; the task was not particularly difficult. The process continued for several more pairs of cards, sometimes with the differences in length of the three lines on the right being somewhat less easy to perceive than with the initial pairs. The experiment proceeded rather routinely and somewhat dully for a number of such pairings. But then the situation changed, at first in a fairly modest way but then rather disturbingly. The fifth subject was placed into an enigmatic situation: all the preceding participants had routinely reported "1," "1," "1," and "1," when it looked to the fifth participant as though "2" must be the correct choice. The next pair of two would not have this problem, but then there would be a pair in which the other participants unanimously chose, say "2," while it was clear to the fifth participant that this was wrong, and that line "3" was the same length as the test line on the left. These kinds of anomalous situations continued for several more pairs, with the other participants unanimously reporting a match that was clearly inconsistent with what the fifth participant could see. How would the fifth participant deal with this situation? Many of the participants in the fifth position in the sequence were clearly disturbed, fidgeted, and were hesitant in making their report; a few of them stuck to their guns and reported what they actually saw even if it disagreed with the reports of all the other participants, but many also, apparently with some reluctance, gave the same report as their colleagues, even if they could see that the reports did not match their own clear perception.

This situation was produced by having all of the participants other than the fifth one being, unbeknownst to the fifth participant, secret accomplices of the experimenter. They had all been instructed beforehand how to respond to the successive pairs; only the fifth participant was the true naive participant in the experiment. This kind of deception produced a severe conflict for the one true participant, and part of my job as Asch's research assistant was to debrief them after the experiment was terminated, try to help them relieve the anxiety that was engendered by the procedure, and reassure them that what they had done was okay because their reactions were similar to those of others who had been placed into this challenging situation, and were normal. Many participants were quite shaken by their experience, but many also found that it was a useful one— whether or not their own reports had been consistent with those of the majority or had been what they had actually seen. For many, it had been a rather traumatic experience. The experiment did succeed in demonstrating the power of the effect of majority opinion on the individual, even if in later years objections have been raised about performing deceptive experiments of this kind on unsuspecting participants that may be emotionally challenging to them. One clear conclusion of the experiments was that the actual perceptual experience of people is not changed by a majority opinion inconsistent with their own perceptions, but reports about such perceptions can indeed be affected by contrary majority opinion.

Part of my job was to do variations of Asch's experiment by varying the size of the majority and by adding an accomplice whose responses accorded with the actual participant's perception. It turned out that having at least one participant before the critical participant who gave the same report that fitted the true participant's perception greatly reduced compliance with the majority, and that the size of the unanimous majority was not very important: a "majority" of two was almost as effective as a group of four, six or even eight, but having at least one other participant who gave the same responses that the true participant knew was right greatly reduced the tendency to go along with the majority report. One other finding of substantial interest was that even those participants who had gone along consistently with the majority by making the same report did not claim that their perception had been altered in any way; they knew that their report did not match their perception.

I remember spending at least a part of the summer that year after the spring semester at Swarthmore in Center Moriches at my mother's and Schani's house, where, feeling somewhat presumptuous, I dictated the reports of the Asch experiments into a fancy dictating machine that recorded them on small purple discs. These discs were sent back to Swarthmore, where they were duly transcribed by someone. The substance of these reports was used to become part of the text of a successful social psychology textbook that Asch published a few years later; I remember feeling somewhat chagrined that Asch did not provide any acknowledgment of my contributions to those experiments, nor to the reports about them that I had written or dictated (though I think he may have given me minor credit in a footnote).

I think I also occasionally had some interactions with Hans Wallach during

5-8 Hans Wallach *(courtesy of the Friends Historical Library of Swarthmore College)*

5-9 Richard "Dick" Held *(courtesy of Julie Held)*

that 1949 spring semester. I remembered him fondly from my earlier undergraduate years there; he was an awkward, tall, thin man with a posture that reminded me of a question mark. That last characteristic struck me as singularly appropriate, since I remembered his teaching technique, which I found very effective. In seminars he would discuss some issue and then raise questions about it to which he requested the students to respond (even though it later turned out that he knew the answers well himself). He would make some hesitant tentative remarks, gulp, and wait for student reactions. It did make his students think. He had been a bachelor for years, but then had married quite late. His wife, I believe, died not long after a son was born to them. There were some developmental issues with his son, and for years he took care of him at home. I don't know what became of Wallach's son.

There were two students of psychology at Swarthmore at that time whom I remember, both of whom later had distinguished careers but recently passed away. Richard "Dick" Held was working on a master's degree, and co-authored some major papers with Köhler on the latter's theory of satiation, which I will return to shortly. Held later had a distinguished career as a psychologist at MIT, the Massachusetts Institute of Technology. Ulric "Dick" Neisser was an undergraduate student who later became a pioneer in the field with his groundbreaking book *Cognitive Psychology*.

Neisser performed a well-designed experiment on extrasensory perception (ESP) for his undergraduate honors candidacy. If I remember right, he used the classic Zener cards, a deck of 25 cards composed of five sets of cards each containing a star, a triangle, or some other symbol; these cards had already been used in many prior experiments on ESP. Neisser had one person serve as a sender, who successively stared at and concentrated on each of the 25 cards, and a number of receivers who were to guess at the symbol on each of the cards while the sender concentrated on them at carefully timed intervals. His experiment was intended to determine whether ESP worked according to the inverse square law, in other words whether accuracy in identifying the symbols varied systematically according to the square of the distance separating sender and receiver. He had one receiver sitting back to back with the sender, another across the room, a third in the same building but several rooms away, a fourth somewhere across campus from the sender, another some distance away in the same town, and a final one some states away, or some such arrangement. His hope was that the closer to the sender the receiver was sitting, the greater that receiver's accuracy would be. He repeated the experiment with numerous senders and receivers, but I fear that the main result of all this careful procedure was that virtually none of the receivers, irrespective of how close or far away from the sender they were, were able to recognize any of the symbols at more than a chance level. I doubt that Neisser ever published a report of the results of this well-controlled study—and my own memory of its having been performed at Swarthmore may be wrong; it may have been carried out at Harvard University instead.

At the time, Köhler, Wallach, Held, and others were doing research on figural aftereffects, a kind of illusion in the perception of a given figure produced by prolonged visual inspection of a previously pre-sented figure. Köhler's theory was that the inspec-tion of the initial figure produces a change in the cerebral structures stimulated by that figure in such a way that the resistance induced could dis-tort the perception of a subsequently presented figure, the brain correlate of which would be stim-ulation of an adjacent locus in the brain. If one stares at a fixation point with a horizontal rectan-gle to the right of it, the corresponding part of the occipital lobe in the brain would become "satiat-ed" or increased in resistance to later stimulation. Thus a pair of little squares in a subsequent test figure, just above and just below the location of the previously "satiated" rectangle, should look farther apart vertically than identically spaced

5-10 Ulric "Dick" Neisser
(courtesy of the Archives of the History of American Psychology, The Drs. Nicholas and Dorothy Cummings Center for the History of Psychology, The University of Akron)

squares on the left, because the resistance of the location in the brain corresponding to the space between the squares on the right had increased as a result of
satiation with the inspection rectangle. Köhler and Wallach had done many experiments on this figural aftereffect. Köhler thought that it might be possible to
produce the same kind of electrochemical resistance in the occipital visual cortex
artificially by a weak electrical current through that part of the occiput that was
presumably affected by "satiation" with prolonged visual exposure to an inspection figure, and asked me whether I would be willing to serve as a participant in
an experiment to test this idea. I immediately concurred.

So Köhler attached some electrodes to my occiput at the back of my skull in
places that would result in brain stimulation corresponding to where he considered that satiation would be induced by prolonged inspection of a visually presented figure. He first checked whether there would be an appropriate distortion
of a test figure by prolonged inspection of a visually presented satiation figure;
there was. So he assumed that the relevant part of my occipital brain had indeed
been satiated in a way that was consistent with his theory. Thereafter, after the
visually induced satiation had had enough time to dissipate so that the two vertical distances between pairs of little squares above one another to the right and
left of the fixation point in the test figures again appeared equal, he tried to induce the same satiation and distortion in my brain by passing a very weak electrical current through that same part of the occipital brain via the electrodes attached to my skull. My recollection is that there was no resulting perceptual
distortion at all; the two right-hand squares looked just as far apart vertically as
the pair of squares on the left. The experiment didn't work. All that resulted was
that I suffered a minor headache that was gone within less than an hour.

One other memory concerns an event which occurred while I was back at
Swarthmore in the spring of 1949. I know that my mother and Schani were almost always short of funds. I remember proudly lending Schani $200 to help him
buy a car. Whether or not that loan was ever repaid, I don't recall, but I do remember being proud to have the financial resources to lend my impoverished
stepfather some money.

Having just thought of this incident reminds me of another event related to
money that also occurred while I was spending some time with my mother and

stepfather on Long Island, but must have tran-spired several years earlier. I remember naively going to a nearby bar because I needed some cash, and asking the bartender if he would cash a check for me. I

5-11 Schani and Anni, probably on Long Island, 1950 *(family archives)*

had brought a check along and was about to fill it out when I was so startled by his response that I actually burst into tears. He stared at me with incredulity and fire in his eyes, slammed his fist down on the bar, and sneered, "Get the hell out of here." It was a rude encounter with the fact that not everyone trusts every stranger. I even remember some regulars at the bar laughing at me as I slunk out of the bar, mortified.

Vacation times, Christmas, other holidays, and summer weeks that I wasn't at the camp were spent in successive houses in which my mother and Schani lived, first in Caldwell and Essex Fells, NJ, and later in Center Moriches and Brookhaven on New York's Long Island. One summer in Brookhaven I remem-ber having a brief affair with a fairly young divorced girl, a Marilyn whose last name I don't remember, who was the daughter of one of my mother's lady friends. I remember my mother encouraging the relationship with this girl, whom she called "Marilyn Monroe" when talking about her with me. The affair didn't last long; as I recall, she ended up a few months later marrying someone we didn't know.

This may be a reasonable spot to offer a comment about instructional styles, and modes of testing for student understanding with various kinds of material. I remember being somewhat appalled by the contrast between Swarthmore and then Hopkins; and my later graduate experience at Harvard was no better. Going from college to graduate school was like going back to high school. Tests were again multiple choice or true-false questions, and other rather automatic and superficial devices, and the typical teaching mode was again lecture.

At Swarthmore the Socratic method prevailed in seminars in the honors program; there were discussion, debates, student-generated papers, and mainly student presentations, and "objective tests" were not the rule. Somehow Swarthmore had encouraged respect among students and respect for students on the part of instructors, while the teaching and student evaluation techniques at the prestigious graduate schools belittled the student and acted as though the instructors' obligation was to try to help fill the poor empty heads of students with things they didn't know but needed to know, using drill, repetition, and other methods to pour the wise and mature older instructors' wisdom into the incompetent students. I think my shock at the contrast between my Swarthmore honors program experience and my disappointment with instruction in graduate school helped me develop my own later teaching style, in which I tried to show my respect for students and my support of students' efforts to raise questions about a teacher's views about a given subject matter; perhaps this may help explain why, somewhat to my surprise, I received several awards for teaching during my later career.

5-12 The dining room at the Hopkins Faculty Club *(courtesy of the Johns Hopkins Club)*

Another memory of Hopkins that seems worth recording is that graduate students who were teaching assistants were eligible to use the Faculty Club. This club had facilities for playing ping pong and billiards, of which I took advantage, and also had a dining room in which, for $1.75, one could get a multiple-course hot meal

at lunch time. That is
where (in addition to my
breakfast of toast and
coffee—with additions
from my host and hostess
at the house where I was
renting a sleeping room) I
typically ate my main
meal of the day. I remem-
ber that I basked in the
opportunity to interact
there not only with fellow
graduate teaching assis-

5-13 The game room in the Hopkins Faculty Club *(courtesy of the Johns Hopkins Club)*

tants, but also with many impressive mature scholars in other fields who ate lunch there and typically treated us graduate students as colleagues—and would even deign to play table tennis or billiards with us.

Although I learned some advanced statistics, learned about generosity from my landlord and landlady, became more conversant and comfortable with psychophysics and with designing, conducting, and writing up experiments and other empirical work, and also engaged in some further explorations and escapades with attractive members of the female gender, those two years (1½ at Hopkins and half a year back at Swarthmore) in my twenties don't feel all that memorable in terms of my growing up, maturation, education, or becoming who I think I now am.

6 Graduate School: Harvard

While I am not sure how I managed to get into the doctoral program in experimental psychology at Harvard University, an exclusive program that only accepted three or four new students every year, once again Wolfgang Köhler may have played a role; and I know that my father had had some mutually respectful correspondence and interactions with Edwin Garrigues Boring, a prominent Harvard professor in what was now the department of experimental psychology. Just a short time before I got to Harvard, the earlier Department of Psychology had split into two separate departments: Experimental Psychology, and a new Department of Social Relations which encompassed social psychology, cultural anthropology, social psychology, and clinical psychology.

I rented a modest apartment in Cambridge near the campus with a fellow Swarthmore graduate, Pete Dodge. I don't remember what his field of study was, nor what became of him. Within a few weeks of my arrival in Cambridge I had effectively moved in with a fellow graduate student in experimental psychology, Nancy MacKaye. She was a talented artist and absolutely brilliant student. More—much more—about her later.

Almost all my working time in Cambridge was spent in the basement of Memorial Hall, "Mem Hall" to its denizens; that is where the Department of Experimental Psychology was housed. I remember sharing an office with another student, Bill McGill, who later became president of Columbia University.

There happened to be some kind of conveniently placed horizontal pipe near the ceiling above

6-1 Pete Dodge *(courtesy of the Friends Historical Library of Swarthmore College)*

6-2 Bill McGill *(courtesy of the University Archives, Rare Book & Manuscript Library, Columbia University Libraries; photo by Manny Warman)*

© Springer Fachmedien Wiesbaden GmbH, part of Springer Nature 2020
M. Wertheimer, *Facets of an Academic's Life*,
https://doi.org/10.1007/978-3-658-28770-2_6

6-3 Memorial Hall *(from https://commons.wikimedia.org/wiki/ File:Tower_with_Clocks,_Memorial_Hall,_Harvard_University.jpg)*

my desk, and I remember keeping a small cardboard box of provisions that hung from a rope above my desk that was slung over that pipe. Condensed mushroom soup, crackers, and dried fruit were the source of meals like lunch or supper when I didn't have the opportunity to eat those meals elsewhere. All I had to do was untie the knot holding the rope slung over the pipe, lower the box, and there was my meal.

I had a "Parker Fellowship" (I don't know what benefactor endowed that fellowship, nor who helped me apply for it and obtain it) for my first year at Harvard; I remember that the $800 it provided seemed like an immense amount of money—and indeed sufficed to cover all my costs, including tuition, books, housing and food. I soon also was a teaching assistant for E. G. "Gary" Boring, for courses in introductory psychology and the history of psychology. I don't remember what other financial support I had later, but all through my higher education I was supported by grants, scholarships, fellowships, or various kinds of assistantship. Possibly my father's benefactors, the Elkans, helped support me financially during my first year or two at Swarthmore, but after that I believe I always managed to make my way financially myself—including the $200 loan I had proudly managed to make to Schani for a car, as mentioned earlier.

During the first year there was a graduate "Pro-Seminar" which all new students were required to take, taught for several weeks each by all the members of the faculty. It was an intensive advanced introduction to contemporary experimental psychology. One of the most impressive instructors was Karl S. Lashley, a world-famous physiological psychologist who knew his field cold and who spent most of his time in Florida running the Yerkes Laboratories of Primate Biology. A brilliant lecturer, he spoke quickly without notes and in clear, articulate, grammatically impeccable sentences that included citations of relevant recent literature as though he were reading from a carefully edited version of a scholarly manuscript that had been published in an important peer-reviewed journal.

6-4 Edwin Garrigues ("Gary") Boring *(courtesy of Harvard University, Department of Psychology)*

Boring had recently published a letter to the editor of the prestigious house organ for the American Psychological Association, the *American Psychologist*, in which he touted the eighty-hour week for aspiring and contributing psychologists. Any psychologist or graduate student hoping to have a successful career should be prepared to spend at least 80 hours a week working, and he strongly encouraged this practice in his students and colleagues, as well as doing it himself. I was no exception, and almost blindly followed his recommendation. Early every morning I showed up in the basement of Mem Hall, and I wouldn't leave it again until late in the evening to go home to sleep for a few hours, and then show up early the next morning at Mem Hall

6-5 Karl S. Lashley *(courtesy of Harvard University, Department of Psychology)*

again. Often I was even unaware of the weather; it might have been bright and sunny in the early morning when I got to Mem Hall, and then there could be several inches of snow on the ground when I left late in the evening to go to bed; there were no windows in the basement of Mem Hall to let its denizens know what was going on outside. And it didn't matter. Almost every waking hour was devoted to study or research or a seminar. My time was totally consumed by my graduate work. Just as I had never explored Baltimore or the rest of the Johns Hopkins University campus while I was there, all I explored of Cambridge and Harvard, with very few exceptions such as used book stores, was my immediate surroundings during my studies.

I remember little about other seminars I took, but there were some. I also soon was doing research in the Psycho-Acoustic Laboratory, a well-equipped facility that was high-tech for its time and was set up to do research primarily in auditory psychophysics. It was directed by S. Smith ("Smitty") Stevens, who I believe was the incumbent of a special professorship in psychophysics that had been created just for him. He was to become the supervisor of the research I did later for my doctoral dissertation.

Boring made it a point routinely to have a one-on-one luncheon at the Harvard faculty club with each new graduate student in the department. I remember little of that lunch other than his expression of respect for my father and his Gestalt theory, even though he himself disagreed vehemently with the theory. In fact, my dismay with the theoretical disagreements among respected mentors that had already become so striking at Hopkins, where the behaviorist atmosphere conflicted so severely with the Gestalt perspective that had been ingrained in me since childhood, was further exacerbated at Harvard. Just as Swarthmore had been a major center for Gestalt psychology, and Hopkins carried on the tradition of behaviorism, there were strong traces of the structuralist tradition at Harvard. Boring had in fact been one of the most prominent students of E. B. Titchener, the founder of the structuralist school, an approach that was profoundly elementalistic and subjective, and against which both Gestalt theory and behaviorism, each for very different reasons, had rebelled. First I had been taught that Gestalt theory had the truth, then behaviorism, and now structuralism. The final result was that I became quite eclectic in my theoretical orientation, although I did retain a lifelong respect for the Gestalt orientation and a strong tendency to value clear, objective experimental evidence—a value shared by all three schools. I have been and am a firm believer in the scientific method as the best epistemological tool, as the most trustworthy source of reliable knowledge, and my later identification with cognitive psychology during the last four or five decades of my career was consistent with my continuing adherence to a Gestalt approach.

I don't recall much detail about my work as Boring's teaching assistant for introductory psychology or history of psychology, except that he used texts he had co-authored ("Boring, Langfeld, and Weld" for the introductory course, and his classic, monumental *History of Experimental Psychology* for the history course). Boring almost always had a kind of strange, artificial fixed smile on his face, which somehow appeared untrustworthy. I recall being quite startled to see that smile while he lectured, on the day after a tremendously traumatic day: his daughter had just committed suicide—and that smile was there, undaunted, on the face of the presumably stricken father. It was indeed a deeply disturbing, almost ghoulish experience for me; I don't know how Boring managed to maintain his composure in the way he did, when this time must have been so tragic for him.

John G. Beebe-Center was a "dollar-a-year" member of the experimental psychology department faculty who had inherited a huge fortune from the Heinz 57 company, and taught and did scholarly work for the university simply because he enjoyed doing so. He was the author of a successful text on feeling and emotion, and I think he taught a course or seminar on that topic, too. What I remember most about him, though, is that he induced me to read an obscure German monograph by a German scholar, von Senden, that summarized the not very extensive world literature of documented cases of the experience of people who were born blind but later regained sight. Donald Olding Hebb had just published an influential book, *The Organization of Behavior*, in which he claimed that developing the ability to recognize or even just to see visual objects requires extensive learning, and Hebb cited von Senden's book as providing evidence to support his conclusion about the necessity of learning to see. Beebe-Center had skimmed von Senden's book and had tentatively concluded that few if any of his cases actually corroborated Hebb's hypothesis. Knowing that my native language was German, he suggested that I

6-6 John G. Beebe-Center *(HUP Beebe-Center, John G. (1), Harvard University Archives; courtesy of Bachrach Portraits)*

read the monograph carefully, and come to my own conclusions about how accurate Hebb's use of von Senden's material actually was. It turned out that Beebe-Center was right. Much of the case material in von Senden's book contradicted rather than corroborated Hebb's view.

Beebe-Center convinced me to write a brief note for publication about this matter. I remember his infinite patience as I prepared successive drafts of the note. He would painstakingly go word for word with me in his office over every sentence in the first page or two of each draft, asking, "Is this word really the right one here in this place?," "This sentence implies such and so; do you really intend to have that implication?," "Doesn't this point require a bit more elaboration?," or "Can't this point be made more effectively in fewer words?" I don't remember how many drafts there were before both he and I were satisfied that it actually did say what we wanted it to—probably at least a half dozen.

Especially impressive to me was the consequence of his suggestion that I send the draft to Hebb himself (who was president of the American Psychological Association in 1950 or so) for his comments before submitting it to a journal; I assumed that this was just a bit of professional courtesy, but the outcome was startling to me. It gave an immense boost to my respect for some of the leading scholarly psychologists of the time, among whom I definitely count both Beebe-Center and Hebb, whose selfless devotion to the efforts of a mere graduate student were deeply, deeply appreciated. Hebb responded within less than a week to the request for comments about this note, the central point of which was a rather severe criticism of Hebb's own work, by making both stylistic and substantive suggestions that *strengthened* my argument against him. His scholarly integrity was truly astonishing and amazing. He set an instructive example of selfless scholarly integrity for me unmatched by anyone else, an example which I admired and still admire immensely. The multiply-revised manuscript was duly published in the pres-

6-7 Donald Olding Hebb
(courtesy of the University of British Columbia Archives [UBC 5.1/3771])

tigious *American Journal of Psychology* before I was 25 years old.

Edwin B. ("Eddie") Newman had visited our house in New Rochelle when my father was still alive, and had, indeed, spent some time in Germany earlier when he was a graduate student himself studying with Wolfgang Köhler and my father in Berlin and Frankfurt. He had become chairman of the new Harvard department of experimental psychology, and I remember him in effect taking me under his wing when I first got to Cambridge. I learned later that his multi-year chairmanship of the department was made in the somewhat unflattering way that the appointment was always on an annual basis; his colleagues in the department in effect had the power to unseat him at the end of any academic year if they were dissatisfied with what he was doing for them. He apparently did the job of keeping his colleagues reasonably happy well enough to continue for several years in that role of the relatively powerless department chair.

6-8 Edwin B. ("Eddie") Newman *(courtesy of the American Philosophical Society)*

At one point I also served for a while as a research or teaching assistant to Burrhus Frederick Skinner, better known as B. F. Skinner, or "Fred" to his colleagues and his graduate students. His systematic psychology, "descriptive behavioristics," became immensely popular with a large number of devoted followers both nationally and internationally, and some historians have claimed Skinner as the most influential American psychologist of the second half of the twentieth century. His approach to psychology ostensibly eschewed any theory at all, and concentrated instead on the purely objective description of behavior and its determinants. Under what conditions does an organism emit what kinds of responses, and how is the probability of the reoccurrence of these responses affected by their consequences in the environment? Environmental events that increase the subsequent probability of those preceding responses are labeled positive reinforcers—and Skinner analyzed in detail how this simple mechanism can explain an immense range of human (and animal) behaviors. Skinner also

6-9 Burrhus Frederick Skinner
*(from https://commons.wiki
media.org/wiki/File:B.F._Skinner
_at_Harvard_circa_1950.jpg)*

offered a graduate seminar in which I enrolled; he challenged the students to come up with any human behavior which couldn't be accounted for fully with his simple descriptive principles. All the students, including myself, tried hard to find any such behavior, but none of us succeeded.

He even wrote a popular novel, *Walden Two*, which became an international best-seller, and which describes a human community based on his principle of reinforcement: actions which enhance individuals' own competence, and which altruistically are helpful to the well-being of the entire community, are reinforced, leading to a kind of utopia. Several "experimental communities" were in fact set up by volunteers in a variety of places in this country and abroad, trying to follow Skinner's principles, and some of them survived and even flourished for a number of years. Skinner's approach was often unjustly accused of being somewhat authoritarian because people's behavior was viewed as determined not by free will but by the environmental consequences of their actions, as though some evil dictator could induce people to do whatever the dictator wanted—but Skinner actually advocated that people can, by well-planned and proper reinforcement schedules, be encouraged to become the best that they can be.

Incidentally, Skinner also enjoyed playing the harpsichord. And I remember attending a cocktail party somewhere during my stay in Cambridge that Skinner also attended. I have a clear image of Skinner, after having indulged in some two or three martinis, raising a cocktail glass with a flourish, and quietly and immodestly declaring, "Psychology began—with B. F. Skinner."

I helped train pigeons for Skinner in an ingenious piece of apparatus intended to demonstrate the establishment of competitive behavior. He had already induced cooperative behavior in some pigeons with another device, which had two bird cages placed right next to each other; each cage had two distinctively colored buttons at which the two hungry pigeons could peck. They had learned before to peck at such buttons to receive small amounts of food in an automatically supplied feed tray that provided this reinforcement for pecking at the buttons. Soon the test changed; the pigeons, which could easily see each other, now didn't get fed unless they pecked the same keys at the same time. If one of the neighbors pecked the red key in its cage and the other one pecked the green one in its cage, neither got fed, but if they both pecked the red key or both pecked the green key, they both got fed. To cooperate successfully, they each had to see which key the other bird was pecking, and had to emit the same key-pecking behavior as the other bird. It turned out not to be difficult to produce this cooperative behavior with this procedure.

To generate competitive behavior, Skinner ingeniously used a small modified ping pong table, and managed in effect to train pigeons to play ping pong. At first the birds were trained on a device that held a plywood half of a small ping pong table that sloped upward from above the floor where the hungry pigeon was standing. An automatic mechanism started a ping pong ball rolling down from the top of this inclined plane toward the pigeon. If the ball dropped off the end of the table where the bird was standing, the pigeon did not get fed, but if the bird managed to peck the ball hard enough to send it back over the top of the panel so it fell off on the other side, the pigeon did get fed. In this way, it became possible to train several birds to become quite proficient in pecking at the ball so it did not fall down their end of the half ping pong table, but disappeared over the top of their end down the other side. Now it was just a matter of placing two well-trained hungry birds at opposite ends of a ping pong table that had a raised center; an automatic device placed the ball at the top center, and it would begin to roll at random down one side or the other toward one of the pigeons. If the ball fell down on the floor of the apparatus on the side on which one of the birds

6-10 Pigeon ping-pong table *(courtesy of the B. F. Skinner Foundation)*

was standing, the pigeon at the other end of the table received a reinforcement; if it fell down on the floor at the other end, the other hungry pigeon got fed. The birds did indeed end up playing ping pong in the sense that each one did peck at the ball as it rolled down toward them, trying to hit it hard enough to roll over the top and down the other end of the table so they would get fed. I remember Skinner showing this demonstration of competitive ping pong playing by pigeons to several fascinated classes.

One minor complication with this procedure was that soon—actually following Skinner's own principle of reinforcement—the birds learned to cooperate instead of compete. Since the machine that randomly "served" the ball made it start to roll about an equal number of times to one side or the other, both pigeons were fed somewhat more often if neither of them bothered to peck at the ball, so the competitive ping pong "game" soon stopped; the birds simply let the ball fall down on their own side if it happened to come that way, and waited for it to roll off the table on the other side soon thereafter. That way they both got reinforced more often over time than if they continued to peck at the ball and tried to make it go down on the opposite side of the table. The reinforcement schedules resulted in the hungry pigeons being fed more often than if they persisted in the competitive behavior. They soon learned to cooperate instead.

I didn't know many students in Cambridge when I first got there. I do remember that the ones with whom I interacted in seminars or labs or at parties were generally cordial and welcoming. One was George Heise, also in psychophysics; I don't know what became of him. Dick Neisser, pictured on page 91, whom I had gotten to know at Swarthmore, came as a student after I'd already arrived in Cambridge; he ended up having a distinguished career as a pioneer cognitive psychologist. I saw Douwe Yntema again, who had been a friend at Swarthmore; he may have been doing graduate work at MIT rather than at Harvard; I don't remember. Lar-

6-11 Ward Edwards *(courtesy of the Friends Historical Library of Swarthmore College)* ry Weiskrantz, earlier my roommate at Swarthmore, also became a graduate student in the experimental psychology department at Harvard. And Ward Edwards, who had once dated my sister, Lise, while all three of us were students at Swarthmore, was also a fellow graduate student in the same department. He later went to California, where he had a distinguished career in decision theory. He became a pioneer in the new field of cognitive psychology by developing how Keynesian theory could be applied to decision making, generating many later works based on his original insights.

By the time I got to Harvard, Ward was married, and his wife Ruth and he invited me to their Cambridge apartment for dinner within a few days after my arrival. They introduced me at that dinner to another graduate student, from Ann Arbor, MI, who had been in Cambridge several months before I got there: Nancy Mac-Kaye, alias Lavinia Steele MacKaye, alias

6-12 Nan and me, early 1950s *(family archives)*

"Nan" to all her friends and acquaintances. We were immediately attracted to each other. In September, 1950, we were married. More about that later.

The topic I chose for my doctoral dissertation turned out to be a bit of evidence about how poor my judgment was at the time. It was consistent with my imprudent ranting about behaviorism and Gestalt theory when I railed against the theoretical perspectives of Cliff Morgan, the department chair back at Hopkins. I decided at Harvard to test a basic assumption that my mentor, Smitty (S. S.) Stevens, was advocating at the time: that absolute thresholds of sensation vary randomly over time: the so-called quantum theory of the variation of absolute sensory thresholds in the human sensory system. I proposed testing this assumption by measuring the absolute thresholds (the minimum amount of physical energy required for the sensory modality to detect it at all) in hearing, vision, and

6-13 "Smitty" (S. S.) Stevens
(courtesy of the Harvard University Archives and the Emilio Segrè Visual Archives, Physics Today Collection)

pain. Stevens' assumption was that these variations are random; I suggested measuring them over time to see whether, according to a variety of measures, they actually are.

My proposal to Stevens, only about a page long, was to measure absolute visual, auditory, and pain thresholds in a small number of participants over various time periods, and then to assess whether these changes were or were not correlated over modalities, and whether or not they displayed any systematic variations. Stevens looked at my proposal, seemed to think it was okay, and asked me to prepare a more fleshed-out proposal. A few days later I gave him one that was some four or five pages long, and he told me to go ahead and do the experiments. He said I could use the psychoacoustic lab for my work, and told me to come back to him when I had some results. He left me almost completely on my own, without providing any detailed supervision. It seemed a bit strange and difficult to me at the time, but it did engender a kind of independence in my work that I later found useful. It got me to pursue any question that interested me in whatever way that seemed to me appropriate, which resulted in my publishing dozens of articles about a broad range of topics for the next several decades. I don't know if this was his intent with his minimal supervision, but it worked in getting me to publish a lot of different experiments and other work which I'm sure helped further my career.

I remember inventing a simple signaling device in a modality I wasn't testing, touch, to indicate to the research participant when a stimulus was being presented for vision, audition, or pain. It was an apparatus attached to the participant's wrist, which had a small lever that would make a metal wire gently touch the back of the participant's hand when I pushed a button in the control room at the anechoic chamber in the soundproof, dark psychoacoustic lab. The participant had been adapted to the dark for at least a half hour before testing began, and the visual stimulus was a small circle of light next to a fixation point; this was used to measure the visual threshold. The auditory threshold was measured with a faint pure tone at a middle frequency presented through ear phones. Pain threshold was measured by directing a beam of light at a round black spot painted on the participant's forehead; long enough exposure to this radiation produced a mild sensation of pain, and the pain threshold was measured in terms of the length of time the radiation was on before the participant noticed the first hint of pain. The participant's task was to push a button held in the participant's hand if the participant sensed the visual, auditory, or pain stimulus after the tactile stimulus had been activated.

6-14 Carl Leventhal *(courtesy of the Office of NIH History and Stetten Museum, National Institutes of Health, Bethesda, Md.)*

The participants in this study, which was performed over a period of several months, were Nan, myself, and an undergraduate student at Harvard at the time who had been one of the campers in my tent in an earlier summer, Carl Leventhal, who later became a physician. Analysis of the measurements was carried out on a Marchand calculator, a mechanical hand-operated gadget with buttons and a small rotating arm that was much slower in carrying out complex calculations than modern computers; I think it typically took me a good hour to analyze the data from a 15-minute session. I used several different ways to determine whether the variations in the thresholds in the three modalities were random or not. All demonstrated that they were not random after all, showing that Stevens' assumption that they are random was disproven. Disproving one of a supervisor's pet theoretical assumptions is not a wise project for a dissertation thesis; it is not a prudent choice, but that is what I had proposed and performed.

Meantime, I had begun to feel that my graduate training had been rather one-sided, so I had crossed the street from Mem Hall to attend a graduate class with Robert W. White, a brilliant, quiet clinical psychologist who had recently published a well-received text, *Lives in Progress*, which subtly, compassionately, and thoroughly described the lives of some former Harvard undergraduates. Boring and Stevens disapproved of my bothering to have anything to do with the rival Department of Social Relations, with which there had recently been a rather

6-15 Robert W. White *(courtesy of the University of Nebraska-Lincoln Department of Psychology and the Nebraska Symposium on Motivation)*

acrimonious split. But I found White to be a wise and congenial psychologist, and became convinced that I should become better acquainted with the "softer" side of psychology.

I applied for and obtained a clinical psychology internship at Worcester State Hospital, about forty miles west of Cambridge in Massachusetts, and I succeeded in getting financial support from a United States Public Health Fellowship in Clinical Psychology. Back then the requirements for eligibility for a clinical internship were much less stringent than they are now. There was no need for prior practica, seminars, or such things as courses on psychological testing or psychotherapy. In the early fall of 1951, Nan and I moved to a pleasant large apartment with a fireplace, high up in one of the staff towers at the enormous imposing state hospital building in Worcester—and I even found a berth for a tiny sailboat (that I had bought earlier), at a pier on tiny Lake Quinsigamond, next to the hospital grounds.

Previously I had sailed on Great South Bay on the south side of Long Island near Schani's and my mother's house, on a tiny canvas fold-up hull that I fitted with leeboards, a rudder, and sail gear in the form of a short wooden mast, a boom made of a broomstick, a small mainsail, and a tinier jib. I also remember having rented a much larger gaff-rigged catboat on Great South Bay one time; it had a lee helm (meaning it spontaneously drifted in a direction away from the wind) and, as a consequence, I managed to tip it over. Fortunately the water was only a few feet deep, so I was able to lower the huge sail, right the hull, and return the boat to where I had rented it, without doing any damage.

The boat I took with me and sailed on Lake Quinsigamond, named the *Ktchoo*,

6-16 Bridge over Lake Quinsigamond, Worcester, MA *(courtesy of Dan Malloy, Hopedale History - hope1842.com)*

was a "Moth," a class of sailboat with a teardrop-shaped hull that was only nine feet long from stem to stern but had a wide beam and very shallow draft. Its mast was a full eighteen feet high and it carried a single large triangular fore-and-aft sail with boom that made the vessel surprisingly fast for its small size. I remember that there was only about a foot or less clearance between the top of the mast and the bottom of the middle of a bridge in the center of Lake Quinsigamond where a major east-west highway crossed the narrow, long north-south lake; sailing the *Ktchoo* on this lake was a pleasure, including the challenge of going under the bridge without losing wind and without having the top of the mast hit

6-17 Me on the Moth *Ktchoo (family archives)*

the bottom of the bridge. I didn't have the opportunity to sail there very often, but I did enjoy it immensely whenever I did.

The experience at Worcester as a clinical psychology intern was instructive and occasionally disturbing. It did result in my becoming somewhat dubious about much of clinical psychology; its beliefs and practices, my experience taught me, were obviously not as thoroughly based on solid empirical evidence as experimental psychology is.

One experience that clashed with my training at Swarthmore, then Hopkins, and then Harvard, all of which emphasized empirical evidence rather than mere opinion, was an event involving my supervisor at Worcester, Leslie Phillips. He was an advocate of the utility of the Rorschach Ink Blot Test for revealing significant aspects of an individual's personality, and had recently completed writing a well-received book on Rorschach interpretation. One of his convictions was that "eye" responses on the Rorschach could be pathognomonic of paranoid ideation.

If the person being tested reported seeing "eyes staring at me out of the gloom," or some such interpretation, this was a sure sign of paranoia.

I did a simple empirical study using the extensive file of many dozens of cases with detailed psychiatric history and close to verbatim Rorschach records available at the hospital, and recorded for each case whether there were eye responses on the Rorschach and evidence in the personal history of any kind of paranoid ideation. Even though the results of the Rorschach test had been used to determine a diagnosis for many of these patients, there turned out to be no relation whatever between eye responses on the Rorschach and diagnoses of paranoia or evidence of suspiciousness in the case history.

I told Phillips about the result of my statistical analysis, and indeed even ended up publishing this finding about the lack of a demonstrable relationship between eye content responses on the Rorschach and any evidence of suspiciousness or paranoia in the case history. Not long thereafter, Phillips was making a routine demonstration of expert Rorschach analysis to psychiatry interns and interns in clinical psychology at the hospital. He read the protocol of a set of Rorschach responses from a patient and noticed an eye content response; the patient saw threatening eyes that were staring at him. And Phillips said, "This patient's description of the Rorschach inkblot is a clear sign—your opinion to the contrary, Mike, notwithstanding—that the patient suffers from extreme suspiciousness and possibly paranoia." His persistence in his belief despite contrary empirical evidence was unconscionable to me; it flew in the face of all of my preceding educational experience, which had always championed the dispassion-

6-18 Worcester State Hospital *(courtesy of the Massachusetts Department of Mental Health)*

ate evidence resulting from well-controlled scientific studies. It wasn't just my "opinion" that eye content responses are unrelated to suspiciousness or paranoia in a patient's case history or diagnosis, it was an assertion based on empirical evidence. Phillips' reaction has, I'm afraid, soured my impression of clinical psychology ever since.

At Worcester I also was given the opportunity to do psychotherapy for several patients. Most of the patients there were chronic psychotics, who had been in the hospital for many years. Supervision of the psychotherapy sessions was minimal; I was largely thrown on my own resources, and didn't really have any clear instruction in how to engage in successful psychotherapy. I remember that we interns were supposed to wear a starched white linen jacket whenever we interacted with patients, and always to be addressed as "Doctor," even though we had not yet earned that degree; this did make me uncomfortable. Nevertheless, we were to be "Doctor" for any patient, whether for psychotherapy sessions or for testing. I performed many intelligence tests and personality tests (including the Rorschach) on a wide variety of patients during my year's internship.

I remember several psychotherapy sessions with a recently admitted young woman patient who was diagnosed with paranoid schizophrenia. I managed to establish some beginning rapport with her when I picked her up from her ward and brought her to the interview room by falling in step with her as we walked down the halls and up and down some stairs; she noticed what I was doing and smiled, and seemed to enjoy the innocent game. During the psychotherapy session, she reported, among other things, being terrified by the grain in the wood at the door opposite the bed in her room at the hospital appearing to flow down next to the hinges; I had no idea what this was about. She also claimed that her husband was sitting in an empty chair in the interview room and was listening to our conversation. When I challenged her hallucination by asking her what color tie her husband was wearing, she laughed out loud and apparently was at least temporarily relieved to acknowledge that the chair was actually empty.

During the stint at Worcester I became aware of some recently published articles indicating that prefrontal lobotomy of some monkeys rather regularly produced a substantial weight gain in the operated primates. Since the patients at the hospital were routinely weighed once a month, it occurred to me that I could find out whether the same finding would be demonstrable in humans. The case records showed which patients—and there were many of them—had received a prefrontal lobotomy and when the surgery had been performed; it was a fairly frequently used operation in cases of severe psychosis at the time. Data from empirical studies showing that this kind of "psychosurgery" ("the benefits of a prefrontal lobotomy") was typically not really effective, and might instead result in serious, deleterious side effects, were just beginning to be made available in the technical literature.

I duly recorded the measured weight of these patients monthly during the year following the lobotomy, and found that indeed there was a statistically significant gradual increase in their weight during that year. I wrote up my finding for possible publication and showed my draft to Nan, who gently pointed out that some controls were needed. What had been the weight history of these patients during the year preceding the surgery? What was the weight history of patients for whom the operation had been proposed, but on whom it had not been performed because relatives' approval had not been obtained or there were other problems? Nan's astute and incisive scientific competence was immensely helpful; I had not thought of these controls until she pointed them out. It turned out that during the year before lobotomy the weight of patients who had received the surgery was increasing just as quickly as after the operation, and that the gradual weight gain over time also occurred in patients who had been recommended for the surgery but had not received it. Clearly the lobotomy had nothing to do with the weight gain after all; something like the fairly heavy food at the hospital and the rather sedentary lifestyle of the patients was doubtless responsible instead.

There was little contact between staff at the hospital and people working at nearby Clark University in Worcester. I do remember some contact with the Clark faculty on at least two or three occasions in which there were at least brief visits with Heinz Werner (whom I respected very much; he was the author of the

6-19 Heinz Werner *(courtesy of the Clark University Archives)*

6-20 Seymour ("Sy") Wapner
(courtesy of the Clark University Archives)

monograph on speech physiognomy that had impressed me as an undergraduate at Swarthmore) and with his younger colleague Seymour ("Sy") Wapner; at the time, the two were doing extensive empirical research on what they called the sensoritonic theory, an approach which was modestly influential for a little while but which soon lapsed into oblivion. It concerned the presumed effects of certain muscular activations on simultaneous perceptual, usually visual, processes.

At the hospital we also became acquainted with several of the psychiatrists. One, a Dr. Hraba of Czech origin, once made the insightful comment that one can have both fleas and lice, indicating that multiple psychiatric problems could simultaneously be afflicting the same patient. Another, whose native language was Spanish, Dr. José Amador y Morales, became a warm friend. He brought a younger brother, Maño, to live with him in his staff apartment at the hospital, and he too became a good friend. (He took the picture on page 111 of me on the *Ktchoo.*) But while we were living there, Maño was killed in an automobile accident, and I remember José—and Nan and me—mourning his death. To express my sorrow at losing him I improvised a loud impromptu dirge in a minor key for him on a piano available at the hospital.

Nan and I went skiing several times with Smitty Stevens while we were in Massachusetts. Smitty owned a fairly large house in Conway, NH, close to a ski area on Mt. Cranmore, and invited various graduate students and others for weekends at the ski resort. As I remember it, Smitty was married, but his wife had developed some kind of incurable chronic condition that required her continued stay at an assisted living facility. Being a Mormon, he did not believe in divorce. Meantime his secretary at Harvard, a competent, attractive young woman who was also a good skier, Didi Stone, had become his constant companion, and served as a welcoming hostess at the ski resort house.

Stevens was an avid skier and at the time was devoting attention to what he cleverly called a "new twist on skiing," about which I think he actually published an article in a ski magazine. He even asked to borrow my pair of old hickory skis to modify them in this new way. His clever idea was to twist each of the skis from front to back in such a way that placing more weight on the right ski would cause the skier to begin automatically turning to the left, while weighting the left ski more than the right would begin a turn toward the right. The tip of the right ski was steamed and gently twisted toward the left while its back end was twisted in the opposite direction, in effect twisting the ski so that its bottom surface was the beginning of a screw pointing to the left, with the mirror image treatment being performed on the left ski. I remember poor Smitty breaking off the tip of one of my skis while trying to get it properly twisted; chagrined, he immediately bought me a new pair of skis.

To be admitted to candidacy for the doctoral degree, a graduate student had to pass some preliminary written examinations. I had taken these exams about a year after I got to Harvard, I think in general psychology, the history of psychology, sensation and perception, and physiological psychology, and had passed. Several times during 1951, I had asked Stevens to look at results I obtained in my threshold studies or at drafts of parts of my dissertation as I was working on them, but he consistently refused, and told me to show him the thesis when it was completed. I finally did so, late in the fall of 1951, and he duly saw to the appointment of an examining committee, which consisted of three members of the department. Stevens was chair of that committee, and the other two members were Gary Boring and William Verplanck, an instructor with a strong behavioristic bias who had recently joined the department.

The standard practice then was to give the three members of the examining committee a week or so to study the dissertation, after which there would be an oral examination of the candidate. So I prepared three copies of my thesis and delivered them to Stevens, Boring and Verplanck, whereupon Nan and I went off to Vermont for a week of skiing.

6-21 William ("Bill") Verplanck later in his career *(courtesy of Jorge Campo, Conductual)*

On returning to Cambridge, I asked Stevens when the oral exam would take place. He told me there would be no oral; the thesis was not considered ready for the final oral examination. Puzzled and frustrated, I wondered what to do next. I asked Stevens, and he said that he thought the problem I had set for the dissertation wasn't very good, but that my methods for testing the problem were fine. Verplanck told me that the problem was excellent, but that the methods weren't as good as they could have been. And when I went to Boring for advice, all he could do was shrug and say that since Stevens and Verplanck thought the thesis wasn't ready for an oral, he just went along with them. I asked all three for advice about what to do next, but none of them made any clear suggestions. So I simply performed a few more minor variations of my basic empirical procedures, undertook some additional analyses, and revised the text. I resubmitted it later in the fall of 1951, and an oral was scheduled for early January, 1952. After a brief oral exam followed by my waiting no more than five minutes for the examining committee to complete its deliberations, Boring came out the door of the examining room smiling broadly, held out his hand for me to shake, and said, "Congratulations, Dr. Wertheimer!" I was 24, two and a half months short of 25 years old.

6-22 Wood carving by Nan on the occasion of me earning my PhD *(family archives)*

7 Wesleyan

Early 1952 turned out to be a good time to receive a doctoral degree from a prestigious university. The job market favored the applicant; there were many openings available for appropriately qualified job-hunters. I remember applying for jobs at several institutions. One of them was Haverford College, a neighbor of Swarthmore and a comparably small and high-prestige liberal arts college. Its president at the time was a respected young geographer by the name of Gilbert White, who had become one of the world's experts on floods and other natural disasters. As it happens, he later became a colleague at the University of Colorado at Boulder when I was there too. I don't remember much about my application to teach at Haverford, but do recall that my interview with White was very warm and cordial. But that visit did not result in an offer.

Another school to which I applied for a faculty position was the University of Idaho. I don't remember why I pursued that one; probably I responded to an ad that I had found in the *American Psychologist*, the official monthly house organ issued by the American Psychological Association, which carried announcements every month of job openings in academia as well as in other settings. When I began applying to other institutions as well, I notified the department at Idaho that I was withdrawing my application, and received a courteous letter from the chair there, saying "I don't blame you one bit" and wishing me well.

Nan was still working on her own doctoral dissertation when I received my PhD and it was clear that it wouldn't take much longer to fulfill all the requirements for her doctorate as well. I don't know whether this fact played a role in our decision to try to remain in New England, but it may have done so. Indeed our decision to spend a year at Worcester State Hospital wasn't just to give me experience I wanted in clinical psychology; Worcester was also a convenient place for Nan to

7-1 Gilbert White *(courtesy of Mary White)*

© Springer Fachmedien Wiesbaden GmbH, part of Springer Nature 2020
M. Wertheimer, *Facets of an Academic's Life*,
https://doi.org/10.1007/978-3-658-28770-2_7

7-2 David C. McClelland *(from https://commons.wikimedia.org/wiki/File:DavidMcClelland.jpg)*

continue her research for her dissertation, which concerned capillary structure in schizophrenics. I may have applied to several other institutions for my first post-PhD job, but I don't remember doing so. Incidentally, the practice of taking one or two postdoctoral interim positions before applying for a long-term tenure-track academic job that has become the rule in most natural-science fields now was not yet common during the early 1950s.

I don't recall how I applied for, and got, a tenure-track job at Wesleyan University in Middletown, CT. The department chair there at the time, David C. McClelland, had spent some time, just before coming to Wesleyan himself, at Harvard in the Department of Social Relations, and I may have become acquainted with him there. At any rate, by the fall of 1952 Nan and I were ensconced in a pleasant modest apartment in a temporary green wooden two-story building, part of a complex of several such buildings which had been built following the Second World War as housing for war veterans, married students, and faculty at Wesleyan; it was less than a mile from campus.

As was the standard practice in those days, my initial appointment at Wesleyan, even though I already had earned my doctoral degree, was as a tenure-track full-time instructor. The expected promotion to assistant professor occurred soon thereafter. My degrees were all from prestigious institutions, Swarthmore, Hopkins, and Harvard, and I already had a number of publications in well-regarded peer-reviewed technical journals. In those days, the success of an academic career was measured to a large extent by the number of

7-3 Our residence community in Middletown *(family archives)*

publications and the quality of the journals in which those papers were published, and not yet by the number of research dollars which a faculty member brought to an institution with research grants, as tends to be a more frequently-practiced criterion today, at least at the more prestigious institutions of higher learning. I never did manage to master the now highly-valued skill of applying for, and receiving, massive research grants.

I did do a bit of outside work as a consultant to the nearby Long Lane School for Girls, whose inmates were problem children brought there because of serious behavioral issues. I was paid to do psychological testing on some of these girls. But that was only during my first year or so in Middletown. My salary from Wesleyan wasn't opulent, but it was enough for Nan and me to live on without needing additional income. I was teaching courses such as introductory psychology, perception, and history and systems of psychology, and had not only a private office in a pleasant ivy-covered old stone building on campus, but ample laboratory space in which I could do research. And I had a talented, brilliant, loving wife. Life was good.

When meteorological conditions permitted, which wasn't often, I sometimes used my skis to commute between the apartment and the campus. At the time, my skis had adjustable bindings: for downhill skiing, the heels of the boots could be firmly held down on the skis, but for cross-country use the cables going around the back of the boots could be loosened so that the toes were held down but the heels were free to rise several inches above the ski.

Among fellow members of the psychology faculty in addition to Dave McClelland was Joe Greenbaum, a pleasant, supportive colleague who later became chair of the psychology department at the New School for Social Research in New York, where my father had taught for a decade many years earlier.

7-4 Joseph ("Joe") Greenbaum *(courtesy of the New School Marketing and Communications records, The New School Archives and Special Collection, The New School, New York, NY)*

7-5 Richard ("Dick") de Charms
*(courtesy of the Friends
Historical Library of
Swarthmore College)*

The psychology department at Wesleyan boasted a modest program leading to the master's degree as well as an undergraduate major that attracted a large number of students. Among students during my three years at Wesleyan was Richard de Charms, who I remember was my teaching assistant at one point, and who had a charming wife. They later divorced; I don't know what became of them later. Then there was a loving young couple, Elliot and Vera Aronson, who lived in a different apartment in the same complex we did, and whom we enjoyed interacting with socially. Elliot and I did a minor research project that resulted in a joint publication; later he became a very prominent social psychologist with a prestigious professorship at the University of California, Santa Cruz; his textbook, *The Social Animal*, became a long-time bestseller. Another student, Richard ("Dick") Alpert, always wore a formal dark suit with a vest, and a white shirt and tie, while he was at Wesleyan. After leaving Middletown, he became involved in the then-popular LSD craze, changed his name to Ram Dass, and turned himself into a major guru with an enthusiastic international following in the counter-culture. I don't think he ever wore a

7-6 Elliot Aronson *(from
https://en.wikipedia.org/wiki/File
:Elliot_Aronson_1972.jpg)*

7-7 Richard ("Dick") Alpert, later
Ram Dass *(from
http://www.timothylearyarchives.o
rg/timothy-leary-and-harvard-
reunited-at-last/ and
https://www.ramdass.org/cropped
ctr_ram_dass-web/)*

suit and tie thereafter. Many years later my son Benjy, then a professional musician, considered it a great honor to come to know Ram Dass and to perform with him on the occasion of several retreats and spiritual gatherings.

I also remember a young couple who lived in the apartment directly above Nan's and mine; they had a rather tumultuous relationship, often shouting at each other loudly enough for us to hear them fighting. I don't remember their first names, but their last name was Wenzlau.

It was at Wesleyan that I worked on the book with David Beardslee mentioned on page 71, though I don't think that he ever taught at Wesleyan. While I was at Wesleyan I also published several articles based on my dissertation research in the *National Hearing Aid Journal* and in the prestigious *Journal of Experimental Psychology*. I was doing research as well on kinesthetic figural aftereffects, and on individual differences in figural aftereffects. In addition, I had gotten involved in both the regional psychological association, the New England Psychological Association, and the national American Psychological Association, and attended conventions of both of these. Ira Hirsh (pictured on page 404), who at the time was a young faculty member at Harvard, initially encouraged me to become a member of these associations, to attend their conventions, and to present papers at their meetings; during my career, I did present

7-8 Jerome S. ("Jerry") Bruner *(courtesy of the Archives of the History of American Psychology, The Drs. Nicholas and Dorothy Cummings Center for the History of Psychology, The University of Akron)*

dozens of papers at psychology association conventions.

One of the areas which was a fad at the time was the effect of motivation on perception, and I remember getting involved in several symposia and debates about the topic, as well as publishing some articles about it. Jerome S. Bruner and Leo Postman, both at Harvard, had

7-9 Leo Postman *(courtesy of the University of Nebraska-Lincoln Department of Psychology and the Nebraska Symposium on Motivation)*

championed this field, at the time called "a new look in perception." Bruner, who was in the department of social relations at Harvard, encouraged my work, and I maintained some form of contact with him for several years. He even visited me in Boulder, Colorado, after I had moved there; at the time he was wooing a wealthy divorcee who was living in a luxurious house in Boulder several blocks away. I recall swimming in the lavish swimming pool at the rear of that house.

My interactions with Leslie Phillips at Worcester, my experience in administering Rorschach tests there, and my interest in perception also got me to start thinking about the implications of the Gestalt theory for how people describe the Rorschach inkblots, leading eventually to a paper on perception and the Rorschach that was later published. And the contact I made with a mature lady psychologist whose name I don't recall impressed me with the potential utility of the dispassionate use of the results of rigorous research in applied settings. I think her job was with a major insurance company in nearby Hartford; it was her task to help in selecting among candidates for jobs as an insurance salesperson. I remember her chatting with me about her research, which included correlating information on the application form with the later sales record of the agents, and pointing out that it could be very useful to the company to use as criteria for selecting among applicants any variable that could be found to be related to a statistically significant degree with the number of dollars of insurance sales accomplished by the agent after being hired by the company—even if the correlate happened empirically to be something as unexpected as the first letter of the applicant's last name.

7-10 Pup tent used to camp at the Montreal congress *(family archives)*

While I was at Wesleyan, a major international congress of psychology was held in Montreal, Canada. I remember taking three or four students along to attend the conference. Because the attendees at the congress from Middletown were rather impecunious, we took along pup tents to camp in during the several days of the convention. We managed to bring

7-11 Jean Piaget *(from https://it.wikipedia. org/wiki/File:Jean-piaget.jpg)*

our tents, sleeping bags, and other camping gear in the car in which we all drove up to Montreal. I had expected that my rather extensive prior study of French would make it relatively easy for me to converse with nearby farmers or other people out in the country near the city of Montreal, to request permission to set up our tents on their land, but was astonished to discover how different Canadian French was from the French I had learned in high school and college. It was essentially the French of several centuries ago. Nevertheless I did manage to communicate well enough for us to be able to set up our modest camp for the duration of the congress.

The congress turned out to be an impressive event for the Wesleyan contingent. Many famous psychologists attended, and I managed to catch several of them on film with a small 8-millimeter movie camera that I had brought with me for the purpose. Jean Piaget, a famous Swiss psychologist, was there, as were many of the psychologists from Harvard including Boring, Stevens, Newman, Bruner, Postman, McClelland, and others as well as some from Johns Hopkins. I also got brief shots of Dick de Charms, and an earlier fellow Hopkins graduate, Eckhardt Hess, whom I had helped with the statistical analysis of some of the data for his doctoral dissertation; he was to become quite well known for work on the imprinting of ducklings of various species on their mothers. There were also even several Russian psychologists at the congress whom I photographed briefly: I don't think I ever heard their names, but I do remember that I was somewhat surprised by their attendance and by their apparently open interactions with colleagues from

7-12 Eckhardt Hess *(courtesy of the Archives of the History of American Psychology, The Drs. Nicholas and Dorothy Cummings Center for the History of Psychology, The University of Akron)*

other lands. After all, this was the era of McCarthyism, the national "red scare" in the United States, and the beginning of the Cold War. Altogether, the outing to Montreal was, as I recall, quite a success.

7-13 "Honey" Dwyer
(family archives)

The secretary of the psychology department during the time I was at Wesleyan was a young, pleasant, attractive woman by the name of "Honey" Dwyer. I don't think I ever met her husband, if any. I do remember seeing her pushing a baby carriage at one time, but I don't know whether the passenger in the carriage was her baby or someone else's. She had a fetching smile and clearly was very competent at carrying out the duties of her job. She also came up with a simple theory of personality that soon informally became the rage among psychology students and faculty at Wesleyan, as well as many couples living in the temporary housing facility where Nan and I were renting our apartment. Her theory was a typology: people are either "slobs" or "bastards." "Slobs" are emotional people who don't think much about the effect of their actions on the future, but give in to their feelings almost all of the time. "Bastards" are cold, calculating rational beings who dispassionately decide what to do in any situation on the basis of strict, objective evidence. Her theory was that any successful dyad, any pair of people who have a lasting important relationship, is composed of one "slob" and one "bastard." The "slob" supports the emotional side of the relationship, and the "bastard" is responsible for making the rational decisions that assure the well-being of the couple. This theory was gleefully applied to any couples people knew, trying to decide for any lasting dyad which one was the "slob" and which one the "bastard." It was the topic of many cocktail party chit-chats and kaffeeklatsches, including predictions about which couples would last and which ones were doomed because there was no clear way to determine which one was fulfilling which role. It was a lot of fun.

7-14 Me "working" *(family archives)*

7-15 Characteristic sketch by Nan, from our early years *(family archives)*

The biggest events during my time at Wesleyan were the birth of Nan's and my first two children. We congratulated ourselves on our successful family planning. We had gotten married in the fall of 1950, I essentially completed the requirements for my doctorate in 1951, and we succeeded in our intention to have our first child in 1952; Karen Anne Wertheimer was born that November. Then Nan completed her own doctoral requirements in 1953, and our second planned offspring, Mark David Wertheimer (alias "Duffy"), was born in the summer of 1954.

Changing from a household of two young adults to one with first one and then two youngsters produced an enormous difference. Our life before had been devoted to our studies, our work, music, interactions with friends (including playing bridge, which I had first learned at Swarthmore, and which Nan and I had occasionally played with Ward and Ruth Edwards) and visits with Nan's parents and with Anni and Schani, as well as Nan's art projects, but now both our lives were largely focused on the well-being of our kids. We loved it. Both of us interacted extensively with them, and our own moods

7-16 Nan and me, 1952 *(family archives)*

7-17 Nan's mother Lavinia, me, Karen, and Nan in 1952 *(family archives)*

and emotional feelings were to a large extent affected by how Karen and then Duffy were feeling and acting. Because of my anosmia I was often given the task of changing diapers and of washing the diapers and hanging them out onto clotheslines to dry in the sun. I recorded some of Karen's first spontaneous sounds on a wire recorder, and composed several lullabies for her.

I have many fond memories of my children when they were very young. Karen typically had a small weighted plastic cup of milk and another with orange juice in it set out for her on a chair as a "table" that was low enough for her to reach when she drowsily came to that chair to have her drinks after her regular afternoon naps. And I remember carrying her around in my left arm, with her right hand firmly wedged at my back so she couldn't suck her right thumb, while I carried out various household duties such as cleaning, cooking, or making butter by continuously shaking a glass peanut butter jar with a tight-fighting metal screw-on-lid that was filled with cream poured off the top of glass milk bottles that werc delivered almost daily to our front door. The resulting butter (after vigorous shaking for about an

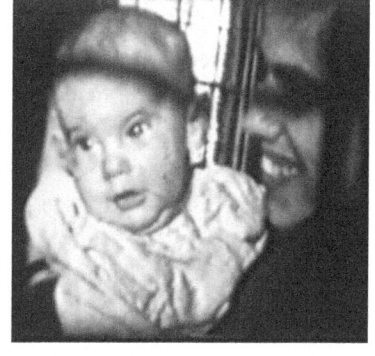

7-18 Duffy and Lise, 1954 *(family archives)*

7-19 My vegetable patch in Middletown *(family archives)*

hour) was surprisingly delicious and sweet, and the buttermilk was quite tasty as well.

I also cultivated a quite productive, fairly large vegetable patch near our apartment; I've managed to have some kind of vegetable patch all my life since childhood. These mini-farms have produced much pleasure throughout the years.

Babysitting was exchanged voluntarily and enthusiastically with other families with young children, and there were quite a few of them at the temporary housing that included our apartment. We participated in this practice, and I took short films with my movie camera of the kids in playpens, interacting with other youngsters, and being cared for by a variety of people.

Projects unrelated to career or kids included a few modest additions to my "bibliophilia," or collection of old books I had started building in Cambridge at a used book shop (where some remarkable older volumes were available often for as little as a couple of dollars, or a dollar, or even only 50 cents), and working on the upkeep of the

7-20 Karen in 1954 *(family archives)*

7-21 Shadrach, Karen, and me outside our home in Middletown *(family archives)*

used 1935 Chevrolet that Nan and I had bought, including rebuilding its relative-
ly simple engine. The car was named "Shadrach"; later cars duly were named
"Meshach" and "Abednego" after three men who, according to Chapter 3 of the
Book of Daniel in the Bible, survived after being thrown into a fiery furnace by
Nebuchadnezzar, King of Babylon.

Before completing my education, I had held a few temporary jobs which did
help my usually somewhat precarious financial situation; I early developed a
pattern of frugality which has persisted throughout my life. It also fit with Nan's
mother's dictum; Lavinia MacKaye Fox sometimes said, "Waste not, want not,"
and that principle has perhaps become a general life tenet for me. I have managed to be financially quite responsible and prudent all my life.

One early job was delivering new telephone books, which I remember doing
on Long Island. Another was a brief stint as a drummer in a summer dance band
at a dive in Center Moriches. I also helped install asbestos insulation in the attics
of homes one summer; the intense heat in these infernos was barely tolerable,
and I wondered later whether it wouldn't have been far less stressful to do this
work in the winter season when the worker wouldn't have to suffer in such a hot
work space—aside from the fact that later it became clear that asbestos is not a
suitable substance for this kind of insulation. Another job that lasted only a week

or so was working at a small factory that manufactured little round indicator dials for display in aircraft cockpits. I sat at a small shop desk in the center of which a knob protruded. "In" trays of photographically exposed plastic dials arrived to my left, and I was to place the discs one by one on the knob. A knee switch activated a machine that made the knob and attached disc rotate, while I had two "guns" with triggers that squirted chemicals at the rotating discs, one a photographic developer and the other a fixative; the guns were attached to tubes that supplied those liquid chemicals. My job was to squirt each dial with the developer until lines and numbers appeared clearly on the disc face, then to squirt them with the fixative to stop the chemical reaction that had been pro-duced by the developing fluid. When I finished with a disc, I stopped its rotation and placed it in an "out" tray to the right of the work space. My anosmia pre-vented me from noticing very much the evidently strong acrid smell of these chemicals. On the third or fourth day my supervisor came by, appalled that I hadn't turned on a switch (that no one had told me about) that activated a power-ful blowing mechanism, a large fan that diverted the foul air outside and that dissipated the chemical fumes. He excitedly shouted, "Are you trying to blow the place up?" Apparently the fumes were dangerous to breathe and also highly flammable, but nobody had bothered to warn me about that. Not surprisingly, I left that job quickly, but I don't recall whether I was fired or just quit.

Three annual academic ceremonies at Wesleyan University required the fac-ulty members to show up in full academic regalia. The first few times I rented the requisite gown, hood, and cap with tassel, but I soon realized it would be cheaper in the long run if I bought the costume for repeated use. So I ended up buying a long black gown festooned with three diagonal black velvet stripes on each side in front to symbolize the doctoral degree, a black hood with a re-splendent crimson lining the color of which proudly represented Harvard Uni-versity, and a black mortarboard cap that boasted a special tassel featuring real gold. This regalia was used not only at Wesleyan but then also at least annually later at the University of Colorado in Boulder for graduation ceremonies and other festive occasions. I still own that regalia; it is kept in the same box in which it arrived in 1952, complete with the protective sheets of tissue paper used in packing the items; the tissue paper is now in largely torn strips and ragged pieces, but the cloth garments are still almost in the same pristine shape they were in when I first bought them.

7-22 "Cap'n" (Percy MacKaye)
(family archives)

Weekends and vacations times were often spent with friends and relatives. I remember more than one Thanksgiving feast with Lavinia (Nan's mother, Dr. Lavinia Gould MacKaye Fox) and Zare (Nan's stepfather, Ezra G. Benedict Fox, whose nickname is an anagram of "Ezra"), in Tenafly, NJ, typically also with Zare's children Greg, Judy, and Zoan, as well as later Zoan's expert tennis-playing husband Bill. Zare would carve the magnificent turkey that Lavinia had prepared; I recall his irreverently referring to the turkey's anatomical rear as "the Pope's nose," a cut which was considered especially desirable. He also called a beer can opener a "church key."

There were visits to various places in New York City and in upstate New York along the Hudson River with other relatives of Nan. There were her grandfather, Percy MacKaye, who was a rather imperious but famous retired playwright living in Manhattan, and her great uncle, Benton, a bachelor who was largely responsible for the creation of the Appalachian Trail. I remember "Uncle

7-23 Benton MacKaye ("Uncle Benton") *(courtesy of Appalachian Trail Conservancy Archives)*

Benton" as a modest, gracious older gentleman who always sent "home-made birthday cards" consisting of gently decorated penny (later three-cent) postcards for relatives' birthdays. After family dinners in upstate New York, Uncle Benton would shove "the youngsters" out of the kitchen, and insist on doing all the dishes and cleanup himself.

I don't know what Nan's relation was to a prominent marine biologist, Huxley Langlois, who lived at Put-In Bay on Lake Michigan, but I recall a visit with him at one time; I think he let me sail a boat there that he owned. He was

7-24 Robin MacKaye, 1955
(family archives)

probably a long-time family friend of Lavinia and that side of Nan's family. For that matter, the modest Moth sailboat that I had kept on Lake Quinsigamond east of Worcester came with us to Middletown, where it was occasionally sailed on the Connecticut River.

By a rather remarkable geographic coincidence, Karen was born in the same Grace-New Haven Hospital in which Nan was born. New Haven was not far from Middletown, and Lavinia was married to Robert Keith MacKaye, Percy MacKaye's son and Nan's father, when he attended the Yale School of Drama. Robert ("Robin") had suffered a major psychotic break not long after his and Lavinia's daughters, first Jean and then Nan, had been born, and he spent the rest of his long life in institutions and then later in protected farm environments. We did visit him several times in upstate New York, but I remember little of those visits beyond seeing that he was a tall, lithe, athletic, handsome but rather taciturn man who did recognize his daughter but otherwise was not very responsive.

Schani did not enjoy large groups of people or family get-togethers; he typically would escape to go to his job as a physicist at the Brookhaven National Laboratory as quickly and as long as possible when any of us were there. Pete and Lise had particularly difficult relationships with Schani; this did improve somewhat over time with Lise, but less so with Peter. For some reason, Schani tolerated me, and later Karen, better than most other relatives. I even remember his not objecting all too strenuously to my joining my mother and Schani for several days one summer in a small cabin they usually rented for their summer vacation in Richtown, near Southeast Harbor on the

7-25 Nan's mother, Lavinia
(family archives)

7-26 Mount Desert Island, Maine *(photo by Lee Edwin Coursey)*

south shore of Mt. Desert Island in Maine; my mother later often reminded me that I had enjoyed that stay on the rocky salty seacoast of Maine so much that I had said, "Hier geh' ich nie wieder weg," or "I'll never leave here again." I did and do enjoy the cool, dramatic summer Maine seacoast very much; indeed Marilyn, my wife of some 50 years, and I spent our honeymoon in the same cabin that my mother and Schani had regularly rented years before, and Marilyn and I spent two weeks each summer for more than twenty years on Monhegan Island, Maine, a remote small island that has some of the most rugged cliffs on the New England coast, has no cars on it, and is mostly undeveloped wild land. My mother and Schani had spent a week on Monhegan back in the mid-1930s; my mother raved about the beauty of Monhegan for years thereafter, but she never returned to it.

My mother and Schani also occasionally visited us in Middletown; so did Peter, Lise, and also Val and his wife Bobbie and their daughter Ellen, who was born about a year after Karen. I have an old movie of Schani, who was always very camera shy, at the temporary housing complex where Nan and I were living, as well as one from a visit by Val and his family, which includes a brief sequence of Val assiduously rubbing on a little spot on the hood of his car. There are also family pictures from that time, of Peter playing on the reed organ in our apartment, Duffy in a playpen in the yard outside the apartment, and other family doings.

It was some time during our stay at Wesleyan that Lise suddenly suffered a rather severe psychiatric breakdown. I remember Schani calling late one evening, asking me to come immediately to Long Island to help get her transferred to a nearby psychiatric hospital in Islip. I drove Shadrach as fast as I could in the wee hours of the morning to my mother's and Schani's house. Lise was clearly very

7-27 Pete at my reed organ; boat bookcase in the rear *(family archives)*

distraught when I got there, and was understandably very reluctant to be taken away to a psychiatric facility. She finally agreed to come with me in Shadrach, as long as she was free to move as she wished in the front passenger seat; Schani had wanted to restrain her in the back seat between himself and my mother, but Lise refused. We did manage to get to the Islip state hospital without a mishap, and Lise was, rather wild-eyed, duly admitted. I remember being quite tearful myself when she ended up entrusted to the hospital staff.

Later Lise was transferred to a mental hospital in Manhattan, Columbia Presbyterian Hospital, which had a fine reputation both as a treatment center and as a research institution. Indeed one of the prominent research psychiatrists there, a Dr. Zubin, took her on as a research assistant for a project he was directing, even though she was also a patient at the time. She had already completed much of the work for her doctoral degree in psychology as a graduate student at the University of Kansas, in Lawrence. Probably in part because of my experience as a clinical psychology intern in Worcester, I recall discussing treatment options with my mother and Schani and they wisely refused to permit any major intensive treatment such as the electric shock therapy that was popular at the time. Lise had not been eating regularly and in a nutritionally prudent way for several months before in Kansas, and it was assumed that some kind of a nutritional deficiency might have triggered her psychiatric breakdown. At any rate, she soon went into spontaneous remission of her troubling symptoms, and got noticeably better within a short time. I have a brief movie sequence I took when Nan and I once visited her in the hospital in Manhattan with Karen (who was dressed in one of the comfortable knitted full-body bags that had arms but only a bag for both legs and feet that Nan had made for her); everyone in that brief snippet was clearly smiling and in good shape. Lise soon recovered completely and never again was stricken with a similar problem. During one of her visits to us in Middletown, Lise produced an amateur but beautiful oil painting of the pasture and barns visible from the front door of our apartment there; it has been displayed in a prominent place in my house ever since. I think she used a set of oil paints that had been given to me years before, with which as a teenager I had painted a fantasy landscape; that too has continued to be displayed in my house.

7-28 Lise's painting of the view from our Middletown home *(family archives)*

8   Early Years in Colorado

One gift I was given, probably by Nan for my birthday in March 1955, was a book by an enthusiastic Australian mountain climber, Douglas Busk, entitled *The Delectable Mountains*. I have loved mountains since my early childhood vacations in the Swiss and Italian Alps, and Nan and I had frequently taken hikes in mountain areas as well as often gone skiing. I had also enjoyed some very modest amateur rock climbing as a child on the beach of New Rochelle in western Long Island Sound. Busk's book had separate chapters on climbs of various mountains around the world, including one on the ascent of 14,255-foot Longs Peak in Colorado's Rocky Mountains. And as it happens, a few days later I received out of the blue a telegram from the University of Colorado in Boulder, asking whether I would be interested in a tenure-track job there as an assistant professor. The department chair in Boulder, Victor Raimy, had contacted Robbie MacLeod about an opening at the University of Colorado for someone to teach introductory psychology and the history of psychology, and MacLeod had recommended me to Raimy. The copious library at Wesleyan happened to have in its collection a catalogue for the University of Colorado at Boulder, the cover of which was an enticing photograph of part of the university campus with the impressive Flatirons, prominent steep slanting slabs of rocky cliffs over a thousand feet high, in the background. If I recall correctly, the telegram offered a salary of four thousand dollars a year.

Back in those days, the process of making people aware of academic openings, and filling them, was much less cumbersome than it has become since then. I got the job offer to come to the University of Colorado at Boulder via literally the "old boys network." Raimy had an opening, called his friend MacLeod

8-1 Flatirons over the University of Colorado at Boulder *(courtesy of Casey A. Cass/University of Colorado)*

© Springer Fachmedien Wiesbaden GmbH, part of Springer Nature 2020
M. Wertheimer, *Facets of an Academic's Life*,
https://doi.org/10.1007/978-3-658-28770-2_8

8-2 Nan, Karen, and Duffy's playpen in Knezzar on the way to Colorado *(family archives)*

asking for suggestions for someone to fill it, and MacLeod recommended me. Apparently (fortunately for me) negotiations between Raimy and a well-qualified candidate at the University of Pennsylvania, Henry Gleitman, had fallen through late in March or early in April, because Gleitman had wanted at least an associate professorship, to which Raimy had agreed, but the Dean of Arts and Sciences at Colorado at the time, Jacob van Ek, had insisted that the appointment could initially not be higher than at the assistant professor level. It could be that Raimy felt pressured because it was already so late in the middle of the spring semester, and he had been unsuccessful in hiring Gleitman. Perhaps this time pressure contributed to the quick, informal action of sending me a telegram with his offer.

I had had no correspondence about the position with Raimy when the telegram arrived. He did not even ask me for a curriculum vitae, nor had he called me on the telephone; there was no mention of my coming for a visit to the campus and giving a colloquium, to see whether they would want me at all, or whether I would be interested in a job at Colorado if it were offered to me. As far as I know, other than Gleitman there was no other candidate being considered for the opening. Within a day or two after receiving Raimy's telegram I studied the catalogue from the University of Colorado, remembered the excitement I had

8-3 A section of the view looking west over Boulder; Longs Peak at right *(family archives)*

first felt when I heard that fascinating Longs Peak was located less than 40 miles from the campus, admired the picture of the Flatirons on the catalogue cover, discussed the matter with Nan at some length, and without any negotiations by the university or by me, sent a telegram to Raimy accepting the offer. I have never since regretted the decision.

We owned an old light-grey Plymouth station wagon named "Knezzar" (short for Nebuchadnezzar), and decided to use that as our "covered wagon" to make the trip west that summer from Connecticut to Colorado. Nan fitted out a one-half size wooden playpen in the "way-in-back" of the car to accommodate Duffy, who was one year old, and we took a tent for us parents; Karen slept as far as I remember on the back seat of the station wagon. The camping trip across the US that summer was relatively smooth and uneventful, and I recall our excitement when we first saw the Rocky Mountains stretching majestically from far south to far north as we approached Boulder. The highway into Boulder from the east had a parking area high on a hill above Boulder overlooking the Boulder valley below, and I think we stopped there to admire the view before rolling down into town. Longs Peak dominated the northwestern sky, and one could see the jagged

mountains of the Continental Divide all the way down to 14,000-foot Pike's Peak a good hundred miles to the south. An impressive, awesome vista it was.

The first year in Boulder, 1955-1956, we lived in a pleasant rented apartment on Athens

8-4 Apartments on Athens Street *(courtesy of Occupancy Management, University of Colorado at Boulder)*

8-5 Crossing Boulder Creek on the walk from our apartment on Athens Street to the university campus *(photo by Dennis Teel)*

Street in a complex housing both student and faculty families. The "commute" to my office in Ketchum Hall on the campus was a fifteen-minute walk. After crossing a foot bridge over Boulder Creek, which flowed just a short distance south of our apartment, a steep path led up the hill to Macky Auditorium and then it was flat from there to my office and to the various classrooms in which the courses I taught met. I usually came home for lunch or carried a brown-bag lunch to my office, and Nan essentially stayed home taking care of our two young children, Karen (age three) and Duffy (age one), and engaged in a wide variety of highly creative artistic projects, painting and wood-carving.

The department of psychology was much smaller in the mid 1950s than it became during the next few decades. There were three new members as of the fall of 1955: Bill Scott, another man whose name I've forgotten and whose contract was not renewed after three years, and myself. There were only seven others who had already been there: Victor Raimy, chair at the time and a prominent clinical psychologist; Karl Muenzinger, a distinguished experimental psychologist who had essentially built the department during the preceding years while serving as chair; Maury Smith, a behaviorist experimental psychologist who studied primarily animal learning processes; Marvin Nachman, responsible for coordinating the teaching of the huge

8-6 Macky Auditorium *(from https://commons.wikimedia.org/wiki/File:Mackey_Auditorium_-_Colorado.jpg)*

sections of the introductory psychology course and
who left a few years later to join the department at
the University of California at Riverside; Kenneth
Hammond, a devoted follower of Egon Brunswik
who developed an illustrious scholarly career on
such issues as decision making and who continued
publishing influential books until he was well into
his nineties and had already been retired for decades; Howard Gruber, who was interested in the
psychology of scientific creativity; and Richard
Jessor, an Ohio State PhD and disciple of Julian
Rotter, whose unusually long career in clinical and
social psychology and as director of a highly successful Institute of Behavioral Science, only loose-
ly affiliated with the department of psychology,
ended very recently when he retired in his late

8-7 Victor ("Vic") Raimy
*(courtesy of the Special
Collections and Archives,
University of Colorado Boulder
Libraries)*

eighties. All of the colleagues were cordial and supportive of me and my efforts
during my early years in Colorado.

Victor Raimy and his wife Ruth made us all feel welcome in Boulder. I remember they had a son who had already left home and was living in Boulder,
working at a local radio station. The Raimys had a pleasant home sitting diago-
nally on a large lot on Baseline Road about 2/3 of a mile south of the campus.
Raimy was prominent in a variety of elective roles in the APA, including serving
on its prestigious board of directors. I remember visiting him one afternoon,
arriving unannounced and unexpected; he was busily cleaning up small branches
in his back yard, breaking up kindling for his fireplace. He invited me inside, and
offered me a martini; with his typical warm and unobtrusive sense of humor, he
explained that the cocktail should be mixed gently with a fork, so as not to
"bruise it." At some time a year or so later, since I was teaching courses on sensation and perception as well as introductory psychology and the history of psychology, he asked me to present an invited lecture on perception and the Rorschach inkblot test in a clinical course he was teaching on personality assessment. Preparation for that lecture resulted in one of my earlier publications, in

8-8 Karl Muenzinger *(courtesy of the Department of Psychology and Neuroscience, University of Colorado at Boulder)*

1957 in the *Journal of Projective Techniques*. In many ways, Raimy, whom I had first met at Worcester State Hospital where he was an occasional consultant while I was a clinical intern there back in 1951-1952, turned out to continue to be a good friend and a wise but gentle mentor for decades.

Karl Muenzinger and his wife lived in a beautiful, dark, fairly modest home on a densely wooded lot atop a hillside almost a mile west of campus that had a gorgeous view of Flagstaff Mountain to the west and the spectacular Flatirons to the southwest. Having been introduced to the history of psychology by Boring at Harvard, and encouraged in that field by MacLeod and then other colleagues, I audited Muenzinger's Boulder course on the history of psychology that was required of all undergraduate students who majored in psychology.

Muenzinger, before Raimy took over, had been for many years chairman of the department. He was a highly effective teacher who assured every student's rapt attention by peppering his lectures with occasional questions; *after* he had raised a question, he would without warning call out a student's name requesting that student to answer it. He also developed a creative original master outline of the history of modern experimental psychology, showing how it evolved from three philosophical and five scientific trends prominent in eighteenth and nineteenth century European thought. I was greatly impressed by Muenzinger's approach to and organization of the history of psychology and ended up taking copious notes at all of his lectures. Those notes, with Muenzinger's deathbed blessing, became the basic outline, flesh and blood (with, admittedly, quite a few omissions and additions) for a book first published in 1970, the fifth edition of which was issued in 2012; at the publisher's request, a sixth edition is already in preparation. Over the years, it has netted me a total of more that $60,000 in royalties, and I am deeply grateful to Karl Muenzinger for his encouragement in

turning his lecture course into a textbook. During
his last year of teaching, not long before his death,
Muenzinger also asked me to do occasional "guest
lectures" in his history course; I recently discovered
an uncashed check for $20 from him for such an
"invited lecture."

Maurice P. Smith, while he managed to get
many graduate students to prepare their PhD disser-
tations about rats running mazes—even graduate
students in clinical psychology—under his direction, did not manage to publish enough of his own
work to rise above the level of associate professor.
He had a charming, vivacious European wife, Agnes, a son who became a chef, and a warm and
friendly daughter, and he enjoyed the Colorado
outdoors as a hiker and mountaineer. Shortly before

8-9 Maurice P. ("Maury") Smith
*(courtesy of the Special
Collections and Archives,
University of Colorado Boulder
Libraries)*

I left Boulder for a year's sabbatical in Washington, DC, during the 1970-1971
academic year, he developed a serious illness for which he was hospitalized. I
"lent" him a batch of books I owned about mountaineering (including, I think,
the Busk volume that had tempted me with Longs Peak) just before leaving for
the year. He died that fall, and I'm afraid I was never able to retrieve those precious books. Maury's widow Agnes and Nan became good friends, for a friendship that lasted for decades.

8-10 Marv Nachman *(courtesy of
Marvin Nachman)*

Marvin Nachman, as I mentioned before, was in
charge of the introductory psychology course
(which typically had more than 1,000 students
enrolled in it every year), and left for California
several years after I came to Colorado. I remember
at least two mountaineering escapades in which we
were both involved. Dick Jessor introduced Bill
Scott and me to rock climbing on the Third Flatiron, using ropes, pitons, carabiners, and the rock
climbing gear common during the middle and late

8-11 Me at the Colorado Mountain Club cabin near Brainard Lake *(family archives)*

1950s, and I think Marv came along on that adventure; I recall poor Bill Scott rappelling down while in an almost horizontal position toward the end of that outing, and vowing never to try roped climbing again. He kept his word. The other occasion was a cross-country ski trip during the cold, snowy winter of 1955-1956 for an overnight stay at a rustic log cabin owned by the Colorado Mountain Club above Brainard Lake at about 9500 feet elevation, just below timberline. Dick Jessor, Kurt Gerstle (a professor of civil engineering), Marv Nachman, and I were along on that outing. Skiing in the several miles uphill to the cabin was more taxing than several of us had expected, but once we had roaring fires going in both the stove and the fireplace, the cabin was warm, cozy, and inviting. In fact, years later I often took the children up to the CMC cabin near Brainard Lake for overnight stays (but not in winter!) before we had our own cabin built in Ward in 1971. I pretty much lost contact with Nachman after he left Boulder.

Ken Hammond was about as involved in the relatively new Institute for Behavioral Science as Dick Jessor was. Lee Jessor, Dick's wife and, like him, an Ohio State PhD, was also an integral part of the Institute of Behavior Science for many years. They succeeded in winning major successive outside grants to fund institute research projects, and Ken invited me to become a member of the institute too. But I never had any sufficiently substantial outside grant or contract money to warrant inclusion of one of my projects as part of the institute's pro-

8-12 The back of our Columbine Avenue house *(family archives)*

grams. Ken also suggested fairly early after I came to Colorado that I should run for election to become department chair, but that never came to pass. Robbie Mac-Leod had told me once that it is a faculty member's obligation at least at some time during an academic career to serve an administrative role such as being department chair, but the closest I came to that was being director of the undergraduate psychology department honors program for decades, chairing doctoral programs in experimental and in sociocultural psychology, and agreeing to be considered for directing the entire general honors program in the College of Arts and Sciences at the University of Colorado at Boulder—for which I was one of the last two nominees, but for which the other was appointed.

After Nan and I had moved in 1956 to a pleasant little house on Columbine Avenue, which we had bought from a professor of French, Pierre Delattre, Ken Hammond came riding on his horse down Columbine Avenue from his house

8-13 Kenneth Hammond *(courtesy of Pamela Hammond)*

several blocks west of our new house, and greeted us from his saddle. He dismounted and offered Karen a ride on his horse, which she eagerly accepted. I took a brief moving picture shot of her on Ken's horse on Columbine Avenue (still partially an un-

8-14 Ken Hammond leading his horse (with Karen riding it) on Columbine Avenue *(family archives)*

8-15 Dick Jessor *(courtesy of Patrick Campbell)*

paved dirt road at the time, but long since paved) with my old 8-millimeter movie camera.

Dick Jessor was an enthusiastic hiker, mountaineer, and rock climber. Several times he, with his wife Lee and their son and daugh-

8-16 Lee Jessor *(courtesy of Kim Jessor and Tom Jessor)*

ter, took our whole family with them on walks along the Mesa Trail, heading from Chautauqua Park just east of the Flatirons and other rock formations southward through forest and over grasslands toward Eldorado Springs. I also took some movies of at least one of those outings. And as I mentioned when writing about Marv Nachman, he also introduced Bill Scott and me to roped rock climbing on the Flatirons, as well as bringing us to the Brainard Lake CMC cabin in midwinter. He continued his mountaineering ventures, including international ones, until he was well into his eighties.

At one point during my early years at Boulder, there were some fairly acrimonious rifts between Ken Hammond and the Jessors on one side, and the rest of the department on the other. I don't remember what the issues were, but I recall both Hammond and Jessor trying to persuade me to join them. I don't think whatever was the crucial matter was ever resolved to everyone's satisfaction, but the Jessors and Hammond essentially retreated to their Institute of Behavioral Sciences and for years had relatively little to do with the rest of the psychology department faculty.

The Jessors had a dramatic house built for them about a mile west

8-17 The Jessor house on Sixth Street *(imagery: Google 2019)*

of campus at the foot of Flagstaff Mountain. Designed by modernist Boulder architect Tician Papachristou, most of its walls are round rather than square. Unfortunately, Dick and Lee broke up. Dick has, I believe, remarried a couple of times since; and I understand that Lee moved to San Francisco and became active in social advocacy. As mentioned a bit earlier, Dick retired very recently from a highly successful productive career as primarily a scholar, researcher, and administrator.

Dick Jessor really got me started on rock climbing. But soon I took it up fairly seriously on my own. I became involved in the Colorado Mountain Club and the Rocky Mountain Rescue Group. By the late 1950s, having bought the requisite equipment from the Holubar Mountaineering shop in Boulder—a 120-foot-long nylon climbing rope, pitons, piton hammer, carabiners, rope slings, rappelling brake, etc.—I was teaching rock climbing for the Colorado Mountain Club. I remember a full-page photo on the cover of the Friday magazine in the local Boulder newspaper, showing me instructing some neophytes in how to do rock climbing, with proper equipment, on an imposing rock wall near Boulder Falls in Boulder Canyon. I was proud of that picture, but no longer have a copy of it. I'll present some more details about my involvement with CMC and RMRG a little later.

Some of my early rock climbing companions were graduate students in the psychology department. One was Bob Elder, a tall, taciturn student of, I think,

8-18 The Flatirons; Third Flatiron on the left *(courtesy of Phillip Yates)*

clinical psychology. He joined me in at least several rock climbs, and I remember a particular ambitious project on a modest rock outcropping part way up Flagstaff Mountain, at which he and I were helping Al Bernardin, a graduate student who was totally blind, to do some modest roped rock climbing.

I also recall that both of those graduate students and I had performed some kind of experimental study which I thought was worth publishing. I submitted a paper on that project, with all three of us as

8-19 Bob Elder climbing a Flatiron *(family archives)*

co-authors, to the *American Journal of Psychology*. The manuscript ended up on the desk of Eddie Newman at Harvard University. Several months after I had submitted it without having heard anything about its status, I wrote to Newman,

8-20 Me on the summit of the First Flatiron; Boulder below *(family archives)*

asking whether the paper had been accepted, needed further work, or was rejected, but only received a rather impatient response, saying that he, as the editor to whom the paper had been referred, would let me know in good time what would become of the article. Since having publications in prestigious outlets like the *American Journal of Psychology* would be a useful plus in a graduate student's curriculum vitae when applying for a job (and hoping to expand my own list of publication for my own career as well), I was

8-21 Pat Capretta climbing a Flatiron
(family archives)

anxious to get that manuscript, or a revised version of it, published. It is now more than a half century since that article was submitted, and meantime Eddie Newman died. I never did hear anything more about that manuscript. Apparently it died on Newman's desk long before he died. As for Bob Elder and the other co-author of that unfortunate article, I lost track of both of them long ago.

Another graduate student with whom I did some climbing was Pat Capretta. He and I did climbs of several of the Flatirons. It may have been with him that I made (what I believed at the time to be) the first ascent of the "Hammer," a small separate pinnacle on the south side of the Third Flatiron. I also remember one attempt that Pat and I made on a prominent rock formation, the Devil's Thumb, on the skyline south of the Flatirons. Near its top is an overhang at about 110°, some 12 feet high. Although we had taken along what we thought should have been sufficient hardware, such as pitons, slings, carabiners, and piton hammer, neither of us felt safe in attempting to lead over that overhang. We descended

8-22 Left: The Devil's Thumb as seen from our patio *(courtesy of Edward Kahn)*

8-23 Bill Scott *(courtesy of the Special Collections and Archives, University of Colorado Boulder Libraries)*

again without reaching the summit, perhaps only another 50 or so feet above the top of the overhang. I never again tried to climb the Devil's Thumb; even though I have climbed many of the other rock formations west of Boulder, quite a few of them a number of times, the Devil's Thumb is one climb I have attempted that I didn't succeed at. As it happens, the Devil's Thumb is prominently visible, to the southwest, from the pleasant little patio outside our apartment at the retirement community where we now live. It is an ambivalent reminder of my successes—and failures—in my identity as a (certainly now former) rock climber. I enjoy seeing it daily, and having it remind me that I should remain humble about my mountaineering career.

As has been true of so many of my acquaintances during my earlier years, I soon lost track of Pat Capretta too. But I know that he managed to publish a relatively short textbook on the history of psychology that for a while threatened to compete with my own brief history of psychology. I don't know how well his book was received, and I heard nothing further about Pat other than that he passed away a few years ago.

Bill Scott joined CU's psychology department faculty at the same time I did. He moved into a pleasant rustic motel suite at the mouth of Boulder Canyon, and became a good friend and colleague. A divorced bachelor when he came to Boulder, he soon married Ruth, a wonderful lady he had known at the University of Michigan in Ann Arbor, where he had obtained his PhD in social psychology with a special emphasis on statistics. He and Ruth often played bridge with Nan and me, and we often had dinner together at our house or at theirs after they moved into a beautiful large house at the southwestern edge of Boulder. He and Ruth adopted a girl, and soon thereafter had two biological children, a boy and then a girl.

Bill was hired away to become chair of a university psychology department in Townsville on the northeast coast of Australia in 1970, and we had little contact with his family after that, other than exchanging Christmas cards and a few visits from Ruth after Bill died. A rather heavy drinker, Bill had severe kidney problems during his last years; this doubtless contributed to his early demise.

In the summer of 1957 the family together with Bill and Ruth Scott moved to pleasant accommodations for two months in the mountains east of Albuquerque, in Tijeras Canyon, while Bill and I were participating in a broad general behavioral science conference at the University of New Mexico sponsored by the U.S. Air Force; this work resulted in my getting deeply immersed in study of how people form impressions of other people, or person perception, about which I produced several publications and generated a large bibliographic card file that itself never did lead to anything further, although I had once been tempted to write a thorough, detailed review of the entire literature on this subject (which I never got around to).

After I had several times taught an undergraduate honors seminar on preparing an empirical honors thesis, and a beginning graduate seminar on how to do psychological research, I thought there might be a market for a book on the subject, concentrating on such matters as how to choose a topic, how to design empirical studies about the topic, how to measure things, how to write up the results, and how to get the results published. I wrote a first complete draft manuscript for such a book in the late 1950s, but didn't include very much about the statistical analysis of the results. Knowing that Bill had a much more thorough background in statistics than I did, I invited him to look over, add to, and revise

my manuscript, and join me as a co-author.

Meantime Nan and I took a sabbatical year off, spending it at Rockland State Hospital in Orangeburg, NY, where we had already spent several

8-24 Rockland State Hospital *(from https://www.flickr.com/photos/scoutingny/5386607998/)*

8-25 George A. C. Scherer
(courtesy of the Department of
Germanic and Slavic Languages
and Literatures, University of
Colorado at Boulder)

summers doing research. Bill's revision of my manuscript resulted in a much longer manuscript concentrating primarily on sample selection, statistics, and other mathematical issues. I re-revised the manuscript, and we finally came up with a kind of compromise that neither of us liked all that much, but that we both found tolerable. The book was published in 1962, was reasonably successful, and was even translated into Spanish several years later.

From 1960 to 1966 I was rather deeply involved with a colleague in the German department at CU, George A.C. Scherer, who had obtained a substantial research grant for evaluating the "audio-lingual method" of teaching the German language to American students, a method he was convinced was superior to what he called the traditional "grammar and translation" method that was typically used in high

schools and colleges. The method involved the spoken language from the start; Scherer thought that this would enhance the development of the connection between the sounds of the foreign language and their meaning better than other methods would. He had set up a quasi-experimental design, with several sections of introductory German at CU being taught by the audio-lingual and several by the traditional method, and had asked Stuart Cook, then chair of the psychology department, to suggest someone in the department to help him measure the competence of the students in German as a result of their exposure to the two different methods at the end of one, two, three, and even four semesters. Cook asked me if I would be interested and I indicated that I would be.

8-26 Stuart W. Cook *(courtesy of*
the Archives of the History of
American Psychology, The Drs.
Nicholas and Dorothy
Cummings Center for the
History of Psychology, The
University of Akron)

I found the resulting collaboration with Scherer pleasant and rewarding, and did come up with a variety of techniques (aside from the usual traditional quizzes and examinations) for measuring the immediacy and accuracy of understanding messages in the new language. These ranged broadly from evaluating the truth or falsity of assertions in the foreign language (such as "Parents are younger than their children") through a variety of other techniques to asking how often the students dreamed in German. The collaboration led to a book published in 1964 by McGraw-Hill, *A psycholinguistic experiment in foreign language teaching*. We planned to apply for another grant to support a new study to

8-27 Glenn Terrell *(courtesy of The Lewiston Tribune)*

test the widely believed hypothesis that people who learn a foreign language before puberty might learn to speak it like a native without an accent, but that people who begin study of a foreign language after puberty will always still have an accent that gives away that they are not native speakers. We did submit that proposal to the Department of Education, which had funded the audio-lingual study, and I believe that it was indeed accepted. But Scherer, who was principal investigator for that grant, died before the study was begun, so it was never carried out. But I did greatly enjoy my work with Scherer on the audio-lingual project.

Other members of the psychology faculty during my early years at CU included Glenn Terrell and O. J. Harvey. Terrell and Gruber asked me to be a co-editor of a book based on a conference about creative thinking that was held in Boulder under the department's sponsorship. Terrell became department chair and then was enticed away to become

8-28 Howard Gruber *(courtesy of the Archives of the History of American Psychology, The Drs. Nicholas and Dorothy Cummings Center for the History of Psychology, The University of Akron)*

8-29 O. J. Harvey *(courtesy of Terry Minton)*

president of Washington State University where his long service became somewhat controversial; and Gruber, who finally published a biography of Darwin that he had been working on for decades, joined the psychology department at the New School for Social Research in New York. I lost contact with both of them soon after they left Colorado; I think both have since passed away.

Harvey too has died; he and I had many rewarding interactions, primarily about the history of psychology, which both of us taught at different times for several years. An admiring student of Muzafer Sherif, Harvey published influential works on social psychology and personality. He and his warm and supportive wife Chris had no children, but were deeply involved in efforts to improve the lot of the Native American Oglala tribe. O. J. was devastated when Chris died, but survived thereafter for a few more years, a rather introverted and reclusive retiree who moved from a spacious home with copious land (in which he and Chris had hosted many grateful graduate students as well as a number of rousing faculty and student parties) to a modest apartment in Boulder.

When I arrived in Boulder, both the psychology department and the entire College of Arts and Sciences of which the department was a unit were run in a democratic manner, with faculty members making most of the important decisions by vote after extensive discussions. The issues included such crucial matters as the undergraduate requirements for graduation and the requirements for completing a major in a particular field; a minimum number of courses in the natural sciences, the social sciences, and the humanities; the nature of the foreign language requirement; the necessary sequence of courses in the major department; the minimum requirements for a minor field; and so on. Such decisions were at the time made by faculty vote, and the discussions preceding such votes, especially in physical meetings of the College of Arts and Sciences, were often extensive, articulate, and heated. I attended many of those meetings, and often joined in on the debates. One figure who stands out in my memory as one of the more eloquent contributors to these discussions was a gaunt, tall, thin older professor of English, Jack Ogilvy, who could (and would) talk convincingly and with a fetching sense of humor on almost any topic.

The amount of interdisciplinary and interdepartmental interaction during the late 1950s far exceeded the amount later, when faculty members typically had few opportunities for contact with fellow faculty from any department other than their own. During my long career in academia, the decision-making process gradually but inexorably moved from the faculty to the administration— and the ranks and income of administrators

8-30 Jack Ogilvy *(courtesy of the Special Collections and Archives, University of Colorado Boulder Libraries)*

swelled enormously, typically at the expense of faculty and staff recompense.

The extremely rewarding experience I had had at Swarthmore in its honors program led me to look into the honors program at CU Boulder almost as soon as I got there. A professor of philosophy, Joe Cohen, had initiated in 1952 a general honors program in CU's College of Arts and Sciences that soon became nationally prominent and was imitated in slightly altered forms at many other institutions of higher learning. Joe directed a national center for college honors programs for several years, and edited what I think was a monthly newsletter for the center, called something like *The Superior Student*.

The CU honors program differed from what I had experienced at Swarthmore. There, as mentioned before, instead of taking any courses during the last two undergraduate years, honors students signed up for two seminars during each semester, one each in the major and one in either of two minors, resulting in a total of eight seminars by the end of the senior year, four in the major and two in each of two minors. Outside examiners evaluated performance on both written and oral examinations at the end of the senior year, and no local professors issued any grades for any of the seminars. By contrast, the CU program permitted students to "read for honors" either in general studies or in the major, or both. To

be a candidate for general honors, the student had
to have completed at least four seminars in fields
outside the major, to prepare an honors thesis, and
to take a general honors written and oral examination; departments decided what the requirements
would be for departmental honors candidates (usually several seminars in the major, an original honors thesis, and both written and oral examinations
in the major). The final decision about every candidate was made by an honors council, composed
of all directors of departmental honors programs as
well as the director of the general honors program,
based upon recommendations from the relevant
examining committees. Candidates for honors at

8-31 Joseph W. ("Joe") Cohen
*(courtesy of the Special
Collections and Archives,
University of Colorado Boulder
Libraries)*

CU also had to complete all the regular course requirements as well as the requirements for the honors distinctions they were seeking. The final result of
candidacy for honors at Swarthmore as well as at CU could be highest honors
(summa cum laude), high honors (magna cum laude), with honors (cum laude), -
- or no honors, if the graduating senior did not appear to deserve any special
recognition.

I soon became director of the psychology department's undergraduate honors
program, a role I enjoyed tremendously for decades. Psychology was the major
declared by more students than any other major in the College, and during a
number of years there were more successful honors graduates in psychology
even than graduates in the general honors program. Most psychology honors
graduates went on to graduate school, and many ended up later having reasonably successful careers in psychology.

The top students didn't bother to try for honors, but there was a large second
tier of capable students who weren't all that sure of their competence. Successfully completing several seminars; designing, carrying out, and writing up an
original empirically-based thesis; passing challenging written examinations; and
orally defending the thesis provided many previously unsure students with an
experience that helped convince them that they indeed were competent scholars

after all. Advising them all individually and serving as mentor for them was one of the most rewarding chores in my academic career. Many of them became good friends with whom I continued to have contact for years after they graduated.

As departmental director of honors for psychology, I also was a member of the honors council, and served on many examining committees for candidates for general honors and for departmental honors in other disciplines, including sociology, anthropology, philosophy, French, German, and even chemistry, biology, and physics. I also became acquainted with, and even occasionally friends with, colleagues on the honors council from other departments. These contacts further cemented my conviction about the value of a broad liberal arts perspective.

I also taught a few general honors seminars, including one on personality and once an introduction to psychology that was conducted in German. In the first few years that I was involved with the honors program, under Joe Cohen's direction, the teaching of honors courses was not included in a faculty member's regular teaching load, nor was one paid for conducting these seminars. Being allowed to teach in the honors program was viewed as a coveted privilege for those permitted to lead a seminar in the program (and not all who volunteered were allowed to do so). This changed a few years later when philosophy professor Walter Weir (pictured on page 399) became director of the program; now being permitted to teach an honors seminar was still regarded as an overload, but paid first $200 and later $300 for the semester in which it was taught.

Inevitably, I became, like every other faculty member, a participant in a variety of departmental and college committees, including not only honors but such foci as the university library, the undergraduate and graduate foreign language requirements, distribution and graduation requirements, criteria for faculty promotion and tenure, academic freedom, and others I have forgotten. I believe I was serious and conscientious in trying to fulfill the duties required by such committee appointments, but I don't remember any particular committee issues that seem to be worth reciting in any detail now. But participation on these committees did help cement cordial relationships with other faculty members in the psychology department as well as faculty in other disciplines.

*
**

Outdoor activities have been a source of pleasure since my childhood. Gardening—mostly in the form of raising vegetables—was already there in the childhood "victory garden" in New Rochelle, continued at Wesleyan, and has been essentially an annual project ever since. In winter, skiing was enjoyed enthusiastically until very recently; as mentioned before, my college roommate Stefan Machlup came annually for a week or so to ski the Colorado mountains with us. I even rather selfishly convinced patient and obliging Nan to serve as a kind of automobile ski lift on snow-covered Flagstaff mountain for me one year, driving me several times back up to the summit after picking me up along the road about halfway down.

But especially in the early years in Colorado, mountaineering became a major focus of my life. I soon became a member of the Colorado Mountain Club, and even became a member of the Boulder chapter's executive committee. Over the years I led many outings for the CMC, including some 25 attempts on Longs Peak (of which about half were successful; many had to be aborted due to weather), many climbs of the faces of all three Flatirons, and, one summer, ascents on

8-33 Left to right: Karen, Benjy, Duffy, 1963 *(family archives)*

8-32 Me coiling climbing rope *(family archives)*

successive weekends of the
three main Flatirons and the
two large rock faces south of
them.

Several months of training
were required before I became
accepted as a "fully qualified
member" of the Rocky Mountain Rescue Group, i.e., permitted to lead a rescue mission. I participated in many

8-34 Me with Duff's son Noah in the Agnes Vail hut on
Longs Peak *(family archives)*

missions, most of which were
successful, in the sense that a
lost or injured hiker or climber
would be found and brought to
safety. The camaraderie engendered by these missions
was intense and tremendously
rewarding (probably similar to
the camaraderie developed by
missions of military units), as
was the concrete fact of saving

8-35 Duff, Noah, and me enjoying canned sardines on the
summit of Longs Peak *(family archives)*

a life (in some ways a fitting
complement to the much more
abstract, abstruse, and even
somewhat ambiguous academic successes such as a reasonably well delivered lecture or
acceptance of an article for
publication by a prestigious
journal). Calls to lead or participate in a rescue mission
could come at any time of the

8-36 Me, Karen, and Karen's friend Don Leaver on the
summit of Longs Peak *(family archives)*

8-37 The free rappel on the descent of the Maiden *(photo by Cleve McCarty)*

day or night, and if there was no competing obligation such as a teaching commitment I always tried to be available for these emergencies.

Among the more memorable climbs in which I participated was one led by chemistry professor Harold Walton, an accomplished climber who among other things led outings for the Iowa Mountaineers to the summit of Aconcagua, a mammoth South American peak in excess of 20,000 feet elevation. A soft-spoken Quaker scientist born in England who had joined the CU faculty years before I had come there, he was a short, agile, extremely adept climber. The goal was the Maiden, a sister crag of the Devil's Thumb, soaring into the skyline above the Boulder foothills a short distance south of the Devil's Thumb. The climb was absolutely spectacular. The rock is a thin east-west slab some 300 or so feet tall. The ascent was hair-raising, including an almost horizontal traverse of the almost vertical north face, but the descent was even more spectacular. To the west of the summit extended a bird-like beak, and the descent involved a free rappel for about 100 feet in midair down to a narrow ledge only a few feet wide, from which a second almost verti-

8-38 Harold Walton
(courtesy of the Heritage Center, University of Colorado Boulder)

cal rappel for another 100 feet or so landed one on a fairly sound rock outcrop from which one could descend rather easily. I never tried to do this route alone or with anyone else after Walton's lead.

As for my adventures with the rescue group, there were at least two tragic missions that remain vividly in my memory. One involved a student named Prince Willmon. He had been the top student in my section of the introductory psychology course with an enrollment of some three or four hundred, and I had become acquainted with him and his interest in mountaineering. A few years later he was a graduate student in English at CU. For spring break, he and three other students had headed south for some rock climbing on Ship Rock in Arizona, and then drove back overnight for an ascent of Longs Peak. The weather had been warm that April, and the four of them were totally unprepared for a major spring snowstorm that caught them unawares in their tee-shirts on the summit of Longs Peak. They attempted to rappel from the summit, but set the rappel rope in a wrong place. Believing that it reached down to solid ground, one of the two girls in the party rappelled down, and noticed that the rappel rope ended some twenty feet above the snow-covered steep rocky gully that it was supposed to have reached. She took a chance, dropped down into the snow, and managed to land without any injury, then continued the long trek back to the ranger station, reach-

8-39 Prince Willmon *(photo by Dave Lewis)*

ing there intact except for some frostbitten fingers and toes. She reported that her three companions were still in the park and probably needed help, but the park service decided that the blizzard conditions were too hazardous for any rangers to go in or even to permit the Rocky Mountain Rescue Group to undertake a mission to help them. Two days later, the RMRG was given the go-ahead; there were initially no signs of Prince Willmon or his two remaining companions. I happened to find the bloody remains of Willmon in the snow and rocks far beneath the end of the rappel rope; he clearly had hit his head when he let go of the end of the rope. I helped carry out the litter containing his remains. The other two had also perished, but as leader, Willmon had dutifully tried to make sure that all three of his companions were safely down before he tried unsuccessfully, probably with frozen feet and fingers, to descend to safety himself.

The other mission was above Fourth of July campground on the flank of Arapahoe Peak. We brought down the remains of three hikers who had been killed by lightning at an exposed rock outcrop. Rodents had already attacked the corpses, having consumed their eyes and other parts of their faces and bodies. It was indeed a gruesome mission.

The little house on Columbine Avenue with its pleasant yard was a comfortable home for one year, until Nan found a larger one with a larger yard west of the CU campus, at 1313 Seventh Street, which we bought. We converted its garage into a pleasant den with a fireplace, and enjoyed that for a few years. It was here that our third child, Benjy, was born, in 1958. Then we moved once again in 1962 into a yet larger house, 546 Geneva Avenue, on a mature triple corner lot exactly one mile west of the campus at the foot of Flagstaff Mountain, several blocks south of the Seventh Street house. Except for an occasional year or so elsewhere, 546 Geneva Avenue was a wonderful home for me for half a century, until the move into a welcoming small retirement community three miles south of there in 2011.

8-40 1313 Seventh Street, Boulder *(imagery: Google 2017)*

8-41 546 Geneva, Boulder, in 1962 *(family archives)*

8-42 Left to right: Duffy, Nan, Lavinia, Karen, me, Benjy *(family archives)*

During the early Colorado years I taught introductory psychology, the history of psychology, perception, often a junior and a senior honors seminar, some general honors courses, and a few graduate courses; life was good—in that family, teaching, research, friends, and outdoor activities all brought pleasure, satisfaction, and fulfillment. Those were mostly good years. But soon disaster came, as my marriage started to break up.

9 Later Years in Colorado

Several appendices present details on my scholarly efforts, involvement in various professional associations, and travels. The present chapter is intended to report about memorable events during the years after the first decade or so in Colorado. Although I have lived in many different places in my life (in Germany, where I was born, and in a number of places in the northeastern United States), I have been in Colorado longer than anywhere else, and Colorado has become my home state. With the exception of a year in Pearl River, NY, in 1958-1959, a summer in Hawaii in 1966, and a year in Washington, DC, 1970-1971, I have lived in Boulder since 1955.

The mid-1960s were a disaster for me. My marriage with Nan deteriorated, and we soon divorced. My world almost fell apart. With major turmoil in the family, I moved for a while to a small basement apartment several blocks east of Geneva Avenue, where I had places for all the kids to sleep whenever they were with me, and then I bought a small house (with room for the children too, of

9-1 739 Lincoln Place, Boulder *(imagery: Google 2017)*

© Springer Fachmedien Wiesbaden GmbH, part of Springer Nature 2020
M. Wertheimer, *Facets of an Academic's Life*,
https://doi.org/10.1007/978-3-658-28770-2_9

9-2 546 Geneva Avenue, Boulder, 2010 *(courtesy of Chuck Opperman)*

course) at 739 Lincoln Place, about half a mile southeast of the Geneva House, where I stayed until Nan sold me the Geneva house again when my mother came to join me in 1969 after my stepfather Schani had died. All the rest of the time until the move to a retirement community in 2011, except for the 1970-1971 sabbatical year in Washington, DC, was spent in the Geneva house, which was truly a home I greatly enjoyed for five decades.

I've mentioned my first wife, Lavinia Steele MacKaye, alias "Nan," often in this account so far, but haven't presented all that many details about her. While I don't think it would be useful to write a lot more about her, here's a bit more about this highly talented, brilliant woman with whom I had a complex set of relationships over the years. It all began, as I've mentioned, when I came to Cambridge, MA in the fall of 1949. Ward and Ruth Edwards were graduate students in the psychology department when I arrived at Harvard. I had known Ward back at Swarthmore where he too had been an undergraduate student and had dated my sister Lise briefly, and Ward and Ruth had already become acquainted with Nan, who had come as a graduate student to the Harvard department of experimental psychology from Ann Arbor, MI a short time before I did. They praised Nan to the skies as brilliant, gorgeous, an inspiring artist, and a rigorous creative scientist. Clearly Ward and Ruth Edwards had given Nan the same kind of propaganda spiel about

9-3 My favorite picture of Nan, taken when she was six *(family archives)*

me that they presented to me about her. Then they invited Nan and me for a meal at their place, and within a few weeks I had moved in with Nan in her apartment a few steps away from Harvard Square. She had, frankly, been somewhat promiscuous during the preceding few years (as I'm afraid I, too, had been), and we were almost immediately embroiled in a passionate and deeply loving mutual relationship. We shared meals and bed in her apartment. We subsisted on a modest budget. I remember going somewhere in downtown Boston with her fairly often to shop for our rather frugal meals; one staple was broken hotdogs which were available very cheaply at a weekly flea market we frequented, but often splurged for I think something like $1.50 on breakfast at a nearby modest restaurant, where we would indulge in coffee and two poached eggs each on whole wheat toast; I remember the waiter's shout to the cook when we entered, without waiting for us to order: "Drop two twice on wheat."

I brought Nan to Long Island for a vacation, and both my mother and Schani were impressed by her. Then, during the following summer, she joined me as a fellow counselor at the Ethical Culture School Camp in upstate New York, and we were married that September, 1950, by Nan's stepfather, Ezra G. Benedict Fox ("Zare"), who had enjoyed a long successful career as a prominent lawyer and judge, in the back yard of the house in Tenafly, NJ, where he and Nan's mother Lavinia lived. Lavinia was a pediatrician, who had raised Nan and her older sister Jean ("Jeanie") alone after Nan's father had a severe schizophrenic breakdown when Nan was only two years old. Nan's mother, Zare, and Zare's

9-4 Nan's mother, Lavinia, 1946 *(family archives)*

children Greg, Judy, and Zoan were all warm and supportive of Nan and me, as were Jean, her husband Lynn, and their children, all of whom we occasionally visited during the early years of our marriage. So were other relatives, including Nan's grandfather Percy MacKaye and his brother, Uncle Benton.

As I described already, in my life at Harvard almost all of my time was devoted to either my lab work or literature searches or studying for the seminars or courses I was taking. I remember trying

9-5 Nan's father, "Robin" (Robert Keith MacKaye) *(family archives)*

to bone up carefully before I was to take an exam for a course by conscientiously studying for it for many hours every day; I typically earned a B or a B+ or at most an A- in tests I took at Harvard. By contrast, Nan,

9-6 Nan's and my wedding, Tenafly, 1950 *(family archives)*

9-7 My mother's wedding plaque for us, painted on a paper plate and covered with cellophane *(family archives)*

who was a talented artist as well as a brilliant scientist and who spent considerable time creating beautiful works of art in a variety of media (sketching, painting, colored glass, wood carving, etc.) would hardly bother to do the readings assigned in a course or seminar until the evening before a test and would almost invariably earn a high A on

9-8 Duffy, Nan, Karen, Jeanie with her children (youngest to oldest: Betsy, David, Peter, Steve), and me, 1956 *(family archives)*

the same test. She was indeed incredibly intelligent and competent in many ways.

And she was very sensitive to the wishes of her fellow human beings, too. For example, knowing that my father had owned and played a reed organ, a harmonium, during much of his life, which I had told her about, and that I too yearned to have such an instrument, late during our life together in Cambridge she found a beautiful eighteenth-century harmonium that was in good working order but that was missing a few upper decorative wood parts that had nothing to do with the sound quality of the instrument. This bit of missing decoration was a reason the second-hand store where she found the organ was willing to sell it for a mere $20.

One other reminiscence, triggered by my memory of $20 for the organ, is a practice which troubled me from the start in my relationship with Nan, but which I went along with because it clearly was important to her. Although very devoted to me and for years a truly loving and supportive spouse, she insisted that a $20 bill should be left hidden but available in a desk drawer for her to use should she want to "escape" for a few days. $20 in the middle of the twentieth century was a rather substantial amount for an impecunious young academic couple just start-

9-9 Nan in the 1980s *(family archives)*

ing out on a career, the equivalent in purchasing power of several hundred dollars today. I don't remember Nan ever using the $20 to go anywhere, but somehow the threat was always there: if she felt she would want to—or have to?—leave, here was the financial support that would make it possible for her. She insisted on her independence. Often in later years she would demonstrate her independence in other ways, such as by persisting in some creative artistic or scientific endeavor when there was some strong immediate demand for her to do something else, such as answer the telephone or even feed a child.

The marriage had some rocky features to it almost from the start, but they did not become overwhelming until some nine or ten years later. Nan was brilliant, and inadvertently made me feel quite inferior. She also began to develop some fairly intense relationships with some other men, and I did the same with some women other than Nan. This didn't seem to bother Nan much, but it didn't fit at all with my idea of what a marriage should be. We had many long, intense discussions that left both of us exhausted and me in despair.

One night I found myself badly drunk, climbing without protective gear about halfway up the face of the steep cliff, the First Flatiron. Finally realizing the danger I was in, and how devastating a fatal fall would be to Nan and the kids, not to mention the rest of my family, I decided to seek some outside help once I got back down off that rock safely. Nan agreed to join me in a few sessions with a psychiatrist, who ended up recommending that I undertake a psychoanalysis. I did this for a year or so, despite my skepticism about the effectiveness of such treatment. There were weekly visits to an analyst in Denver, and he did not advise against my decision that year to move out and eventually suggest divorce to Nan. At first Nan was opposed to the idea of divorce, but eventually she met me on the campus of the university and handed me a congratulatory bottle of champagne, saying that she now wanted a divorce. My intense ambivalence led me immediately to smash the bottle on the ground.

The years 1963 to 1970 continued to involve a lot of emotional turbulence in my life, as I sought to establish meaningful relationships with women other than Nan, as well as with Nan. There was a short-lived disastrous marriage to Duffy's elementary school teacher, Jody Breyfogle, who joined the kids and me in Hawaii during the summer of 1966 with her own two children, Laurie and Dave, and there were several other short-lived and unsuccessful liaisons. In 1969, after Schani died, my mother came to Boulder and lived with me and the kids at 546 Geneva, which Nan had again sold to me. My mother, determined to help me find a suitable mate, made several dates for me with what turned out to be completely inappropriate ladies, and I requested that she make no further attempts of this kind.

My mother was attending some graduate seminars given by the CU German department, and became acquainted with Marilyn Schuman, having consulted her several times in the reference department of the university library. Without telling me that she was doing so, she invited Marilyn to join her for lunch at the university memorial center cafeteria—and without letting Marilyn know about it, she invited me to have lunch with her there on the same day. This time her strategy worked. Marilyn and I "clicked" immediately, and by the end of the lunch I asked Marilyn to join my mother, me, and the kids for a skiing jaunt the next weekend, which she immediately accepted. It was just a few months later that I casually asked her to marry me as we were walking across a parking lot to have lunch at the University Club, and by the time we got to the club she had accepted. We were married September 1970 in Washington, DC, with Pete arranging much of the wedding ceremony.

Marilyn and I spent that academic year 1970-1971 in a pleasant rented house belonging to an economist friend of Pete's in the northern tip of the District, with my mother, Duffy, and Benjy as well as two dogs. By this time Karen had begun college.

9-10 Anni with Marilyn and me at our wedding, Washington, DC, 1970 *(family archives)*

I became concerned that the schools in which the boys were enrolled that year had much lower standards than the Boulder schools, but we agreed to their pleas to stay in these schools in part because of their experience in student diversity, which we expected might be useful. The schools had about a fifty-fifty split of Caucasian and minority kids, and Duffy had proudly reported that when he was chosen to participate in after-school touch football games, his fellow students called him "nigga" almost as often as they used that appellation with each other.

The marriage with Marilyn has turned out to be a heaven-sent blessing. We have enjoyed almost a half-century of peace, love, mutual support, and quiet serenity, for which I am immensely grateful. She became a beloved surrogate mother, grandmother, and great-grandmother, whom the offspring refer to as "Mamalyn," "Grandmamalyn," or "Great-Grandmamalyn," and she now is clearly the greatly respected matriarch of the family—even though she sometimes refers to the kids as "Michael's children," which makes both them and especially me uncomfortable. The kids, kids-in-law, grandkids, etc., are not *my* kids, but *our* kids even if Marilyn still hasn't fully realized and accepted it.

As for Nan and my relationship with her, it gradually improved over the years after our divorce, and we even again became good friends without the tensions in our relationship that had helped tear the marriage apart. We visited each other regularly, were both deeply concerned with the welfare of our children, and shared conversa-

9-11 Marilyn and me in our later years *(family archives)*

tions about politics and philosophy, about which we remained in agreement. And, unlikely as it may sound, Nan and Marilyn became good friends, with frequent visits as well. And then when Nan died a few years ago, I was greatly touched when her will made me the executor of her estate.

9-12 Nan and me *(family archives)*

Relationships with females have been a focus of much of my emotional experience, often very intense and sometime almost all-consuming, from my childhood until well into my thirties and forties. There is no point in providing further details about all these adventures, from girlfriends at the summer camp, through significant others during my years in college and graduate study, to almost desperate quests between my divorce from Nan until the wonderful, stable serenity I have had the blessing to enjoy with Marilyn. But to repeat, these kinds of relationships consumed much of my emotional and social interactions, especially during the first four or five decades of my long life.

In the fall of 1971, after Marilyn and I returned to Colorado from Washington, DC, with the boys, Lyle Bourne approached me about joining him in buying some mountain property. He was a fellow professor of psychology and later became chair of the department. He was a good friend who had asked me, among other things, to teach him how to sail. He enjoyed that, and so did I. Now he had found a thirty-acre lot at an elevation of about 9500 feet near the small mountain town of Ward, which began as a mining community. He, Ray Miles (another professor in the psychology department), and I bought that land.

A small group of hippies asked us to give them ten of the thirty acres in exchange for building us a cabin on the remaining twenty. Camp Audubon for Boys at Brainard Lake nearby came to the end of its 99-year lease just then, disbanded, and made the materials from its cabins available for the taking. The hippies used those materials to build a cabin to our specifications in the shape of a large T with a loft over the crossbar. It was completed in the summer of 1972 with a wood-burning cookstove in the crossbar and a second stove for heating in the single-story section. (The cookstove was designed to use either wood or coal; we always used wood.) There was plenty of firewood available nearby, but the cabin remained very primitive: no water, no electricity, no gas, no phone. Heating was done with the two stoves, and lighting came from candles and sometimes kerosene lanterns. Obtaining permits for building the cabin itself turned out not to be difficult, but I believe we got the last permit for an outhouse issued by Boulder County, after many, often frustrating visits to the relevant county officials. The outhouse was built over an old mine, a pit which should suffice for several centuries.

The cabin became a treasured weekend destination for many years. Often Marilyn and I would go up on a Friday, carrying jugs of water and other supplies, and not come back until Monday morning. The one-mile trek from the nearest paved road to the cabin on foot in winter, on a one-lane dirt road, was challenging. Snowdrifts might be four or five feet high. We used these weekends for pleasure, working on a manuscript, reading, preparing a book review, etc. We were also there for several Thanksgiving weekends and even one Christmas celebration with various family members, including my mother. It also proved to be a wonderful icebreaker for students and occasionally colleagues, including foreign visitors from Germany and elsewhere. The cabin hosted dozens of overnight outings for psychology undergraduates. Our kids and grandkids also ended up spending a fair amount of time there. One winter, Duff lived in the cabin for

9-13 Our cabin near Ward, with my granddaughter Malca; known as "BMW" for the initials of the three psychology professors who originally had it built *(family archives)*

9-14 The kitchen area in our cabin (a montage of two photos) *(family archives)*

about a month, adding insulation to not only the roof, but also the walls and the floor. This made the cabin much more comfortable in all seasons.

Initially, Bourne, Miles, and Wertheimer took the cabin for rotating weeks and weekends, but eventually we bought out the other two. Over the years it provided a great deal of pleasure and satisfaction. In 2006 we decided that we were quite frustrated at having to clean up previous use by grandchildren, friends of grandchildren, and others even less connected with us. We decided to sell the cabin. It was bought by a missionary couple who spent half of each year in northeastern Africa, building clinics, schools, and hospitals in poverty-stricken villages and the other half of the year in Colorado, mostly to try to raise funds for their endeavors in Africa. For several years thereafter, they invited us for a summer lunch at the cabin, which they had greatly improved with new windows, doors, outdoor decking, etc. They also added a generator for electricity, though the cabin remained without plumbing. They in fact invited us to use it any time they were not there, but we never did.

My career continued to evolve productively during these years. From 1964 until 1983 I was a member (chair from 1979 to 1981) of the Examination Committee of the American Association of State Psychology Boards. The AASPB was an organization devoted to national concerns about the practice of psychology, including such matters as reciprocity (the acceptance of a psychologist who has been certified or licensed in one state for certification or licensure to practice in another state) and certification and licensure in the first place. State boards for qualifying or licensing individuals for the practice of psychology used different methods for evaluating psychologists' competency, often including oral examinations and a variety of written techniques such as presenting diagnostic material on test cases to candidates for them to use in suggesting potential interventions for these cases. But many states also wanted a national examination, preferably an objective one, to be used as part of the procedure in evaluating candidates for certification or licensure. It was the task of the Examination Committee to prepare such an annual test, which came to be called the Examination for the Professional Practice of Psychology, or EPPP. The committee for preparing this test (which for obvious reasons had to be changed every year) typically met for several days, usually in pleasant resort places, for doing its work. My involvement in this committee was very rewarding, with trips to nice places and making the acquaintance of a variety of interesting colleagues as fellow members of this committee, as well as accomplishing a task that I believed was worth accomplishing.

From 1965 to 2006, or a total of some four decades, I was a member of the Board of Advisors of the Archives of the History of American Psychology at the University of Akron. I had become acquainted early during my career with John Popplestone and his wife Marion White McPherson, who had both been instrumental in founding and then facilitating those archives at the University of Akron, and John and I were active for a number of years in efforts to help the APA decide what to do with its own archives. Over the years the collection, its funding, and its physical facilities expanded immensely, first under John's and Marion's leadership and then under David Baker, who took over after John and Marion retired, and who has managed to make enormous improvements in the size,

9-15 Marion White McPherson and John A. Popplestone
*(courtesy of the Archives of the History of American
Psychology, The Drs. Nicholas and Dorothy Cummings
Center for the History of Psychology, The University of
Akron)*

modernization, funding, and housing of the Akron archives. I didn't play much of a role on that board of advisors, other than recommending that a number of retiring psychologists consider donating their personal papers to that archive, and Baker appropriately suggested that I step down from the board in 2006, to make room for younger and more active members. The archives were also immensely helpful to me, in that they not only were delighted to receive my collection of my father's papers after I had finished working on his biography, but have also accepted more than 100 substantial cartons of my own papers, including innumerable ephemera such as board and committee agenda books. I had been a packrat in keeping all this stuff, and was immensely relieved when the Akron archives agreed to accept any and all of what I was willing to get rid of, and offered even to sort and inventory that material, to keep what they considered appropriate, to send to other archives papers concerned with Psi Chi or particular APA divisions—and to see to the discarding of irrelevant stuff. This has saved me the immense amount of time it would have required for me to sort all this stuff myself.

Back in the summer of 1966 I had the opportunity to take advantage of an arrangement Vic Raimy had organized several years earlier, to exchange courses and homes

9-16 David Baker
(courtesy of David Baker)

9-17 The Pali ridge on Oahu, HI *(from https://commons.wikimedia.org/wiki/File: Cliffs_of_the_Koolau_Range,_Oahu_58.jpg; photo by Lukas KURTZ/ LuxTonnerre)*

with a member of the psychology department faculty at the University of Hawaii. He couldn't do it himself that summer, and offered me the opportunity to do it. We had the use of a pleasant home in Kailua, as well as of a car in which I could commute across the mountainous Pali ridge to the university campus in Honolulu to teach a course in introductory psychology there. The house was near a beautiful almost deserted palm-rimmed sandy beach, where the kids and I swam almost

every day. We also took in a number of cultural displays and events; for example, I learned to make "sennit" (cordage braided

9-18 A husk fresh off a coconut *(courtesy of Diane Hamel)*

9-19 The sennit I braided *(family archives)*

9-20 Mats Björkman *(family archives)*

of plant fibers) from the husk which grows around a coconut.

And then during the summer of 1968 I was invited to be a participant in an "International Seminar on Learning and the Educational Process" in Stockholm, Sweden. I had agreed two years earlier to be an "instructor" in that seminar, so enrolled in Swedish language classes at CU during the two years before that. Meantime a program of instruction in a foreign language (Spanish) that my two older children had enjoyed beginning in third grade had been phased out, and there was talk of having my younger son Benjy skip a grade in school because he was doing so well. For purposes of his social development and because he already had warm friendships with classmates, we decided instead that he wouldn't skip a grade after all, and that he would attend the CU Swedish classes with me instead. He typically came home for lunch during those two years so that he and I could do the homework for the classes together—and he ended up (at ages 9 and 10) getting consistently higher grades in those classes than most of the regular undergraduate students in the class.

During that summer in Stockholm I became acquainted with a number of people who would become good friends and colleagues, including Marianne Bauer at the University of Stockholm and Mats Björkman at the University of Umeå in northern Sweden. Visits to an island in the Skärgården, a group of mostly privately owned islands east of Stockholm, were idyllic experiences during those months, but I'm afraid that the results of that seminar didn't produce much of an impact on my later life, even if some research programs were designed there that may have benefitted several of the European participants.

In 1970-1971, while I was acting administrative officer for educational affairs at the APA Central Office, I was invited to be a "national consultant" for a program on the preparation of social science teachers at Illinois State University, which involved several visits that year to Bloomington, IL. But I fear that I didn't really provide much useful input to that program.

From 1972 to 1993 I was officially a member of the Social Science Education Consortium which was housed in Boulder and directed by Professor Haas of the CU school of education; I was also named as half-time associate director of its Center for Education in the Social Sciences. I was involved in several projects at the center for a while, including writings on the teaching of psychology in secondary schools and a few modest research endeavors.

9-21 John Haas *(courtesy of the University of Colorado)*

For Cheiron, the international society for the history of the behavioral sciences, I served as chair of the committee to review proposals for its annual convention program in 1974, and its convention in 1977 was held in Boulder. I was local host for this convention, tasked with supervising arrangements for housing as well as for the venues of the various paper sessions, symposia, lectures, and other events associated with that convention. As I recall, various staff members at CU were very helpful in making that convention run smoothly, and my contribution was relatively modest.

I have been a member of the editorial boards of several journals, including *Gestalt Theory* since 1980 and the venerable German *Zeitschrift für Psychologie* since 1981. I was even (knowing precious little about computers) on the editorial board of the journal *Computers in Human Behavior* from 1984 to 1993 and of *Philosophical Psychology* from 1987 to 1994. I evaluated many articles submitted to other journals as well when editors of those periodicals asked me to review them. And I'm still on the editorial board of APA Division One's journal, *Review of General Psychology*, as I have been for several decades.

There were also two international exchange delegations during the 1980s, one to China and one to Russia. My wife Marilyn was invited to present papers for both of those delegations, and they even included me as a courtesy member who also presented papers on librarianship for academics in a number of different venues in the two countries where we met with local librarians. A report Marilyn prepared on reference librarianship for the China trip was so well appreciated that a translation of it was published in a Chinese library journal. And I had at-

9-22 Philip Zimbardo *(courtesy of the Archives of the History of American Psychology, The Drs. Nicholas and Dorothy Cummings Center for the History of Psychology, The University of Akron)*

tended a daily intensive Chinese language class at CU for a month or so just before we went on that trip and had learned enough very rudimentary Mandarin that at the end of all exchange sessions I was asked to express our thanks and gratitude to the local hosts who had welcomed us. My use of the tones in that language, I soon learned, was much too exaggerated, in a style used in formal Chinese theater, so that my brief comments, while there was bowing in thanks, and smiling, also typically aroused laughter among our Chinese counterparts.

From 1986 to 1989 television channel WGBH and the Annenberg Foundation, in Boston, prepared a 26-session set of half-hour programs on psychology, intended both for potential classroom use in the English-speaking world and for occasional airing on public broadcasting programs. I was invited to be an advisory board member for that project, and played a rather minor role on it, including helping in the selection of the primary lecturer for it, Philip Zimbardo of Stanford University, a brilliant professor well known for his spellbinding lecturing. We did manage to convince him to accept that position, and his performance in all 26 programs, if anything, exceeded the hopes and expectations of the advisory board.

9-23 Lothar Sprung *(from https://commons.wikimedia.org/wiki/File:Sprung,_Lothar.jpg by Reinhard Ferdinand)*

One memorable occasion in 1988 was that the Deutsche Gesellschaft für Psychologie invited me to come to its annual convention in Berlin, Germany, to accept in his stead their posthumous award of its most distinguished recognition, the Wilhelm Wundt Medal, to my father, Max

9-24 Wolfgang Schönpflug *(courtesy of Wolfgang Schönpflug)*

9-25 Viktor Sarris *(courtesy of Viktor Sarris)*

Wertheimer. The ceremony was appropriately resplendent, and I also presented a well-attended invited lecture there on my father. This trip also permitted me to visit with several German colleagues among whom I have managed to find some long-lasting relationships and even friendships. These included Lothar and Helga Sprung,

9-26 Horst Gundlach *(courtesy of Armin Stock)*

Wolfgang Schönpflug, Lothar Spillmann (pictured on page 387), Viktor Sarris, and Horst Gundlach, among others.

There were other events as well listed in my curriculum vitae (Appendix D), but there is no need to comment on them further, except that maybe I should mention that on their invitation I consulted with psychology departments at several colleges and universities about possible improvements to their undergraduate and graduate training programs. I was also invited to consider moving to a few other institutions in the northeast and the northwest, but none of these resulted in my receiving an offer that I accepted. The one I came closest to accepting was an offer to become head of the department at the University of British Columbia in southwestern Canada in 1971, but I have never regretted that I chose to stay in Colorado.

One privilege of being in the psychology department at the University of Colorado was that my work was supported by several excellent secretaries. The one who stands out during my last few decades in the department is Mary Ann Tucker, who somehow was typically able to return to me drafts and revisions of drafts within hours rather than weeks or

9-27 Mary Ann Tucker *(courtesy of the Department of Psychology and Neuroscience, University of Colorado)*

9-28 Val, Lise, Anni, Pete, and me, 1978 *(family archives)*

days. She quickly transformed my paper-and-pencil scribblings into electronic files. Unfortunately, she passed away some time ago already.

My birth family has been an important and consistently reliable source of pleasure, warmth, and identity over all these years. This of course includes my father, who died when I was only 16 years old, but who has continued to play a large role in my career as well as other parts of my life, including a general Weltanschauung and love of music. My mother, an almost seductive woman who somehow managed to convey to anyone with whom she interacted that that person was the most important and fascinating

9-29 Christmas in Boulder in the 1970s: me, Pete, Anni, and Val *(family archives)*

9-30 Bobbie *(family archives)*

person in the world, seemed to have infinite faith in me. She died when I was 60. My siblings, Val, Lise, and Pete, were visited frequently during the earlier years but I continued to feel a strong, uninterrupted intense warmth with them even when visits had become infrequent. Their doings and families were and continue to be a source of pride in my family. Val already passed away suddenly at the much too early age of 53 in 1978, and his wife Bobbie (née Mayer) died not long after that, but

Dec. 15, 1978

Dear Mike,

   Lisa sent me the dreadful news of Val's death, and I am deeply grieved.

   Lillian and I send to you and your family, our deepest sympathy.

   Altho, I think of all of you very often, Val had been on my mind for several days.

   Lisa also sent me a picture of the family get together, and it is very nice, and she explained who every one is, I think I got it straight, and I am very pleased to have it.

   Very best regards
   Most sincerely
   Rosa

9-31 Letter from Rosa when Val died *(family archives)*

I remember many pleasant interactions with them in Middletown, CT, and also at their pleasant weekend and summer retreat near Lakeville in northwestern Connecticut.

Lise, who was still teaching at Duke University until very recently, has had an impressive career in psychology and philosophy, and she flattered me a few years ago by asking me to meet with a class of hers at Duke while I was on the APA Board of Directors. That experience was apparently appreciated by Lise and by the class, and certainly by me. As for Pete, I visited him and his family often during my many trips to Washington, DC, and also spent many very happy days with them in their wonderful rustic places in the country west of DC, as well as in Brazil both at Christmas time in 1980 and then many years later on the occasion of their daughter Monika's wedding there to Claudio Campos. Monika and Claudio now have two charming and unusually competent and capable kids (their son Nicholas even had lunch with the first lady, Michelle Obama, at the

9-32 Pete and Susan *(family archives)*

9-33 Lise and Mike *(family archives)*

White House when he won a national prize in a recipe contest!); they are making a reasonable living by translation from English to Portuguese and vice versa, and are now living in a house they bought in Edwards, Colorado, near the ski resort of Vail.

Pete and his wife Susan (née Bratley) have remodeled a substantial house in Virginia, west of DC, at Flint Hill, where they are now living. They still own a fine mansion in Cleveland Park in northern Washington, DC, of which they have retained the use of an apartment in the basement while the upper two floors are rented out to a tenant; they stay in that apartment when they want to spend a night or two in Washington. After retiring from a successful downtown law practice of which he was a co-founder, Pete devoted himself to the role of artistic director of an amateur theater company near Flint Hill; Marilyn and I have attended not only rehearsals of some of the plays Pete was directing in the refurbished church used as its venue by that company, but also have seen some of the plays he directed there or in which he was an actor. It turns out that he has a real flair for both convincing acting and insightful, unobtrusive casting and directing, as well as flamboyant story-telling.

9-35 Lise and Mike's daughter
9-34 Monika, Chloe, Nicholas, and Claudio *(family archives)*   Rachel with her son Jason *(family*

Our contacts with Val and Bobbie's children, Ellen and Dave, have been spo-radic and rare, but always most enjoyable. Ellen became a prominent professor of law, and Dave has had an illustrious career in counseling, mental health care, and championing the rights of gays and lesbians. Meantime Lise and Mike Wal-lach's daughter Rachel, after a long, tumultuous, and tragic relationship has be-come a single mother of an adopted son; she has built an impressive unique career as a writer and a champion of civil and racial rights causes. And meantime the children of Ellen and her fellow law professor husband Mark Rahdert are doing reasonably well: Christopher, an adopted son who has been problematic from the start, is managing to make do on his own, and their brilliant daughter Lise Elizabeth completed law school and recently got married. And Ellen's brother Dave is married to Paul Beaudet, who, like Dave, is engaged in a career of deciding for a huge non-profit foundation how best to use its resources in supporting worth-while causes.

Then there are my own chil-dren, Karen (now Karellynne or K Watkins) born in 1952, Duffy (originally and now again Mark) born in 1954, and Benjy, born in 1958. Even though they have

9-36 Ellen and Dave in 1969 *(family archives)*

9-37 Karen, Duffy, and Benjy in 1964 *(family archives)*

long since "grown up," with the life of these three following remarkably different trajectories, they all still somehow have being my child as a part of their
identities, and I can't help thinking of them all as my children as well. I love and
admire each and every one of them, and am proud of what they all have done
with their lives.

Karen has been the breadwinner for her family with a variety of technical jobs
involving mastery of esoteric computer and technological skills that are way
beyond my ken, as well as a career as a wordsmith following her highest honors
in English at Swarthmore College and then a PhD in English at Yale University.
Duffy was a successful elementary school teacher who later became an assistant
principal and then principal of elementary schools, and he apparently inherited

my love of the moun-
tains, with far more, and
more challenging, as-
cents to his credit than I
ever made. He recently
retired, but a year later
became principal of an-
other charter elementary
school entering its se-
cond year of operation.
And Benjy, after some
shaky starts and a failed

9-38 Karen and her husband Jim, 1976 *(family archives)*

marriage that was devastating to him, has with his wife Heather (née Klinger) become a highly respected brilliant musician in much demand for his knowledge of the classical music of northern India and for his own successful compositions in that style; his mastery of the tabla, the esraj, and other musical instruments as well

9-39 Duffy with his wife Carla and their oldest three kids, 1989 *(family archives)*

as the difficult esoteric art of throat singing has led not only to many concerts and performances at yoga studios and elsewhere, both nationally and internationally, but also to lively sales of his performances on tape, CD, DVD, and other modern technological devices.

Several people have commented independently about the life trajectories of my childrend along two dimensions: my own interests, and their religious diversity. It has bee claimed that Karen personifies my devotion to writing and to literature, that Duffy continues my fascination and concern about education, not to mention moun-

9-40 Benjy and Heather *(courtesy of Shantala)*

9-41 Me with my first grandchild, Rivka, in
1980 *(family archives)*

9-42 Me with my first great-grandchild,
Cassidy, in 2008 *(family archives)*

taineering, and the Benjy is the fruition of my own love of producing and hearing music.

As for religion, at least two of the three and possibly actually all three are a result of a combination of my religious tolerance and my own skeptical agnosticism. Karen, largely following the lead of her husband Jim, has become a progressively more and more traditional Jew; Duffy, perhaps partly because of a rather wild adolescence with drug experiments, but also because of a pious wife, became a "Jesus freak" or "born-again Christian," but this identity has become much less obtrusive in recent years; and Benjy endorses an amalgam of Buddhist, Hindu, and Quaker beliefs. Karen and Jim's youngest daughter is following her parents' practices, having married a Jew in Manchester, England, where she is raising their sons in a strict Jewish household. Karen and Jim's second

9-43 My grandson Noah and me, 1981 *(family archives)*

child, Svi, follows his father's practices when he is at his parents' house, but has become essentially the same kind of non-practicing agnostic as most of his academic friends and acquaintances; after a bit of exploration in selling used cars, house painting, and juggling firesticks for a circus, he completed his PhD at the University of California at Santa Barbara, and, after a two-year post-doctoral experience at Stanford University in an esoteric biophysical chemistry field, is now well employed as an expert in translating basic scientific findings into practical applications. He recently got married. Karen and Jim's eldest, Rivka, while respecting her father's strong identification with Judaism, is also apparently essentially an agnostic; she is well launched in a specialized computer trouble-shooting and problem-solving career after a master's degree in database management. Meantime, Duffy and Carla's five children all have taken on the Christian identity of their parents; they too don't seem to be all that extreme in their religious identification, at least when they are around Marilyn and me—but that may be in part because they know that neither Marilyn nor I like to "show

9-44 Rachel helping me reshingle the shed in back of 546 Geneva, 1977 *(family archives)*

our religion on our sleeve." For a while the political consequences of these different religious beliefs and practices were a bit troublesome to family interactions, but such problems have decreased in recent years. Still, Marilyn and I and most of our friends, as well as Benjy and Heather, are staunch left-wing liberals strongly supportive of the Democratic party, but Jim and Carla are equally staunch conservative Republicans. Malca, in England, isn't someone with whom we have political discussions; Duffy and Carla's children, as far as we know, probably are all Republicans, following their parents' lead. But we have reached a stage with Duffy and even recently with Jim in which discussions of political issues are no longer taboo, and they now do occur occasionally with mutual respect and open-minded consideration of opposing perspectives.

There is much more that could be said about my large family, which continues to be a central focus of my everyday life. But there is no need for me to provide much more detail about all that here, except that it feels appropriate at least to list them all here. Aside from my siblings and their spouses and offspring, my own descendants are numerous: three children (Karen, Duffy, and Benjy), their three spouses (Jim, Carla, and Heather), eight

9-45 My grandson Svi watching Pete and me in 1987 as we reached a tie in a game from our childhood *(family archives)*: two players stand at arm's length, and each tries to unbalance the other far enough to move a foot (or fall down). The only touching allowed is clapping palms with the opponent. Much of the play consists of feints and dodges. In this photo, we had just clapped palms forcefully; in the next moment each of us stepped back to keep from falling.

grandchildren (Rivka, Svi, and Malca through Karen and Jim, and Noah, Michael, Ruth Mae ("Ruthie"), Joey, and Mary Rose through Duffy and Carla—the first three as their biological kids and the last two by adoption), five grandchildren-in-law (Svi's wife Teddi, Malca's husband Jon, Noah's wife April, Mike's wife Lizz, and Ruth Mae's husband Jared), and twelve great-grandchildren: Svi's step-daughter Danielle, Malca's sons Ezra and Benjamin and Asher, Noah's four adopted children AJ, Lily, Aliviya, and Maliyah, Michael's children Cassidy and Eli, and Ruthie's sons Gabriel and Benen. And then there is of course Marilyn's only remaining "blood relative," her brother Jack Schuman, who has no offspring. We often traveled with Jack (and his wife Dorinda, née Shearer, until that tormented marriage ended some time ago after many troubled years), and he visited us a number of times in Boulder until he no longer enjoyed traveling; since then, we have typically visited him in southern Oregon twice a year for two weeks each time. These visits were originally to his and Dorinda's house in Pullman, WA, where Jack was a faculty member at Washington State University teaching art history, then after his retirement to his house in Phoenix, OR, and most recently to his cottage associated with an independent living community, aptly named Emeritus but recently bought by Brookdale, in north Ashland, OR, into which he moved in 2013 and in which he lets us stay in one of the bedrooms in his cottage. We have enjoyed many live music performances in Ashland with Jack, as well as superb theater performances, not necessarily of Shakespeare's

plays, at the deservedly world-famous Oregon Shakespeare Festival, which operates four usually sold-out theaters throughout most of each year.

Interactions with family members have been dearly valued aspects of

9-46 Dorinda and Jack *(family archives)*

9-47 Pete, Lise, me at family reunion in 2013 *(family archives)*

my life since my childhood. Even now we still have frequent contact with them, mostly with offspring. Karen and Rivka have been visiting us in our retirement community apartment regularly at least once a week and Jim now comes often too, and we have sometimes driven to Denver to be with Karen and Jim or to Windsor to be with Duffy and his family—and other members of the family come to visit us as well. Pete and Susan have stayed overnight with us at our retirement apartment, and several of Duffy and Carla's children and their family have visited us there. In 2012 we even had a meal in our retirement community private dining room attended by some 18 relatives as a birthday party for me. And Jim and Duffy arranged a 90th birthday bash for me at our retirement community, with some 75 attendees: more than 20 relatives, some 30 Boulder colleagues or friends, and lots of retirement community residents. Our children (other than Benjy and Heather, whose residence is in Portland, OR) live about an hour's drive north or south of Boulder, so in recent years we have had the opportunity of frequent visits to or from them, while not having lived close enough for us to be frequently asked to provide babysitting for them. It has been a convenient situation.

For many years, I have tried to acknowledge every birthday and wedding anniversary in the family, and I hope that I've succeeded in that endeavor.

Interactions with various friends have also greatly enriched my life. Friendships important in my earlier years did not last beyond physical proximity, as I moved away, from Germany to Czechoslovakia to New Rochelle, then to Swarthmore, Baltimore, Cambridge, Worcester, and Boulder, including a few houses in which my mother and Schani lived in New Jersey and then on Long Island. Probably

9-48 My birthday cake with Flatirons photo, 2017 *(family archives)*

the longest lasting one was with my Swarthmore roommate Stefan Machlup, who passed away a few years ago. And I also count my varied interactions with my wife and then ex-wife Nan as one of my longest friendships. My contacts with friends, colleagues, and students often continued at least in the form of annual exchanges of Christmas cards for many years, usually with a short one-page insert reporting significant events of the preceding year. For a time, there could be as many as 100 or so families or people to whom we sent cards and from whom we received them, but in recent years, with correspondents passing away or our just losing contact with them, that number has shrunk down to about 70, about one third of them people Marilyn knew before we met, about another third people I knew before 1970, and the rest people we both knew. And we continue to have frequent contacts with many friends on a regular basis, both local and some further away. Since we moved into our retirement community apartment in 2011, we have also become acquainted enough with a number of fellow residents there to be able to call them friends as well.

As mentioned earlier, some form of gardening has provided pleasure since my childhood. There was a fairly large vegetable patch at our New Rochelle house and also near our apartment in Middletown as well as at our house at 546 Geneva Avenue in Boulder, and there have been many smaller vegetable patches in between. Our small patch a hundred feet or so from the patio of our retirement apartment has also provided us with a surprisingly ample crop of tomatoes, green beans, Swiss chard, zucchini, and mild garlic during the last few years. And at 546 Geneva, fruit trees planted before we got there yielded goodly supplies of apples and plums, and for a while the grape vines there generated several gallons of home-made grape juice, and sometimes we also had peaches, pears, rhubarb, and asparagus. I've always enjoyed "playing with food," in the form of shopping for it, growing some of it, and cooking; it has been a valued complementary activity to the more abstract, esoteric, and more cognitively challenging tasks in academia.

I have enjoyed reading since my childhood; Val was such an effective teacher that under his guidance I had learned to read quite competently by the time I was four years old. During my undergraduate and graduate years, I amassed a fairly substantial collection of what I call my "bibliophilia," books going back to the 17th century, in multiple languages. While I certainly haven't read (or been able to read) very many of them, I greatly enjoy their look and feel. And we also collected over the years a rather substantial home library of maybe 1500 books, including biographies, classics, books on psychology and on Marilyn's specialty Russia and Russian literature, and many books on art and on travel. When we moved into our retirement community, we had to give up some 1000 books or so, but we still kept a lot of them too. Since my retirement, I have also been able to spend more time reading for pleasure than I managed to before, and I have typically been able to read quite a few books each year. One practice that Marilyn and I have both enjoyed (partly due to my perhaps somewhat

9-49 Marilyn on the deck at 546 Geneva *(family archives)*

presumptuous interest in theater) is my reading books in which we're both interested aloud to her.

Many other events during my later years in Colorado could also be described here, but I believe that this is a reasonable place to stop providing further details about my life which, despite some desperately depressing times, has also been filled with an enormous number of very pleasant and even blessed events and circumstances. It has been a very rich and varied life indeed, and I am especially grateful for the serenity that I have been able to enjoy during the last five decades with Marilyn. Life is good.

In November 2011 we moved into a small retirement community about three miles south of the 546 Geneva Avenue house, and we have found our new home very congenial. Our large ground-floor two-bedroom apartment has a patio outside a big sliding-glass door through which we can see a peaceful lawn with trees sloping up gently some 200 feet toward the parking lot of a Catholic church. We have a surprisingly private view of it; we hardly ever see any cars or anyone else there other than some rabbits, squirrels, and birds as well as a few occasional dog walkers. The apartment itself is filled with many treasures we saved from our house, and parts of it are like a museum, with innumerable mementos from earlier times and from many places around the world. Bookcases are filled with travel and art books, many of Marilyn's books about Russia, and much "bibliophilia," plus one small bookcase filled with books I edited, wrote, co-authored, or co-edited. Our old cuckoo clock still faithfully calls out the hours and half-hours, and we enjoy our gas log fireplace. House plants in south-facing windows are thriving, and a few of Marilyn's most spectacular photographs adorn the walls. We do have a new home. And to repeat, life is good.

10 Years in a Retirement Community

After a broad variety of roles and settings, from a youngster transported to a foreign culture speaking an unfamiliar language, to a retired academic playing major roles in his national professional association, I now find myself in a new role and a new setting: I'm one of just over a hundred residents in an independent-living retirement community. It is indeed a setting that is very different from any I had experienced before in my long and variegated life.

Every major life change is a challenge, but this one turned out to be relatively easy. It's not that my many previous often major transitions have somehow made me more resilient than before (although that too may have played at least a small role), but mainly that the new role and setting are so pleasant and not at all difficult to adjust to.

I was blessed with a childhood during which I felt safe and loved, and was warmly encouraged to explore the almost infinite-appearing variety of fascinating activities and possibilities that young life offered. The transition to a new culture was exciting and rewarding, and school was a never-ending source of wonder, learning, friendships, and the opening of doors to new vistas I never before knew existed and could not even have imagined without the stimulus of excellent teachers, books, fellow pupils, and a plethora of new experiences. True, the trauma of my mother abandoning me, my siblings, and my father was a painful experience which took years to overcome (if I ever actually did overcome it), but the heady excitement that came with attending Swarthmore College soon became central in the next phase of my life. The intense pleasures of intellectual inquiry, explorations with the opposite sex, learning foreign languages, sports, variegated social activities, music, the outdoor life, efforts at various kinds of creative endeavor, skiing, writing, and editing all dominated my life for many years. My life has included many a period of profound satisfactions.

Graduate school was a challenge, and my days there were almost totally devoted to work and study. But there was time for my beloved summer camp, and the development of an intense relationship with a woman who almost right away ended up dominating my life even more than my mother had done. Nan and I

© Springer Fachmedien Wiesbaden GmbH, part of Springer Nature 2020
M. Wertheimer, *Facets of an Academic's Life*,
https://doi.org/10.1007/978-3-658-28770-2_10

married, had children, and co-operated in various professional activities that were related to my efforts to build a career that not only would be satisfying for me but also would make it possible to earn enough to support Nan and the children.

The year in Worcester was part of this effort. Then the time at Wesleyan and early in Colorado got me well launched on a career in academia. I succeeded in amassing a reasonably respectable list of publications in professional journals, was apparently an acceptable college teacher (although I never was trained for that role and never truly felt competent as a teacher during my long teaching career—despite winning various awards for teaching), and earned enough so that we didn't have to skimp too much. Nevertheless Nan and I were constantly careful to be frugal in our spending habits, a pattern that has continued down to the present for me and that was clearly responsible for Nan's ability to support herself, and also often the children, after our divorce, as well as amassing a small fortune (and preserving a substantial inheritance from her mother) which she passed on to the children both during several decades and then when she died.

10-1 Karen, Benjy, Nan, Duffy, and me in Pearl River, 1958 *(family archives)*

That pattern also helped me to save enough that I now have an estate and income during retirement that means I should never have to depend on my offspring for financial help and that I may even be able to leave them at least a small inheritance when I'm gone.

The working years were very busy, as I strove for promotion, tenure, and recognition while trying to support my family. I put in up to 70 or 80 hours a week on my work and career, while also making time for interactions with my beloved children (who grew up much too fast), endless stimulating and often frustrating talks with Nan, visits with friends and family mem-

10-2 My office at the University of Colorado, in the building named for Karl Muenzinger *(family archives)*

bers, and enjoying an active outdoor life.

Then, even as I was beginning to achieve some coveted goals such as being elected to prestigious posts in my national professional association and being rapidly promoted, a new and exceedingly difficult time began as my relationship with Nan deteriorated. After a year's separation, we were divorced, and I was despondent. My self-esteem, already weak before, plummeted, and for several years (despite continuing success in my career) I was almost incapacitated. I engaged in a brief totally imprudent marriage to someone who was quite incompatible, got involved successively in a series of other stupid romantic attachments, and even came so close to attempted suicide that I sought outside psychiatric help. Whether that help really was appropriate or truly successful, I still don't know, but at least I did manage to survive a desperate decade that was the nadir of my entire life. I now am deeply grateful that I did manage to make it, somehow, through those awful years.

The second half of my life brought a kind of fulfillment and serenity that had been totally lacking before. My marriage to Marilyn has been the godsend of my life. With her, there was a renewed period of enthusiasm, pleasure in work, wonderful relationships with the kids, extensive travel, rewarding social activities and, best and most valued of all, a new conviction that maybe I might not be justified in having such a miserable opinion of myself. She has restored my self esteem, and raised it to a level I had never experienced before, a feat on her part for which I am extremely grateful.

That stage of my life, which has lasted more than four decades, has included substantial recognition in my career, the expansion of my family to four generations, and a stable, fulfilling life until my retirement in 1993. Although I did officially retire at that time, my scholarly contributions (books, articles, roles in professional associations) continued for another two decades or so, and I retained an office at the university past my ninetieth birthday (though by the time the department asked me to clear it out, I had hardly used it any more for two or three years).

But then came a time when I'd had enough of all that, and I now am retired de facto as well as de jure. And while I did obtain a great deal of satisfaction from my career, I do not miss the activities, responsibilities, and recognition that it involved. I've started, gratefully, on a new phase of my life, genuine retirement. And I'm enjoying it immensely.

In September 2011 we started renting an apartment at the Meridian, an independent retirement community some three miles south of the house I'd lived in off and on for half a century, and in November of that year we moved permanently into that apartment. It has turned out to be an ideal setting for us, and has become a cherished home. Life here is different from any life I've had before, and it is deeply appreciated and very good.

Marilyn and I had explored various retirement communities in the Boulder region for several years before we decided to try to move to the Meridian. There

10-3 The sign by the road for the Meridian
(courtesy of Brookdale Meridian Boulder)

was a wide choice, from small ones like the Meridian to others that had as many as 450 residents. Some were downright elegant and very expensive (requiring a down payment of hundreds of thousands of nonrefundable dollars), while some others appeared to be somewhat dilapidated. Some required purchase of an accommodation, but others were on a purely rental basis. While we had managed to put away some funds regularly for retirement while we were still working, funds that would assure us a modest income during retirement years, we were not blessed with an enormous accumulation that would have permitted us to move to one of the more expensive communities. So in 2009, believing that we might still want to stay in our beloved 546 Geneva Avenue house for a few more years, we put down a small (refundable) deposit at the Meridian; this deposit could be used to cover part of the first month's rent if we should decide to move into one of those Meridian apartments. We knew there was a fairly long waiting list, that apartments became available only sporadically, and that there was quite a variety in the kinds of apartments that made up the Meridian community. We were in no hurry. We had become acquainted with the Meridian several years earlier, in part through a friend who had joined us on a trip to Norway and who was now a resident there, and in part through a retired physics professor with whom we played tennis for a number of years and who, with his wife, was also a resident there.

Among the attractions of the Meridian was the fact that the financial arrangement is a rental rather than a purchase; that it is within short walking distance of a large shopping area with an excellent grocery store, a branch of our bank, restaurants we both enjoy, and many other resources including bus stops; that we knew and enjoyed several of the residents; and that it is only some three miles due south of where we had lived before, a region which we had gotten to know a good bit over the years. During a period of a couple of years several apartments did become available, and we were given the option of renting them. Some were smaller than we wanted (only one bedroom and one bathroom) but had fine views of the Flatirons to the west; others were larger but looked out on a parking lot. Some had a fireplace but most did not. Some were along a long hall with many neighbors and others were more private. Some had extra storage space and others did not.

Then when we returned in September 2011 from our annual anniversary two-

10-4 The Peck House in Empire, Colorado *(courtesy of Sally St. Clair)*

night stay at the Peck House in Empire, Colorado (where we'd gone every year for a couple of decades for our anniversary celebration), we had a voicemail on our phone informing us that another ground-floor two-bedroom apartment with a patio had become available. Still not really expecting to move for another year or two—we really did enjoy our home at 546 Geneva Avenue, even though with its huge yard and six bedrooms it was clearly much too big for us—we decided to go ahead and look at it. It was at the southwest corner of the community, had a pleasant private sunny patio with a large storage shed, had a gas-log fireplace, was just around the corner from the public dining room, lounge, and living room, was next to the playground of an elementary school just to the south, shared a private short hallway with only one other apartment, had large windows with a southern exposure, had a semi-private lawn area with a few trees, extending several hundred feet uphill to the west with a modest unobtrusive small church and its parking lot, and while not cheap, was available for rent. And the rent included weekly cleaning, 180 meals a year for each of us, all expenses for water, gas, and electricity, yard maintenance, innumerable activities from several weekly movies to daily exercise classes such as tai chi, yoga, and strength train-

10-5 The northern portion of the "back yard" outside the patio of our retirement home, in summer *(family archives)*

10-6 The southern portion of the "back yard" outside the patio of our retirement home, in winter *(family archives)*

ing, live music performances, a maintenance crew to fix any problems that might arise, free parking, and a number of other amenities.

We rented it on the spot. And we have not regretted it; over the years we have been in this apartment, we have grown progressively more and more fond of it. We have seen many of the other apartments in the complex, and the one we rented is without doubt the best one for us in the entire community. Its privacy is unmatched (we hardly ever see anyone in "our" big back yard other than an occasional dog walker or gardener). Our big double glass patio door is used by many of our offspring as our front door when they come to visit; it is almost as though we have our own private cottage in the country that happens to be attached to an almost invisible facility with many amenities. And the rise to the west means that even from our patio, while we can barely hear the traffic on the nearby main road, we cannot see the cars. The square footage of the apartment is almost half what we had available in our entire house, and we managed to fur-

10-7 The dining room at the Meridian *(courtesy of Brookdale Meridian Boulder)*

nish our new abode with many of the treasures we brought with us from the house. These treasures help provide continuity, and help bring back many fond memories.

We have become acquainted with many of our fellow residents, and a number of them have become good friends. We frequently share some meals in the Meridian dining room with them (the food and service are generally very good, including several options at most meals, as well as a fine soup and salad bar), go to tai chi, balance, yoga, strength training, and "stretch and flex" classes almost daily (the leaders of these groups have also become friends), attend more movies (usually well-chosen classic films) than we have in decades, and join occasional outings to local parks and restaurants. I also participate in such other activities as live music, monthly sing-alongs, for several years monthly slide shows by Marilyn, current events discussions, weekly bridge games, occasional ping pong, a weekly sign language class, weekly Friday evening cocktail parties, "resident chats," elaborate Sunday buffet brunches, foreign language lunches, meetings with members of the management team, tending our little vegetable patch, receptions for new residents, and various lectures.

My time has been so well filled with community activities, reading, food preparation, dealing with mail, and so on, that even though we moved in some eight years ago, I still have several boxes full of stuff brought to the apartment from our house that I haven't yet gotten around to opening. Until the summer of 2017 I still had some office space on the campus of the University of Colorado; until I learned to use a shared computer in the Meridian library, I used to go there a couple of times a week, to check e-mail on a computer "lent" to me when I became a member of the APA board of directors, which is now so old that they don't want it back. I now use that computer at home, or else the computer in the

Meridian library, so there's no point any more in my keeping an office at the university.

Our new circle of friends includes people with a variety of backgrounds. There is a fairly large number of retired academics. As I mentioned before, there was a retired CU physics professor and his wife who had already been good friends for several years before we moved in to the Meridian, but they moved out to an assisted living facility a couple of years ago. A retired CU professor of music whom I barely knew before we moved here became a good friend; his wife, an accomplished artist, passed on two years after we moved in and had also become a good friend. Two retired CU math professors recently moved in; one was born, raised, and educated in Vienna, was an avid skier and had a pleasant American wife, and the other was a legendary rock climber who back in 1960 had won considerable fame in the local mountaineering community by being a member of a two-man team that was the first to climb directly up the center of the imposing 90° vertical 1000-foot Diamond that makes up the northeast face of 14,000-foot Longs Peak. And the widow of another CU math professor who had become a highly respected dean of the College of Arts and Sciences also fairly recently moved in to the Meridian. One of my former colleagues in the CU psychology department and his wife also moved in some time ago; unfortunately his wife died just a month after they had moved here.

This is of course one of the realities of being in a retirement community: it is not unusual for there to be either residents who move out into a facility where they can receive more everyday help—or residents who die. Indeed a new resident who moved in a little while ago, who had been a

10-8 The lily pond at the Meridian *(family archives)*

10-9 Marilyn and me on a horse-drawn carriage ride
(courtesy of Theresa Reed, Brookdale Meridian Boulder)

near neighbor at the Geneva house, died suddenly and unexpectedly a month or so after he moved in. Another longer-term resident, who served for years as the unofficial self-appointed "welcome ambassador" to all new residents, including us, and who participated enthusiastically in many community activities, also died suddenly and rather unexpectedly some time ago.

Such events are still not easy to deal with, but they have become a part of everyday life in a retirement community. We have heard that the average tenant at the Meridian is here for about five and a half years—but there is one current resident who is still in remarkably good shape both mentally and physically, who moved in here with her CU business school professor husband when the facility first opened more than thirty years ago, and there are a few other residents who have lived here almost that long too.

Another resident whom we've gotten to know is the widow of a CU history professor, and several residents were associated with CU's Norlin Library. There are also academics retired from other colleges and universities. A geologist with Swedish ancestry who was an expert on reefs retired here from the University of Nebraska, and there is a cultural anthropologist who is an expert on native American tribes and languages who retired from Oklahoma State University. An Air Force World War II veteran who was responsible for economics education in the state of Wisconsin contributed well-informed, balanced, and articulate comments, discussion, and questions to current events discussion sessions and turned out to be a warm, friendly, and stimulating companion at meals in the Meridian dining room. Recently moved in is an MIT-educated meteorologist who also taught mathematics at the Colorado School of Mines, at Boulder High School, and the Boulder County Jail, who has turned out to be a brilliant intellectual, a fine bridge player, and a good friend. A woman who was born deaf, who was an administrator at Gallaudet College and spent her career helping deaf and hard-of-hearing people, participates enthusiastically in exercise classes, is an expert Scrabble player, and also turned out to be a good friend. And there are still others who had connections with academia.

Many without such connections have also become good friends. A retired dentist who was an avid gardener, and his wife, became good friends even though their political opinions differed strongly from ours; he too passed on suddenly a while ago, but his widow, who was a serious bridge player despite frustrating problems with her vision, was also a very good friend. Our next-door neighbors the Epsteins, with whom we share a short private hallway at the southwest end of the community, have become close friends. Dick Epstein suffered a disabling illness some years ago and was confined to a wheelchair, but until his recent death still participated actively in current events discussions and bridge games, and his wife Judy, born in Switzerland and raised in France, is an excellent artist, gardener, and widely respected and beloved extraverted member of the community; everyone here loves her, she has taken care of our house plants when we were away, and altogether has turned out to be an ideal neighbor. These neighbors have also introduced us to other word games like "Boggle."

Then there are many other residents whom we've gotten to know, and

10-10 Marilyn, me, and Judy Epstein on a Meridian picnic in the mountains *(courtesy of Theresa Reed, Brookdale Meridian Boulder)*

with whom we are on good terms. One wealthy Republican was a retired businessman. A long-time member of Marilyn's church moved in a little while ago, and we joined her for some meals as well as in some modest exercise classes. There is also a group with whom I have become close because we often play bridge together; bridge can be a good ice breaker. We have also gotten to know several newer couples of whom we've become quite fond: a retired research chemist and his wife, a retired professor of hospital management and finance from the University of California at Berkeley and his wife, a high school math teacher and his spouse, and a recent move-in couple who knew me during my time of misery a half-century ago.

And then there is William ("Bill") Weber, who was a resident here quite a few years ago, moved out because of the expense (he was helping his daughter buy a car), and moved back in a few years ago when the car was paid for. A centenarian as of late 2018, he is a professor emeritus of botany who is probably the world's greatest expert on lichen. He still is publishing papers on such things as plant species that only propagate locally, but of which specimens were found both in New England and in Great Britain—providing further evidence of continental drift. As it happens, my older son took some classes from Weber at the University of Colorado, and considers him absolutely brilliant.

Marilyn knows the names of almost all the dogs who live here—though not necessarily the names of all their owners (oops: "guardians" in Boulder). New residents are permitted to bring along a cat or dog as long as the pet weighs 25

pounds or less, but many of the current pets clearly have exceeded that weight. Among the canine pets are tiny "Lollypop," who is taken for five or six walks outside our patio daily by her gaunt lady guardian;

10-11 Bill Weber *(courtesy of Cliff Grassmick)*

"Suzy" was the large friendly mongrel dog of the now deceased dentist and his now vision-challenged wife; "Molly," the pet of a retired professor of nursing; "Ellie May," the carrot-loving beagle of the retired high-school math teacher and his wife, who clearly

10-12 "Night on the Nile" at the Meridian *(courtesy of Theresa Reed, Brookdale Meridian Boulder)*

enjoys people and for whom Marilyn and I have occasionally done dog-sitting in our apartment (and on walks outside) when his mistress went to take her husband to the doctor; at least two golden retrievers, and a variety of others too. But we haven't gotten acquainted with any of the cats, although we have occasionally heard about them and their antics from their guardians.

The management team at our community is most impressive. The executive director clearly has the well-being of the residents as her first priority. She hosts a monthly "tea with the ED" and a monthly general meeting open to all residents, "The View," at which she reports on events and issues of interest to all and in which she opens the floor for any resident who wishes to do so to raise any issue whatever. She responds immediately and with both good humor and a good sense of humor to each such comment, and indeed follows through as well as she can, given the constraints of budget and of her immediate superiors. The Meridian is one of some 500 or more retirement communities in the US that was bought in early 2014 by Brookdale, and the Canadian company that owned this group in the summer of 2014 completed the purchase of some 600 or so additional retirement communities including the Emeritus ones (in one of which, in Ashland, OR, Marilyn's brother Jack has now been living for several years), so that now Brookdale is by far the largest such company, managing about 1164 communities nationally. It turns out that the Boulder Meridian ranks second in this entire group (after one in Arizona) in terms of how long it has been full and how large the waiting list is. And in a resident satisfaction survey in the fall of 2016, our community ranked highest in the entire Western region. We're not surprised; our executive director does a superb job of running this place. She is truly an expert at multi-tasking, taking care of a myriad of issues at the same time.

We also have an excellent director of financial affairs, who makes it a point to be available and helpful to each and every resident at all times. He spends many overtime hours at the facility whenever that is necessary, filling in for various other staff members whenever needed. He (as well as the executive director) even help serve coffee and other drinks in the dining room if the dining room staff is short-handed.

The activities director is an enthusiastic, extraverted, energetic lady who puts together and arranges an enormous set of activities each week, including well-selected movies almost every evening, and participates in many of the activities to the extent that her busy schedule permits. She too is very open to suggestions from residents, as is the executive director.

The executive director and financial director appear to be the ones most involved in hiring staff: the maintenance crew, housekeepers, kitchen workers, dining room wait staff, receptionists, night workers and others. Whatever criteria are used in selecting personnel, the results are surprisingly good. Hired staff are uniformly polite, competent, warm, and friendly with residents, indeed consistently treat the residents— even the more

10-13 Marilyn and me at an "Anniversary Dinner" *(courtesy of Theresa Reed, Brookdale Meridian Boulder)*

challenging ones—with respect and deference. And the hired staff also clearly are highly competent in carrying out the tasks they have been employed to do. Almost all of them also seem—miraculously—to learn the names of all residents almost immediately.

Moving into the Meridian, and my "de facto" retirement, have indeed involved a major transition in my life. A fairly detailed description of the apartment, and of our daily rituals since retirement, is presented in Appendix I to document how clearly this place has managed to provide continuity in my and my wife's lives. Many features of this residence, and many of its contents, serve to preserve a lot of the positive aspect of earlier parts of our long, fulfilling lives.

While the Meridian is officially an "independent living" facility, a number of additional services are available through a "personalized living" program that offers paid outside assistance to residents who need help getting around, or keeping up with medications, or enjoy massage or need physical therapy, and so on. We haven't made use of such services (yet), but their availability means that quite a few long-term residents who otherwise might have had to move into an "assisted living" or "long-term care" facility could remain in a community that for years or decades has been home for them.

11 Epilogue: Who Am I?

The first few chapters of this chronicle were drafted quite a few years ago, and Appendix B on *The Wertheimer Times* was written several months later. Then I looked at a fairly recent CV, intending to start writing about the post-Wesleyan years, but got distracted by thoughts about all the various names that I've been called during my long life, and how these names have been associated with my identity, with who I am. Like probably almost every other human being, I have in some way been many different people, depending on circumstances, environment, setting, and with whom I'm interacting. Was I really the same person when I taught sailing on Lake Otsego in northern New York State at the Ethical Culture School Camp, when I was on a mission with other members of the Rocky Mountain Rescue Group to try to find a boy lost in the Colorado foothills, when I played harmonica at an amateur hour on Monhegan Island, Maine, when I recorded my Sonata Number ½ on the piano when I was 17 years old, when I took care of one-year-old Peter when I was a nine-year-old child early in the morning at 12 The Circle, New Rochelle, when I gave the presidential address for the Division on the History of Psychology at a convention of the American Psychological Association, when I lectured on something or other during a course at the University of Colorado at Boulder or on my father at a psychology convention in Germany, and when I fixed "gooshy-goshy French toast" or "egg in the bread" for a bevy of appreciative children and grandchildren on a wood stove at 9500 feet elevation in our rustic cabin in the Colorado mountains? Like everyone else, I have had multiple roles during my life, and it feels as though each one has, in its own way, helped enrich the overall tapestry of my life story. So rather than continuing to narrate what seemed to be significant events chronologically in my life, I became tempted to muse a bit about my names, my identities, my self image—and maybe also the image that others have had of me. Who am I?

I'm a son, a brother, a brother-in-law, a husband, a father, a grandfather, a great-grandfather, an uncle, a sailor, a mountaineer, a former president of several professional associations, an author of lots of books and technical articles, an editor, a champion of the history of psychology and a skeptic about the so-called practice of psychology, an award winner for teaching and other activities, an amateur bridge player, an avid and modestly effective gardener, a not very good skier, an anosmic cook with an undeserved reputation for gourmet cookery, the son of a famous father, a pipe smoker, an outdoorsman, an amateur musician and composer and lover of classical western music as well as of old German and American folk songs, someone who has unsuccessfully tried to keep my weight down for three quarters of a century, a professor emeritus, and recently the president of the resident council at a retirement community. None of these captures the essence of who I am, yet they all clearly are part of who I think I am.

And all this is only a truncated initial list. There is so much more. I've been a teaching assistant, a research assistant, a presumed expert on sensation and perception, a world traveler, a graduate student of Asian art while traveling the world with a CU art professor, a multilingual interpreter and translator, a fervent amateur etymologist and linguist, a stand-in recipient for a prestigious award to my father from a German psychological society, a modest Ken-Ken and Sudoku puzzler and an avid crossword puzzler (but one stumped by the hyper-sophistication of Sunday *New York Times* puzzles), a modest tennis player, a former member of the Board of Directors of my national professional association, an agnostic or Quaker or humanist or eclectic, an ocean kayaker, an expert underwater swimmer and worker, the undergraduate host of a multilingual poetry radio program, an actor, a play director, a reluctant clinical psychologist, the president of a university chapter of the venerable honor society Phi Beta Kappa, a monetary skinflint but donor of generous financial gifts to relatives and to innumerable charities, a presumed expert on UFOs, and someone who has shaken the hand of legendary physicist Albert Einstein.

What variegated identities! None of them captures the essence of who I am (if there is such a thing; do any other species ever wonder about "who they really are"?), yet each of them does capture a facet of who I am, or at least of who I have been.

It might be worthwhile to continue these musings by considering all the names I've been called; each one has rich, intricate implications. Indeed at least in western society (and probably everywhere throughout the world) there typically are very strict rules, as well as major taboos, about who can use what names for whom under what circumstances. Use of the "wrong" name can lead to such consequences as feeling insulted, or even violated; use of the "right" name appears to be among the strictest rules in human verbal behavior.

When I was a child, like most kids I had a few nicknames. Under ordinary conditions, I was usually referred to as "Michel" or even the diminutive "Michelchen." Then later, in the US, I was often called "Mikey" by my mother and others. Comparably, my sister was "Lise" or "Lischen," and my older brother was "Val" or "Valli," and only rarely, if ever, Valentin.

In elementary school, as I've mentioned, I had a classmate who often came to our house to play in the afternoons; I called my friend "Smokey," in reference to an admired firefighter from a newspaper comic strip, "Smokey Stover," and it was only much later, to my chagrin, as I've mentioned before, that I realized that he might have thought I was derisively referring to his skin color: he was an African American, and I certainly didn't intend to use a racial slur for his nickname.

At summer camp, I was almost always just "Mike" to everyone—whether it was initially in my role as a camper or later as a junior counselor or regular counselor. At college I was also almost always "Mike," although on rare occasions it was "Mike Wertheimer" or even only "Wertheimer." I was never "Werthy" or anything like that, but I do remember my mother affectionately calling my father "Heimere," a diminutive of the last two syllables of Wertheimer, especially used when we children were still very young. One collective variant used by my stepfather Schani during later years when we were visiting him and my mother, when he wanted us to stop being noisy, was "Kindersch!," a takeoff on the semi-diminutive "Kinderchen" or "Little children," when he would exasperatedly shout at us, "Kindersch! Ruhe!" or "Kids! Be quiet!"

I've also mentioned that there was a fellow graduate student at The Johns Hopkins University by the name of Michael Leyzorek. He was a strapping fellow, much taller than I, and I don't know what became of him. Soon after we got acquainted, we fell into a pattern of greeting one another whenever we met in the lab or the hall or the classroom: I would say "Hi, Mike!" (high Mike) and he would respond, " 'Lo, Mike!" (Hello or low Mike), acknowledging that he was a big Mike and I a littler one.

At Harvard, I consistently was Mike, and sometimes some faculty members called me "Wertheimer." Then at Worcester State Hospital, as I've also reported, while I was an intern in clinical psychology, I was required to wear a starched white jacket whenever I interacted with a patient, and was told to ask the patients to refer to me as "Doctor," even though I had not yet complete the requirements for the PhD. While I complied with the local practice of having the pre-PhD interns called "doctor," I did feel uncomfortable about doing so; it felt like a kind of uncalled-for fraud.

For a few years after actually completing my PhD, I felt comfortable and proud to be called "Dr. Wertheimer" or, after promotion from instructor to assistant professor, "Professor Wertheimer," but this pride didn't last very long. Indeed, late in my career, following the example of one of my most admired professors, Robbie MacLeod, my preferred name other than "Mike" or "Michael" became simply "Mr. Wertheimer."

One name I enjoyed during my role as faculty advisor to the Boulder chapter of the national honor society Psi Chi and as director of the psychology departmental honors program at the University of Colorado at Boulder was one that some undergraduates bestowed upon me and typically used when I took undergraduate students for ice-breaking overnight trips to our primitive mountain cabin (no water, electricity, gas, or phone); it was "Dr. Mike." Somehow it managed simultaneously to convey both respect and a warm, friendly sense of informality. But I did find "Herr Professor Doktor Michael Wertheimer," continually used on me at psychology conventions in Germany, a bit too elaborate, formal, and stultifying—although I must confess that I was pleased and surprised by overhearing one elderly psychologist at a convention in Germany once say to a colleague that the young German colleagues should follow "Herr Wertheimer's model" of speaking proper excellent traditional German (after all, my German was that of a speaker some 70 or so years earlier, practiced only occasionally with my mother and used periodically at international conventions or in some of my research and scholarly projects).

I don't know how it happened that my two sets of grandchildren ended up with two different names for me. My children consistently called me "Pa" or "Papa," but my daughter's children used the American "Grandpa" and my son's children have always used the German "Opa" (although for some reason for a short time my grandson with the same name as mine called me "Opu," which I greatly enjoyed). For that matter, I still find flattering, and somewhat over-whelming, as well as surprising, what happened when that boy was born on July 4, 1982. Our daughter-in-law, his mother, called a day or so after the birth to report that both mother and child were doing fine. I inquired whether he had been named yet, and when she said no, I asked whether he might become "Inde-pendence Wertheimer" in recognition of the day of his birth. She laughed and repeated that he hadn't been named yet. Several days later, I was informed that he had been given the same first, middle, and last name as mine: Michael Mat-thew Wertheimer. I was stunned, and still don't quite know how to deal with that revelation. There wasn't a "junior" in our family, he wasn't "Michael Matthew Wertheimer II" or "the second"; my name had skipped one generation, but now there was another human being, genetically related to me, who had the same name as I. I still don't know what led my son and daughter-in-law to name him after me, but some part of me is still deeply grateful and somewhat awed. And I must say that I am very proud of him, a professional nurse, recovering cancer patient, loyal husband, and devout and devoted father of two children of his own, who are of course two of my many great-grandchildren.

For that matter, our youngest son early came up with a name for my second wife, "Mamalyn," which was quickly adopted by our other two children, and appropriately become "Grandmamalyn" and "Great-Grandmamalyn" when later generations were born. And my own "Opa" or "Grandpa" did become "O-Opa" and "Great-Grandpa" with grandchildren and great-grandchildren. These names were used not only by direct descendants, but also by children-in-law and grand-children-in-law, with one exception. My daughter's husband has constantly called me "Mike" since he first became acquainted with me. I don't know how come this usage developed, but so it is. And it doesn't bother me.

For some reason, Marilyn has always called me "Michael," as have virtually all acquaintances and colleagues and friends for more than 40 years. Only my brother and sister, their spouses, various nieces and nephews, and friends and acquaintances I've known for a half century or more still refer to me as "Mike." But that's all okay with me too. As is true of most naming rituals, I've gotten used to these practices, and their "rules" are almost never, if ever, broken.

One naming incident which rankled me a bit and which I've never forgotten must have occurred a bit over half century ago in Germany. My first wife and I were traveling in a rented car in Europe in a final attempt to reconcile our troubled marriage. We had a modest meal at a modest restaurant somewhere in Germany, and I impatiently waited for what seemed to be for much too long for the waiter in the almost-empty restaurant to give me the bill. Finally we decided just to get up and get ready to leave, hoping this way to arouse the waiter's attention. As he saw us apparently about to leave, he quickly came over and scowling, said, "Du hast ja noch nicht bezahlt!" ("You haven't paid yet!"), using the highly impolite familiar version of the second person pronoun "Du" instead of the required polite "Sie." I was truly offended, and did pay him—even giving him a much larger tip than he deserved. I don't remember a single other instance of the extremely impolite and inappropriate use of the informal second person pronoun ("Du" in German, "du" in Swedish, "tu" in French, "tu" in Spanish) on me on any occasion during many trips to foreign lands in which the language had the two forms of the second person pronoun.

Other names I've been called of course include "Sir" or "Mister" or "Hey, you," like any other male in this society. I've also sometimes been addressed as "Professor" or even "Prof." And collective names in addition to Schani's use of "Kindersch" include "guys," as when a waitress asks the variegated group of restaurant customers what the assemblage of males (and now females too) of different ages would like to choose from the menu: "What would you guys like for breakfast today?" I've been called "lover," "loverly," "darling," or "sweetheart" by waitresses in England, where the use of such terms had different implications than when my wife uses one of the last two as an intimate name.

A joke among fellow oldsters has become popular in recent years, and is making the rounds of retirement homes. Memory, including for names, especially those recently learned, notoriously deteriorates in older people. An old geezer is walking down a street and encounters another tottering old-timer. He says,

"Great to see you again!," and his companion responds, "Yes. Good to meet again. But I'm sorry, I've forgotten your name. What is your name?" Whereupon the other says, "Uh…how soon do you have to know?"

As the lists earlier in this chapter indicate, I have had a wide variety of roles in my life, all of which have been part of who I am. Most of this entire memoir is at least indirectly and implicitly devoted to exploration of these roles. But even if it is just a disorganized potpourri of unrelated items, it might be fun to elaborate a bit further on some of them. They all contribute to the attempt to characterize who and what I have been, and who or what I still am.

Early in my life I was a brother to my older brother Val and my younger sister Lise, and later to Pete as well. Val was to some extent my protector and instructor (he taught me to read, to play chess, and many other things), but also became a kind of superior competitor, who was so much better than I at badminton and at chess. And I've already mentioned remembering games of Monopoly with him and Lise, during which Val would make tempting-sounding proposals to Lise but which would provide even more benefit to him—and I would catch on to them and warn Lise that they really were to her disadvantage. But the three of us played many cooperative games which we all enjoyed tremendously; we were a very close-knit trio. And we performed various skits and plays, for which my mother and father served as a remarkably patient and appreciative audience. Val and I also constructed kites and balsa-and-tissue model airplanes that we proudly would fly in our back yard or on the big lawn across the street from 12 The Circle.

At evening meals around the dining table, as I also reported earlier, current politics were often the topic of conversation, typically in both German and English, and my father managed to involve all three of us children in the discussion, sometimes asking us for our opinions—and gently insisting that we defend them more or less articulately. All of our assertions were not only requested but also respected. This of course encouraged all of us to develop a positive self-respect.

My relation with Peter, some nine years my junior, were somewhat different from those among Val, Lise and me, who were much closer together in age. During his first year or so, as reported elsewhere in this account, I was given the job of taking care of him early in the mornings after my mother had fed him and had gone back to her room to sleep for another hour or two. I would play with him in numerous ways we both enjoyed, and when he was a little older I would bring him bits of food, often elaborately served in a small bowl on a small plate on top of a larger plate, etc., on a tray. We became very close early on, and that closeness has persisted for many decades. He also claims that he remembers my teaching him to sail at the Ethical Culture School Camp during later summers, when he and Lise were still campers and I had become a counselor who, among other things, had duties at the waterfront that included teaching swimming, canoeing, rowing—and sailing.

When we were very young, there often was singing of German and, later, American folk songs after dinner, with my mother playing the guitar or my father playing the piano. For a time we also had a miniature "family orchestra," for which Val played clarinet, Lise a recorder or metal bells (a kind of xylophone), and I a drum.

My father also occasionally told us modest stories about characters he had either made up himself or had learned about when he himself had been a child, and the stories often included roles for each of us children. A similar practice, using similar characters, was carried on later by me in telling stories to my own children and grandchildren. He also occasionally gave us puzzles to solve, including simple versions of problems he used in his lectures to demonstrate the role of insight in problem-solving. His role, not surprisingly considering his age when we were young children, was more that of a grandfather than that of a father, but it always clearly exuded his love—and respect—for us.

In public elementary school in New Rochelle's Mayflower School, I enjoyed the subjects, and was early taught English by accommodating teachers and fellow pupils. Although I was initially a foreign student, of course, I soon felt accepted and never felt like an alien. There I learned many songs, arithmetic, geography, some science, and all the other usual topics, and was introduced to linguistics and grammar (in third grade we were taught how to parse sentences) and to other foreign languages (French and Spanish). I went on in French and Spanish in high school at Fieldston School, where I also had a year of Latin and Greek. My strong interest in languages was kindled during my childhood early schooling, and has stayed with me throughout the rest of my life. I later studied Swedish, and a bit of Portuguese, Icelandic, and even Chinese Mandarin.

I don't remember all that many other things about my schooling during elementary and high school, other than that I was skipped early (from first grade to second grade during my first year in school), which made me younger and smaller than my classmates during most of my education. Younger and smaller, yes, but I was also comparatively a bit weak and pudgy, seeing myself as a kind of embarrassed "Mr. Four-by-Four," short and heavy and inept; this image of myself as overweight has persisted throughout my adulthood down to the present. For many decades I have wished I were ten or twenty pounds lighter than I am, but have rarely succeeded in shedding even just a few undesired pounds.

One course mentioned earlier that I found valuable and enjoyable at Fieldston School was the weekly small-group get-together for a half hour, required of all students in all the grades (or "forms," as they were called at Fieldston), labeled "Ethics." It typically involved a rather informal discussion by all who were assembled of a timely issue, often based on some current event. The discussion focused on alternative ways to deal with the issue, and the pros and cons of each alternative. The effort was directed less at finding the one best solution; what was explored were the consequences and desirability of each alternative. I believe it did help develop all students' critical thinking abilities, as suggestions were thoroughly and carefully evaluated by the group. It was indeed an effective venue for teaching ethics, in line with Fieldston's focus as an "Ethical Culture" school. It served as a kind of substitute for religious training as carried out in many other kinds of private schools.

Another course I enjoyed was "shop," in which the pupils (almost only boys; the girls instead had "home economics," mostly devoted to cooking and housekeeping) had the opportunity to work creatively with wood and metal, using saws, lathes, hammers, and other tools. I've already mentioned that I remember making a rather ingenious floor lamp out of wood; it could be raised or lowered to a variety of positions, determined by appropriate hooked cuts into a vertical member engaged by a dowel suspended from the main vertical board. This lamp, the design of which I didn't invent, is still in use by my brother Peter in his home in Virginia. I also remember making some ash trays for my father out of metal circles pounded with a ball-peen hammer.

The most memorable aspect of my high school years, though, was my involvement with the Ethical Culture School Camp, about which I've reported at some length already earlier in this manuscript. ECSC was on a large piece of property on the northeast end of Lake Otsego, a small lake about eight miles long north to south and about a mile wide. Campers came for a full two months during the summer, and I thrived in the role of, first, camper, then junior counselor, and finally full-fledged counselor. There I learned to become a sailor, a proficient swimmer, a junior Red Cross water safety instructor, a reasonably proficient camper, and a minimally expert tennis player, and in later years I had the role of instructing all these acquired skills. In early years we also had horseback riding and vegetable gardening. At camp I learned many wonderful songs; the camp director had created clever new lyrics for a wide variety of traditional folk songs and classical tunes, and these were regularly sung there; most evenings there was a general camp sing in the "social hall" after dinner. There also was some square dancing and social dancing, as well as various skits and other productions.

The camp experience taught me to enjoy a wide variety of activities, sports, and creative endeavors that have enriched my life ever since. I also learned to play the harmonica there, a skill that has been appreciated by my kids and grandkids, that was used at our mountain cabin and as an icebreaker on many trips to foreign lands; as mentioned before, I have also played at amateur hours on Monhegan Island, and have presented several harmonica recitals at the retirement community where I now live, based on Christmas carols and on folk songs from Germany, France, the US, England, and elsewhere.

The director of the ECS camp apparently took a fancy to me while I was a student at Fieldston; he and a colleague, Phillips Houghton, both of whom taught shop, spent their summers at the camp. For several summers during my last years at the camp, the director, Willys P. Kent, asked me to come for an extra week before the camp opened, and an extra week after it closed, to help him set up and dismantle the waterfront. As elaborated before, this required rebuilding and later taking apart a rather complex set of docks or wharves going from shore out into the lake, with separate docks, at right angles to the main one, to designate shallow areas for use by kids who had not yet learned to swim, for intermediates, and for those who could handle deep water, and to provide mooring places for the rowboats and sailboats. Construction of these long plank walks required reconstruction of square piers made out of criss-crossed logs, like Lincoln Logs®, from the bottom up, with the logs impaled on heavy vertical steel poles screwed into strategically-placed bases permanently on the bottom. My job was to take each numbered log and attach it successively to the appropriate poles and thus build up the supports for each of the piers until these piers came above water, so that the long planks of the docks could be securely attached to them. At the end of the season, the entire structure was taken down again, because the ice buildup on the surface of the lake during winter would have damaged it. I felt rather proud that my ability to hold my breath for relatively long periods of time, and not only to swim but to work underwater, was valued enough for me to have been given this particular job.

The summer camp, as I've mentioned several times before, also was where I first became aware of, and started to act upon, my fascination with girls. I enjoyed dancing with them, gawked at them in their bathing suits, and even engaged in some "puppy love" activities with several female fellow campers and, later, with fellow female junior counselors and counselors. In many ways, the camp was an idyllic venue for such romantic encounters.

At Swarthmore College I had several memorable roommates. My interactions with them also helped me develop various new roles. My best friend there was Stefan Machlup, the son of a prominent Viennese political economist. Stefan took me as it were under his wing when I first arrived on campus, and we were lifelong friends. He persuaded his parents to take me along on several ski trips while we were students, and years later he came to Boulder almost annually for a week or so to go skiing with us. On summer trips east with my children, we often stopped for the night with him in Cleveland when we were going to Long Island for a vacation with my mother and Schani for a month or two; the stops on the way at "Motel Machlup" were always gracious and pleasant.

Another roommate was Larry Weiskrantz, an impressive quiet scholar who later became a professor at Cambridge in England and had an illustrious career in psychology. And there was Howard Chandler Robbins ("Robbie") Landon, H.C.R. Landon, who became the world expert on Haydn. Often accompanying records of Haydn symphonies, he would, as I reported earlier, tune a single tympanum to two different tones on opposite sides, and play along enthusiastically with the record player on this double-tuned drum. He vowed to get all of Haydn's symphonies recorded during his lifetime—and achieved that goal as well as writing a biography of Haydn that is still considered a definitive classic.

Others included Pete Dodge, who later was briefly my roommate in Cambridge, MA, too when I went to Harvard, and John Rosselli, an accomplished cartoonist from Great Britain who became a highly-respected British journalist.

I continued in my fascination with the opposite sex, experiencing with various girlfriends a succession of often somewhat torrid love affairs, some of them actual and a few of them imaginary.

At Swarthmore, as mentioned earlier, I also tried my hand at radio productions, with a weekly 15-minute poetry show one semester during which I presumptuously read poems in English, German, French, and Spanish, and my directing of a radio play version of Marlowe's *Dr. Faustus*. I also played the role of Grumio in a stage production of Shakespeare's *Taming of the Shrew*, for which I was praised by none other than the poet W.H. Auden in a review of the play he wrote for the college newspaper while he was a visiting faculty member at Swarthmore one year.

It was at Swarthmore, too, as I reported earlier, that I was introduced to Quakerism. The school had a Friends origin, but there was no longer any special emphasis on Quakerism while I was there. I don't remember when it was, nor who it was that suggested that I do so, but I attended the meeting on campus. I found the experience very rewarding. Silent worship in a peaceful, quiet group, with only an occasional simple reverent thought expressed by someone in the group moved to do so, and with the emphasis on "that of God in everyone," appealed to me, and to the extent that I am involved in any religious activity other than being a kind of agnostic, I can perhaps classify myself at least as an attender at Friends' meetings. While I have gone to other religious services on various occasions, and sometimes accompanied my wife to Christian Science church events, as well as having lectured at a Unitarian Church in Boulder and attending an occasional Sunday service on Monhegan Island and now at my retirement community, my religious side is probably more attuned to a kind of Quakerism than to any other organized religion. Hinduism, Buddhism, including Zen, and other mystical religions have a modest appeal for me, but the mystical, esoteric aspects of these religions I find as problematic as I find the fascination with the crucifixion and the apparently almost cannibalistic sharing of the body and blood of Christ in some traditional orthodox Christian rituals. Does religion play a major role in "who am I?" I don't think so, except that I do share a true awe and wonder at existence, at life, at love; there obviously is so much more to the world and to the experience of it than one individual's modest sensations and perceptions. Life is full of miraculous wonder at hearing profound music, seeing majestic structures such as Notre Dame Cathedral in Paris, contemplating a gigantic mountain, reveling in a loving relationship—but I don't feel any need to believe in or worship some kind of God or magical creator, on the basis of faith alone.

Indeed I find faith without clear evidence from sensation or rational empirical thought to be dangerous, even abhorrent: think of all the ugly and horrible things that have been done to and by people in the name of religious faith.

But the practice and modest acceptance of a kind of Quakerism is something that has after all been a part of me. My encouragement of even an occasional private little Quaker meeting with my children when they were young was apparently enough to make my youngest son become a much more serious Quaker than I have ever been, and he even asked me to officiate at a Quaker ceremony for his wedding, which I was happy and proud to do. And the funeral memorial service for my first wife was appropriately, I feel, held in Boulder's Friends Meeting House. Recently, too, I have arranged for biweekly half-hour "Friends meetings" in our apartment; they have typically been attended by about a dozen residents of our retirement community.

By the time I was at Swarthmore, it had already become clear to me that, for whatever reason, I was tolerated by my stepfather Schani more than any of my siblings were. I don't know how this happened, but this too became part of my "me." Schani was intolerant, even cruel I fear, to Lise, who had to leave the house on weekends while she was finishing school and living with my mother and Schani, so that Schani's house could be free for any activities he wanted to engage in without interference from distracting children. And Peter was treated even more intolerantly and cruelly. But somehow it was okay for me to be around, even if Lise's and especially Pete's presence were not permitted when my mother and Schani wanted to be alone together. Was I somehow more considerate, more accepting of my mother's and Schani's relationship, or somehow more tolerable, than Lise or Pete? I doubt it. Val was already safely away in college, and I had this inexplicable privilege. Why? I still don't know, but at the time it was part of what made me wonder who and how and what I was.

All my life I have been aware that I am a son of Max Wertheimer. In my earliest years, this didn't mean much other than having an overwhelming sense of security by being the son of a warm, impressive, supporting and caring grandfather-aged father. It wasn't until I was well into my teens that I realized that my father was a truly remarkable much-admired scholar, but soon the many admiring visitors to our house in New Rochelle convinced me of that. By the time I went to college, my identity as a son of an eminent psychologist had become salient; I'm sure that several of the professors there were very cognizant of my heritage. Hans Wallach, who had been a student of my father's in Europe, treated me with respect. Wolfgang Köhler, a fellow founder of the Gestalt school of psychology, who had himself become perhaps an even more prominent Gestaltist than my father, in effect took me under his wing. And I'm convinced that being my father's son also played a significant role in my being accepted for graduate work at The Johns Hopkins University and then at Harvard University. It doubtless helped get me scholarships and fellowships, as well as job offers I might not have had if I hadn't been Max Wertheimer's son.

For a few years I reveled in that privilege, but soon I also began to yearn for my own independent reputation as a competent aspiring psychologist. Yet I know that my being the son of a famous psychologist inevitably ended up playing a role in my own advancement in the field. I resented having in effect to compete with my father for a while, and was even proud when the number of my publications in refereed technical psychology journals exceeded his. But it has always been clear to me that the quality and influence of his relatively few publications far exceeded the quality of any of mine. His contribution to psychology is, and will continue to be, far greater than mine. But now, towards the end of my years, that is a relief rather than a burden. I have been blessed with so many more years than he (he died at age 63; I'm still alive in my early nineties; and his later years were almost without exception more challenging than any of mine), and have had so many more blessings than he during my much longer and less stressful life. Now I can accept being the son of an eminent, still-famous scholar and psychologist without any remaining feelings of pride or resentment or resignation; it just happens to have been my fate. It no longer is a very significant part of who I feel I am today. It doesn't make me any more special than any other human resident on this globe.

Soon after I arrived at The Johns Hopkins University, I was made a teaching assistant in an introductory psychology course. My job was to conduct weekly discussion and laboratory sections composed of small groups of students, some of whom were not only the same age I was, but even older. I felt intimidated and somewhat presumptuous in the role of instructor or "leader" of these groups, but somehow I managed nevertheless.

Another role at Hopkins was as a research assistant. I was given the task of determining the visibility of blips on several different designs of radar scope screens, which gave me valuable experience in experimental design and psychophysics. But the project was "classified," meaning "secret," because of the potential utility of the results for military applications. As I reported earlier, a routine visit from an Air Force officer produced a demand for evidence that I was a loyal American citizen, who had been cleared to undertake such sensitive work for the military. Production of my birth certificate, showing that I had been born in Berlin, Germany, had the opposite of the desired effect. Was I essentially a foreigner, an enemy alien who was actually doing this classified work? My supervisor rushed me from Baltimore to Washington, in the company of an Air Force guard who was charged with keeping a careful eye on me, in order to establish that I was truly a citizen. Fortunately I was able to document that my parents had indeed become citizens in 1939, and that I was indeed their son, so I soon managed to obtain an official certificate of derivative citizenship, and everyone was able to breathe a sigh of relief. My involvement in this nationally sensitive project did not constitute a danger to the country after all.

I spent a semester at Swarthmore College again after completing my master's degree at Hopkins. As I have pointed out on several occasions, the dominant theoretical perspectives at the various schools I attended were impossible to reconcile. At Swarthmore, as had been the case informally at home since my early childhood, it was taken for granted that the Gestalt approach was correct; it contrasted sharply with behaviorism and structuralism, as well as the misguided psychoanalytic approach, which were all hopelessly wrong. Then at Hopkins behaviorism was taken for granted as the only true orientation to psychology; all the other "schools" were unscientific, and a waste of time—including the Gestalt theory that I had venerated since childhood. Then when later I got to Harvard, the vestiges of structuralism dominated the scene, and Gestalt, behaviorism, and psychoanalysis were all ridiculed. Finally, during a year's clinical internship at Worcester State Hospital, and in a few clinically-oriented courses I attended (over the objection of the faculty of the experimental psychology department at Harvard) at the relatively new department of social relations at Harvard, I was exposed to the implicit acceptance of a psychoanalytic orientation and derision regarding the other approaches.

This successive exposure to each of the four major theoretical orientations current in psychology at the time in four different venues led to substantial confusion in my own theoretical identification. Eventually this did result in a kind of somewhat uncomfortable eclecticism in my own theoretical bent, but with a high value on empiricism, experimentalism, objectivity, and a respect for convincing evidence and rational argument—and also a hefty dose of Gestalt thought. When cognitive psychology evolved as a respectable way to identify oneself late in my career, that was the label I generally used for myself. It seemed—and seems—to include almost all of what I believed myself in my version of eclecticism.

This theoretical turmoil may seem somewhat esoteric to someone outside the field of academic psychology, but it did constitute a rather major concern in my own identity as a psychologist and as a research scholar. And those terms, "psychologist" and "research scholar," have been fairly central in my own identity.

My return to Swarthmore after my Hopkins master's degree was made possible by an offer from a close friend and admirer of my father, Solomon Asch, to serve for a semester as his research associate. Asch was of course very aware that I was the son of a prominent Gestalt psychologist; Asch himself had become a social psychologist and an ardent advocate for Gestalt theory. I almost certainly got this job because I was my father's son. A gentle, brilliant, humble, soft-spoken scholar, Asch gave me some freedom in designing and carrying out variants of a famous set of experiments he was conducting on the effects of group pressure upon individual behavior. I spent the summer of 1949 dictating in detail the results of the experiments I had conducted under Asch's supervision, and, as I reported earlier, I was somewhat disappointed—actually feeling a bit cheated—when Asch published the results of these studies (among many others) in a book a while later, without giving me explicit credit for my role in them. The book has become a classic in social psychology and Gestalt theory.

At Harvard again it was clear that as a graduate student almost everyone saw me as "a son of Max Wertheimer." The nominal chair of the department, Eddie Newman, who was in that role annually subject to approval by the other members of the department of experimental psychology, had been a visitor to the Wertheimer house in New Rochelle when I was a child; I already mentioned that he hung a bird house in a tree in the back yard at 12 The Circle. He had also studied briefly with my father back in Germany. "Gary" Boring, or E. G. B., functionally the true head of the department, had engaged in extensive correspondence about Gestalt issues with my father more than a decade before I came to Harvard; he and his colleague S. S. Stevens, with whom I was to complete my doctoral project, both were very skeptical about Gestalt theory but clearly also deeply respected my father—and were very aware that I was his son. It did give me a kind of privileged position in their eyes, and they doubtless expected comparable brilliance in Max Wertheimer's son. I suspect they were somewhat disappointed when I didn't fully live up to their perhaps unrealistic expectations. And altogether, being one of only a small number of graduate students in a department filled with famous faculty such as B.F. Skinner, E. G. Boring, and S. S. Stevens—and Georg von Békésy, who soon after I left won a Nobel Prize—

made me feel as though I should have been more exceptional than I ever turned out to be.

At Swarthmore and Harvard I also experienced my first two serious love affairs, with Silvia Rosselli at Swarthmore and then Nancy MacKaye at Harvard. Both of them turned out to be problematic, but they also played a major role in my trying to find out who I am. The obsession with Silvia dominated my last undergraduate year at Swarthmore, and doubtless interfered to some extent with my studies. My marriage with Nan produced many very positive results, including three wonderful children, but her sheer brilliance, creativity, and competence inadvertently and tragically ended up making me doubt my own abilities. Among other things, she gently but convincingly was able to point out to me various serious flaws and problems with controls in several studies I conducted and had already written up for publication, flaws of which I had been unaware before she made me aware of them.

But discussion of such things doesn't really belong here in the consideration of "who am I?"—though they have indeed contributed to self-doubt and serious concerns about my own worth, issues which have deeply troubled me for decades. My wife Marilyn has finally, to my infinite gratitude, after many years begun to convince me that maybe I, my life, my career, my personality may have some value after all. Perhaps the feelings of inferiority which Nan, totally unintentionally and totally inadvertently, had encouraged in me as a central part of my identity are unwarranted after all.

Then there are the familial roles of husband and of father, father-in-law, grandfather, grandfather-in-law, and great-grandfather, all of which became rather major ingredients in my perceived identity. These are of course a central part of my core. I continue to be deeply interested in and concerned about the welfare of all my descendants and descendants-in-law, but with a different, and unique, relationship with each of these precious people. Interactions with them are less frequent than at earlier times, as is appropriate to the trajectories of each of their lives. But to repeat, these relatives, my unbelievably tolerant, supportive, competent, and incredibly gorgeous girlfriend Marilyn (who has also consented to be my wife) as well as my brother, sister, brother-in-law, nieces, nephews, etc., and friends are integral to who I am. To a large extent, they define "me."

On a much more superficial level are various other roles that I have held or that have been thrust upon me, e.g., such titles as president of Psi Chi, of the Rocky Mountain Psychological Association, of divisions of the APA devoted to general psychology, the teaching of psychology, the history of psychology, and of theoretical and philosophical psychology, and of the Alpha chapter of Colorado of Phi Beta Kappa, and being a fellow of APA's division of experimental psychology and numerous other APA divisions, being chair or member of innumerable APA boards and committees, at meetings of which I always tried to achieve Quaker consensus rather than taking votes, not to mention being the recipient of numerous awards and recognitions such as officially becoming a professor emeritus. While all of these professional roles are, or were, part of my identity at one time or another, they are far less central to the "me" that I am now than many of the other sources of identity I have indicated already. Somehow all the professional roles and honors are now—gratefully—just a part of my past. While I did enjoy a tremendously rewarding career, I have no regrets about it being over. I don't miss the many paid-for trips to Washington in my roles with the APA (including some 16 or so annually while I was for three years on the Board of Directors). Rewarding they were, and I did enjoy them immensely (and they did make me feel in some ways not "inferior" but even almost reasonably competent), but that's been more than enough. That's all, mercifully, over.

My father died when he was 63. My brother Val died many years ago, when he was only 53. I remember the occasion all too well. And I remember the bit of foreboding I felt when some internal clock made me aware later that I was approaching the exact same age as Val was when he died. When that date passed, I felt a bit of relief. But soon that changed to being incensed for a while at the unfairness of fate. Why was I still alive, when he had already been snuffed out at a much younger age? It didn't take long for that in turn to change into a sense of inestimable gratitude for my sheer existence. Here I am decades older than Val (and even my father) was ever permitted to become, and I'm still around, still somewhat compos mentis, and incredibly grateful for every single day. Life, experience, love, sheer *being* are unbelievably valuable blessings given to us in some incalculable and mysterious, ineffable way. My son Benjy manages to convey this unbelievable blessing of human existence and awareness, this gift of being, so beautifully to his audiences with his music and his humble, devout, simple expressions of gratitude, awe, and wonder at the miracle of being a living, feeling human.

Ultimately, it doesn't matter what my answer is to the question, "Who am I?" At this stage in my long, wonderful life I no longer really care who I am. I am just exhilaratingly and infinitely grateful that I have been blessed with such a miracle of life and that I have continued to be blessed with it for so many years.

Appendix A: *Die Schöpfung der Welt*

A unique handmade book dated 1937, *Die Schöpfung der Welt; für Wertheimer's Kinder* (*The Creation of the World: for Wertheimer's children*) is one object which I fortunately have kept for many years. Written and provided with vivid watercolor illustrations by Lisbeth Stern, sister of the famous German artist Käthe Kollwitz, it retells the story of much of the Book of Genesis in simplified German. The sheer existence of this beautiful book is one piece of information about the remarkable relationship between my father and Lisbeth Stern. It claims no author and is accompanied by an unsigned, typewritten letter dated only "1936." Here is an attempt at a translation of it:

```
1936
    I have tried here to show you the world in little
pictures, from very early until now. And as I
sketched and ruminated back and forth, I have always
had to wonder about how much bickering and fighting
there has been always and everywhere in the world, as
if there really couldn't have been anything more im-
portant than that.
    Naturally, one would like to be able to say: But
it couldn't be like that! and this was certainly not
right—and that was not!—But it's easy to talk -; they
just did it! And finally, you will quietly find peace
with all your "justice" and "injustice"—especially
when you've gotten old, as I am now.
    The animals don't do it any differently; they
fight and bite each other, and then they help each
other again with the same hot zeal with which they
just fought.
    And there it is now like a miracle: if the
fighting was so bad that you had to think that every-
thing that wanted to grow there had been trampled,
then, if it became quieter again afterwards and you
look right at it, then you see how here and there the
```

© Springer Fachmedien Wiesbaden GmbH, part of Springer Nature 2020
M. Wertheimer, *Facets of an Academic's Life*,
https://doi.org/10.1007/978-3-658-28770-2

young stalks have come out fresh again and not even
so few — no, quite strong and beautiful!
    This secret power in nature, which wants to grow
again and again, must not be forgotten. And even if
nature has made earthquakes, famines, and wars, it
also makes beautiful rain, healthy people and also
peace!
    You're not allowed to forget this—and you should
think of the rainbow that God drew across the sky
when the Great Deluge was over.
That's what one has to do!

The typewritten text of the book, in somewhat biblical German, begins with the seven days of creation: of heaven and earth, light and darkness, firmament and waters, grass and herbs, beasts and birds, man and woman, and a day of rest. It goes on to the story of the Garden of Eden, including God's admonition not to eat of the fruit of the Tree of Knowledge—and the serpent convincing Eve and Adam to eat of it, resulting in the Fall of Man. Summarized next is the fable of Cain and Abel, and God's destruction of the Tower of Babel. There follows the saga of Noah and the Ark and the destruction of all other life in the great storm that lasted forty days and forty nights. Finally the dove that Noah sent forth returns with an olive leaf, showing that it was now safe to leave the Ark, which had landed on top of Mount Ararat. It ends with Noah gratefully building an altar the burnt offering of which so pleases God that He creates a huge rainbow and promises to curse the earth no more: "As long as the Earth remains, sowing and harvest, cold and heat, summer and winter, day and night shall not cease."

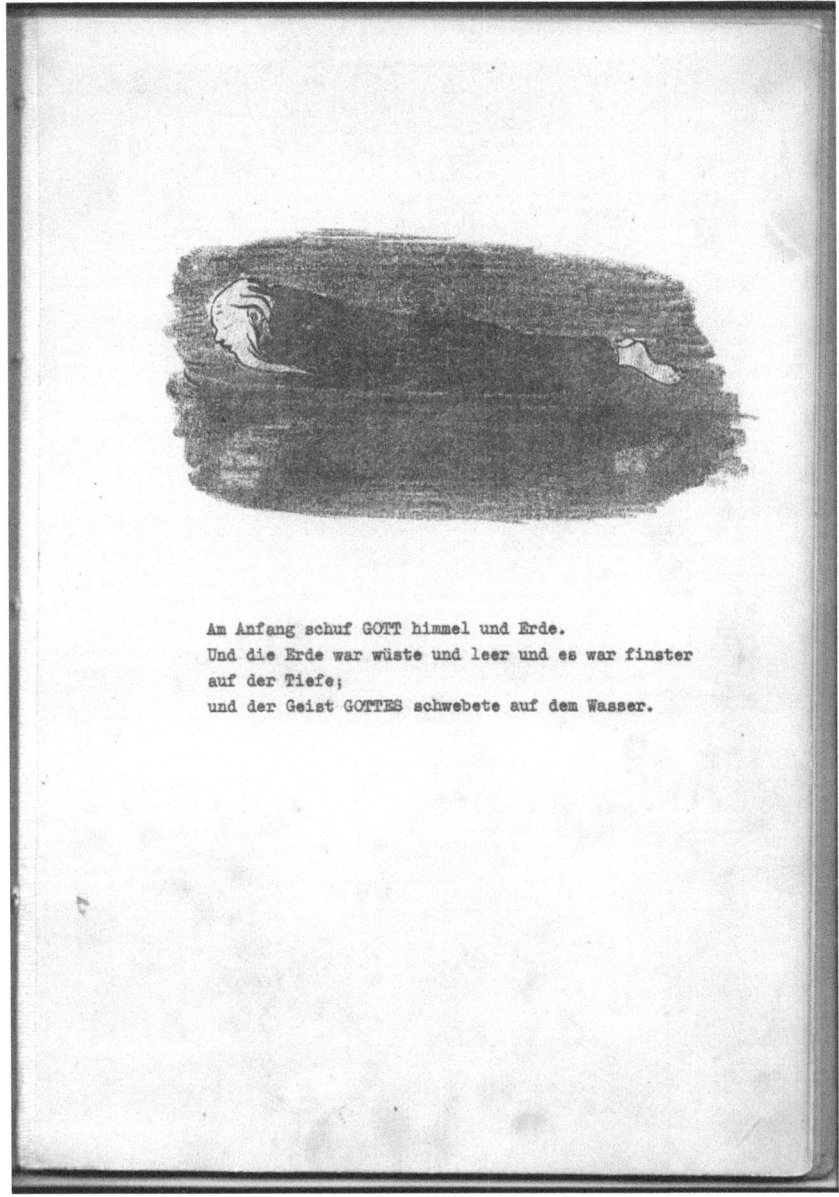

Am Anfang schuf GOTT himmel und Erde.
Und die Erde war wüste und leer und es war finster
auf der Tiefe;
und der Geist GOTTES schwebete auf dem Wasser.

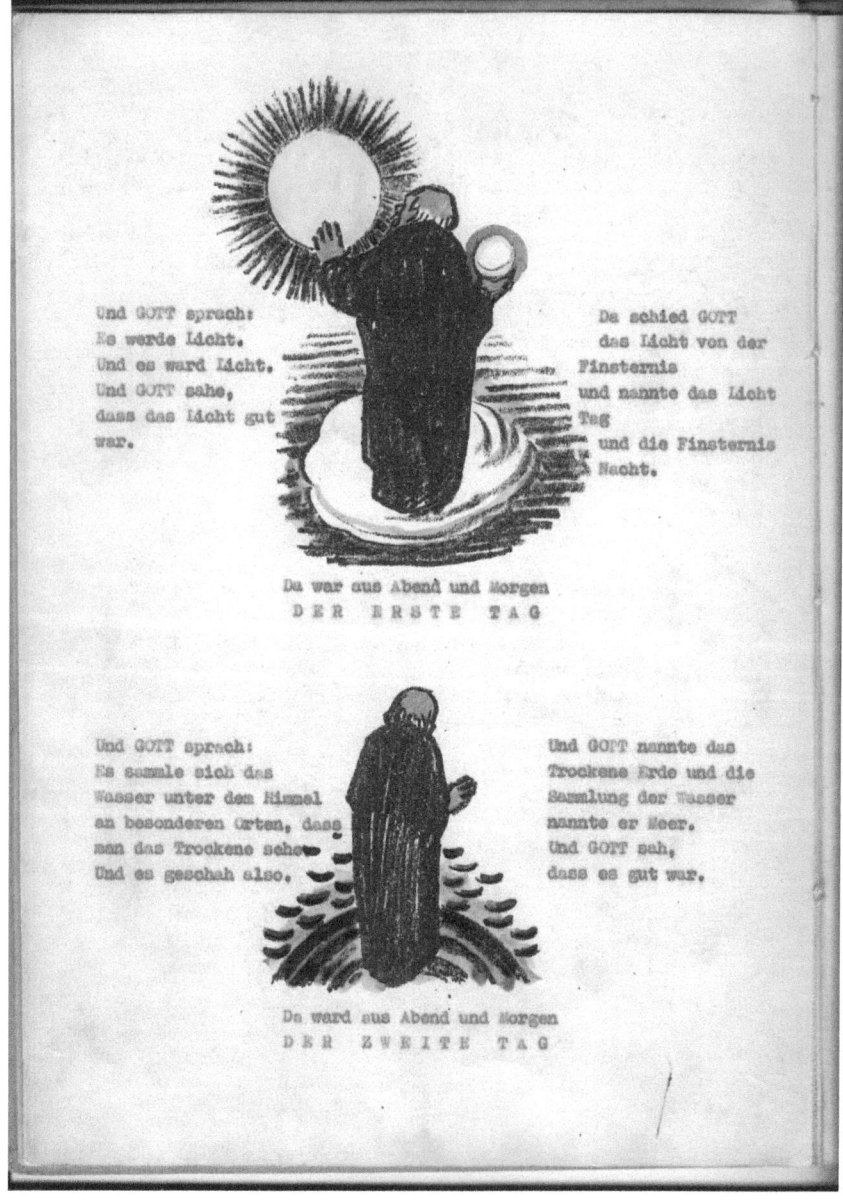

Und GOTT sprach:
Es werde Licht.
Und es ward Licht.
Und GOTT sahe,
dass das Licht gut
war.

Da schied GOTT
das Licht von der
Finsternis
und nannte das Licht
Tag
und die Finsternis
Nacht.

Da war aus Abend und Morgen
DER ERSTE TAG

Und GOTT sprach:
Es sammle sich das
Wasser unter dem Himmel
an besonderen Orten, dass
man das Trockene sehe.
Und es geschah also.

Und GOTT nannte das
Trockene Erde und die
Sammlung der Wasser
nannte er Meer.
Und GOTT sah,
dass es gut war.

Da ward aus Abend und Morgen
DER ZWEITE TAG

Und GOTT sprach:
Es lasse die Erde aufgehen Gras und Kraut, das sich besame; und fruchtbare Bäume, dass ein jeglicher nach seiner Art Frucht trage und habe seinen eigenen Samen bei sich selbst.

Und es geschah also. Und die Erde liess aufgehen Gras und Kraut, das sich besamete, ein jegliches nach seiner Art. Und GOTT sah, dass es gut war.

Da ward aus Abend und Morgen
DER DRITTE TAG

Und GOTT sprach:
Es errege sich das Wasser mit webenden und lebendigen Tieren und mit Gevögel, das unter der Veste des Himmels fliegt. Und GOTT schuf grosse Walfische und allerlei Getier, ein Jegliches nach seiner Art.

Und GOTT segnete sie und sprach: seid fruchtbar und mehret euch und erfüllet das Wasser im Meer und das Gevögel mehre sich im Himmel.

Da ward aus Abend und Morgen
DER VIERTE TAG

Und GOTT sprach:
Die Erde bringe
hervor
lebendige Tiere,
ein jegliches
nach seiner Art,
Vieh, Gewürm
und Tiere auf
Erden, ein
jegliches
nach seiner Art.

Und es geschah
also.
Und GOTT sahe,
dass es gut
war.

Da ward aus Abend und Morgen
DER   FÜNFTE   TAG

Und GOTT sprach:
Lasset uns Menschen
machen, ein Bild, ·
das uns gleich sei,
die da herrschen über
die Fische im Meer und
über die Vögel unter
dem Himmel und über das
Vieh und über die ganze
Erde und über alles Gewürm,
das auf Erden kriechet.

Und GOTT schuf den
Menschen ihm zum
Bilde, zum Bilde
GOTTES schuf er ihn.
Und er schuf sie ein
Männlein und ein
Fräulein. Und GOTT
segnete sie und sprach
zu ihnen:
Seid fruchtbar und
mehret euch und füllet
die Erde.

Und es geschahe also.
Und GOTT sahe an alles, was er gemacht hatte und siehe da,
es war alles sehr gut.
Da war aus Abend und Morgen
DER   SECHSTE   TAG

Also war vollendet Himmel und Erde mit ihrem ganzen Heer.

Und also vollendete GOTT am siebenten Tag seine Werke, die er machte, und ruhete am siebenten Tage von allen seinen Werken, die er machte; und segnete den siebenten Tag und heiligte ihn darum, dass er an demselben geruhet hatte von allen seinen Werken.

Also ist Himmel und Erde geworden, da sie geschaffen sind, zu der Zeit, da GOTT der Herr Erde und Himmel machte.

Da ward aus Abend und Morgen
DER SIEBENTE TAG

Und GOTT der Herr pflanzte einen Garten in Eden, gegen Morgen, und setzte die Menschen darein. Und GOTT der Herr liess aufwachsen allerlei Bäume, lustig anzusehen und gut zu essen, und den Baum des Lebens mitten im Garten. Und GOTT der Herr gebot dem Menschen und sprach: Du sollst essen von allerlei Bäumen im Garten; aber vom Baum der Erkenntnis sollst du nicht essen. Denn welchen Tages du davon issest, wirst du des Todes sterben.

Und die Schlange war listiger, denn alle Tiere auf dem Felde, die GOTT der Herr gemacht hatte, und sprach zu dem Weibe: Ihr werdet mit nichten des Todes sterben sondern ihr werdet sein wie GOTT und wissen, was gut und böse ist. Und das Weib schauete an, dass von dem Baum gut zu essen wäre, und lieblich anzusehen, dass es ein lustiger Baum wäre, weil er klug machte; und nahm von der Frucht und ass und gab ihrem Manne auch davon und er ass.

Und sie höreten die stimme GOTTES des Herrn, der im Garten ging, da der Tag kühl geworden war. Und Adam versteckte sich mit seinem Weibe vor dem Angesicht GOTTES des Herrn unter die Bäume im Garten. Und GOTT der Herr rief Adam und sprach zu ihm: Wo bist du? Und er sprach: Ich höWrte deine Stimme im Gartenund fürchtete mich; darum versteckte ich mich.

GOTT sprach: Hast du nicht gegessen von dem Baum, davon ich dir gebot, du sollst nicht davon essen?

Da sprach Adam: Das Weib, das du mir zugesellt hast, gab mir von dem Baum und ich ass.

Da sprach GOTT der Herr zum Weibe: Warum hast du das getan? Das Weib sprach: Die Schlange betrog mich also, dass ich ass.

Da sprach GOTT der Herr zu der Schlange: Weil du solches getan hast, seist du verflucht vor allen Tieren auf dem Felde. Auf deinem Bauch sollst du gehen und Erde essen dein Leben lang.

Und zum Weibe sprach er: Ich will dir viel Schmerzen schaffen, wenn du schwanger wirst; du sollst mit Schmerzen Kinder gebären. Und zu Adam sprach er: Dieweil du hast gehorcht der Stimme deines Weibes und gegessen von dem Baum, davon ich dir gebot und sprach: Du sollst nicht davon essen: Im Schweisse deines Angesichts sollst du dein Brot essen, bis dass du wieder zu Erde werdest, davon du gekommen bist. Denn du bist Erde und sollst zu Erde werden.

Und Adam hiess sein Weib Eva, darum dass sie eine Mutter ist alles Lebendigen.

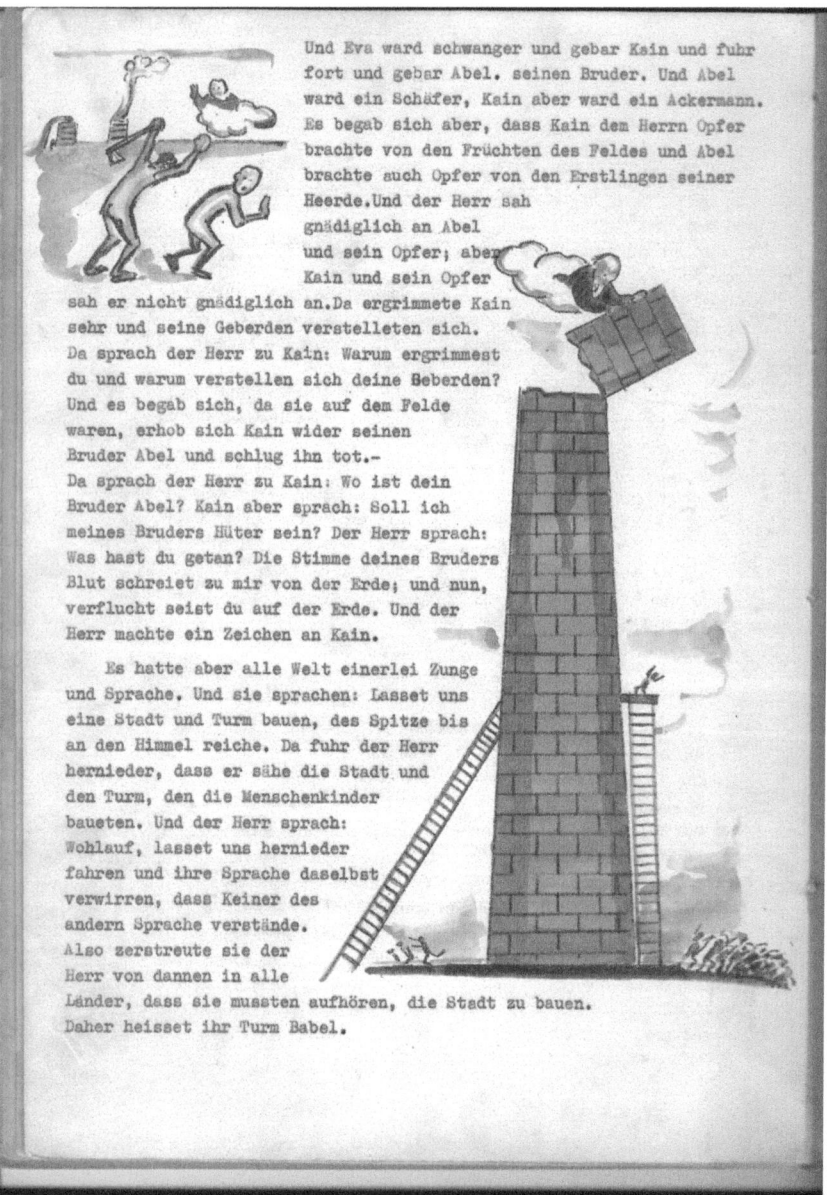

Und Eva ward schwanger und gebar Kain und fuhr
fort und gebar Abel. seinen Bruder. Und Abel
ward ein Schäfer, Kain aber ward ein Ackermann.
Es begab sich aber, dass Kain dem Herrn Opfer
brachte von den Früchten des Feldes und Abel
brachte auch Opfer von den Erstlingen seiner
Heerde.Und der Herr sah
gnädiglich an Abel
und sein Opfer; aber
Kain und sein Opfer
sah er nicht gnädiglich an.Da ergrimmete Kain
sehr und seine Geberden verstelleten sich.
Da sprach der Herr zu Kain: Warum ergrimmest
du und warum verstellen sich deine Geberden?
Und es begab sich, da sie auf dem Felde
waren, erhob sich Kain wider seinen
Bruder Abel und schlug ihn tot.-
Da sprach der Herr zu Kain: Wo ist dein
Bruder Abel? Kain aber sprach: Soll ich
meines Bruders Hüter sein? Der Herr sprach:
Was hast du getan? Die Stimme deines Bruders
Blut schreiet zu mir von der Erde; und nun,
verflucht seist du auf der Erde. Und der
Herr machte ein Zeichen an Kain.

Es hatte aber alle Welt einerlei Zunge
und Sprache. Und sie sprachen: Lasset uns
eine Stadt und Turm bauen, des Spitze bis
an den Himmel reiche. Da fuhr der Herr
hernieder, dass er sähe die Stadt und
den Turm, den die Menschenkinder
baueten. Und der Herr sprach:
Wohlauf, lasset uns hernieder
fahren und ihre Sprache daselbst
verwirren, dass Keiner des
andern Sprache verstände.
Also zerstreute sie der
Herr von dannen in alle
Länder, dass sie mussten aufhören, die Stadt zu bauen.
Daher heisset ihr Turm Babel.

Aber der Herr sah, dass der Menschen Bosheit gross war auf
Erden und alles Dichten und Trachten ihres Herzens nur böse
war immerdar.
Da reuete es ihn, dass er die Menschen gemacht hatte auf
Erden und er sprach:
Ich will die Menschen, die ich geschaffen habe, vertilgen
von der Erde, von dem Menschen an bis auf das Vieh und bis
auf das Gewürm und bis auf die Vögel unter dem Himmel, denn
es reuet mich, dass ich sie gemacht habe.
Und der Herr sprach zu Noah: Mache dir einen Kasten von
Tannenholz und mache Kammern darinnen und verpiche sie mit
Pech inwendig und auswendig.
Denn siehe, ich will eine (Eine) Sündflut mit Wasser kommen
lassen auf Erden, zu verderben alles Fleisch darinnen ein
lebendiger Odem ist. Alles was auf Erden ist, soll unter-
gehen. Und du sollst in den Kasten gehen mit deinem Weibe
und deinen Kindern. Und du sollst in den Kasten tun
allerlei Tiere je ein Paar, Männlein und Fräulein, dass
sie lebendig bleiben bei dir.
Und Noah tat alles, was ihm GOTT gebot.
Und der Herr sprach zu Noah: Gehe in den Kasten, du und
dein ganzes Haus. Denn ich will auf Erden regnen lassen
vierzig Tage und vierzig Nächte und vertilgen von dem
Erdboden, alles, was ich gemacht habe.
Und Noah ging in den Kasten mit seinem Weibe und seinen
Söhnen, dazu allerlei Tier nach seiner Art, allerlei
Gewürm, das auf Erden kriecht, nach seiner Art und
allerlei Vögel nach ihrer Art.
Das ging alles zu Noah in den Kasten bei Paaren. Und das
waren Männlein und Fräulein von allerlei Fleisch und
gingen hinein, wie GOTT ihnen geboten hatte.
Und der Herr schloss hinter ihm zu.

Die Sündflut

ARARAT

Da kam die Sündflut vierzig Tage auf Erden; und die Wasser
wuchsen und hoben den Kasten auf, dass der Kasten auf dem
Gewässer fuhr.
Da ging alles Fleisch unter, das auf Erden kriechet und
das Gewässer stand auf Erden hundert und fünfzig Tage.

Da gedachte GOTT an Noah und an alles Vieh, das im Kasten
war und liess Wind auf Erden kommen und die Wasser fielen.
Und das Gewässer verlief sich von der Erde und nahm ab nach
hundert und fünfzig Tagen.

Nach vierzig Tagen tat Noah das Fenster auf
an dem Kasten, den er gemacht hatte und
liess einen Raben ausfliegen, der flog
immer hin und wieder her.

Darnach liess er eine Taube ausfliegen, damit
er erführe, ob das Gewässer gefallen wäre auf
Erden. Da aber die Taube nicht fand, da ihr
Fuss ruhen konnte, kam sie wieder zu ihm in
den Kasten; denn das Gewässer war noch auf
dem ganzen Erdboden. Da tat er die Hand
heraus und nahm sie zu sich in den Kasten.

Da harrete er noch andere sieben Tage und
liess abermals die Taube herausfliegen
aus dem Kasten. Die kam zu ihm um die
Vesperstunde und siehe, ein Ölblatt
hatte sie abgebrochen im Munde.

Da redete GOTT mit Noah und sprach: Gehe aus dem Kasten, du
dein Weib und deine Söhne und allerlei Getier, das bei dir
ist, das gehe heraus mit dir; und seid fruchtbar und mehret
euch auf Erden.
Noah aber bauete dem Herrn einen Altar und opferte Brandopfer
auf dem Altar.

Und der Herr
roch den
lieblichen
Geruch und
sprach in
seinem
Herzen:
Ich will
hinfort nicht
mehr schlagen
Alles, was da
lebet,
wie ich getan
habe.

So lange die Erde steht, soll nicht mehr aufhören Same

und Ernte, Frost und Hitze, Sommer und Winter, Tag und Nacht.

Appendix B: *The Wertheimer Times*

Found among old letters and papers that had somehow been kept, without ever having been looked at for more than half a century, was a cardboard box with a tight-fitting foil-bedecked cover, containing copies of several issues of the "Wertheimer Times," together with various bits of correspondence and other documents related to that short-lived periodical. It offers a rather detailed account of everyday occurrences in the Wertheimer household, mostly in 1939, and of events concerning friends and relatives during that period that were considered of interest to the Wertheimer family and its acquaintances. Proudly proclaimed as "The Editor" was Michael Wertheimer, and at various times other individuals were added to a list of editors, including Valentin and Lise, as well as Karin Köhler (daughter of Wolfgang Köhler) and Judith Brodsky (a girlfriend of Val's; her father was a dentist in New York City and her mother an editor who published a book on freedom which contained an essay by Max Wertheimer). The correspondence was from a conglomeration of Wertheimer acquaintances, mostly from the New Rochelle-New York City-Swarthmore region, but also including, in Germany, Anni's aunt Mile and uncle Fritz Rosenberg, as well as Lisbeth Stern.

The issues of the newspaper, and the correspondence, when rearranged from the haphazard order in which they were in the box into proper chronological sequence based on dates on the issues and postmarks or dates on most of the letters, provide a detailed portrait of the then eleven-to-twelve-year-old "editor," and of how he viewed his world, that could not have been retrieved from fallible memory. Hence this appendix presents this set of documents with the occasional German material translated into English, and with a few explanatory comments about individuals and events to the extent that current memory was able to retrieve details from more than three quarters of a century ago.

B-1 Karin Köhler *(courtesy of the Friends Historical Library of Swarthmore College)*

© Springer Fachmedien Wiesbaden GmbH, part of Springer Nature 2020
M. Wertheimer, *Facets of an Academic's Life*,
https://doi.org/10.1007/978-3-658-28770-2

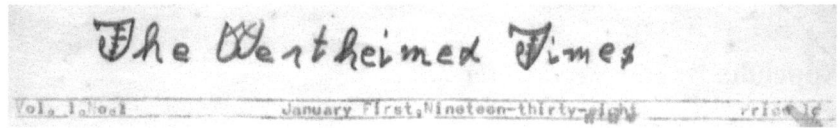

B-2 Masthead of Vol. I, Issue 1 of *The Wertheimer Times (family archives)*

Volume I, Issue 1

The first page of the first issue of the newspaper, two columns of purple text on off-white paper, had as its centered major title *The Wertheimer Times*, handwritten in a semi-Gothic ornate style that obviously was an attempt to imitate the masthead of *The New York Times*, with the capital letters W and T awkwardly and elaborately decorated but still clearly recognizable. Between two horizontal ruled lines below that was "Vol. 1. No. 1" on the left, "Price 1¢" on the right, and centered "January First, Nineteen-thirty-eight" (with "n,", "n," and "e" partly typed over "eight," to try to make the "eight" into a "nine"). The typewriter used for producing the newspaper had a clean, simple, highly readable typeface; it clearly was the Corona typewriter someone had given to Max Wertheimer to type his magnum opus, *Productive Thinking*, now donated to the Archives of the History of American Psychology at the Cummings Center for the History of Psychology at the University of Akron in Ohio.

A somewhat awkwardly hand-printed headline covered the entire space atop both columns: "Mrs. Beno Elkan Makes This Paper Possible." The Elkans were acquaintances and benefactors of the Wertheimers who lived in Larchmont, NY, a suburb of New York City very close to New Rochelle, NY, where the Wertheimers were residing in the huge house at 12 The Circle. The first name "Benno" is consistently misspelled throughout the issue as "Beno." For a few years the Elkans financially supported the Wertheimer household, regularly supplementing Max's fairly meager salary from the New School for Social Research in New York, where he was teaching. No readily available documents nor memories indicate how the Elkans had managed to develop the financial resources to support the Wertheimer family, how substantial that support was, why they provided it in the first place, nor when their generous financial beneficence started and ended.

The text of the story took up all the left column of the first page of the first issue. It reads as follows:

> Mrs. Beno Elkan, who resides at 75 Prospect Avenue, in Larchmont, made a donation to the Editor that made this paper possible. It is, in detail, a gelatin tray, some special 'Ditto' ink, and some special carbon paper. In short, it is a hectograph gelatin printing set. The Editor gives many thanks to Mrs. Elkan, as he is grateful to have the opportunity to learn to print.
> The former newspaper which had almost a name exactly like this paper, was supposed to come out every week, printed on a typewriter [presumably with the copies of the "former newspaper" provided by the use of carbon paper]. For the first six weeks it did come out. But on the fourth week, the staff [who this "staff" was—probably Val—was not reported, nor was the name of the "former newspaper"] quit the newspaper, leaving the Editor to report and do everything connected with the newspaper alone. For the last two weeks of the newspaper's history the Editor kept on, but he finally stopped at the sixth copy, it being too hard to write alone. The newspaper was doomed for the time.
> At Christmas, the Editor received this, on which this paper is printed, from Mrs. Elkan. The staff has joined the Editor again, with the addition of another one person added to the staff, (Con't page 2).

Unfortunately no trace of this earlier version of the "newspaper" remains in readily available documents nor in memory. Presumably this earlier version was produced in the summer and fall of 1938, when the "editor" was eleven years old. The spacing of the lines is flush on the left margin of the first column and clearly efforts were carefully made by adding spaces as needed between words so that the right margin of the first column is close to flush as well.

The top of page two of the first issue has, underlined all the way from the left edge of the sheet to the right edge, all in capitals, "THE WERTHEIMER TIMES, NEW ROCHELLE, N.Y., SUNDAY, JANUARY 1, 1938, PAGE TWO"; not surprisingly, the editor made a frequent error by not indicating that the year had in fact changed to 1939. The top of the left column of page two is entitled "MRS. BENO ELKAN (continued from page 1)." The text beneath that reads:

> the zealed [sic] reporter Lise Wertheimer. The first copy of this newspaper is a demonstration of what we hope to do every month.

The Editor gives acknowledgment not only to his staff, Lise and Valentin Wertheimer, but also a giant acknowledgment to Mrs. Elkan once more. Three cheers for Mrs. Elkan, Hip, hip, Hooray! Hip, hip, Hooray! Hip, hip, Hooray!

B-3 A hectograph just like the one on which *The Wertheimer Times* was published *(courtesy of Gregory F. Reeson)*

The "hectograph" was an 8 ½ x 11 inch metal tray with flanges about an inch high, containing about a half inch of yellow-greenish gel. The printing procedure involved typing a master sheet with special ink, pressing the master sheet rather vigorously onto the gel with a roller, removing and discarding the master, and then pressing clear paper onto the gel with the roller to make a print. This process could be repeated some thirty or forty times before the material became illegible. After the final legible copy had been made, the gelatin tray had to be heated until the gelatin melted, absorbing and melting the remaining ink from the master fairly uniformly throughout the gel. Once the gel had cooled and coagulated again, it was ready to be used to print the next page. Quite a few dozens of pages could be printed in this way before the gel became so saturated with remaining ink as to become unusable. Whether the gel was ever replaced is unknown.

At the top of the right-hand column on page one of this first issue, under the main hand-lettered headline, was a horizontal rule below which, in capitals, it was announced that "APPENDICITIS STRIKES GERTRUD COURANT." The text of the story reads:

> Gertrud Courant, best friend of Peter, and also a great friend of the family, was stricken with appendicitis on the early morning of December 23, 1938. Around 1 P.M., it was decided that she would have to be operated on. The appendicitis specialist, Dr.

Zandzeen, who operated on the editor about
a year and three months ago, operated on
Miss Courant at 4 P.M. that day. She came
out of the drug about 1 A.M. and was put
to sleep with a certain hypodermic. She
woke on the morning of the next day in a
nice room with a fellow patient, a woman who
was there because of kidney trouble. (Con't
page 2).

B-4 Gertrud ("Du-du")
Courant in later years
(courtesy of Klaus Moser)

Gertrud was the older daughter of Richard Courant, a prominent professor of mathematics at, I think, New York University. She had two older brothers, Ernst and Hans, and a younger sister, Lori, who was a close friend of Lise's. The Courant family lived a mile or two north of 12 The Circle, west of North Avenue and just north of the New Rochelle High School on a hill. Gertrud was often hired as a babysitter and playmate for Peter. And as it happened, the incision which Dr. Zandzeen had made earlier on "the Editor," to remove his appendix, had developed an infection which, while not serious, resulted in a lifelong unsightly scar, as mentioned on page 39.

"GERTRUD COURANT (Continued from page 1)" appears on page two, right after the last "Hip, hip, Hooray!" and three well-spaced asterisks, completing the left column on that page.

On the third day, the Editor went to see her in the hospital,
and she was still in a rather blurred, dizzy mood. The Editor
had to leave New Rochelle Hospital after about five minutes because Miss Courant was still too tired, and it was too great a
strain on her. Since then, the Editor has been to seee [sic] her
almost every day, talking with her when she was in a tired mood
and playing games with her when she felt better. The last time
the Editor was there, Miss Courant felt so well, that he, the
patient and Miss Courant played a game together. We are sincerely hoping that she will be well soon, and are extra sad that she
had to get it in the Christmas Season. Merry Christmas and a
Happy New Year, Gertrud! P.S. She is coming home on Monday, Jan
3, 1939.

This time the year was correct.

The last story starting on the front page of the first issue of *The Wertheimer Times*, entitled, all in capitals, "WERTHEIMERS TAKE CITIZENSHIP TEST,"

began eight lines from the bottom of the
right-hand column, following a row of
three carefully spaced asterisks. The text
reports:

> Mr. Max Wertheimer and Mrs. Anni
> Wertheimer took the test for the
> second citizenship paper, on
> Wednesday, December 28, 1938, at
> the Court House of White Plains,
> the county center of Westchester.
> [This time the year was correct
> again.] They went together with
> Mr. Beno Elkan and (Con't page
> 2).

B-5 Clara Woolie Mayer *(courtesy of the New
School Marketing and Communications
records, The New School Archives and Special
Collections, The New School, New York, NY)*

The right-hand column of page two is
devoted to the continuation of this
story: "CITIZENSHIP TEST (Con't
page 1)." How the Editor came up with the abbreviation "Con't" for "continued"
is lost in the mists of the past.

> Miss Clara Woolly Mayer, the witnesses for Mr. and Mrs.
> Wertheimer at the court.
> Mrs. Wertheimer was tested first at 1 P.M. The questions asked
> her were as follows—in the same order.
> Question: What kind of government does our country have?
> Answer: A republican sort.
> Question: When the president dies, who takes his place?
> Answer: The vice-president.
> Question: How many senators are sent to Congress from this
> state?
> Answer: Two.
> Mr. Wertheimer took his test at 1:30. There were the following
> questions—in the same order.
> Question: Are you acquainted with the form of government of this
> country.
> Answer: Yes.
> Question: What are the branches of government?
> Answer: The Legislative, Executive, and the Judicial.
> Both Mrs. and Mr. Wertheimer passed the test, getting every-
> (Con't 3)

And there the page ended.

Page three was headed "THE WERTHEIMER TIMES, NEW ROCHELLE, N.Y., SUNDAY, JANUARY 1?, 1939 PAGE THREE." Why the question mark appeared in the date is unclear. The story was completed about a quarter of the way down the right-hand column of page three, under the heading "TEST (Continued from page two)":

```
one of the questions correct.
They both ask us to give much of the credit to the two witness-
es. Everything went well in the Court House, so that the
Wertheimer family will probably be citizens in three or four
months.
```

Why the process would require a few more months to be completed was not explained. Nor was it explained why this story was not the lead one in this issue. No mention is made in the story of the fact that my father had carefully studied a lot of material about the U.S. government, expecting a much more detailed exam, and was startled by the simplicity of the questions he was actually asked.

All of the left column and the seven lines at the top of the right-hand column on page three were devoted to "P E T E R ' S   C O L U M N," with double spaces between all the letters in the title. The first story in the column had the headline, "PETER VISITS 'DU-DU'." "Du-du" was Peter's version of Gertrud Courant's first name, and soon caught on with the whole family as her nickname. The story reports:

```
On the 31st of December Peter visited Gertrud at the hospital
for the first time. Anni and I are afraid he was too loud. He
got a Santa Claus box, which opened and had candy in it. The
candy Master Peter soon dropped on the floor, and busy hands
picked it up.
He did not want to go. Anni and me he pushed out, exclaiming an-
grily: "Go-way!" Finally, however, we persuaded him to go. Du-du
wanted him to come again, but we doubted he would, because he
was too loud.
```

After three carefully horizontally spaced asterisks began another story, headlined "MASTER PETER OUT SHOPPING":

```
The car was away, so we did not go to the market we usually went
to, being too far away for a comfortable walk with Peter. In-
stead we went to "King Kullen".
First "my little nuisance" was a good boy.
```

Then he got cranky and wanted all the candy. He loves to see
"bĕbys" (as he calls babies) and at last I found one for Peter
and showed him to Peter.
Master Peter and I watched him for a while; then he got a piece
of cake. This was too much for my little fellow, and he called:
"Cooky! Want a cooky!" A colored man standing near said: "You
can get 'em free dare. I jes' got meself one. They're for sample." I thanked him and ran with Peter to get some pieces of
cake. For him I got one, and I got one for [continuing to the top
of the right-hand column] myself. When the sales lady saw him she
said: "I have something special for you.", and gave him a cook-
ie. I enjoyed the remainder of Peter's cake and took some more
samples of the cake. Thus, we wnt [sic] home from shopping.

Whether there was anything purchased during this "shopping trip" remains
unclear. Furthermore, apparently there were no qualms in the reporter helping
herself (and Peter) to the "samples." And that one of the characters in the story is
called a "colored man" and how that person spoke in a kind of caricature of a
dialect was unfortunately a rather accurate reflection of the stereotypical way in
which African Americans were typically viewed in suburbs of New York during
the late 1930s. Racial prejudice was rampant in all everyday interactions there at
that time, and apparently the reporter herself was far from immune to these practices.

The last part of page three was devoted to "A GOOD JOKE":

Reporter: You said you had so many headlines. Tell them to me.
Editor: About Mrs. Elkan, about the citizenship test, and about
the Gertrud.
Reporter: What do you mean?
Editor: Oh, I see I mean the Gertrud Courant.
Reporter: Say! What's the idea?
Editor: Oh! Gertrud Courant! I don't mean the Gertrud Courant, I
[mean] the Gertrud Courant story.

This "good joke" may remain somewhat opaque to a reader of modern English even if one mentions that the definite article was frequently used in the
Wertheimer version of German at that time when referring to a person by name,
such as "the Gertrud," "the Valentin," or "the Lise."

Page four of the first issue had a wide column on the left and a narrower one
on the right. The left-hand column was devoted to two "POEM SELECTIONS"
and an index. The first poem, entitled "HAPPY NEW YEAR!," read:

Happy New Year! Happy New Year!
This, let us cheer!
We are happy, and our faces shine;
As we drink of our goblets filled with wine.

The second was called "CHRISTMAS":

On this holy Christmas Day,
A baby was born and lain in the hay.
Some shepherds in the fields, while blowing a horn,
Saw an angel come to them and say "Christ is born."

They went to see the child,
Lying in the hay, so soft and mild.
A holy Boy; a Son of God;
And at last the shepherds homeward trod.

In the index, a total of seven items (including the title of "Peter's Column") were credited to Lise, three to the editor himself, two to Val—and one to Carlo Collodi.

The narrow right-hand column of page four contained Lise's report on "OUR NEW YEAR PARTY" and the beginning of Val's book report. Lise wrote:

B-6 Index for Volume I, Issue 1 of *The Wertheimer Times (family archives)*

On Christmas Eve I asked the Wertheimers to sing. For some reason we could not. I asked them the next day; they still could not. And so it went on, until New Year's Day, when Anni Wertheimer told me we could sing. [Why singing wasn't permitted earlier, and who prohibited singing must forever remain a mystery.] Valentin and I ran into the cellar to get fuel for the fireplace, as we wanted a fire while we sang. Finally we got settled; I had unpacked Mrs. Wertheimer's guitar, for we loved to sing to it. We began with "Ihr Kinderlein Kommet," my favorite German song. We sang other German songs; then turned to a few English ones. When it became late we drank our wine, and wished everyone: A HAPPY NEW YEAR!

That young children were permitted to drink wine was somewhat surprising.

Val's book report on *Revolution 1776* by John Hyde Preston begins on page four and is completed on page five:

> Here you have a very interesting history of the Revolutionary
> War where the author does not believe in heroic deeds like Paul
> Revere's Ride, etc. but he just believes in those with a tremen-
> dous amount of proof. He writes it as thouhg [sic] you really
> live in the book. It is very exciting, and tremendously educa-
> tional. I would advise you to read a school history before, be-
> cause you would get a strange point of view of the Revolutionary
> War if you did not. I really advise you to read it if you are
> interested in the Revolutionary War. (The book retails at $1.49
> at most book stores)

The rest of the top half of the last page of this first issue is filled by an excerpt from Collodi's "PINOCCHIO." It is not clear how much editorial license was used in this particular version.

> Once upon a time there was… "A king!," you will exclaim. No, you
> are mistaken. Once upon a time there was a piece of wood. It was
> not the best wood, but just a common piece of kindling, such as
> one uses to kindle fires. I can't say how it came about, but the
> fact is, that one fine day this piece of wood happened to be in
> the shop of the old carpenter, Mr. Cherry. [Wasn't it Gepetto in
> the original version?] As soon as Mr. Cherry saw this piece of
> wood, he saw it was just what he needs for a table leg. But just
> when he raised his axe for the first blow to shape it. But just
> then a voice said: "Do not strike me too hard!" Imagine Mr.
> Cherry's surprise! (To be cod)

And there the excerpt ends, complete with the ungrammatical third-from-the-last sentence. In a number of ways, a slightly inaccurate bit of borrowing. The lower half of the page is a hand drawing of a cottage and several trees, with "Happy New Year" written in large letters on the left. The monogram W, clearly Val's combination of a V and a W, is proudly placed just right of center at the bottom of the picture.

Chronologically the next item in the box was an envelope postmarked February 1, 1939, from "Friedrichs, Apt 3B, 435 Webster Ave, New Rochelle, New York," with a cancelled 2¢ stamp (that's what first-class local mail cost back in the late 1930s). The envelope contained a small paper envelope for a coin or a stamp—from which the contents had long since been removed—and

THE WERTHEIMER TIMES, ... ROCHELLE, N.Y., JANUARY 1, 19??   PAGE 2?...

B O O K REPORT(CON'T 4)

Revere's Ride,etc,but he just believes in these with a tremendous amount of proof . He writes it as thouhg you really live in the book. It is very exciting,and tremend-ously educational. I would advise you to read a school history before,because you would get a strange point of view of the Revolutionary War if you did not . I re-ally advise you to read it if you are in-terested in the Revolutionary War. (The book retails at 1.49 at most book stores)

*   *   *

P I N C C C H I O

Once upon a time there was... "A king," you will exclaim. No,you are mistaken. "nce

upon a time there was a piece of wood. It was not the best wood, but just a common piece of kin-dling,such as one uses to kin-dle fires. I can't say how it came about,but the fact is,that one fine day this piece of wood happened to be in the shop of the old carpenter, Mr.Cherry. As soon as Mr.Cherry saw this pi-ece of wood,he saw it was just what he needs for a table leg. But just when he raised his axe for the first blow to shape it. But just then a voice said:"Do not strike me too hard. Imagine Mr.Cherry's surprise!(To be con

Happy New Year

B-7 *The Wertheimer Times*: Volume 1, Issue 1, page 5 *(family archives)*

nothing else. The Friedrichs were acquaintances of the Wertheimers who had dutifully remitted the price for the first issue or two.

Another envelope had no address or stamp; written on it was "Lise and Michael from Karin." The neatly handwritten short letter in the envelope was dated Feb. 1, 1939; it obviously was from the then nine-year-old daughter of Wolfgang Köhler. Since there was no address on the envelope, the message must have been delivered by hand by someone visiting 12 The Circle from Swarthmore, PA:

> Dear Lise and Michael,
>
> I would like to be editor in your paper. I will write things that happen in Swarthmore, and I can write a few poems if you want me to, maybe some stories. Can you tell me what you write [sic].
> Many greetings to your mother and Peter.
>
> Karin

Volume I, Issue 2

The second hectographed issue of *The Wertheimer Times*, dated simply "February, Nineteen-thirty-nine," featured a realistically quadrupled subscription price of 4¢. The main front-page story of Vol. I No. 2 proclaimed, "Dr. Erwin Levy Marries."

```
Erwin Levy had been a student of Max Wertheimer at the Universi-
ty of Frankfurt am Main. Already a psychiatrist with an MD at
the time, he had seen to the packing and shipping of many of the
Wertheimers' belongings to the United States in September, 1933,
and had himself managed to come to New York not long thereafter.
A frequent visitor to the house at 12 The Circle, he had managed
to develop a practice in New York City. Erwin Levy, M.D., one of
the greatest friends of the family, married this month, to a la-
dy called Alice Wertheimer. This Miss Wertheimer is, strangely,
of no known relation to the Editor's family, the name being the
same. These two had their engagement on the twenty-second of
last December. They married in the N.Y. City Hall on the six-
teenth of January. Their honeymoon started on the day of their
marriage, until a week later. They spent their honeymoon at Pat-
terson, New York, traveling most of the time in their car. Their
residence is now at Hastings Hillside Hospital in a cottage near
there, as Dr. Levy works at the hospital, which is in Hastings-
on-Hudson, New York. The staff sends the best wedding wishes to
Mr. and Mrs. Erwin Levy.
```

The Wertheimer Times

Vol. I No. 2   February, Nineteen-thirty-nine   Price:

Dr. Erwin Levy Marries

Erwin Levy, M.D., one of the greatest friends of the family, married this month, to a lady called Alice Wertheimer. This Miss Wertheimer is, strangely, of no known relation to the Editor's family, the name being the same. These two had their engagement on the twenty-second of last December. They married in the N. Y. City Hall on the sixteenth of January. Their honeymoon started on the day of their marriage, until a week later. They spent their honeymoon at Paterson, New York, traveling most of the time in their car. Their residence is now at Hastings Hillside Hospital in a cottage near there, as Dr. Levy works at the hospital, which is in Hastings-On-Hudson, New York. The staff sends the best wedding wishes to Mr. and Mrs. Erwin Levy.

*   *   *   *

GERTRUD COURANT WELL AGAIN

Gertrud Courant, who, as was told in the last issue, had appendicitis. Having come home on Jan. 2, she got up on Jan. 4.

She went to school for the first time again on Tuesday, Jan. 10.

She and Peter are together often again, to Peter's great joy.

A NEW MUSICAL INSTRUMENT

Michael Wertheimer, the editor of this newspaper, has thought up a new musical instrument.

It is made of a long rubber band(a), some strips of metal(b), and a thin metal device.

It is played by plucking the rubber band, which has been tuned to the first seven notes of the scale. This instrument may be seen and inspected at the editor's office.

*   *   *

VALENTIN WERTHEIMER OFF STAFF

Valentin Wertheimer, who was on the staff in the last issue, has quit the staff because of his being too busy with school work. The editor and the staff permitted it.

Three other brief stories comprise the content of the first page of this issue. "GERTRUD COURANT WELL AGAIN" reports:

> Gertrud Courant, who, as was told in the last issue, had appendicitis. Having come home on Jan. 2, she got up on Jan. 4. She went to school for the first time again on Tuesday, Jan. 10. She and Peter are together often again, to Peter's great joy.

Apparently the Editor had not caught the grammatical problem in the first sentence of this story. The second front-page story, immodestly entitled: "A NEW MUSICAL INSTRUMENT," describes a device I contrived for producing sound by plucking stretched rubber bands. The final bottom-right front page article, titled "VALENTIN WERTHEIMER OFF STAFF," reports:

> Valentin Wertheimer, who was on the staff in the last issue, has quit the staff because of his being so busy with school work. The Editor and the staff permitted it.

Across the top of page two of this issue, emblazoned in large red hand-written capital letters, is "BIG CONTEST!" underlined in red. The rest of the page in the one extant copy is so poorly printed as to be close to illegible in most places. The contest fills the entire page. The list of prizes includes:

First Prize
DIARY WITH REAL PHOTOGRAPH OF LABRADOR BY SIR WILFRED GRENFELL WITH A HANDPAINTED COVER

Second Prize
BLACK CLOTH-BOUND FIVE YEAR DIARY

Third and Fourth Prizes
WORLDS FAIR GOLD PLATED SOUVENIR KEY CHAIN

These key chains must have been obtained at the 1939 World's Fair in Flushing, NY. Beneath this list of prizes was written:

Here's all you have to do

ALL YOU HAVE TO DO IS TO FINISH THIS SENTENCE IN 25 WORDS OR LESS: I LIKE THIS PAPER BECAUSE.. .
SEND IN TO: THE EDITOR, THE WERTHEIMER TIMES, 12 THE CIRCLE, NEW ROCHELLE, NEW YORK BEFORE FEBRUARY 25. THIS CONTEST IS ABSOLUTELY FREE! ENTER IT TODAY TO WIN THE HANDPAINTED DIARY! FILL IN THE COUPON ON THE RIGHT TO ENTER THIS CONTEST. IF YOU DON'T WANT TO CUT OUT THE COUPON YOU MAY MAKE A FACSIMILE. ENTER THIS CONTEST NOW!

B-9 Headline announcing the contest in Volume I, Issue 2 of *The Wertheimer Times*; the paper has yellowed and the hectographic ink has faded, but the red hand-lettering remains bright. *(family archives)*

The coupon had typed on it, "Dear Sir: Here is my entry to your big FREE contest: I like this paper because:" followed by three lines for writing in the entry, as well as space for "SIGNED" and "ADDRESS."

Page three is entirely devoted to items in "PETER'S COLUMN." The first is entitled "HE IS A LITTLE NUISANCE BECAUSE," and lists several pranks of the then 27-month-old boy:

1. He puts all the lights on in the daylight.
2. He screws the bulbs out of the lamps.
3. He opens and closes all of the doors.
   And of course, he is also a nuisance for what most other little children are. Anyway, "nuisance" certainly fits that little boy!

The next story, entitled "PETER'S JOKE," reports:

Michael was hitting Peter slightly with a rubber band. "Don't hit me," dejectedly said Peter. Michael hit himself. "Don't hit 'Maggy,'" Peter said. Michael stopped. A moment later, Peter pounded Michael with his fists! ('Maggy' is what Peter calls Michael)"

A third item lists three "NEW ACHIEVEMENTS MADE BY PETER."

1. He talks mostly German to Anni (who talks German to him) and mostly English with Rosa (who talks English to him). [Rosa Mae Anderson (later Dixon) was the dedicated, warm, beloved maid for many years at 12 The Circle, who was in charge of the kitchen. Clearly at this early stage of his life, Peter was already functionally bilingual in English and German, and

knew which language to use with the various members of the household.]

2. He knows how to open doors (some people aren't so glad about that).

3. He climbs on a chair by himself.

A fourth Peter story, entitled "SLEDDING," reports:

Peter goes sledding now. To be pulled always? No, not at all. When nobody is on the sled, he usually pulls it himself, and he pulled me once, but it wasn't quite he who made the sled go. I let him think so, as even pulling is good for him; and I pushed with my hands. Anni took him to go down a hill. It was very hard to slide, and Peter was very happy!? they slid at all, which shows what a "good sport" he is.

A fifth bears the headline, "LIEBER PAPA":

Peter: Papa 'lēf' noch? (Ger: Papa schläft noch? Eng: Father still asleep?)
Anni: Nein.
P: Papa ausge'lafen? (Ger: Papa ausgeschlafen? Eng: Father slept enough?)
A: Ya. [sic]
P: Papa hosies an? (Ger: Papa hosen an? Eng: Has father pants on?)
A: Ya
P: Lieber Papa (Nice [literally "dear" or "beloved"] father.)

And the next story, "HIS 'PEEP-PEEPS'" continues on to the top of page four:

When Peter eats Anni sometimes asks, "Smeck gut?" [German "schmeckt's gut?" or English "Does it taste good?"] Peter usually answers "'Meck gut." ["Schmeckt gut," or "tastes good."] Anni then says "Das freut mich." ["That pleases me."] So when bathing he made believe his "Peep-peeps" (birds) [small waterproof toys] drank. He asked "'Meck gut?" He answered for them "'Meck gut." Then he said, beaming: "Das freut mich!"

And the final Peter's column story for February 1939 is entitled "GOING TO SLEEP IN A NEW WAY":

When Peter goes to bed on the porch in the morning he says: "One, two machen." ["Do one-two."] That means to push him back and forth. Anni does it. [The origin of this expression is unclear, nor is it clear what it involved.] But now he said: "Nicht one, two machen." ["Don't do one, two."] "All right, Peter," was Anni's

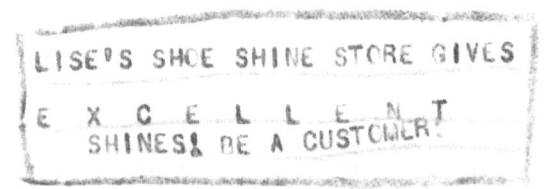

B-10 Lise's shoeshine advertisement *(family archives)*

reply. "Turn around," said Peter. Anni turned him a little.
"Mehr." ["More."] He repeated this until he stood so that he
could see the sky and trees. Then he was satisfied.

Just what this story was all about remains a bit unclear.

A poem entitled "SNOW" fills part of page four:

The snow is falling gently down,
It gives the earth a fluffy gown,
We hurry to get our sleds and our skis,
Then we go-with the snow up to our knees.
Happy, are we children, with the snow,
And cannot wait sledding and skiing to go.
We also go sliding, and on our sleds riding-
But best of all is to play
In the clean white snow, today.
Happy, are we children, with the snow,
And cannot wait sledding and skiing to go.

Next, a brief item entitled "PINNOCHIO" [sic] reports that "this story will
not be continued- so if you want to read, it [sic] you can easily get it at any library."

There is an index that gives the page number on which each item in this issue
begins, but does not provide the name of the author of any of the stories. And
bottom right is an advertisement: "LISE'S SHOE SHINE STORE GIVES
E X C E L L E N T SHINES! BE A CUSTOMER!" The lines are separated by
much-faded underlining, probably with a red pencil which was also used to add:
"IT'S WORTH THE NICKEL!"

Correspondence About the First Two Issues

Five one-time entries to the "big contest" were included in the box of documents. They were apparently evaluated by the Editor himself, who had scribbled
"none," "runner-up" in two cases, "2nd," and "1st" on them. The one categorized

as "none," submitted by Mrs. Wertheimer, read "I like this newspaper because: I like the Editor so very much." The two runners-up were from Rosa ("I like this newspaper because it tells me about the family I like best, and especially Peter") and from Max Wertheimer—but all in the Editor's handwriting ("I like this newspaper because: many items were really nice, because I feel a trend in it to become still nicer and because it's real somehow real work"). All three of these entries were facsimiles. The obverse of the first was blank; the obverse of the second had hectographed on it, all in capitals, "DEAR READERS: WE ARE VERY SORRY TO HAVE TO DO THIS, BUT WE MUST CALL YOUR AT-TENTION TO THE PRICE OF THIS PAPER. THE EDITOR"; and the third had typed on the obverse "DO UNTO OTHERS AS YOU WOULD HAVE DONE UNTO YOU." The remaining two entries were on coupons clipped from the paper. The one marked "2nd," from "K.S. Safranski at 21 Maywood Road," read "I like this paper because: it is the best of its kind. 99 44/100 % pure" (ob-viously plagiarizing a then popular advertisement for Ivory Soap); and the first prize entry, from "Mrs. B. Elkan, 75 Prospect Ave., Lchmt," read "I like this paper because: it gives me all the latest news of my best friends in a peppy + straightforward way."

An unstamped hand-tinted picture postcard of an "Old Spanish Court Yard in The Old Quarter of New Orleans" had only "For Michael" in the address space, and bore the message:

> My dear Mr. Editor,
> I want to tell you that I enjoyed your last number very much. I believe I have to send in for the next numbers. Please take this stamps [sic] and let me know how much I owe you. I wish you success and I am looking forward for the next issue.
> > Fondly yours,
> > Mara

When this material had been delivered to the Editor, and by whom, is un-known. The name "Mara Politzer" rings a very faint memory, probably an ac-quaintance of the Wertheimer family. A slip from Rosa had the handwritten message "In payment for the Wertheimer Times," undated; and there was an empty envelope with a 3¢ stamp postmarked "Feb. 3 1939 1:30 PM Larchmont,

N.Y." with the Elkan return address (perhaps used by Mrs. Elkan for her contest entry).

An extravagantly encouraging testimonial from Safranski, in German, is dated 8 February 1939 and arrived in an envelope postmarked "Feb. 9 12-M Grand Cent. ANNEX, N.Y.S." Addressed "To the Editors at The Wertheimer Times," it can be translated as follows:

B-11 Kurt Safranski (center right front of picture)
(courtesy of the Missouri Photo Workshop)

Most honored editorial board,
I have not sent my thanks for the shipment of the first issue—and now the second issue already gives me pleasure! I greet the appearances of the "Wertheimer Times" wholeheartedly and am looking forward eagerly to every one of the forthcoming issues. Finally here is a paper from which one can find out about news events in the way in which one wants to learn about them—things that are so much closer and more important to one than what the wide world calls so "important." Isn't it much more significant to hear that Miss Courant is well again, that Dr. Levi [sic] marries an unrelated Wertheimer and that Valentine [sic] has left the staff—than e.g. that Judge Manton took $225,000 in bribery funds? Continue to report with veracity and industry about the large things in the small realm, to tell us about Peter and his deeds and misdeeds, and whatever else the times may bring. As an earlier colleague I have a full understanding of your problems. I hope that the modest subscription price will at least in part solve these problems. It is to be hoped that the other subscribers will also pay promptly. From earlier years I know what a puzzling point this always is! Readers are not always payers! But I am certain that the competent leadership of the "W.T." will succeed in overcoming these and other difficulties that it will encounter on its path.
With the best wishes for the continuing success of the "Wertheimer Times,"

Your very grateful
Safranski

A postscript adds:

> Would the 'staff' be able to find the time somehow to chat with me
> about newspaper problems with a cup of chocolate? Attachments to the
> staff, such as Mr. and Mrs. Prof. W, Peter, Valentin, etc., etc. would be
> heartily welcome!

A second envelope from Safranski, with the same postmark date and time, was addressed to the "librarian of the Wertheimer Times." Although now empty, it must have held fairly substantial contents because it had three canceled 3¢ stamps; on the back, in German, was written "A small contribution to the Reference Library of the W.T."

A third envelope several days later from Safranski contained two separate sheets (and must have included his contest entry). The first brief note said, "here is my entry to your big contest.—The copy I received last time was hard to read—blurred and words missing. Please speak with your printing depart.—Still looking forward to seeing you. Yours sincerely, K.S. Safranski." The second was headed, "Believe it or not," underlined. "Did you ever see a piece of iron floating in the air?? (I don't mean an airplane... just a plain piece of steel...)" Next is a diagram of one brick-like object above another, with rays emanating from them. The text goes on to say, "To be seen only by appointment. K.S.S." It is not known whether the visit with hot chocolate ever occurred, nor whether the Editor ever saw Safranski's demonstration of what must have been magnetism.

A note from Rosa to "Miki" from the middle of February may have accompanied her entry to the "big contest." "My dear Miki, Your Valentine was real nice. I liked it very much. It was nice of you to think of me, Rosa."

A submission in English to the "big contest" was received in an envelope with a 5 Pfenning stamp postmarked "Berlin-Charlottenburg" on February 27, 1939. Quite likely the delay was due to the relevant issue not having arrived in Germany in time for the submission to have been received before the deadline. "I like this paper because: it informs very well about the Wertheimer family, it has amusing stories, it has nice poems, all that for little price!" The name on the cut-out coupon was "Uncle Fritz and Aunty Mile," and in the space for the address was typed "unknown." Anni's relatives were obviously trying to be cautious. But

Berlin, March 13th 1939.

Dearest Michel,

Last year I was with you on the 20th of March, and I still remember how nicely you laid the table for your birthday party; and the little gifts everybody got! To day I only congratulate you by letter wishing you many happy returns of the day, and many fine presents (gifts!) for to day. And this time Peter will not be sick again; and you can make as much noise as you want to!

On my secretary there is the calendar you gave us for X'mas. Three windows are already open, and it makes great fun to us. But the kite with the string is the prettiest thing I ever saw. I wonder what I'll find behind the other windows. —

Are you drinking chocolate with the whole party and has Rosa baken a big cake with your name written with creame?

I'll think of you the whole day! By-by, and have a good time! Love from Lili.

Dear chief editor!

I read in a newspaper almanack, that You have your birth-day next time and being a greatful reader of your much interesting "W. times", I feel myself obliged to congratulate You and to send my best wishes for You and for Your enterprise! Respectfully Yours Mr. fritz

B-12 A letter from the Rosenbergs (*family archives*)

both of the Rosenbergs probably either committed suicide or perished in a Nazi concentration camp gas chamber about two years later.

Volume I, Issue 3

A third issue, dated March 1939 on page one but February 1939 on the rest of its pages, contained, like the second issue, four pages. The main story of the front page, headlined "Mr. Wertheimer Takes a Trip" across the whole page, takes up the left column:

> Professor Max Wertheimer, father of the editor, left for Prince-
> ton from the Pennsylvania station at noon on January 26. He ar-
> rived at [Albert] Einstein's home in the early afternoon. He
> stayed at the house of Einstein until Saturday morning, having
> many interesting discussions with Dr. Einstein. The Saturday
> lunch was eaten at the house of the Director of the Psychology
> Department at Princeton, Dr. [Herbert] Langfeld. That afternoon
> Dr. [Edwin B.] Newman, a good friend of Dr. Wertheimer, took
> him to Swarthmore, to visit the [Wolfgang] Koehlers. He met
> psychologists [Karl] Duncker, [Hans] Wallach, [Richard] Crutch-
> field, etc. He also met philosopher [Maurice] Mandelbaum and
> mathematician [Hans?] Rademacher. After days of interesting
> discussions, he came back to New York on Friday, February 3 with
> Duncker. He enjoyed his trip, and also was glad to see our new
> reporter, Karin Koehler. On Monday, the 6, his lectures started
> again.

The results of the "big contest" in the second issue are presented in detail in the right column of page one, continuing onto the next page. Page two also contains five other brief stories.

> ANNI WERTHEIMER SICK
> Mrs. Anni Wertheimer, the mother of the editor, got a bad cold
> Friday, February 26. Next morning she had a high temperature:
> 102. On Tuesday, she had no temperature anymore. Wednesday she
> got up because Peter was sick. During most of her sickness she
> lay in Lise's room, the first day in Valentin's.

Next was "THE EDITOR RECEIVES AN OFFICE," a story in two short sentences:

> The editor received his own room and a desk to make an office to
> write this paper in. The other children all also have their own
> rooms.

Which room the editor "received" as "his own" is not known.

"VALENTIN WERTHEIMER TAKES A TRIP" completes the left column of page two:

> Valentin Wertheimer left for Weston on Friday, the 17, and came back on the 24. He had a good time there with the Kortners, who live there. Weston is near Westport, Connecticut. He had a school vacation all 1st [sic] week.

Fritz Kortner was a prominent German actor, director, and movie star, and had two children: Peter who was about Val's age and Manni who was about Lise's age. Val and Peter Kortner had both been "home-schooled" together years before, when the Wertheimer and Kortner families spent about a half

B-13 Fritz Kortner *(from https://commons.wikimedia.org/ wiki/File:Bundesarchiv_B_145_ Bild-P047613,_Curt_Bois_und _Fritz_Kortner_im_Schiller-Theater.jpg)*

year together in Marienbad, Czechoslovakia, during the first half of 1933.

The right-hand column of page two begins by proclaiming "KARIN KOEHLER NEW REPORTER ON SWARTHMORE, PENN."

> Karin Koehler, who has recently joined the staff, lives in Swarthmore, the daughter of Prof. Koehler. She will have a column each monthe [sic] entitled 'News From Swarthmore.' She will be editor of this.

The next story, which completes the page, doubtless refers to the contents of the now-empty envelope that was received in February from Kurt Safranski: "A GREAT EDITOR MAKES A CONTRIBUTION TO A LITTLE EDITOR":

> Mr. K.S. Safranski, famed editor of many newspapers and magazines, is an [sic] publisher in New York. He is a subscriber to this paper and has made a great contribution to our files. It consists of a series of nearly 30 pamphlets about many of the famous scientists of the world. Some examples are: Roger Bacon, Gutenberg, Johann Kepler, Galileo, William Harvey, Newton, Dalton, Pasteur, Roentgen, Edison, Marconi, Wright brothers, etc. They are very interesting and we invite you to see them. As it is very worth while. We can not extend our gratitude enough to Mr. Safranski for this great contribution to our newspaper.

"PETER SICK," reports the first story in Peter's Column on page three:

Peter was sick with stomach trouble and a cold. Soon after it began, Anni got sick too. Then Peter got ear trouble, and is not up yet.

The next story is "PETER MAKES ANNI EAT":

A few days ago, at lunch ,Anni didn't want to eat. But we made her a slice of bread, still she wouldn't eat. Finally Peter took it in his hand and held it in front of Anni's mouth. "Beiss ap," he said. (Bite off.) Anni could not refuse this, and ate it. So when Michael and I failed, Peter had done it.

Headed "EXCUSE ME...," the next item reads:

But Peter didn't have many adventures this month, being sick most of the time, so I am sorry, but I cannot write anymore about him this month.

Next is "FLOWERS: (A POEM)":

Now the flowers will waken,
And to our house they'll be taken.
Buds here, buds there, buds everywhere!
In all places (tis so fair)."

Then "SPRING (ANOTHER POEM)":

Spring is here! Spring!
The flowers beginning!
Now we can play
In the sun—every day!
Happy is everyone, that spring is here,
And that the flowers are blooming, near.

This is followed by "P.S. I hope you all enjoy the spring!"

The proud headline "THIRTY SUBSCRIBERS" introduces a brief story:

Our newspaper now has thirty subscribers—all over the place—some right here, some in Larchmont, some in New York, and some in Swarthmore. We also have a reporter in Swarthmore! We thank everyone precisely [odd adverb!] for their co-operation with this paper!

No mention is made of Berlin, Germany (the Rosenbergs).

The page ends with a coupon offering "Free: Tom Thumb history of the United States cloth-bound!"

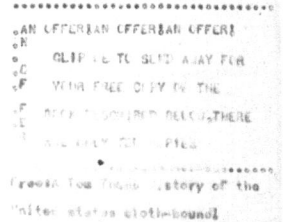

B-14 Coupon for a free book
(family archives)

Page four for the first time provides a kind of "masthead" for the paper:

The Wertheimer Times [ornately hand-written]
NEW ROCHELLE, NEW YORK, FEBRUARY, 1939
                THE STAFF
EDITOR-IN-CHIEF MICHAEL WERTHEIMER
PETER'S COLUMN EDITOR LISE WERTHEIMER
POETICAL EDITOR LISE WERTHEIMER
POLITICAL EDITOR MICHAEL WERTHEIMER
SWARTHMORE COLUMN EDITOR KARIN KOEHLER
FOUR CENTS FOR EVERY REPRINT RECEIVED

"Reprint" is an odd term in this context. This is followed by "SO SORRY!" which reports:

Last time we forgot to print who wrote what—here it is:
Michael Wertheimer wrote: Dr. Erwin Levy, Gertrud Courant, musical instrument, Valentin Wertheimer, Big Contest.
Lise Wertheimer wrote: A Nuisance, Peter's Joke, New Achievements, Sledding, Lieber Papa, Going to sleep, Snow, [sic]

There follows the "INDEX TO THIS COPY," with the three Peter stories and the two poems attributed to "L. Wertheimer" and all the remaining items attributed to "M. Wertheimer."

"THE LIFE OF BICY ICE (PART ONE)" completes the rest of the last page of this issue.

Bicy Ice was born in a big refrigerator out of some water from the refinery. When Bicy was two minutes old, he was put in a big truck, which stopped at the front of a big house. A man got out of the truck and put Bicy on a piece of cloth and [he] was brought to the third floor of an apartment house. He was put into a refrigerator on top of a bottle of wine. 'Boo-hoo!' whined the wine, 'you are squeezing me!' So finally the bottle was freed from Bicy's sight and said a polite 'Thank you.' But now the wine bottle was on top of the wonderful Camembert's cheese. After quite some shoving and pushing the cheese and bottle were free of each other. All this started a conversation among them...(Cont.)

Further Correspondence about *The Wertheimer Times*

A letter from "Karin Köhler, 401 Walnut Lane, Swarthmore, Pa.," addressed to Lise and postmarked "Mar. 2, 1939 6:30 PM," contained two sheets. The first sheet said:

Dear Lise,

I am very sorry I didn't send anything, but I thought I should send it on March 20. But I will send things as soon as I am ready. I liked your paper very much but I think you could improve it by telling about things more clearly for people who don't know some of your friends so well. Would you please explain about that contest.

Karin

P.S. Some more things are coming.

The second sheet, entitled "Rose Valley School News," reported:

We are studying the Stone Age and so we started this game that I am going to tell you about. The object of the game is to make models out of clay or any material. It has to have something to do with the Stone Age. There are three parts Early, Middle, and Late Stone Age and Food, Shelter and Tools. Each person has a thing to do. I have Food in the Middle Stone Age and Shelter in the Early. Food means you can make a little bear out of clay or something like that and for Shelter you could make a cave. Each object counts a certain amount of points. There are two sides and the one that gets most points wins.

If you want to make it shorter you can scribble out things you don't think are important.

Karin

Another letter from Karin dated March 7 to Lise indicated "I don't know what I should write about so I won't send anything more. I hope you will be able to use the crossword puzzell [sic] in your paper. Karin." The puzzle was a 6x6 square:

Across
1. Play with mostly singing.
6. Vegetable.
8. The shorter way of writing for example.
9. When talking of yourself.
10. Opposite of stop.
7. Finish

Down
1. Quite a bit of water.
4. Meaning again.
3. Older person.
2. Something to write with.
10. Note in the scale.
11. Negative.
5. Form of the verb 'to be.

Also in the envelope was a small sheet carefully folded and sealed with a pin, labeled "ANSWERS." The answers, as revealed in that sheet, were:

A letter postmarked the evening of March 3, 1939, from "Friedrichs, 435 Webster Ave., New Rochelle, N.Y." says "My dear Editor, I am very much interested in your paper + wish to state that this copy is so well printed that I am able to read nearly every word. Yours truly, Nellie Friedrichs."

On April 19, 1939, Nellie Friedrichs wrote again: "Dear Editor: Enclosed I am sending 10¢ for the April copy of your very interesting paper to which I am always looking forward, and 10¢ for the advertisement with which I am greatly satisfied." But no April 1939 copy of the W.T. seems to have survived.

An index card with the message "Enclosed please find 4¢ for the Times. I think that your paper is very lively and interesting. I am looking forward to the next issue. Yours, Ann Ruth Maslow" was in an envelope postmarked Mar 10,

B-15 Abraham Maslow
(courtesy of the Archives of the History of American Psychology, The Drs. Nicholas and Dorothy Cummings Center for the History of Psychology, The University of Akron)

1939 9:30 PM. The return address was 1232 Ocean Ave., Brooklyn, N.Y. The writer of the note was probably a member of the family of Abraham Maslow; Abraham Maslow was a student and admirer of Max Wertheimer whose theories of motivation were to become very prominent in U.S. psychology during the next two decades.

One coupon, from "Safranski," requested a copy of the "Free Tom Thumb History of the United States cloth-bound!"

A note in German, dated 25.3.39, from the sister of noted artist Käthe Kollwitz translates:

Greatly honored gentleman and greatly honored Madame Lise,
I thank you very much for sending me your paper, which I read with great interest. I regret not being able to participate in your contest, since I unfortunately don't have the competence to do so; nevertheless I request that you continue to send me your honored paper, from which I am most pleasantly instructed about events in the Wertheimer family.

With great admiration,
Lisbeth Stern

An undated letter from Anni's sister Lotte reads,

My dear children!
Last week I received the March-news which are as usual very interesting. When I come to USA and earn any money I shall pay your newspaper every number with 40p. But in the next time I shall send you little books for thanks for your industry. And I am eagerly waiting for the next number and if I have time I shall write a little contribution to it. Is there anything special you want me to write about? Please let me know about.

With many greetings,
your Aunt Lotte

B-16 Amateur theatricals by Tante Lotte, center, and her sisters (Anni at right) *(family archives)*

Apparently Anni had tried, so far unsuccessfully, to find more of the gelatin for the hectograph, because a letter to her dated April 20, 1939, on letterhead of the Columbia Ribbon and Carbon Manufacturing Co, Inc. reads:

> Dear Madam:
> —We are in receipt of your card asking us to mail you 1 lb. of composition. Please be advised that we have forwarded your request to our New Rochelle dealer—O. Mueller, 247 Huguenot Street, your city, who will be glad to take care of this order as they keep a full line of our merchandise in stock at all times.

An April 26, 1939 penny postcard postmarked in New York was from "A.M. Kulka," and while the name is dimly familiar, nothing remains in memory about who that person may have been. In German, the somewhat hard-to-decipher message reads:

Dear Michael,

It was only today that I got around to reading your newspaper. I believe that there is hardly any better one and I heartily wish for regular publication. How are mother and you all?

> Many thanks and all the best.
>
> A. M. Kulka

Response requested.

B-17 Erwin Levy *(courtesy of Gerhard Stemberger)*

A letter mailed at 10 AM on July, 1939, from Erwin Levy, M.D., P.O. Box 691, Hastings-on-Hudson, N.Y. contained a message on the letterhead of "The Grove School, Madison, Conn." Apparently in response to a request, it reads:

Sir:

I hereby submit a report on the naturalization of Dr. Erwin Levy, who became an American citizen on Thursday, July 13, 1939. Dr. Levy came to this country on August 19, 1934, from Paris, France. He has become a citizen under a special law which says that if you marry an American citizen, you may become a citizen yourself after three years. If you don't marry, you have to wait five years.

That's why Dr. Levy married! He is now vacationing in Madison, Conn., and had to go to White Plains by car, in order to be sworn. There was a judge who conducted the ceremony, and a reverend who made a very nice speech on the privileges and obligations of American citizens. Dr. Levy had two witnesses from the Hastings Hillside Hospital, Hasting-on-Hudson, N.Y., which is where he lives. I hope, my dear Mr. Editor, that this is the information desired.

> Cordially yours,
>
> Levy

An undated and unsigned story printed neatly in pencil on lined paper, headlined "Wertheimers Get Rabbits" was clearly intended as an item for an issue of *The Wertheimer Times*.

The Wertheimer family has now gotten a pair of rabbits. Their rabbits are albinos. This kind has pink eyes, pinkish white ears, and white fur. They wash like a cat, and are always clean. A very large place is used for them to live in. There is a wire fence around this place and a door to come in by, as the fence is too high to jump. Inside are three tunnels. In the middle of these is a large hole, also covered. The inside of this has hay in it, which the rabbits use for both sleeping and eating. There is also a box with two small holes, big enough for the rabbits to get through. The inside of this is also covered with hay (alfalfa). There is a pan of water, a bunch of greens, and a small pan with oats in it. This is for them to eat and drink. The Wertheimers (mostly the children) always want to go into the rabbits, but, as the latter are not really tame and used to visitors, they cannot go too often. All the Wertheimers were very glad to get these new pets, and like them very [much].

If memory serves, this chicken-wire rabbit enclosure had been built by Rosa's husband Albert, and by later in the summer the two rabbits had multiplied several times. The rabbits had also soon succeeded in digging holes under the fence in several places, so that they could leave and re-enter the enclosure as they wished. But it is not clear who had written the item.

A letter dated July 10, 1939, signed by Margaret Manson and Dorothy B. Nyswander, with the return address of 22 West Street, Mamaroneck, N.Y., was in an envelope on which was typed "To be delivered by Dr. B. Burks." Barbara Burks was a pioneer behavioral geneticist who occasionally studied with and visited Max Wertheimer. Fallible memory is unable to retrieve any information about Manson or Nyswander, although the second name is dimly familiar. The return address for the letter was "SCHOOL HEALTH STUDY COMMITTEE, 12-26 31st AVENUE, ASTORIA, NEW YORK." It reads:

Dear Sir,
Having received the May and June-July issues of The Wertheimer
Times, we would appreciate your listing us as a regular subscriber to
your paper. It was with regret that we read the concluding installment of
'Sir Skilt Swordsman' and we hope that future issues will contain other
ballads of a similar excellence. Your photograph offer is eagerly accepted. We hope that it may be possible to secure photographs of other
members of the family whose interesting events are so colorfully chron-
icled. Enclosed please find twenty-five cents (25¢) for the following:

May, and June-July issues of The W. Times- $.08; Three photographs
(special offer) .14; Postage for mailing photographs .03. Total $.25.

Sincerely yours,
Margaret Manson
Dorothy B. Nyswander

B-18 Autographed photo of Lise *(family archives)*

B-19 Autographed photo of me *(family archives)*

No copies of the indi-
cated issues of the paper
were in the box, but an
envelope marked "5
pictures (autographed) of
Lise; 5 pictures (auto-
graphed) of Micke" [sic]
contains a 3"x5" folded
index card on which was
written "The ten Prints
18¢" and inside of which
were two remaining 1"
by 1½" black-and-white
prints each of Lise and
Michael, the former
signed respectively "Lise
Wertheimer" and "Mi-
chael Wertheimer, Edi-
tor" on the back.

A July 27 letter to the
Editor listed "20¢ for two
editions, with kind regard
from Mrs. N. Friedrichs."

A letter on letterhead
of "Black Star Publishing Company, Inc., Graybar Building, 420 Lexington
Avenue, New York" postmarked "Grand Central Annex, N.Y. 8:30 PM July 31st,
1939," was "dictated by KSS to C" and included a reprint of a four-page August,
1939 issue (Vol. IV No. 4) of *The Institute News*, "published by the Franklin

Institute, Benjamin Franklin Parkway at Twentieth, Philadelphia, Pa." The letter, addressed to "Editor, Wertheimer Times" and signed by Safranski, stated:

> You might be interested in the enclosed INSTITUTE NEWS and especially in the little Electrical Toy, as described on Page 2. I could imagine that Mr. Valentine [sic] and yourself would like to build such a box.
>
> With kindest regards to everybody,
>   Yours
>   Kurt S. Safranski, BLACK STAR

The item entitled "Electric Toy" on page two of *The Institute News* is about a "recently invented… ingenious electrical toy which… illustrates in a novel manner the principles of electrical attraction and repulsion." The next two paragraphs are marked in red:

> The toy consists of a cardboard box six inches square, three inches deep, lined with metal-faced paper and covered with a tightly stretched sheet of cellophane. The box contains a number of small tissue-paper figures and small pith-balls. By passing the fingers lightly and rapidly to and fro across the cellophane surface, it becomes highly electrified and the paper figures begin a lively dance, being alternatively attracted and repulsed.
>
> Any child can construct one of these toys in a short time at trifling cost and will derive a great deal of enjoyment when his companions are mystified at the actions of the little dancers.

B-20 Barbara Burks *(Journal of Heredity, Volume 34, Issue 12, December 1943)*

An undated sliver of paper contains items drafted by Lise for *The Wertheimer Times*. On one side of the paper is:

> Our Visit to Barbara Burks.
> A few weeks ago we went to Barbara Burks who has a cute little house in Cold Spring Harbor. When we went swimming we thought it should be called "Warm Spring Harbor" because the water was so warm. Miss Burks has a funny kind of

boat. it [sic] is sort of a tube with a bottom of cloth. It also had paddles. We ate supper here and then, after a very good time, went home.

On the obverse of the sheet were three items for Peter's Column:

Who Can Run and Who Cannot
Peter and Rosa were crossing the street and:
P: Run Rosa!
R: I can't run, Peter!
P: Rosa, are you too fat to run?
R: Yes Peter.
P: Anni isn't too fat to run. Anni can run.

Ice-cream
Peter loves ice-cream. When his mother goes away for a day, and Peter knows, she comforts him by getting him one.

Flowers
Peter likes flowers. Whenever he finds one, he wants to pick it. Then, if he may pick it, later he gives it to one of us to put in to water.

Volume II. Issue 2

One more issue of *The Wertheimer Times* was included in the box. It is unclear how many issues there may have been between this one and Volume I Issue 3, nor is it known how many issues there may have been after this one. Dated August 1939 and still listing 4¢ as its price, its huge hand-lettered front page story is headlined "DR. LEVY NATURALIZES." Under that, on the left, typed in capitals, is "DR. LEVY SENDS LETTER TO TELL OF NATURALIZATION," then "Editors Note: It is not necessary to write a story, as all the information is contained in the letter. Here we shall publish it." And the full letter, including "The Grove School, Madison, Conn., Sunday" as the return address and "The Editor. The Wertheimer Times. 12 The Circle, New Rochelle, N.Y." as the addressee, as well as "Sir:" verbatim reproduces Levy's entire July letter.

The right-hand column of page one is headlined "OUR TRIP TO THE NEW YORK WORLD'S FAIR." Both this story and the Levy letter go on to the next page, as indicated by "Continued on page two" at the bottom of both columns on page one—and on the next page the continuations are headed by "(CONT. F.P.1)" and "(CONT. FRM. P. ONE)"; no longer the "con't" of earlier issues.

B-21 Bronx Whitestone Bridge *(from https://commons.wikimedia.org/wiki/File:BWBafter_cop y_(13720407785).jpg)*

The World's Fair story is so long that it continues on to parts of pages two, three, and four.

On Saturday, July 22, Lise, Michael, Mother, and I (Valentin) went to the World's Fair. We started out at about 4:00 pm by car. We went via the Shore Road and then the Whitestone Bridge. This bridge and its approaches, I think, is one of the most modern and beautiful structures of the world, including the World's Fair.

Upon our arrival at the fair we decided to park at the City parking field, after paying the 25¢ fee. Then we heard a man shouting "Take your bus now, or walk a mile to the fair." We decided to walk, which we found satisfactory, as it was not far. We then arrived at the ticket booth. This Sat. and Sun. happened to be bargain days, and for paying 50¢ for children and $1.00 for adults, you got: a. Admission, b. A hamburger or frankfurter, c. an ice Tea or Coffee, d. e. f. g. h. Five different tickets to Five different amusements. We bought these and proceeded through the IRT BMT gate. Upon entry we decided to first go to the Perisphere to see the "City of Tomorrow." On our way we wnt [sic] through several interesting exhibition buildings.

As our group arrived at the perisphere our mother bought us admission tickets. We first got on a long and high escalator to take us to the correct elevation. We walked in to the Perisphere (and I better not talk about it lest I spoil the fun of the readers). Then our little group continued on to the Am. Tel. and Tel. building to see the voder in operation. This is really a marvelous machine and I think everybody would enjoy it. (It is a mechanical device which talks by making different sounds.)

THE WERTHEIMER TIMES,NEW ROCHELLE,NEW YORK,AUGUST,NINETEEN THIRTY NINE   PAGE THREE

L I S E ' S   B O O T
  B L A C K   S T O R E
Shoes shined...one pair...........$.05
        V O L U N T A R Y
          STATEMENTS
'You gave me an excellent shine!'
                        Valentin W.
'A really shining shine!'
                  Michael   W.
'Very well done!'
                  Prof.Max   W.
    *   *   *
V A L E N T I N   W E R T H E I M E R
DEVELOPING
    PRINTING
      PHOTOGRAPHING
        NO ENLARGING

SEE   JUNE-JULY   ISSUE   FOR   RATES
      *   *   *
N O T I C E :   :   :
IF YOU PATRONIZE THESE ADVERTISEMENTS
(BOOT BLACK AND PHOTOGRAPHING ADS)YOU
RECEIVE,FOR EVERY ORDER OF FIVE CENTS
OR OVER,ONE COUPON.EACH COUPON IS WO-
RTH TWO CENTS TOWARD THE PURCHASE PR-
ICE OF THIS PAPER ORTOWARD PAYMENT OF
ANY PRINTING ORDER.(EXAMPLE:YOU HAVE
TWO COUPONS,SO FOR THESE YOU MAY GET
ONE ISSUE OF THE WERTHEIMER TIMES.)

OUR VISIT TO BARBARA BURKS
    A few weeks ago we went to Barbara
Burks,who has a cute little house in
Cold Spring Harbor,L.I.
    When we went swimming there we though
it should be called'Warm Spring Harbor',
as the water was so warm.
    Miss Burks has a funny kind of boat.I
is a sort of tube with a canvas bottom.
It also had paddles.We each had a ride.
We ate supper there and then,after a
very good time,went home.
    *   *   *
WORLD'S FAIR (CONT.FROM PAGE TWO)
our hamburgers or franks and iced tea,
sat down,and enjoyed our meal.
    We then headed towards the Amusement
Section.On our way we saw the Westinghouse exhibit.We walked around the Amusement Section and went into the Zoo-
logical exhibit.We then went to 'Old New
York','Penguin Island',and'Strange as it
Seems'.These were all overcrowded.This
spectacle is one thing that can't be o-
verlooked,it is so marvelous.Yes,I mean
the fireworks.Then we went back to the
parking field,which took us one hour to
walk.We piled into the car and almost
fell asleep.After and uneventful trip
(Continued on page four)

B-22 *The Wertheimer Times*: Volume 2, Issue 2, page 3 *(family archives)*

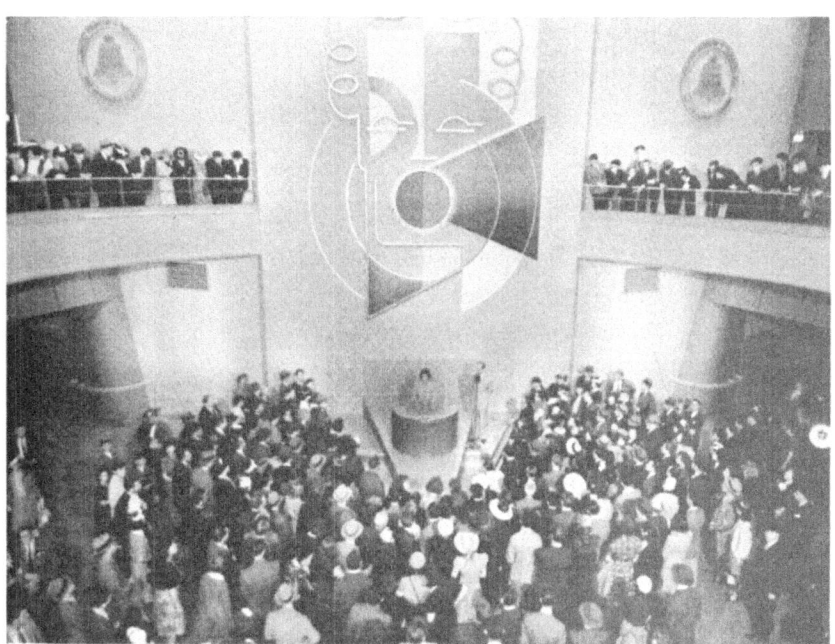

B-23 The "Voder" at the 1939 New York World's Fair *(from https://en.wikipedia.org/wiki/ Voder#/ media/File:VODER_demonstrated_on_1939_New_York_World_Fair_-)*

We went to the Transportation Area, going through the Firestone building first. There we saw how a tire is made and used on a real farm with real animals, etc. This is a very interesting exhibit if you have enough time to go through it thouroughly [sic]. Next was the Aviation building, which is a marvel. There are real, fullsize airplanes standing on the ground and hanging in the air. One can enter almost every plane. There were many other exhibits like motors, etc. to do with Aviation.

The next building on our program was the marine building. We saw many interesting things, including a Coast Guard Life Boat which had really been used.

Since it was getting on supper time we decided to eat. We procured our hamburgers or franks and iced tea, sat down, and enjoyed our meal.

We then headed towards the Amusement Section. On our way we saw the Westinghouse exhibit. We then went to 'Old New York,' 'Penguin Island,' and 'Strange as it Seems.' These were all overcrowded. This spectacle is one thing that can't be overlooked, it is so marvelous. Yes, I mean the fireworks. Then we went back to the parking field, which took us one hour to walk. We piled into the car and almost fell asleep. After and [sic] uneventful trip we went home and to bed. The next morning we

```
found out that the 22nd of July
was  one  of  the  most  crowded
days: 291,000 people admitted by
11 pm!
```

The left column of page three is devoted to advertisements, and the story "OUR VISIT TO BARBARA BURKS," the draft of which is described on page 285, filled the top half of the right column of page three. Lise's Peter's Column items from the same sheet are published on page four. The right column of page four presents the masthead, followed by pricing information:

B-24 New York 1939 World's Fair: Trylon and Perisphere *(from https://picryl.com/media/trylon -and-perisphere-new-york-worldand39s- fair-dfe00c)*

```
MICHAEL WERTHEIMER EDITOR IN CHIEF
MICHAEL WERTHEIMER CURRENT EVENTS
MICHAEL WERTHEIMER STORIES
LISE WERTHEIMER CURRENT EVENTS
LISE WERTHEIMER PETER'S COLUMN
VALENTIN WERTHEIMER CURRENT EVENTS
VALENTIN WERTHEIMER TREASURER
FOUR CENTS PAID FOR EVERY COPY
NOTICE THE PRICE OF THIS PAPER,
STARTING IN SEPTEMBER, WILL BE FIVE CENTS, SO AS TO INSURE NO
DEFICIT.
```

An index credits M.W. with "Dr. Levy," "Notice," and "How Bean Got String"; V.W. with "World's Fair," "Advertisement," and "Advertisement"; and L.W. with "Visit to Burks" and "Peter's Column."

Completing page four is "HOW THE BEAN GOT ITS STRING":

```
Once upon a time there lived together in a house a bean, a
straw, and a coal. They were very happy together. One day they
took a walk. They came to a stream with no bridge so the straw
laid himself across as a bridge. As the coal went across, the
straw buckled up, and the two fell in the water. Then the coal
camp up the bank, dripping wet. Then the bean burst out laugh-
ing. To be continued in September.
```

Additional Documents

Among further items in the box was a complete draft of Val's long story about the World's Fair and a continuation of the earlier story about the Wertheimers' rabbits:

> The bunnies are really an early birthday present for Peter and Lise, the two youngest of the family who both have their birthdays in October. The rabbits are not named yet, because the only difference noticed yet was that one is braver, friendlier, and tamer. But of course one cannot go by this to name them. After a while, though the bunnies will be tamer.

The obverse of the sheet on which this was written carried a "poem," entitled "School":

> In the month of September
> Every school member
> Must return.
> Whether they like it or whether they not
> They soon get used to it
> And are a nice lot.
> School has begun.

An unlined sheet of paper has two Peter stories in pencil:

> Peter and Picture-taking
> Peter doesn't like to have his picture taken. Or maybe he does, but he doesn't act it. Whenever we try to take a picture of him, he wrinkles up his nose, and of course, we don't take him that way.

> Peter Shopping
> Peter likes to go shopping. One day we went and there was a 'Beechnut Circus.' This was very interesting. It really moved Peter, and I watched it for most of the time that we were there. Peter said "I've never seen anything like that before" and I liked it very much.

Two stories by "Judith A. Brodsky and Valentin Wertheimer" are carefully written in ink. "Our Trip to the Lewisohn Stadium" was dated August 25, 1939:

B-25 A concert at Lewisohn Stadium *(from https://digitalcollection s.nypl.org/items/510d47d9-ba0a-a3d9-e040-e00a18064a99)*

On August 25, 1939 Mrs. A. Wertheimer took Lise, Mikey, Judith and Valentin to the residence of the Golds in New York City by automobile. We met the Golds in front of their house and then together walked to the Lewisohn Stadium one block away in order to hear the concert. In the group were Rita, Jenny [the Gold sisters], Mrs. and Mr. Gold [their parents], Doctor Brown [there is no information on who this is], Dr. Levy, the above mentioned and others. We arrived, and then sat down on the hard, cold stone benches. Only the authors had their coats along. So they were the only comfortable people. The program commenced with Beethoven's Leonore Overture which we all enjoyed very much, passing one pair of opera glasses from one person to another. When the overture was completed Mr. Fritz Reiner, the conductor of the proformance [sic] bowed proudly in front of a gigantic audience. Which completed the first part of the proformance. After the intermission was over Mr. Reiner proceded to conduct one of the most famous symphonies ever written, the Beethoven ninth symphony. After a most enthralling program which every one enjoyed immensely we left the stadium very much more enlightened than when we first arrived.

The first sentence of the next item, "Days during Vacation," was crossed out:

~~The first time Judith Brodsky and her family really got to know the Wertheimers was when the Wertheimers went to visit the Brodsky's in Connecticut.~~ The Wertheimers arrived in time for a very delicious and appetizing lunch. After that we all went down to Camp Beach and went swimming but unfortunately Valentin had a cold and was confined to sitting on the beach (which was rocks) to watch the others swim. After everyone decided they were too cold to swim any longer they played a rapid game of ball and then sat down to a very palatable picnic supper on the beach. After supper the Wertheimers left with Judith promising to visit them the following week —A week later true to her promise Judith went to visit the Wertheimers in New Rochelle. When she arrived with her mother (who left shortly afterwards) Micheal [sic] and Lise and Valentine [sic; this must have been written by Judith] and Judith all went on a treasure hunt that unfortunately was interrupted by the discovery that some of the notes (essential to the game) had somehow disappeared into thin air. But the prizes were handed out and all ended happily.

Judith must have been Val's girlfriend; for quite some time Val kept a black and white photo of Judith on his night table, with Judith in a bathing suit striking an almost "pin-up" pose that made her look very attractive.

A letter in German from Dr. Anne Marie Kulka, 112 East 81st Street, New York (presumably the same A. M. Kulka who sent the letter shown on page 282) dated Aug 1 but postmarked Aug 2, in translation reads;

Dear Wertheimers,
Many thanks for the most recent number of the Wertheimer Papers. I read it again with great pleasure and interest. How are you all? I always plan to come to New Rochelle but unfortunately nothing ever comes of it. It is now awful in the city, so that I won't be able to visit you soon. All the best and most pleasant to the whole family."

An otherwise empty envelope postmarked August 20 contained a note saying "with kind regards from Mrs. K. Friedrichs," and a loose slip of paper has Ann Ruth Maslow's address on one side and Theresa Wood's on the obverse (who Theresa Wood was is unknown).

An envelope addressed to "Master Michael Wertheimer, 10 the Circle, New Rochelle, N.Y." from "Alice Levy, c/o CAMP MADISON, MADISON, CONNECTICUT" postmarked August 28

B-26 Kurt and Nellie Friedrichs *(from https://opc.mfo.de/detail? photo id=1243)*

reached its intended destination despite the slightly erroneous address. Alice's letter, on Camp Madison letterhead, reads:

Dear Editor,

I am sending you herewith the camp-paper of Camp Madison.—I hope you enjoy reading it, and if possible I will forward to you an August edition. I plan to go back Aug 31st and of course one of my first visits will be too [sic] New Rochelle,

Herzlichst [most heartily]

Alice Levy

Enclosed with this letter was a four-page carbon copy of "*The Madison Reporter*, Volume 9, No. 1, June 25, 1939," the contents of which suggest that Camp Madison may have been a year-round children's day camp.

A loose letter on the letterhead of "Dr. Ruth Nanda Anshen, 205 West 57th Street, New York   City" is dated September 30, 1939:

B-27 Ruth Nanda Anshen *(from https://www.newspapers.com/ image/149087262)*

Dearest Mikey,

As one editor to another, I hope you will accept my very favorable criticism of the editorial work and policy of The Wertheimer Times. The material which you have selected for publication, the excellent observations of your contributors and assistants are all highly commendable; and I therefore, beg you to permit me the honor of endowing your publication with one dollar now and then, first in order to assure my subscription, since no doubt the great demand on the part of your readers makes it sometimes difficult for you to have your supply equal to the demand, and secondly because I firmly believe that so splendid an enterprise should be endowed. So please accept this humble offering. We all send our dearest love to your collaborators, Valy and Lise, and to your dear parents, too.

Faithfully,

Nanda

Another letter postmarked September 20 addressed to "Mrs. + Mike Wertheimer" contains three sheets. One says :

Dear Mike,

I am sending you an article for your paper. I hope you like it. There are not many things happening just yet and I hope the next one will be more interesting. Hoping you have a wonderful year at Fieldston.

> Love,
> Judith [Brodsky]

The other two sheets contain the following, written cursively in ink:

> New York seems pretty quiet, considering all the commotion that is going on in Europe. It is under the general feeling of school. In the morning children are rushing to catch buses with books under their arms. And in the afternoon they are seen in different groups walking leisurely home. At the corner of 58th Street and Broadway a building is being constructed which is very disturbing to the Brodsky family which will not only, when finished, will [sic] eclipse the view but also the peace of mind while in preparation of being finished. For the past three days, the Coca Cola sign which forcasts [sic] the weather has been incorrect, as most predictions are, of the weather, and politics.

> To the editor,
> When the sky turns Brown—and the moon turns blue, and Hilter [sic] turns a democratic painter. I'll let you know,
> > Sincerely
> > Judith Brodsky

Yet another empty envelope postmarked Sept. 20, 1939, 9 PM from Dr. Ruth Nanda Ashen may have been the one in which she had sent her letter and a one dollar bill. An undated sheet had "HAPPY BIRTHDAY LISE!" in large inked capital letters across typed text for "THE LIFE OF BICY ICE," with the full text interrupted occasionally by small colored sketches of an ice truck, a house, a bottle, a human profile, a ship, and a box labeled "Camembert's." At the bottom of the sheet was "THE END" and a "GOOD LUCK" ring in capital colored letters; the ring surrounded a center circle that said "ON YOUR BIRTHDAY." The rest of the story of Bicy Ice, the first part of which had already been published in *The Wertheimer Times*, reads as follows:

> All this shoving and pushing started a conversation among the three. Bicy was asked to tell his life, and told his short story. Then the bottle was asked to tell his story. "Well, I was born in a bottle factory and was then transported to Italy. There an old man put this delicious wine into me. Then I was brought over here, to the U.S., on a big ship and then was bought and then put in here," said the bottle. The cheese's story

was altogether different. "I was born in a dairy farm. There I was made into cheese out of butter, brought to the store, was bought, and put into this icebox." All this time Bicy had been melting, and now was only half of his original size, and when he awoke next morning he was only ½ in. by ½ in. by 1 in. He knew very much more than he had known when he was born, thanks to his good friends, the bottle and the cheese. Then he melted into water. "Goodbye" was his last word.

An envelope postmarked Oct 24 from Friedrichs was empty. But another one, postmarked Cold Spring Harbor, N.Y. October 25, 1939 ,4 PM, contained a typed letter dated October 24, with the signature and postscript in pencil:

Dear Michael:
It is a very nice issue of your newspaper which arrived today. I believe there are at least three issue [sic] for which I have not paid, so I am sending 15 cents in stamps, and cordial thanks of a loyal subscriber!
                                    Yours sincerely,
                                    Barbara Burks.
Congratulations to Lise on her prize!

It is not clear what prize is referred to here.

Yet another ornate long thin envelope postmarked Oct 30, 1939 contains a very thin sheet of rice paper with "KURT STEPHEN SAFRANKSI" printed in red at its top. Dated the day before, it reads, in elegantly lettered ink:

Dear Sir,
I refer to your offer in the last 'Wertheimer Times' (by the way, an excellent issue again!) and should like to have portraits of VALENTIN, MICHAEL, LISE, and PETER Wertheimer. Please enclose your bill for prompt remittance.
                                    Yours sincerely,
                                    K.S. Safranski
How are the rabbits?"

A second copy of Vol. I No. 3 and of the first page of Vol. II No. 2 were also in the box, as well as one typed page of "PART TWO: THE TASK," subheaded "Chapter five: THE SNOWSTORM," a fanciful obscure story that contains attempts at dialect-style conversation.

There were two more items were in the box, though it is not clear why; they appear to be unrelated to *The Wertheimer Times*. The first, dated Jan 3, 1940, is

B-28 Willys Peck Kent ("Uncle Willys") *(from https://www.newspapers.com/image/85418319)*

from Willys Peck Kent, 6120 Fieldston Road, New York City. Kent taught shop at Fieldston School, which Val and Michael were attending; he was also the director of the Ethical Culture School Camp near Cooperstown, NY, which all the Wertheimer children attended for two months each for several summers. Written on the envelope in pencil in Michael's handwriting are several lines of imperfect French; Michael must have been studying French by this time at Fieldston. Kent's letter, dated "Jan. 1, 1940" was:

> Dear Mike,
> Happy new year and thanks for the calendar. If I get my dates mixed and come to school on Saturday or Sunday instead of Mon. + Tuesday, you can tell all the kids that anyhow it is not your fault.
> Have you made any New Year's resolutions? I have made one. I am determined for the period of 12 months to write 1940 instead of 1939 but I fear I shall not always succeed.
> Do you know Ernest Lopez of the second form? I hear that he was very severely injured in an accident down south somewhere. See you before many days.
> Sincerely,
Uncle Willys.
> My best to your family.

At the summer camp, the director and his wife were known by the campers as "Uncle Willys" and "Aunt Roxie"; and there's no evidence that Ernest Lopez was someone Michael knew.

The last item in the box, postmarked May 22, 1940, was addressed in Max Wertheimer's handwriting to "Mr. Michael Wertheimer, Hudson Guild Farm, Andover, New Jersey," and contained two sheets, one a letter from Max with a note from Anni, the other a letter from Lise. Max's letter, in German, read,

> Dear Michel,
> I think a lot about you and hope that things are going cheerfully and strongly for you, and that you are having really beautiful days there!!
> And I would like to know how your days look—from early morning until evening! + whether everything is good. And would like to have such

a letter from you, but of course you shouldn't use a lot of time for it but write me briefly the [in English:] "essentials and highlights." And however much I'm pleased that you are there in such a nice area, I am looking forward to your being here again and that we'll all be together.

Have a great time!!
—Paps.

Upside down at the top of the letter is" "Today I wrote Poniz a letter, but one can only read it if one can spell in German. Here it is: XND DN ZL DN HB XO GM8 4 Poniz. Can you read it??" Read as German letters and a numeral, this become "Ich sende Dir einen Zettel, den habe ich so gemacht für Poniz" or "I send you a sheet; I made it this way for Ponitz."

In German, in Anni's handwriting, on the obverse of this sheet is "Many greetings and a kiss from Mama. Have a very nice time! Val and Rosa and Peter also greet you heartily!"

Lise's letter is written in clear cursive pencil:

Dear Mike,
How are you? I am missing you. Are you having a nice time at the Hudson Guild? I hope you are. You are lucky that you don't have to go to school. We aren't so lucky. But school isn't so bad. We saw a movie there today on Alexander Hamilton. It was very good. Our Father's Night has been changed to June 7, so maybe you can come. Today Papa drove to school to get me. In the afternoon Anni did, and we drove to Beckwith Beach. Things have been made there. One of these was something looking like a <u>large</u> scow turned upsidedown. We wondered whether it was a boat or a float. Then we drove to Davenport Park and watched branches being sawed off. So we had some fun, even though you weren't there, but I hope you come home soon anyway. Then it will be still better.
Good-bye and good luck from

Your loving sister
Lise

What and where Beckwith Beach or Davenport Park were, what Hudson Guild Farm was, and why Michael was there, all remain obscure.

Apparently someone assumed some time decades ago that all these items were sufficiently worth saving to put them into that box. They do provide some details about everyday life in the Wertheimer household during a period of intense international turmoil: Adolf Hitler was using immense military might to expand his Third Reich and establish what was to be called the Holocaust, leading soon to the Second World War. While political topics were indeed discussed with other current events around the typical dinner table at 12 The Circle, such major international doings had not yet entered the awareness of the Editor of *The Wertheimer Times* sufficiently to make them worth mentioning in its pages. He was still living in the comfortable, safe, secure, warm home of his childhood.

Appendix C: Val's Autobiography

Ellen Wertheimer, Val's daughter, recently discovered an autobiography of her father written in 1937, presumably as a school exercise. Ellen comments, "I think it's pretty amazing on many levels." Clearly after only a few years in this country, Val's command of English was already remarkable. As she notes, "Hearing him speak to us from 1937 is truly incredible." Val was only 11 or 12 years old when he wrote this account, which is reproduced here in his own original handwriting.

While in several ways it parallels the kinds of things mentioned or hinted at in Appendix B: *The Wertheimer Times*, or in the early narrative of this book, it presents in a characteristic fashion the somewhat more mature perspective on the family's early years by my late older brother.

© Springer Fachmedien Wiesbaden GmbH, part of Springer Nature 2020
M. Wertheimer, *Facets of an Academic's Life*,
https://doi.org/10.1007/978-3-658-28770-2

Contents

Chapter I – How my parents, brothers, sister and I came to be.

Chapter II – My life in Germany.

Chapter III – My two school vacations.

Chapter IV – My trip from Marienbad to Cherbourg.

Chapter V – My Atlantic crossing.

Chapter VI – My life in the United States.

Chapter – VII – My Hobbies

Chapter VIII – My ideas about America.

Chapter I

How my parents, brothers, sister,
and I came to be.

I was born in Berlin on
May 12, 1925. I am the oldest
of us children. They are Michael
who was born March 20, 1927,
Lise, my sister who was born
October 12, 1928, and lastly my
baby brother Peter, who was
born October 28, 1936. My little
brother is a very lively baby,
full of play.

My father who is a professor
of psychology was born on
April 15, 1880 in Prague. My
mother, was born on June 16,
1901. She was born in Landsberg

Un der Warte. All this makes a
big family, doesn't it?

Chapter II
My life in Germany.

In Germany, I often visited the Frankfurt airport, the airport of the city where I lived. Also very close was the Taunus Mountain Range where it was very interesting to climb. In the Taunus also was an old fortress of the Middle Ages which was a meuseum which we often visited. When I was six years old I started school. I didn't like those German Schools because they were too strict and you did not have enough liberty. School was every day except Sunday.

I went to school by trolley. It was pretty hard to always get the right trolley and get off in the right places.

So I went to that school two whole years. I always went away in my vacations but that is in the next chapter.

Chapter III.
My two school vacations.

The first one of my vacations
was spent in Switzerland. We
went there by train through the
St. Gotthart tunnel which is the
second largest tunnel in the world.
When we arrived we settled
into a stone cottage. That
was our base of operations.
The town where we lived
was called Ascona which was
bordering Locarno. The town
also had a shore on Lago
Maggiore. (Lake Maggiore).
That was a wonderful lake
to go swimming so we often
went. We also did some boating.

It was a very nice vacation
    One day I took a ride
with my mother and a friend
to a base of a mountain. The
name of the mountain was Mt.
Tamaro and the height was
1967 meters ~ (6556⅔ feet high.
We started at morning and were
back at night. The time from
the bottom to the tip took us
~~exactly~~ 4½ hrs. The ~~few~~ journey
down took only 4 hrs. It was
very nice on the tip so we
took a nap on top. Then we
returned home.
    At the end of my second
school-year we went to
Czechoslovakia never to return
home to Germany ~~because~~ It

Chapter III (continued)
started out to be a vacation
and then we did not like
the government because it had
changed and the government
did not like us.
    And now back to what
I did during the vacation.
There we lived in a house
called the "Golden Hark".
Almost all the houses have
a name in Czechoslovakia
instead of street and number.
We lived close to a few long
paths where we made many
bicycle outings. We also
went swimming there.
The name of that
town was Marienbad.

Somewhere during the vacation we went on a visit to Karlsbad. There we went to see one of the worlds foremost geysers the " Karlsbader Sprudel. It spouts 72 meters into the air at an unbearable temperature. The water is mixed with so many minerals that if you hold a branch or something into the sprudel it would be covered with stone, Then we went back to Marienbad.

Chapter IV

My trip from Marienbad
        to Cherbourg.

We stayed in Marienbad
till the late August and
then we took a train for
Praha (Prague). There we
got tickets for the sleeper car
all the way to Paris. The
train left by 7:30 P.M. By
the time we arrived in Paris
at 9:00 AM we had passed
through part of Czechoslovakia,
all of Austria, all of Sa Switzerland and part of France.
In Paris we went sight-
seeing to several meuseums.

The following day we went on top of the Eiffel Tower. The tower itself is 1000 ft high. The whole contraption sways in a moderate breeze about 6 feet at the top.

You could see all over Paris from on top. Then we went down, It took quite a while to get down because you changed elevator 4 times. They also went very slow.

Then we went by train to Cherbourg

Chapter II

My Atlantic crossing

As we arrived in
Cherbourg we went to
the harbor where we went
on a tender to take
us out to the "Majestic".
It was the largest steamer
in the world before the
"Queen Mary" and "Normandie"
were built. The "Majestic"
has a tonnage of 56,601
tons. The tender is there
because the harbor is too
shallow for the ocean liners
to come in.
When we arrived on board

we immediately went to
our cabins. I had an outside
cabin with my father. There
was a porthole through which
you could see. The next
morning after breakfast we
went on deck

There we looked at
the charts of the oceans
which are very interesting.
We also looked on a chart
which showed our daily progress.
The next days we lay out
on deck, played games and
ate three meals a day.

When we arrived in New
York City it was exactly
5½ days since we left Cherbourg.
The whole trip we had good weather.

Chapter VI

My life in the United
States of America.

When we arrived in
America we went to the
Holley Hotel. We stayed
there for one week. Then
we moved to Larchmont.
There we lived in the
Bevan Hotel for two weeks.
It is situated close to the
beach so we often went
swimming. Then we moved
to our present home in
New Rochelle.
    Then I started school.
The school I went to was

the Mayflower Elementary school. It is a very nice school.

Then I came to the Fieldston school which I am enjoying very much. My personal idea of the school is that it is very complete. I hope to have a grand time there.

Chapter VII

My Hobbies

Since I arrived in America
I built several hobbies one
of them being stamp collecting. Another very interesting
hobby of mine is automobile
collecting. I collect pictures
and booklets about automobiles.
Then I try to memorize
important facts about
the autos.

My favorite of all
now is following the pol-
itics about the different countries.
I read the New York Times
and also have very

exciting and interesting discussions with my father.

Chapter VIII

My ideas about America

I think that America is a very reasonable continent in compare with others.

The United States for instance. They are a progressive, sensible and easy to understand group of states compared to other countries like Japan and Germany.

When you go to school in America for one day and the next day go to a German school the diffrence is enormous. In the German it is much more bossy like. The teacher may boss you around and usually does it while in American schools you are at more of your freedom.

Appendix D: Curriculum Vitae

CURRICULUM VITAE: MICHAEL WERTHEIMER

Personal History

Born Berlin, Germany, March 20, 1927. Immigrated to U.S. September, 1933; naturalized U.S. citizen April, 1939.

Married to the former Nancy MacKaye, 1950; three children, born 1952, 1954, 1958; divorced January, 1965.

Married to the former Marilyn Schuman, September, 1970.

Children-in-law, grandchildren, grandchildren-in-law, and great-grandchildren.

Education

1933-1939	Public Schools of New Rochelle, NY, through seventh grade
1939-1944	High school: Fieldston School, Bronx, NY; class of 1944
1944-1947	Swarthmore College, BA (with high honors in psychology) 1947
1947-1949	The Johns Hopkins University, MA (psychology) 1949
1949-1951	Harvard University, PhD (experimental psychology) 1952
1951-1952	Worcester State Hospital, Worcester, MA, internship in clinical psychology

Professional History

1947-1949	Research & teaching assistant, The Johns Hopkins University and Institute for Cooperative Research
Spring 1949	Research assistant (full time, with S. E. Asch), Swarthmore College
1949-1951	Parker Fellow; teaching assistant and fellow; research assistant, Harvard University Psychology Department and Psycho-Acoustic Laboratory
1951-1952	Research psychologist, Worcester Foundation for Experimental Biology, Massachusetts
1952-1953	Instructor of psychology, Wesleyan University
1953-1955	Assistant professor of psychology, Wesleyan University

© Springer Fachmedien Wiesbaden GmbH, part of Springer Nature 2020
M. Wertheimer, *Facets of an Academic's Life*,
https://doi.org/10.1007/978-3-658-28770-2

1953-1955	Clinical consultant, Connecticut State Vocational Guidance Department and Long Lane School for Girls, Middletown, CT
Summers 1953-1955	Research psychologist, Rockland State Hospital, Orangeburg, NY
1955-1957	Assistant professor of psychology, University of Colorado
1956-1970	Research consultant, Denver Veterans Administration Hospital
1956-1970; 1971-1993	Director, Departmental Honors Program in Psychology, University of Colorado (Co-Director 1987-1993)
1957-1961	Associate professor of psychology, University of Colorado
Summers 1957-1958	Air Force Behavioral Science Conference, University of New Mexico
Summer 1958	American Psychological Association (APA)-National Science Foundation (NSF) Conference on Training for Research, Estes Park, Colorado
1958-1959	Principal Research Scientist (Psychology), Rockland State Hospital, Orangeburg, NY
1960-1961	Human factors consultant, The Martin Company, Denver, Colorado
1960-1966	Research consultant in psycholinguistics, German Department, University of Colorado
1960-1969	APA-NSF Visiting Scientist
1961-1993	Professor of psychology, University of Colorado
1963-1971	Editorial consultant, *Contemporary Psychology*
1964-1983	Member (Chair, 1979-1981), Examination Committee, American Association of State Psychology Boards
1965-1966	President, Division 2 (Teaching of Psychology), APA
1965-2006	Member, Board of Advisors, Archives of the History of American Psychology, University of Akron, Akron, OH
Summer 1966	Visiting professor, University of Hawaii
1966-1969	Representative to APA Council from Division 26 (History of Psychology)
Summer 1968	Instructor, International Seminar on Learning and the Educational Process, Stockholm, Sweden

1968-1970	Member (Chair 1969-1970), APA Committee on Precollege Psychology
1968-1971	Board Member, Consortium of Professional Associations in the Continuum of Teacher Education (CONPASS)
1970-1971	Acting Administrative Officer for Educational Affairs, APA Central Office, Washington, DC
1970-1971	National Consultant, Program on the Preparation of Social Science Teachers, Illinois State University, Bloomington, IL
1971-1974	Member-at-Large of the Executive Committee, Division 24 (Philosophical Psychology), APA
1972-1975	Associate Director (half-time), Center for Education in the Social Sciences, University of Colorado
1972-1975	Secretary-Treasurer, Division 24 (Philosophical Psychology), APA
1972-1993	Member, Social Science Education Consortium
1973-1975	Member (Chair, 1974-75), Education and Training Board, APA
1973-1979	President, Alpha of Colorado, Phi Beta Kappa
1973-1979	Rocky Mountain Regional Vice President, Psi Chi
1974	Chair, Review Committee, Cheiron (International Society for the History of the Behavioral and Social Sciences)
1975-1976	President, Division 1 (General Psychology), APA
1975-1977	Representative to APA Council from Division 24 (Philosophical Psychology)
1975-1978	Member, Ad Hoc Panel on Accreditation Guidelines, APA
1976-1977	President, Division 24 (Philosophical Psychology), APA
1976-1978	Member, Publications and Communications Board, APA
1976-1978	Chair, Research and Development Committee, Publications and Communications Board, APA
1976-1978	Chair, Committee on Psychology in Secondary Schools, APA
1976-1979	Member (Chair, 1977-1978), Committee on Undergraduate Education, APA
1977	Local host, Cheiron (International Society for the History of the Behavioral and Social Sciences)

1977-1978	President, Division 26 (History of Psychology), APA
1977-1978	Chair, Committee on Celebration of the Centennial of the Founding of the First Experimental Psychology Laboratories, APA
1978-1979	Co-chair, Ad Hoc Committee on APA Archives
1978-1980	Member-at-Large of the Executive Committee, Division 24 (Philosophical Psychology), APA
1978-1980	Member, Committee on Celebration of the Centenary of the Founding of Experimental Psychology Laboratories, APA
1978-1983	Member, Advisory Committee on Obituaries in the *American Psychologist*, APA
1979-1983	Member, Examination Policy Committee, American Association of State Psychology Boards
1979-1983	National historian, Psi Chi
1980-	Member, Editorial Board, *Gestalt Theory*
1981	Recipient, award for the best paper in the humanities published in 1980 by a member of the University of Colorado faculty
1981	Member, APA Accreditation Appeal Panel
1981-1982	President, Rocky Mountain Psychological Association
1981-1982	Co-chair, Public Interest Coalition, APA Council of Representatives
1981-1983	Representative to APA Council from Division 24 (Philosophical Psychology)
1981-	Member, Editorial Board, *Zeitschrift für Psychologie*
1982-1983	Chair, Psi Chi/APA Edwin B. Newman Award Committee
1983	Chair, Forum A (academic/research forum), APA Council of Representatives
1983	Member, APA Accreditation Appeal Panel
1983	G. Stanley Hall Lecturer, APA
1983	Recipient, Distinguished Teaching in Psychology Award, American Psychological Foundation
1983-1986	Member-at-Large of the Executive Committee, Division 1 (General Psychology), APA

1983-1986	Member, Fellows Committee, Division 1 (General Psychology), APA
1983-1987	Member, Committee on the History of Psychology in the Rocky Mountain Region, of the Rocky Mountain Psychological Association
1984-1985	President, Division 24 (Theoretical and Philosophical Psychology), APA
1984-1986	Member, Fellows Committee, Division 2 (Teaching of Psychology), APA
1984-1987	Member (Chair 1985-1986), Committee on International Relations in Psychology, APA
1984-1993	Member, Editorial Board, *Computers in Human Behavior*
1985 (Oct)	Member, Delegation of Librarians invited by the Government of the People's Republic of China to visit a dozen libraries in mainland China
1985-1988	Member, Fellows Committee, Division 26 (History of Psychology), APA
1986-1987	Chair, Fellows Committee, Division 2 (Teaching of Psychology), APA
1986-1987	Member, Steering Committee for a Task Force on Deviancy, APA
1986-1988	Representative to APA Council from Division 1 (General Psychology)
1986-1989	Member, Advisory Board for a psychology telecourse, WGBH/Annenberg Foundation, Boston
1986-1993	Archivist, Rocky Mountain Psychological Association
1987	Participant, APA National Conference on Graduate Education in Psychology, Salt Lake City, UT, June 13-19
1987	Recipient, Fifth Annual Faculty Advising Award, College of Arts and Sciences, University of Colorado
1987-1994	Member, Editorial Board, *Philosophical Psychology*
1987-1995	Consulting Editor, *Professional Psychology: Research and Practice*, APA

1988	Recipient, Distinguished Service Award, Rocky Mountain Psychological Association
1988	Substitute Recipient, Wilhelm Wundt Medal, awarded posthumously to Max Wertheimer, Deutsche Gesellschaft für Psychologie
1988	Historian, Division 1 (General Psychology), APA
1989-1990	National president-elect, Psi Chi
1990-1991	National president, Psi Chi
1990	Recipient, Gender Neutral Language Award, Campus Women's Organization, University of Colorado at Boulder
1990	Recipient, Distinguished Career Contributions to Education and Training in Psychology Award, APA
1990-1993	Member-at-Large, Executive Committee, Division 1 (General Psychology), APA
1990-1996	Member, Membership Committee, APA
1991-1992	National past president, Psi Chi
1992	Recipient, Award for Exceptional Service to Division 1 (General Psychology), APA
1993	Recipient, Excellence in Service Award, University of Colorado
1993-	Professor emeritus of psychology, University of Colorado
1994 (Jan)	Participant, National Conference on Postdoctoral Education and Training in Psychology, APA, Norman, OK
1994 (April)	Recipient, Award for Outstanding Service to the RMPA and to Psychology, Rocky Mountain Psychological Association
1994-1996	Representative to APA Council from Division 26 (History of Psychology)
1994-1996	Member of the Executive Committee, Division 26 (History of Psychology), APA
1995-1998	Member, Community Advisory Board, Department of Psychology, Metropolitan State College, Denver, CO
1996-1997	Representative to APA Council from a coalition of Divisions 24 (Theoretical and Philosophical Psychology) and 26 (History of Psychology)

1996-1997	Member, Working Group on the Development of American Psychology, APA Council of Representatives
1996-1998	Liaison to Membership Committee, APA
1996-1999	Member, doctoral committee for W.D. Woody, Colorado State University, Ft. Collins, CO
1996-2000	Member, Advisory Committee on Obituaries in the *American Psychologist*, APA
1997-1999	Representative to APA Council from Division 26 (History of Psychology)
1998	Consultant, Ad hoc committee to consider renaming Porteus Hall, University of Hawaii
1998-2000	Member-at-large of the Executive Committee, Division 1 (General Psychology), APA
1998-2001	Member, Committee on the Structure and Function of Council, APA
1999	Recipient, first Award for Distinguished Service to Division 24 (Theoretical and Philosophical Psychology), APA
1999-2001	Member, Riverside Publishing Co. Bender—Gestalt Advisory Panel
1999-2002	Member, History Oversight Committee, APA
2000	Recipient, Lifetime Achievement Award for Sustained, Outstanding, and Unusual Contributions to the History of Psychology, Division 26, APA
2000 (Aug.)	Representative to APA Council from Division 24 (Theoretical and Philosophical Psychology)
2000-2006	Secretary, Division 1 (General Psychology), APA
2003-2006	Representative to APA Council from Division 1 (General Psychology)
2005	Recipient, C. Alan Boneau Award for "Extended Distinguished Service to The Society for General Psychology, Division 1, APA"
2006	Recipient, Psi Chi Distinguished Member Designation, for "Outstanding Contributions to the Field of Psychology and for De-

voted and Conscientious Efforts toward Achieving the Purpose of Psi Chi"
2006 Recipient, "Recognition Award for truly extraordinary service as officer and Secretary-extraordinaire of this Society in its mission to advance psychology across specialty areas," Division 1 (General Psychology), APA
2007-2009 Member-at-Large, Board of Directors, APA
2009 Recipient, "Award for Distinguished Contributions to Theoretical and Philosophical Psychology," Division 24, APA
2010-2012 Member, Policy and Planning Board, APA

Memberships in Societies

1947- Phi Beta Kappa
1949-1960 The Society of the Sigma Xi
1949-1955 Eastern Psychological Association
1951- American Psychological Association (Fellow, 1966)
1952-2005 American Association of University Professors
1955-1993 Rocky Mountain Psychological Association
1955-1967 Colorado Psychological Association
1960-2010 Psychonomic Society
1969-2010 Cheiron (International Society for the History of the Behavioral and Social Sciences)
1970-1990 Social Science Education Consortium
1973- Psi Chi
1986- Golden Key (Honorary Member)
1989- American Psychological Society (Charter Fellow)

Publications: Books

Beardslee, D. C. and Wertheimer, M. (Eds.) (1958). *Readings in perception.* Princeton, NJ: Van Nostrand.

Wertheimer, M. (Ed.) (1959). *Productive thinking*, by Max Wertheimer (enlarged edition). New York: Harper.

Gruber, H. E., Terrell, G., and Wertheimer, M. (Eds.) (1962). *Contemporary approaches to creative thinking.* New York: Atherton.

Scott, W. A. and Wertheimer, M. (1962). *Introduction to psychological research.* New York: Wiley.

Scherer, G. A. C. and Wertheimer, M. (1964). *A psycholinguistic experiment in foreign language teaching.* New York: McGraw-Hill.

Wertheimer, M. (Ed.) (1965). *Il pensiero produttivo.* An Italian translation by Massimo Giacometti and Rosetta Bolletti of *Productive thinking* by Max Wertheimer, 1959. Firenze, Italy: Editrice Universitaria.

von Fieandt, K. (1966). *The world of perception.* (An English adaptation, by the author, of his *Havaitsemisen Maailma*, with the consultation of M. Wertheimer). Homewood, IL: Dorsey.

Wertheimer, M. (1970). *A brief history of psychology.* New York: Holt, Rinehart, and Winston.

Wertheimer, M. (Ed.) (1970). *Confrontation: Psychology and the problems of today.* Glenview, IL: Scott, Foresman.

Wertheimer, M., Björkman, M., Lundberg, I. and Magnusson, D. (1971). *Psychology: A brief introduction.* Glenview, IL: Scott, Foresman. (translation by M. Wertheimer of original Swedish text)

Wertheimer, M. (1971). *Kurze Geschichte der Psychologie.* A German translation by Elisabeth and Wolfgang Schmidbauer of *A brief history of psychology*, 1970. Munich: Piper.

Wertheimer, M. (1972). *Fundamental issues in psychology.* New York: Holt, Rinehart, and Winston.

Wertheimer, M. (1972). [*A brief history of psychology*]. A Japanese translation of *A brief history of psychology*, 1970. Tokyo: Seishin Shobo.

Bauer, M. and Wertheimer, M. (1972). *Study guide to accompany Psychology: A brief introduction.* Glenview, IL: Scott, Foresman.

Wertheimer, M. and Holmstrom, M. (1972). *Instructor's resource book for Psychology: A brief introduction.* Glenview, IL: Scott, Foresman.

Wertheimer, M. (1972). *Pequena história da psicologia.* A Portuguese translation by Lolio Lourenco de Oliveira of *A brief history of psychology*, 1970.

São Paulo, Brazil: Companhia Editora Nacional, Editora da Universidade de São Paulo.

Mussen, P., Rosenzweig, M. R., Aronson, E., Elkind, D., Feshbach, S., Geiwitz, J., Glickman, S. E., Murdock, B. B. and Wertheimer, M. (1973). *Psychology: An introduction.* Lexington, MA: Heath.

Mussen, P., Rosenzweig, M. R., Aronson, E., Elkind, D., Feshbach, S., Glickman, S. E., Murdock, B. B. and Wertheimer, M. (Eds.) (1974). *Concepts in psychology.* Lexington, MA: Heath.

Kasschau, R. A. and Wertheimer, M. (1974). *Teaching psychology in secondary schools.* Washington, D C: American Psychological Association and Boulder, CO: ERIC Clearinghouse for Social Science Education.

Wertheimer, M. (1975). *Introduction to psychology.* Module A-l of Wayne H. Holtzman (Ed.), *Personalized psychology.* New York: Harpers College Press.

MacLeod, R. B. (1975). *The persistent problems of psychology.* Pittsburgh: Duquesne University Press. (Wertheimer co-authored the preface with Mary Henle, and edited the book and saw it through the press.)

Wertheimer, M. (1977). *Introduction to psychology.* Reissue of 1975 booklet. Westwood, MA: The PaperBook Press.

Wertheimer, M. (1977). *Beknopte geschiedenis van de psychologie.* A Dutch translation by Rob Uiterwijk of *A brief history of psychology*, 1970. Baarn, The Netherlands: Het Wereldvenster.

Mussen, P., Rosenzweig, M. R., Aronson, E., Elkind, D., Feshbach, S., Geiwitz, J., Glickman, S. E., Murdock, B. B., Wertheimer, M. and Harvey, L. O. (1977). *Psychology: An introduction*, 2nd ed. Lexington, MA: Heath.

Wertheimer, M. and Rappoport, L. (Eds.) (1978). *Psychology and the problems of today.* Glenview, IL: Scott, Foresman.

Wertheimer, M. (Ed.) (1978). *Productive thinking*, by Max Wertheimer (enlarged edition). Reissue of 1959 book. Westport, CT: Greenwood Press.

Holtzman, W. H., Cooper, R. G., Forgus, R. H., Harris, C. W., Iscoe, I., Kozlawski, L. T., Spence, D. T., Stephan, C., Stephan, W., Wertheimer, M., Willerman, L. and Young, R. K. (1978). *Introduction to psychology.* New York: Harper and Row.

Wertheimer, M. (1978). *Pequena história da psicologia*. Reissue of 1972 book. São Paulo, Brazil: Companhia Editora Nacional.

Johnson, M. and Wertheimer, M. (Eds.) (1979). *Psychology teacher's resource book: First course*. Washington, DC: American Psychological Association.

Viney, W., Wertheimer, M. and Wertheimer, M. L. (1979). *History of psychology: A guide to information sources*. Detroit, MI: Gale.

Wertheimer, M. (1979). *A brief history of psychology*, rev. ed. New York: Holt, Rinehart, and Winston.

Mussen, P., Rosenzweig, M. R., Blumenthal, A. L., Aronson, E., Elkind, D., Feshbach, S., Geiwitz, J., Glickman, S. E., Harvey, L. O., Murdock, B. B. and Wertheimer, M. (1979). *Psychology: An introduction*, brief ed. Lexington, MA: Heath.

Scott, W. A. and Wertheimer, M. (1981). *Introducción a la investigación en psicología*. A Spanish translation by Pedro Rivera Ramirez and Juan Manuel Beltran V. of *Introduction to psychological research*, 1962. Mexico City: Editorial el Manual Moderno.

Wertheimer, M. (Ed.) (1982). *Productive thinking*, by Max Wertheimer, enlarged ed., Phoenix ed. Reissue, with a new preface, of 1959 book. Chicago: University of Chicago Press.

Eckardt, G. and Sprung, L. (Eds.) and Sinha, D., Tutundjian, M. H. and Wertheimer, M. (Co-eds.) (1983). *Advances in historiography of psychology*. Berlin, East Germany: VEB Deutscher Verlag der Wissenschaften.

Wertheimer, M. (1983). *Breve storia della psicologia*. An Italian translation by Monica Morganti of *A brief history of psychology*, 1970. Bologna: Zanichelli.

Corsini, R. J. (Ed.) (1984). *Encyclopedia of psychology*, four volumes. New York: Wiley. (Wertheimer is listed as an associate editor.)

Webb, W. H., Wertheimer, M., et al. (1986). *Sources of information in the social sciences: A guide to the literature*, 3rd ed. Chicago and London: American Library Association.

Wertheimer, M. (1987). *A brief history of psychology*, 3rd ed. New York: Holt, Rinehart, and Winston.

Corsini, R. J. (Ed.) (1987). *Concise encyclopedia of psychology*. New York: Wiley. (Wertheimer is listed as an associate editor.)

Bartlett, N. R., Spilka, B. and Wertheimer, M. (Eds.) (1988). *History of psychology in the Rocky Mountain Region*. Special issue of *Journal of the History of the Behavioral Sciences*, 24, No. 1.

Kimble, G. A., Wertheimer, M. and White, C. (Eds.) (1991). *Portraits of pioneers in psychology*. Mahwah, NJ: Erlbaum and Washington, DC: American Psychological Association.

Pate, J. L. and Wertheimer, M. (Eds.) (1993). *No small part: A history of regional organizations in psychology*. Washington, DC: American Psychological Association.

Kimble, G. A., Boneau, C. A. and Wertheimer, M. (Eds.) (1996). *Portraits of pioneers in psychology, Vol. 2*. Mahwah, NJ: Erlbaum and Washington, DC: American Psychological Association.

Corsini, R.J. and Auerbach, A.J. (1996). *Concise encyclopedia of psychology*, 2nd ed. New York: Wiley. (Wertheimer is listed as an associate editor.)

Kimble, G.A. and Wertheimer, M. (Eds.) (1998). *Portraits of pioneers in psychology*, Vol. 3. Mahwah, NJ: Erlbaum and Washington, DC: American Psychological Association.

Corsini, R.J. (Ed.) (1999). *Dictionary of psychology*. Philadelphia: Brunner/Mazel. (Wertheimer is listed as a consulting editor and prepared many entries.)

Wertheimer, M. (2000). *A brief history of psychology*, 4th ed. Fort Worth, TX: Harcourt.

Davis, S.F. and Wertheimer, M. (2000). *An oral history of Psi Chi, the national honor society in psychology*. Chattanooga, TN: Psi Chi.

Kimble, G.A. and Wertheimer, M. (Eds.) (2000). *Portraits of pioneers in psychology*, Vol. 4. Hillsdale, NJ: Erlbaum and Washington, DC: American Psychological Association.

Kimble, G.A. and Wertheimer, M. (Eds.) (2003). *Portraits of pioneers in psychology*, Vol. 5. Hillsdale, NJ: Erlbaum and Washington, DC: American Psychological Association.

King, D.B. and Wertheimer, M. (2005). *Max Wertheimer and Gestalt theory*. New Brunswick, NJ: Transaction Publishers of Rutgers University. Paperback (2007).

Benjamin, L.T., Jr., Dewsbury, D.A., and Wertheimer, M. (Eds.) (2006). *Portraits of pioneers in psychology*, Vol. 6. Hillsdale, NJ: Erlbaum and Washington, DC: American Psychological Association.

Metzger, W. (2006). *Laws of seeing.* Translated by L. Spillmann, S. Lehar, M. Stromeyer, and M. Wertheimer. Cambridge, MA: MIT Press.

Wertheimer, M. (2012). *A brief history of psychology*, 5th ed. New York: Psychology Press.

Pickren, W. E., Dewsbury, D. A., and Wertheimer, M. (Eds.) (2012). *Portraits of pioneers in developmental psychology.* (Vol. 7 in the series *Portraits of Pioneers in Psychology*). New York: Psychology Press.

Spillmann, L. (ed.) (2012). Max Wertheimer: *Perception of motion and figural organization.* Cambridge, MA: MIT Press. Translated by Wertheimer, M., et al.

Wertheimer, M. and Puente, A. (in preparation) *A brief history of psychology*, 6th ed. New York: Psychology Press.

Publications: Articles, notes, etc.

Garner, W. R. and Wertheimer, M. (1951). Some effects of interaural phase differences on the perception of pure tones. *Journal of the Acoustical Society of America*, 23, 664-667.

Wertheimer, M., (1951). Hebb and Senden on the role of learning in perception. *American Journal of Psychology*, 64, 133-137.

Wertheimer, M. (1952). A single-trial technique for measuring the threshold of pain by thermal radiation. *American Journal of Psychology*, 65, 297-298.

Wertheimer, M. and Ward, W. D. (1952). The influence of skin temperature upon the threshold of pain as evoked by thermal radiation: A confirmation. *Science*, 115, 499-500.

Wertheimer, M. (1953). Variability in audiometry. *National Hearing Aid Journal*, 6, (6), 4-5; (7), 10; (8), 9-10.

Wertheimer, M. (1953). An investigation of the "randomness" of threshold measurements. *Journal of Experimental Psychology*, 1953, 45, 294-303.

Wertheimer, M. (1953). On the supposed behavioral correlates of an "eye" content response on the Rorschach. *Journal of Consulting Psychology*, 17, 189-194.

Knapp, R. H., Greenbaum, J. J. and Wertheimer, M. (1953). Recent undergraduate origins of scholars in the behavioral sciences. *American Psychologist*, 8, 479-483.

Wertheimer, M. and Wertheimer, N. (1953). A metabolic interpretation of individual differences in figural aftereffects. *Psychological Review*, 61, 279-280.

Wertheimer, M. (1954). Can a trained subject judge his auditory sensitivity? *Quarterly Journal of Experimental Psychology*, 6, 21-22.

deCharms, R., Levy, J. and Wertheimer, M. (1954). A note on attempted evaluations of psychotherapy. *Journal of Clinical Psychology*, 10, 233-235.

Wertheimer, M. (1954). The differential satiability of schizophrenic and normal subjects: A test of a deduction from the theory of figural aftereffects. *Journal of General Psychology*, 51, 291-299.

Martin, S. B. and Wertheimer, M. (1954). A bibliography of recent work on the Wechsler-Bellevue. *Psychological Newsletter*, 6, 10-38.

Wertheimer, M. (1954). Constant errors in the measurement of figural aftereffects. *American Journal of Psychology*, 67, 543-546.

Wertheimer, M. (1955). The variability of auditory and visual absolute thresholds in time. *Journal of General Psychology*, 52, 111-147.

Wertheimer, N. and Wertheimer, M. (1955). Capillary structure: Its relation to psychiatric diagnosis and morphology. *Journal of Nervous and Mental Disease*, 122, 14-27.

Wertheimer, M. (1955). Techniques in teaching abnormal psychology. *American Psychologist*, 10, 826.

Wertheimer, M. (1955). Figural aftereffect as a measure of metabolic efficiency. *Journal of Personality*, 24, 56-73.

Wertheimer, M., Levine, H. and Wertheimer, N. (1955). The effect of experimentally induced changes in metabolism on perceptual measures of metabolic efficiency. *Perceptual and Motor Skills*, 5, 173-176.

Wertheimer, M. (1957). Perception and the Rorschach. *Journal of Projective Techniques*, 21, 209-216.

Dinnerstein, D. and Wertheimer, M. (1957). Some determinants of phenomenal overlapping. *American Journal of Psychology*, 70, 21-37.

Wertheimer, M. and Jackson, C. W., Jr. (1957). Figural aftereffects, "brain modifiability," and schizophrenia: A further study. *Journal of General Psychology*, 57, 45-54.

Selkin, J. and Wertheimer, M. (1957). Disappearance of the Müller-Lyer illusion under prolonged inspection. *Perceptual and Motor Skills*, 7, 265-266.

Wertheimer, M. and Aronson, E. (1958). Personality rigidity as measured by aniseikonic lenses and by figural aftereffects. *Journal of General Psychology*, 58, 41-49.

Wertheimer, M. (1958). The defense mechanisms that students report in their own behavior. *Journal of Genetic Psychology*, 92, 95-96.

Wertheimer, M. and Gillis, W. M. (1958). Satiation and the rate of lapse of verbal meaning. *Journal of General Psychology*, 59, 79-85.

Wertheimer, M. and Leventhal, C. M. (1958). "Permanent" satiation with kinesthetic figural aftereffects. *Journal of Experimental Psychology*, 55, 255-257.

Wertheimer, M. (1958). Influence of time distortion during practice on recall. *Perceptual and Motor Skills*, 8, 95-98.

Wertheimer, M., Groesbeck, B. and Gyr, J. (1958). How can we improve graduate education in psychology? *Psychological Reports*, 4, 23-28.

Wertheimer, M. (1958). The golden split. *Contemporary Psychology*, 3, 80.

Wertheimer, M. (1958). The relation between the sound of a word and its meaning. *American Journal of Psychology*, 71, 412-415.

Mathews, A. and Wertheimer, M. (1958). A "pure" measure of perceptual defense uncontaminated by response suppression. *Journal of Abnormal and Social Psychology*, 57, 373-376.

Mathews, T. and Wertheimer, M. (1958). An experimental test of the Köhler-Wallach and the Osgood-Heyer theories of figural aftereffects. *American Journal of Psychology*, 71, 611-612.

Wertheimer, M. (1959). Introducing graduate students to psychological research. *Psychological Reports*, 5, 181-183.

Wertheimer, M. and Crow, E. G. (1959). Relation between individual differences in figural aftereffects and in rate of lapse of meaning of words. *Perceptual and Motor Skills*, 9, 82.

Festinger, L., Garner, W. R., Hebb, D. O., Hunt, H. F., Lawrence, D. H., Osgood, C. E., Skinner, B. F., Taylor, D. W. and Wertheimer, M. (1959). Education for research in psychology. *American Psychologist*, 14, 167-179. (Report of the NSF Estes Park Conference)

Wertheimer, M. and Arena, A. J. (1959). Effect of exposure time on adaptation to disarranged hand-eye coordination. *Perceptual and Motor Skills*, 9, 159-164.

Soltz, D. F. and Wertheimer, M. (1959). The retention of "good" and "bad" figures. *American Journal of Psychology*, 7, 450-452.

Strassburger, F. and Wertheimer, M. (1959). The discrepancy hypothesis of affect and the association value of nonsense syllables. *Psychological Reports*, 5, 528.

Armstrong, R. G. and Wertheimer, M. (1959). Personality structure in alcoholism. *Psychological Newsletter*, 10, 341-349.

Weiss, P., Groesbeck, B. and Wertheimer, M. (1959). Achievement motivation, academic aptitude, and college grades. *Educational and Psychological Measurement*, 19, 663-666.

Wertheimer, M. (1960). Der Einfluss der Mikrostrukturwahrnehmung auf das Gelbphänomen: Eine experimentelle Untersuchung mit Beobachtungen zu einer möglichen "Helligkeitssättigung." [The influence of the perception of microstructure on the Gelb phenomenon: An experimental investigation with observations on a possible "satiation of brightness."] In *Festschrift für Wolfgang Metzger* and *Psychologische Beitrage*, 5, 273-282.

Wertheimer, M. (1960). Max Wertheimer (1880-1943). *Encyclopædia Britannica*, vol. 23, 514-515.

Wertheimer, M. (1960). Conceptions of chronological age as a function of chronological age. *Psychological Reports*, 7, 450.

Wertheimer, M. (1960). Values in person cognition. In Willner, D. (Ed.) *Decisions, values, and groups*. (Vol. 1), pp. 135-153. New York: Pergamon.

Wertheimer, M. (1960). Studies of some Gestalt qualities of words. In Weinhandl, F. (Ed.), *Gestalthaftes Sehen: Ergebnisse und Aufgaben der Morphologie. Zum hundertjährigen Geburtstag von Christian von Ehrenfels*, pp. 398-405. Darmstadt, Germany: Wissenschaftliche Buchgesellschaft.

Beach, L. R. and Wertheimer, M. (1961). A free response approach to the study of person cognition. *Journal of Abnormal and Social Psychology*, 62, 367-374.

Wertheimer, M. (1961). Psychomotor coordination of auditory and visual space at birth. *Science*, 134, 1692.

Wertheimer, M. (1962). Auditory-oculomotor reflexes at birth. *Science*, 135, 998-999.

Scherer, G. A. C. and Wertheimer, M. (1962). The German teaching experiment at the University of Colorado. *German Quarterly*, 35, 298-308.

Wertheimer, M. (1962). From the 1962 program chairman. *Teaching of Psychology Newsletter*, APA Div. 2, June, 18-19.

Wertheimer, M. (1962). Psychomotor coordination of auditory and visual space at birth. *American Journal of Clinical Hypnosis*, 4, 282.

Wertheimer, M., Lipton, J. M., Herring, F. H. and Greenhouse, A. H. (1963). Theoretical and clinical studies of perception: Figural aftereffects in brain-damaged, schizophrenic, and control subjects. *VA Newsletter for Research in Psychology*, 5, (May) 4-5.

King, W. L. and Wertheimer, M. (1963). Induced colors and colors produced by chromatic illumination may have similar physiological bases. *Perceptual and Motor Skills*, 17, 379-382.

Wertheimer, M. (1964). Gestalt psychology. *Encyclopædia Britannica*, vol. 10, 370-371.

Wertheimer, M. and King, W. L. (1964). Can an induced color produce an after-image? *Perceptual and Motor Skills*, 18, 696.

Bassett, L. G., Bronwell, A. H., Ferrell, J. K., Liebowitz, H., Picha, K. G., Quarles, L. R., Wert, C. A., Wertheimer, M. and Yates, W. R. (1964). Administration and funding. Chap. 3 in Krieth, F. and Allen, J. M. (Eds.), *Honors programs in engineering*, pp. 17-35. Boston: Allyn and Bacon.

Holland, M. K. and Wertheimer, M. (1964). Some physiognomic aspects of naming, or, maluma and takete revisited. *Perceptual and Motor Skills*, 19, 111-117.

Wertheimer, M. (1965). Relativity and Gestalt: A note on Albert Einstein and Max Wertheimer. *Journal of the History of the Behavioral Sciences*, 1, 86-87.

Wertheimer, M., Lipton, J. M., Herring, F. H., Greenhouse, A. H. and Means, J. R. (1965). A reexamination of kinesthetic figural aftereffects in the brain-injured. *Perceptual and Motor Skills*, 20, 518-520.

Cameron, P. and Wertheimer, M. (1965). Kinesthetic figural aftereffects are in the hands, not in phenomenal space. *Perceptual and Motor Skills*, 20, 1131-1132.

Minard, J. G., Wertheimer, M. and Bailey, D. E. (1965). Measurement and conditioning of perceptual defense, response bias, and emotionally biased recognition. *Journal of Personality and Social Psychology*, 2, 661-668.

Wertheimer, M. (1966). Presidential message. *Teaching of Psychology Newsletter*, APA Div. 2, 1, 1.

Wertheimer, M. (1966). The psychologist and the foreign-language teacher. *International Journal of American Linguistics*, 32, 63-74.

Kimmel, D. and Wertheimer, M. (1966). Handwriting analysis and the clinical assessment of personality: A correlational study. *Journal of Projective Techniques and Personality Assessment*, 30, 177-178.

Wertheimer, M. (1966). Discussion. In Jenkin, N. and Pollack, R. H. (Eds.), *Perceptual development: Its relation to theories of intelligence and cognition*, pp. 70-71, 73, 75, 79-80, 226. Chicago, IL: Institute for Juvenile Research.

Wertheimer, M. (1966). Teaching 1966 psychology in 1966. *Teaching of Psychology Newsletter*, APA Div. 2, post-convention issue, 3-5.

Davis, B. and Wertheimer, M. (1967). Some determinants of associations to French and English words. *Journal of Verbal Learning and Verbal Behavior*, 6, 574-581.

Wertheimer, M. (1967). The hot line (letter to the Board of the Colorado Psychological Association). *The Colorado Psychologist*, 1, #3, 8.

Wertheimer, M. and Herring, F. (1968). Individual differences in figural aftereffects: Some problems and potentials. *Journal of Psychology*, 68, 211-214.

Wertheimer, M. (1968). A case of "autostasis" or reverse autokinesis. *Perceptual and Motor Skills*, 26, 417-418.

Sheets, C. A. and Wertheimer, M. (1968). Effect of instructional set on kinesthetic figural aftereffects. *Journal of Experimental Psychology*, 77, 692-695.

Wertheimer, M. (1969). Personality ratings based on handwriting analysis and clinical judgment: A reply to Teut Wallner. *Journal of Projective Techniques and Personality Assessment*, 33, 94-96.

von Fieandt, K. and Wertheimer, M. (1969). Perception. In *Annual review of psychology*. Palo Alto, CA: Annual Reviews, 20, 159-192.

Wertheimer, M. (1969). Perceptual problems. In *Scientific study of unidentified flying objects*. (E. U. Condon, Scientific Director), pp. 559-567. New York: Bantam.

Wertheimer, M. (1969). A case of "autostasis" or reverse autokinesis. *Mental Health Digest*, 1, 24. Also reprinted in Sanford, F. H. and Wrightsman, L. S., Jr. (1970). *Psychology: A scientific study of man*, 3rd ed., pp. 331-332. Belmont, CA: Brooks/Cole.

Wertheimer, M. (1971). Why, what and how: Psychology taught in the public schools. *Illinois Psychologist*, Nov.-Dec., 17-19.

Wertheimer, M. (1972). Gestalt psychology. In *Encyclopædia Britannica*, Vol. 10, pp. 370-371. Chicago: Encyclopædia Britannica.

Wertheimer, M. (1972). Wertheimer, Max. In *Encyclopædia Britannica*, Vol. 23, p. 412. Chicago: Encyclopædia Britannica.

Wertheimer, M. (1973). Toward a phenomenological psycholinguistics of multilingualism. In Krech, D. (Ed.) *The MacLeod symposium*, pp. 69-82. Ithaca, NY: Department of Psychology, Cornell University.

Wertheimer, M. (1973). Brief biographical sketches of forty psychologists, in Wolman, B. B. (Ed.), *Dictionary of behavioral science*. New York: Van Nostrand.

Wertheimer, M. (1973). Robert Brodie MacLeod (1907-1972). *Journal of the History of the Behavioral Sciences*, 9, 287-299.

Wertheimer, M. (1973). High school psychology: Stepchild or offspring? *The Behavioral and Social Science Teacher, 1*, 6-13.

Wertheimer, M. (1974). What is philosophical psychology? *Philosophical Psychologist*, 8, (2, Spring), 2-4.

Wertheimer, M. (1974). The problem of perceptual structure. Chapter 5 in Carterette, E. C. and Friedman, M. P. (Eds.), *Handbook of perception*, Vol. 1, pp. 75-91. New York: Academic Press.

Wertheimer, M. (1975). Minutes of 1974 meetings. *Philosophical Psychologist*, 9, No. 1, 3-10.

Wertheimer, M. (1975). Toward a phenomenological psycholinguistics of multilingualism. *ERIC Clearinghouse on Languages and Linguistics*, Document ED 104115, 17 pp., microfiche.

Reade, W. K. and Wertheimer, M. (1976). A bias in the diagnosis of schizophrenia. *Journal of Consulting and Clinical Psychology*, 44, 878.

Wertheimer, M. (1976). President's message. *Philosophical Psychologist*, 10, No. 2, 1.

Wertheimer, M. (1977). Historical aspects of the psychology of language and cognition. In Rieber, R. W. and Salzinger, K. (Eds.), *The roots of American psychology: Historical influences and implications for the future*, pp. 317-320. New York: New York Academy of Sciences.

Wertheimer, M. (1977). A bright future for general psychology? *Division 1 Newsletter, Division of General Psychology*, American Psychological Association, Summer, No. 22, 1-2.

Wertheimer, M. (1977). Presidential message: A plea. *Newsletter of the Division of the History of Psychology*, American Psychological Association, Nov., 10, No. 1, 9-10.

Wertheimer, M. (1978). Humanistic psychology and the humane but tough-minded psychologist. *Philosophical Psychologist*, 12, No. 1, 5-22.

Wertheimer, M., Barclay, A. G., Cook, S. W., Kiesler, C. A., Koch, S., Riegel, K. F., Rorer, L. G., Senders, V. L., Smith, M. B. and Sperling, S. E. (1978). Psychology and the future. *American Psychologist*, 33, 631-647.

Wertheimer, M. (1978). Humanistic psychology and the humane but tough-minded psychologist. *American Psychologist*, 33, 739-745.

Popplestone, J. A. and Wertheimer, M. (1979). Report of the ad hoc committee on APA archives to the APA board of directors. *Newsletter of the Division of the History of Psychology*, American Psychological Association, Feb., 11, No. 2, 5-8.

Wertheimer, M. (1979). The examination committee of the American Association of State Psychology Boards. *AASPB Newsletter*, March, 15, No. 1, 60-61.

Wertheimer, M. (1979). Dreams and reality about master's-level clinical psychologists. *Professional Psychology*, 10, 135-136.

Wertheimer, M. (1979). AASPB regional workshop at CPA convention generates recommendation for action. *AASPB Newsletter*, August 15, No. 2, 39-41.

Wertheimer, M. (1980). Gestalt theory of learning. In Gazda, G. M. and Corsini, R. J. (Eds.), *Theories of learning: A comparative approach*, pp. 208-251. Itasca, IL: Peacock.

Wertheimer, M. and Meserow, S. (1980). Did Piaget work with Binet? A note. *Journal of the History of the Behavioral Sciences, 16*, 280.

Wertheimer, M. (1980). Max Wertheimer, Gestalt prophet. *Gestalt Theory* (Darmstadt, West Germany: Steinkopff), 2, 3-17.

Wertheimer, M. (1980). Historical research--Why? In Brozek, J. and Pongratz, L. J. (Eds.), *Historiography of modern psychology: Aims, resources, approaches*, pp. 3-23. Toronto, Canada: C. J. Hogrefe.

Wertheimer, M. (1981). Memory and forgetting. In Benjamin, L. T. and Lowman, K. D. (Eds.), *Activities handbook for the teaching of psychology, pp. 75-76*. Washington, DC: American Psychological Association.

Wertheimer, M. (1981). Suggestibility and susceptibility to set. In Benjamin, L. T. and Lowman, K. D. (Eds.), *Activities handbook for the teaching of psychology*, pp. 180-181. Washington, DC: American Psychological Association.

Wertheimer, M. (1981). Chain reaction time. In Benjamin, L. T. and Lowman, K. D. (Eds.), *Activities handbook for the teaching of psychology*, pp. 205-206. Washington, DC: American Psychological Association.

Wertheimer, M. (1981). Psi Chi in fine shape as its second half century begins: Psi Chi National Historian's Report, 1978-1980. *Psi Chi Newsletter*, Spring, Vol. 7, No. 2, pp. 1, 4.

Viney, W., Wertheimer, M. and Wertheimer, M. L. (1981). The authors reply to Josef Brozek's review of their *History of psychology: A guide to information sources. Journal of the History of the Behavioral Sciences*, 17, 432.

Hall, J. E. and Wertheimer, M. (1981). Strategies in validating the examination for professional practice of psychology. *Professional Practice of Psychology*, 2, 21-24.

Wertheimer, M. (1981). Message from the president. *Rocky Mountain Psychological Association Newsletter*, Fall, iv-v.

Wertheimer, M. (1982). Gestalt theory, holistic psychologies and Max Wertheimer. *Zeitschrift für Psychologie*, 190, 125-140.

Ericsson, A., Polson, P. and Wertheimer, M. (1982). Preface. In Wertheimer, M. (Ed.) Max Wertheimer's *Productive thinking*, enlarged ed., pp. xi-xvii. Phoenix ed. Chicago: University of Chicago Press.

Wertheimer, M. (1982). Was Jung the first to diagnose "complexes" with the word-association method? *Rocky Mountain Psychologist*, Fall, 1-23.

Wertheimer, M. (1982). Psi Chi continues strong, takes on expanded international perspective. Psi Chi National Historian's Report for 1980-1981. *Psi Chi Newsletter*, Winter, Vol. 8, No. 1, pp. 1, 3.

Wertheimer, M. (1982). Report of the Council Representative. *Newsletter of the Division of Theoretical and Philosophical Psychology*, American Psychological Association, Fall/Winter, 1981--Spring/Summer, 1982, Combined Issue, 8.

Wertheimer, M. (1982). APA Council tries out a new mechanism--which seems to work. *Newsletter of the Division of Theoretical and Philosophical Psychology*, American Psychological Association, Fall/Winter, 1981--Spring/Summer, 1982, Combined Issue, 9-10.

Wertheimer, M. (1982). Report of the Division 24 Representative to APA Council. *Newsletter of Division 24 of the American Psychological Association*. Fall/Winter, 1982, Vol. 2, no. 1, 9.

Wertheimer, M. (1983). Gestalt theory, holistic psychologies, and Max Wertheimer. In G. Bittner (Ed.), *Personale Psychologie: Beiträge zur Geschichte, Theorie und Therapie*, pp. 32-49. Göttingen, West Germany: C. J. Hogrefe.

Wertheimer, M. (1983). Why we should study the history of psychology. In G. Eckardt & L. Sprung (Eds.) and D. Sinha, M. H. Tutundjian & M. Wertheimer (Co-eds.), *Advances in historiography of psychology*, pp. 11-25. Berlin, East Germany: VEB Deutscher Verlag der Wissenschaften.

Wertheimer, M. (1983). Psi Chi initiates more members than ever before, has another fine year: Psi Chi National Historian's Report for 1981-1982. *Psi Chi Newsletter*, 9, 2 (spring), pp. 1, 3.

Wertheimer, M. (1983). Dr. Frances Culbertson elected midwest regional vice president. *Psi Chi Newsletter*, 9, 2 (spring), p. 16.

Wertheimer, M. (1983). Council Representative's report. *Theoretical and Philosophical Psychology: Newsletter of Division 24 of the American Psychological Association*, Spring/Summer, Vol. 2, No. 2, pp. 3-4.

Wertheimer, M. (1983). Report of the Division 24 Representative to APA Council. *Theoretical and Philosophical Psychology: Newsletter of Division 24 of the American Psychological Association*, Fall/Winter, Vol. 3, No. 1, pp. 6-7.

Wertheimer, M. (1983). Another potential publication outlet for theoretical and philosophical articles in psychology. *Theoretical and Philosophical Psychology: Newsletter of Division 24 of the American Psychological Association*, Fall/Winter, Vol. 3, No. 1, p. 14.

Wertheimer, M. (1984). The experimental method in nineteenth- and twentieth-century psychology. In V. Sarris and A. Parducci (Eds.), *Perspectives in psychological experimentation: Toward the year 2000*, pp. 17-26. Hillsdale, NJ: Erlbaum.

Wertheimer, M. (1984). Topological psychology. In Corsini, R. J. (Ed.), *Encyclopedia of psychology*, Vol. 3, pp. 435-436. New York: Wiley.

Wertheimer, M. (1984). Wertheimer, Max (1880-1943). In Corsini, R. J. (Ed.), *Encyclopedia of psychology*, Vol. 3, p. 469. New York: Wiley.

Wertheimer, M. (1984). Wertheimer, Michael (1927-). In Corsini, R. J. (Ed.), *Encyclopedia of psychology*, Vol. 3, p. 469. New York: Wiley.

Wertheimer, M. (1984). Council Representative's report. *Theoretical and philosophical psychology: Newsletter of Division 24 of the American Psychological Association*, Spring/Summer, Vol. 3, No. 2, pp. 2-3.

Wertheimer, M. (1984). What is philosophical psychology? *Theoretical and philosophical psychology: Newsletter of Division 24 of the American Psychological Association*, Spring/Summer, Vol. 3, No. 2, pp. 15-16.

Wertheimer, M. (1984). History of psychology: What's new about what's old. In A. M. Rogers and C. J. Scheirer (Eds.), *The G. Stanley Hall Lecture Series*, vol. 4, pp. 155-188. Washington, DC: American Psychological Association.

Wertheimer, M. (1984). Psi Chi's traditions--and growth--continue: Psi Chi National Historian's report for 1982-83. *Psi Chi Newsletter*, 10, (4), 29-30.

Wertheimer, M. (1985). A Gestalt perspective on computer simulations of cognitive processes. *Computers in Human Behavior*, 1, (1), 19-33.

Wertheimer, M. (1985). Creative thinking and research. *1984 National Research Conference Proceedings, Delta Pi Epsilon*, 6-7.

Wertheimer, M. (1985). The implicit assumptions of modern psychology. *Theoretical and Philosophical Psychology*, 1/2, 1-3.

Wertheimer, M. (1985). The evolution of the concept of development in the history of psychology. In G. Eckardt, W. G. Bringmann and L. Sprung (Eds.), *Contributions to a history of developmental psychology*, pp. 13-25. New York: Mouton.

Wertheimer, M. (1985). Psychology. In A. J. Goldstein (Ed.), *Peterson's annual guides/graduate study: Book 2. Graduate programs in the humanities and social sciences 1986*, 20th ed., p. 1679. Princeton, NJ: Peterson's Guides.

Wertheimer, M. (1985). Annual report of Division 24 for 1984-1985. *Theoretical and Philosophical Psychology*, 5, (1), 1.

Chiszar, D. and Wertheimer, M. (1986). Margaret Altmann (1900-1984). *Animal Behavior Society Newsletter*, 31, (1), 15.

Wertheimer, M. (1986). Candidates for division elections. *Theoretical and Philosophical Psychology*, 6 (1), 57-59.

Wertheimer, M. (1986). Die experimentelle Methode in der Psychologie des 19. und 20. Jahrhunderts. [The experimental method in the psychology of the nineteenth and twentieth centuries.] In V. Sarris and A. Parducci (Eds.), *Die Zukunft der experimentellen Psychologie* [*The future of experimental psychology*], pp. 29-38. Weinheim and Basel: Beltz Verlag.

Wertheimer, M. (1986). Gestalt psychology. In Goetz, P. W. (Ed.). *The New Encyclopædia Britannica*, Vol. 26, pp. 328-329. Chicago: Encyclopædia Britannica.

Pastine, M., Wertheimer, M., et al. (1986) An international library exchange in China: Academic and research libraries in the PRC. *College & Research Libraries News*, 47, (6), 392-399.

Wertheimer, M. (1986). The implicit assumptions of modern psychology. *Theoretical and Philosophical Psychology*, 6, (1), 5-17.

Watson, R. I., Sr. and Wertheimer, M. (1986). Psychology: Survey of the field. In W. H. Webb, et al. (Eds.), *Sources of information in the social sciences*, 3rd ed., pp. 403-428. Chicago: American Library Association.

Wertheimer, M., Brodie, J., Fendrich, D., Mannes, S., Okuda, C., Sharps, M. and Weisberg, J. (1986). Psychology: Social science, natural science and profession. In S. P. Wronski and D. H. Bragaw (Eds.), *Social studies and social sciences: A fifty-year perspective*, pp. 165-178. Washington, DC: National Council for the Social Studies.

Wertheimer, M. (1986). The annals of the house that Ebbinghaus built. In F. Klix and H. Hagendorf (Eds.), *Human memory and cognitive capabilities: Mechanisms and performances*, pp. 35-44. Amsterdam: Elsevier North-Holland.

Wertheimer, M. (1987). Psychology. In A. J. Goldstein (Ed.), *Peterson's annual guides to graduate study: Book 2. Graduate programs in the humanities and social sciences 1987*, 21st ed., p. 1863. Princeton, NJ: Peterson's Guides.

Wertheimer, M. Obstacles to the integration of competing theories in psychology. *International Newsletter of Uninomic Psychology*, 1987, *3*, 17-24.

Wertheimer, M. (1987). Topological psychology. In R. J. Corsini (Ed.), *Concise encyclopedia of psychology*, p. 1129. New York: Wiley.

Wertheimer, M. (1987). Wertheimer, Max (1880-1943). In R. J. Corsini (Ed.), *Concise encyclopedia of psychology*, pp. 1154-1155. New York: Wiley.

Wertheimer, M. (1987). Wertheimer, Michael (1927-). In R. J. Corsini (Ed.), *Concise encyclopedia of psychology*, p. 1155. New York: Wiley.

Wertheimer, M. (1987). Psychology. In A. J. Goldstein (Ed.), *Accounting to zoology: Graduate fields defined*, pp. 178-179. Princeton, NJ: Peterson's Guides.

Wertheimer, M. (1987). Unification through "fragmentation": An apparently paradoxical solution. *Theoretical and Philosophical Psychology*, 7, 28-30.

Wertheimer, M. (1987). Report on the 1987 midwinter meeting of the APA Council of Representatives. *Division 1 Newsletter, Division of General Psychology, American Psychological Association*, Spring, No. 48, 5-7.

Wertheimer, M. (1987). Some implicit assumptions of modern psychology. *Zeitschrift für Psychologie*, 195, 311-323.

Wertheimer, M. (1987). APA Council, "our" magazine, and restructuring the association. *Division 1 Newsletter, Division of General Psychology, American Psychological Association*, No. 50, 4-6.

Sarris, V. and Wertheimer, M. (1987). Über Max Wertheimer (1880-1943) im Bilddokument: Ein historiografischer Beitrag. [On Max Wertheimer (1880-1943) in pictorial documentation: An historiographic contribution.] *Psychologische Beiträge*, 29, 469-493.

Wertheimer, M. (1987). Psychology. In Moore, T. C. and Sacchetti, R. D. (Eds.) *Graduate programs in the humanities and social sciences 1988*, 22nd ed. *Peterson's annual guides to graduate study: Book 2*, p. 1877. Princeton, NJ: Peterson's Guides.

Lambert, L. E. and Wertheimer, M. (1988). Is diagnostic ability related to relevant training and experience? *Professional Psychology: Research and Practice*, 1988, 19, 50-52.

Bartlett, N. E., Spilka, B. and Wertheimer, M. (1988). The geographical, cultural, and historical context of psychology in the Rocky Mountain region. *Journal of the History of the Behavioral Sciences*, 24, 6-8.

Chiszar, D. and Wertheimer, M. (1988). Margaret Altmann: A rugged pioneer in rugged fields. *Journal of the History of the Behavioral Sciences*, 24, 102-106.

Chiszar, D. and Wertheimer, M. (1988). The Boulder model: A history of psychology at the University of Colorado. *Journal of the History of the Behavioral Sciences*, 24, 81-86.

Wertheimer, M. (1988). Epilogue. *Journal of the History of the Behavioral Sciences*, 24, 117.

Wertheimer, M. (1988). Meaningfulness and memory. In Makosky, V. P., Whittemore, L. G. and Rogers, A. M. (Eds.), *Activities handbook for the teaching of psychology*, vol. 2, pp. 80-82. Washington, DC: American Psychological Association.

Wertheimer, M. (1988). ESP, central tendency, and probability. In Makosky, V. P., Whittemore, L. G. and Rogers, A. M. (Eds.), *Activities handbook for the teaching of psychology*, vol. 2, pp. 199-200. Washington, DC: American Psychological Association.

Wertheimer, M. (1988). Constructing unified theory. *International Newsletter of Uninomic Psychology*, 4, 38-42.

Wertheimer, M. (1988). Obstacles to the integration of competing theories of psychology. *Philosophical Psychology*, 1, 129-135.

Wertheimer, M. (1988). Psychology. In Moore, T. C. (Ed.), *Peterson's guide to graduate programs in the humanities and social sciences 1989*, 23rd ed., pp. 911-912. Princeton, NJ: Peterson's Guides.

Wertheimer, M. (1988). APA task force on centennial celebrations solicits input. *History of Psychology*, 20, 27-31.

Wertheimer, M. (1989). Wundt medal awarded posthumously to Max Wertheimer. *Journal of the History of the Behavioral Sciences*, 25, 204-205.

Wertheimer, M. (1989). Verstehen Lehren aus gestaltpsychologischer Sicht. *Beiträge zur Lehrerbildung*, 7, 149-160.

Wertheimer, M. (1989). Psychology. In Verys, B. (Ed.), *Peterson's guide to graduate programs in the humanities and social sciences, 1990, 24th ed. Peterson's annual guides to graduate study: Book 2*, pp. 939-940. Princeton, NJ: Peterson's Guides.

Wertheimer, M. (1989). Max Wertheimer's challenging legacy. *Psychological Research*, 51, 69-74.

Wertheimer, M. (1990). Sex differences and the "variability hypothesis." In Makosky, V. P., Silco, C. C., Whittemore, L. G., Landry, C. S. and Skutley, M. L. (Eds.), *Activities handbook for the teaching of psychology*, Vol. 3, pp. 298-300. Washington, DC: American Psychological Association.

Wertheimer, M. (1990). Mary Henle (1913-). In O'Connell, A. N. and Russo, N. F. (Eds.), *Women in psychology,* pp. 161-172. New York: Greenwood, 1990.

Wertheimer, M. (1990). Edwin B. Newman: An appreciation. *Psi Chi Newsletter*, Summer, 7-10.

Wertheimer, M. (1990). Good ideas for centennial activities? *Division 1 Newsletter, Division of General Psychology, American Psychological Association,* fall (58), 6.

Wertheimer, M. (1990). Psychology. In vonVerys-Norton, B. (ed.), *Peterson's guide to graduate programs in the humanities and social sciences, 1991,* 25th ed., pp. 929-930. Princeton, NJ: Peterson's Guides.

Wertheimer, M. (1990). Edwin B. Newman: In memoriam. *History of Psychology Newsletter,* 22 (3), 50-54.

Wertheimer, M. (1991). Max Wertheimer, Gestaltprophet. In Walter, H. J. (Ed.), *Max Wertheimer: Zur Gestaltpsychologie menschlicher Werte [Max Wertheimer: On the Gestalt psychology of human values],* pp. 123-170. Opladen, West Germany: Westdeutscher Verlag.

Wertheimer, M. (1991). Trials, tribulations, and triumphs: The woes and wealth of an academic career: Message of the president. *Psi Chi Newsletter,* 17 (winter), 1, 3.

Wertheimer, M., Hilgard, E. R., Spilka, B., Tyler, L. E., Norman, R. D., Loftus, E. F., Brewer, M. B., Ellis, H. C., Wollersheim, J. P., and Kendler, M. H. (1991). A tale of two regions: The Rocky Mountain and the U. S. Western. *Zeitschrift für Psychologie,* 199, 107-119, 191-204.

Wertheimer, M. (1991). Max Wertheimer: Modern cognitive psychology and the Gestalt problem. In Kimble, G. A., Wertheimer, M. and White, C. (Eds.), *Portraits of pioneers in psychology,* pp. 189-207. Hillsdale, NJ: Erlbaum and Washington, DC: American Psychological Association.

von Eye, A., Lienert, G. A., and Wertheimer, M. (1991). Syndromkombinationen als Metasyndrome in der Konfigurationsfrequenzanalyse. [Syndrome combinations as metasyndromes in the frequency analysis of configurations.] *Zeitschrift für Klinische Psychologie, Psychopathologie und Psychotherapie,* 39, 254-260.

Wertheimer, M. (1991). The Psi Chi national convention will be special: Message of the president. *Psi Chi Newsletter,* 17 (spring), (2), 1, 3.

Wertheimer, M. (1991). Will you be ready to commence your life? Message of the president. *Psi Chi Newsletter,* 17 (summer), (3), 1, 3.

Wertheimer, M. (1991). The obligations of excellence: Message of the president. *Psi Chi Newsletter*, 17 (fall), (4), 6-7.

Wertheimer, M. (1991). The third annual convention of the American Psychological Society. *Psi Chi Newsletter*, 17 (fall), (4), 30.

Wertheimer, M. (1991) Psi Chi/APA convention tribute: A celebration of Ruth Cousins's contributions to Psi Chi. *Psi Chi Newsletter*, 17 (special edition), (5), 7.

Wertheimer, M. (1991). Psychology. In B. vanVorys-Norton and P. Williams (eds.), *Peterson's guide to graduate programs in the humanities and social sciences*, 1992, 26th ed., Book 2 of *Peterson's annual guides to graduate study*, pp. 933-934. Princeton, NJ: Peterson's Guides.

Wertheimer, M., King, D. B., Peckler, M., Raney, S. M., and Schaef, R. (1992). Carl Jung and Max Wertheimer on a priority issue. *Journal of the History of the Behavioral Sciences*, 28, 45-56.

Wertheimer, M. (1992). Toward a tough-minded tender-mindedness. *Psi Chi Newsletter*, 8 (winter), (1), 6-15.

Wertheimer, M. (1992). Humanistic psychology and the humane but tough-minded psychologist. In R. B. Miller (Ed.), *The restoration of dialogue: Readings in the philosophy of clinical psychology*, pp. 317-326. Washington: DC: American Psychological Association.

Wertheimer, M., Heissenbuttel, T. J., Keene, E., Lienert, M. J., Meyer, H., Robyn, E. S., and Smith, L. (1991, but issued in 1992). Percentages of pages per period: A simple bibliometric technique. *Zeitschrift für Psychologie*, Supplement II for 1991, 53-58.

Wertheimer, M. and King, D. B. (1992). A history of Division One: General Psychology. *The General Psychologist*, *28*(3), 22-29.

Wertheimer, M. (1992). Society for Gestalt Theory and its Applications (GTA): Goals and purposes. *Gestalt Theory*, *14*, 293-295.

Wertheimer, M. (1993). Foreword. In Viney, W., *A history of psychology: Ideas and context*, pp. xv-xvii. Boston: Allyn and Bacon.

Wertheimer, M. (1993). Psychology. In Peterson's Guides: *Graduate programs in the humanities and social sciences, 1993*, 27th ed., pp. 1061-1062. Princeton, NJ: Peterson's Guides.

Wertheimer, M. (1993). Psi Chi history 1991-1992: A year of transition and growth for Psi Chi. *Psi Chi Newsletter*, fall 1993, vol. 19, No. 4, p. 11.

Wertheimer, M., Suinn, R. M., Jalbert, N. L., Coleman, L. M., Lewis, M. L., and Byers, S. (1993). Can psychology be general without being diverse? *The General Psychologist*, *29*, 9-22.

Wertheimer, M. (1993). On the occasion of the fiftieth anniversary of Max Wertheimer's death. *Gestalt Theory*, *15*, 165-171.

King, D. B. and Wertheimer, M. (1993). The Rocky Mountain Psychological Association. In Pate, J. L. and Wertheimer, M. (Eds.), *No small part: A history of regional organizations in American psychology*, pp. 127-150. Washington, DC: American Psychological Association.

Wertheimer, M. and King, D. B. (1994). Max Wertheimer's American sojourn, 1933-1943. *History of Psychology Newsletter*, Spring, 1994, *26*, 3-15.

King, D. B., Wertheimer, M., Keller, H., and Crochetière, K. (1994). The legacy of Max Wertheimer and Gestalt psychology. *Social Research*, *61*, 907-935.

King, D.B. and Wertheimer, M. (1994). Max Wertheimer at the University of Berlin. *Selected papers from the history of psychology convention at the University of Berlin*, pp. 17-18. Deutsche Gesellschaft für Psychologie.

Wertheimer, M. and Wertheimer, M.L. (1995). Can the gap between psychology's two cultures be bridged? *Psychological Inquiry*, 6, 131-134.

Wertheimer, M. (1995). Wertheimer, Max. *American National Biography*, 3 pp. New York: Oxford University Press.

King, D.B. and Wertheimer, M. (1995). Max Wertheimer at the University of Berlin. In Jaeger, S., Staeuble, M., Sprung, L. and Brauns, H.P. (Eds.), *Psychologie im soziokulturellen Wandel: Kontinuitäten und Diskontinuitäten*, pp. 276-280. Frankfurt am Main: Peter Lang.

Wertheimer, M. and King, D.B. (1996). A history of Division One (general psychology). In Dewsbury, D.A. (Ed.), *Unification through division: Histories of the divisions of the American Psychological Association, Vol. 1*, pp. 9-40. Washington, DC: American Psychological Association.

King, D.B., Montañez-Ramírez, L.M., and Wertheimer, M. (1996). Barbara Stoddard Burks: Pioneer behavioral geneticist and humanitarian. In Kimble, G.A., Boneau, C.A., and Wertheimer, M. (Eds.), *Portraits of pioneers in psy-*

chology, vol. II, pp. 213-225. Mahwah, NJ: Erlbaum and Washington, DC: American Psychological Association.

Wertheimer, M., Yeager, T., and Jones, V.L. (1996). Studying and teaching psychology. In Social Science Education Consortium (Ed.), *Teaching the social sciences and history in secondary schools: A methods book*, pp. 72-104. Belmont, CA: Wadsworth.

King, D.B., Golden, G.L., and Wertheimer, M. (1996). The APA in World War II: The work of the APA Committee on Displaced Foreign Psychologists. *The General Psychologist*, 32, 13-18.

Wertheimer, M. (1996). Four articles: Isomorphism, Topological psychology, Wertheimer, Max (1880-1943), and Wertheimer, Michael (1927-). In Corsini, R.J. and Auerback, A.J. (Eds.), *Concise encyclopedia of psychology*, pp. 500-501, 912, 964, 964. New York: Wiley.

Wertheimer, M. (1996). The August 1996 meeting of the APA Council of Representatives. *Journal of Theoretical and Philosophical Psychology*, 16, 173-175.

Wertheimer, M. (1997). Briefing: A contemporary perspective on the psychology of productive thinking. *Psychology Teacher Network*, Jan/Feb, 2-3, 6, 8, 13.

Wertheimer, M. (1997) Teaching Tips: History belongs in every course. APS Observer, spring.

Wertheimer, M. (1997). Congratulations on the new Psi Chi newsletter format. *Eye on Psi Chi*, 2, 7.

Wertheimer, M. (1997). Briefwechsel: Zum Briefwechsel Wolfgang Metzger–Max Wertheimer 1929-1937. [Postal exchanges: On the correspondence of Wolfgang Metzger and Max Wertheimer, 1929-1937.] *Gestalt Theory*, 19, 263-265.

Wertheimer, M. (1997). Ein kurzer Überblick über die psychologischen Schulen vor dem Zweiten Weltkrieg [A brief overview of the psychological schools before the Second World War]—with comments on the destructiveness of ingroup-outgroup discrimination. In Hassler, M. and Wertheimer, J. (Eds.), *Der Exodus aus Nazideutschland und die Folgen: Jüdische Wissenschaftler im Exil*, pp. 191-206. Tübingen: Attempto Verlag.

Wertheimer, M. (1997). A contemporary perspective on the psychology of productive thinking. U.S. Dept. of Education, ERIC/CASS database, 44 pp.

King, D.B., Cox, M., and Wertheimer, M. (1998). Karl Duncker: Productive problems with beautiful solutions. In Kimble, G.A. and Wertheimer, M. (Eds.). *Portraits of pioneers in psychology*, vol. III, pp. 163-178. Mahwah, NJ: Erlbaum and Washington, DC: American Psychological Association.

Wertheimer, M. (1998). A clash in world views: Interview with Dr. Michael Wertheimer. *NARTH Bulletin*, 6(2), 7-8, 25-26.

Wertheimer, M. (1998). Report on the February 1998 meeting of the APA Council of Representatives. *History of Psychology*, 1, 263-264.

Wertheimer, M. (1999). History belongs in every course. In Perlman, B., McCann, L.I., and McFadden, S.H. (Eds.), *Lessons learned: Practical advice for the teaching of psychology*, pp. 129-134, Washington, DC: American Psychological Society.

Ross, H.W. and Wertheimer, M. (1999). Kenneth Bruce Little (1918-1997). *American Psychologist*, 54, 1126-1127.

Wertheimer, M. (1999). Reorganization and productive thinking. In Benjamin, L.T., Jr., Nodine, B.F., Ernst, R.M. and Broeker, C.B. (Eds.), *Activities handbook for the teaching of psychology*, vol. 4, pp. 218-224. Washington, DC: American Psychological Association.

Wertheimer, M. (1999). Set and information processing. In Benjamin, L.T., Jr., Nodine, B.F., Ernst, R.M. and Broeker, C.B. (Eds.), *Activities handbook for the teaching of psychology*, vol. 4, pp. 225-227. Washington, DC: American Psychological Association.

Wertheimer, M. (2000). Report of the Division 26 representative on the meeting of the APA Council of Representatives August 19 and 22, 1999. *History of Psychology*, 3, 73-74.

Wertheimer, M. and V. Sarris (2000). Max Wertheimers *Produktives Denken*. In Lück, H., Miller, R., and Sawz-Vosshenrich, G. (Eds.), *Die klassiker der Psychologie*, pp. 183-187. Stuttgart: Kohlhammer.

Wertheimer, M. (2000). Two articles: Isomorphism, and Wertheimer, Michael. In Craighead, W.E. and Nemeroff, C.B. (Eds.), *Corsini encyclopedia of psychology*, 3rd ed. New York: Wiley.

Sharps, M.J. and Wertheimer, M. (2000), Gestalt perspectives on cognitive science and experimental psychology. *Review of General Psychology*, 4, 315-336.

Wertheimer, M. (2001). A brilliant, exasperating, and disturbing critique of modern psychology: A review of Koch. S., *Psychology in human context: Essays in dissidence and reconstruction*, Finkelman, D. and Kessel, F. (Eds.). *Contemporary Psychology*, 46, 34-36.

Wertheimer, M. (2001). Five articles: American Psychological Association: History, K. Duncker, C. von Ehrenfels, S.W. Fernberger, and M. Wertheimer. *Oxford-APA encyclopedia of psychology*. New York: Oxford University Press and Washington, DC: American Psychological Association.

Sarris, V., and Wertheimer, M. (2001). Max Wertheimer's research on aphasia and brain disorders. *Gestalt Theory*, 23, 267-277.

Wertheimer, M. (2002). In Memoriam: Psi Chi loses a longtime friend: Neal E. Miller. *Eye on Psi Chi*, 7, 34-35.

Wertheimer, M. (2004). Psi Chi, the national honor society in psychology, celebrates its 75th anniversary. *APS Observer*, *17*, 20-22.

Wertheimer, M. (2005). Raymond J. Corsini, Ph. D., the Marble kid. *The General Psychologist*, 40, 16-17.

Wertheimer, M. (2005). APA Council Report. *The General Psychologist*, 40, 17-18.

Wertheimer, M. (2006). Teachers teach and students learn, right? In Buskist, R., et al. (Eds.), *The teaching of psychology in autobiography*. Washington, DC: Division 2 of the American Psychological Association.

Boneau, C. A., and Wertheimer, M. (2006). Gregory A. Kimble (1917-2006). *American Psychologist*, 61, 632-633.

Michael, K. D. (2007). What I think I may have learned—reflections on fifty years of teaching: An interview with Michael Wertheimer. *Teaching of Psychology*.

Wertheimer, M. (2007). The case of the purloined picture: Rosalind Franklin and the keystone of the double helix. In Gavin, E. A., Siderits, M. A., and Clamar, A. (Eds.), *Women of vision: Their psychology, circumstances, and success*, pp. 259-271. New York: Springer.

Wertheimer, M. (2007). Gestalt psychology. In W. A. Darity (Ed.), *International Encyclopedia of the Social Sciences, Second edition.* Farmington Hills, MI: Macmillan.

Wertheimer, M. (2007). Rudolf Arnheim: An elegant artistic Gestalt. *Psychology of Aesthetics, Creativity, and the Arts*, 1, 6-7.

Wertheimer, M. (2008). Chain reaction time: Measuring the speed of thought. In Benjamin, L. T., Jr. (Ed.), *Favorite activities for the teaching of psychology*, pp. 5-7. Washington, DC: American Psychological Association.

Wertheimer, M. (2008). Set and information processing. In Benjamin, L. T., Jr. (Ed.), *Favorite activities for the teaching of psychology*, pp. 141-142. Washington, DC: American Psychological Association.

Wertheimer, M. (2010). A Gestalt perspective on the psychology of thinking. In Glatzeder, B. M., Goel, V., & von Mueller, A. (Eds.), *Towards a theory of thinking: Building blocks for a conceptual framework*, pp. 49-58. Berlin, Germany: Springer-Verlag.

Wertheimer, M., and Woody, D. W. (2017). The professoriate in the twenty-first century —with some speculations about impending changes. *Scholarship of Teaching and Learning in Psychology*, 3, 284-298.

Ericsson, K. A., Polson, P., and Wertheimer, M. (2017). Preface to Max Wertheimer's *Productive Thinking*. Berlin: Springer.

Sarris, V. and Wertheimer, M. (2018). Max Wertheimer: Productive Thinking (1945). In Lück, H.E., Miller, R., and Sawz-Vossenrich, G. (Eds.), *Klassiker der Psychologie. Die bedeutenden Werke: Entstehung, Inhalt, und Wirkung [Classics of psychology. The significant works: Origin, content, and effects]*, 2nd expanded and revised ed., Stuttgart, Germany, pp. 158-162.

Papers presented at professional association conventions

Wertheimer, M. (1954). Figural aftereffects in schizophrenic and normal subjects. American Psychological Association, 1954. *American Psychologist*, 9, 492. (Abstract)

Wertheimer, M. Metabolic efficiency as a hypothetical construct. Connecticut State Psychological Association, 1954.

Wertheimer, M. and Gillis, W. M. Some determinants of the rate of lapse of meaning of words. Rocky Mountain Psychological Association, 1956.

Wertheimer, M. (1956). Theories and facts about individual differences in figural aftereffects. American Psychological Association, 1956. *American Psychologist*, 11, 420-421. (Abstract)

Wertheimer, M. The influence of subjective time spent in practice on learning. Rocky Mountain Psychological Association, 1957.

Titley, R. and Wertheimer, M. (1957). The effect of hue on apparent distance. Colorado Psychological Association and Colorado-Wyoming Academy of Sciences. *Journal of the Colorado-Wyoming Academy of Sciences*, 1957, 4 (9), 41. (Abstract)

Selkin, J. and Wertheimer, M. (1957). A study of the disappearance of the Müller-Lyer illusion under prolonged inspection. Colorado Psychological Association and Colorado-Wyoming Academy of Sciences, 1957. *Journal of the Colorado-Wyoming Academy of Sciences*, 4 (9), 41-42. (Abstract)

Wertheimer, M., Burns, P., and Gillis, W. M. (1957). The effect of emotionality of a word on the rate of lapse of meaning of the word. Colorado Psychological Association and Colorado-Wyoming Academy of Sciences, 1957. *Journal of the Colorado-Wyoming Academy of Sciences*, 4, (9), 42. (Abstract)

Wertheimer, M. (1957). A preliminary study of the relation between the sound of a word and its meaning. Colorado Psychological Association and Colorado-Wyoming Academy of Sciences, 1957. *Journal of the Colorado-Wyoming Academy of Sciences*, 4 (9), 42-43. (Abstract)

Wertheimer, M. and Leventhal, C. M. (1957). "Permanent" satiation with kinesthetic figural aftereffects. American Psychological Association, 1957. *American Psychologist*, 12, 456. (Abstract)

Wertheimer, M. Graduate education in psychology: Philosophies and research strategies. Contribution to symposium with same title. American Psychological Association, 1957.

Kaiser, L. R., Darnell, R. L., and Wertheimer, M. Accuracy of time estimation as a function of task complexity. Rocky Mountain Psychological Association, 1958.

Mathews, A. and Wertheimer, M. A pure measure of perceptual defense uncontaminated by response suppression. Rocky Mountain Psychological Association, 1958.

Wertheimer, M. The epistemological primacy of individual perception. Wayne State University, Conference on Consciousness and Perception. February, 1961.

Wertheimer, M. The senior integrative course in psychology. Contribution to symposium with same title. American Psychological Association, 1961.

Wertheimer, M. Space perception at birth. Division 3 perception group. American Psychological Association, 1961.

Wertheimer, M. The psychology honors program at the University of Colorado. Contribution to symposium on honors programs in psychology. American Psychological Association, 1962.

Wertheimer, M. The Colorado German-teaching experiment. Division 3 psycholinguistics group. American Psychological Association, 1962.

Wertheimer, M. and Scherer, G. A. C. The audiolingual teaching of German: A psycholinguistic experiment. Psychonomic Society, 1962.

Wertheimer, M. Some transsummative approaches to psychological problems. International Society for the Comparative Study of Civilizations, Salzburg, Austria, 1964.

Wertheimer, M. The psychologist and the foreign-language teacher. Indiana University-Purdue University Foreign Language Conference, 1965.

Cameron, P. and Wertheimer, M. Kinesthetic figural aftereffects are localized in the hands, not in phenomenal space. Rocky Mountain Psychological Association, 1965.

Finnegan, M. and Wertheimer, M. Accuracy of quantitative readings of altimeter designs. Colorado-Wyoming Academy of Sciences, 1966.

Wertheimer, M. Teaching 1966 psychology in 1966. Division 2 Presidential Address, American Psychological Association, 1966.

Wertheimer, M. Rationales for and approaches to the teaching of psychology's history. Contribution to symposium on teaching the history of psychology, American Psychological Association, 1966.

Wertheimer, M. American psychology in 1872 and in 1967. 75th anniversary symposium, American Psychological Association, 1967.

Wertheimer, M. The individual psychologist and the social crisis. Rocky Mountain Psychological Association, Salt Lake City, 1970.

Wertheimer, M. Fundamental issues in psychology. American Psychological Association, Miami Beach, 1970.

Wertheimer, M. Why, what and how: Psychology taught in the public schools. Illinois Psychological Association, Chicago, 1971.

Wertheimer, M. The twentieth-century revolution in the behavioral sciences. Phi Beta Kappa address, University of Colorado, 1972; same paper delivered as part of the Social Studies Lecture Series, Western State College of Colorado, Gunnison, 1972.

Wertheimer, M. Toward a phenomenological psycholinguistics of multilingualism. Colorado State University, 1972; same paper delivered at Linguistic Circle of Colorado, 1972; and at Rocky Mountain Modern Language Association, Tucson, AZ, 1972.

Wertheimer, M. High school psychology: Stepchild or offspring? American Psychological Association, Honolulu, HI, 1972.

Wertheimer, M. High school psychology. Rocky Mountain Psychological Association Convention, Las Vegas, NV, 1973.

Wertheimer, M. Robert Brodie MacLeod. Cheiron: The International Society for the History of the Behavioral and Social Sciences, Plattsburgh, New York, 1973.

Wertheimer, M. Conversation-Contact Hour, American Psychological Association, New Orleans, 1974.

Wertheimer, M. Contemporary philosophical issues in psychology. Contribution to panel with same title, Rocky Mountain Psychological Association, Salt Lake City, 1975.

Wertheimer, M. Getting into graduate school and getting a job in psychology: The view from the chair of the E & T Board. Rocky Mountain Psychological Association, Salt Lake City, 1975.

Wertheimer, M. Crises in modern psychology. Contribution to panel with same title, Rocky Mountain Psychological Association, Phoenix, 1976.

Wertheimer, M. Division 1 President's invited panel on psychology and the future. American Psychological Association, Washington, DC, 1976.

Wertheimer, M. Historical aspects of the psychology of language and cognition. Conference on the Roots of American Psychology: Historical Influences and Implications for the Future. The New York Academy of Sciences, 1976.

Wertheimer, M. The emergence of psychology as a separate experimental discipline. Panel sponsored by the Committee on the History of Science, University of Colorado, Boulder, June, 1977.

Wertheimer, M. Humanistic psychology and the humane but tough-minded psychologist. Division 24 Presidential Address, American Psychological Association, San Francisco, 1977.

Wertheimer, M. Wertheimer and Wertheimer: Two cultures. Contribution to symposium: Boring, Dunlap, Lewin, and Wertheimer: In my father's steps. American Psychological Association, Toronto, Canada, 1978.

Wertheimer, M. Max Wertheimer, Gestalt theorist. Division 26 Presidential Address, American Psychological Association, Toronto, Canada, 1978.

Wertheimer, M. A quick (?) and easy (?) way to get rich: Write a book! Contribution to symposium with same title, Rocky Mountain Psychological Association, Las Vegas, 1979.

Wertheimer, M. Humanistic psychology: Is it humane, is it psychology? Invited address as "provocateur" for a symposium: The great humanistic debate. American Psychological Association, New York, 1979.

Wertheimer, M. A Gestalt approach to scientific creativity. Contribution to symposium: Prospects and progress toward a psychology of science. American Psychological Association, New York, 1979.

Wertheimer, M. Why we should study the history of psychology. Invited address, XXIInd International Congress of Psychology, Leipzig, East Germany, 1980.

Wertheimer, M. Conversation-Contact Hour, American Psychological Association, Montreal, Canada, 1980.

Wertheimer, M. Gestalt theory, holistic psychologies, and Max Wertheimer. Centennial Lecture, American Psychological Association, Montreal, Canada, 1980.

Wertheimer, M. The experiment in nineteenth and twentieth century psychology. Invited contribution to international symposium on experimental psychology in the year 2000. Bad Homburg, West Germany, 1981.

Wertheimer, M. Was Jung the first to diagnose "complexes" with the word-association method? Invited address, Western Psychological Association, Sacramento, CA, 1982.

Wertheimer, M. Was Jung the first to diagnose "complexes" with the word-association method? Presidential address, Rocky Mountain Psychological Association, Albuquerque, NM, 1982.

Wertheimer, M. An honors program in psychology. Contribution to symposium on innovative instruction in undergraduate psychology. Rocky Mountain Psychological Association, Albuquerque, NM, 1982.

Wertheimer, M. The evolution of the concept of development in the history of psychology. Invited address, International Symposium on the History of Developmental Psychology, University of Jena, East Germany, 1982.

Wertheimer, M. Conversation hour on communication across the iron curtain. Invited presentation, International Council of Psychologists, San Francisco, CA, 1983.

Wertheimer, M. Max Wertheimer: Cognitive psychology and the Gestalt problem. Invited address, American Psychological Association, Anaheim, CA, 1983.

Wertheimer, M. History of psychology: What's new about what's old. Invited address as part of the G. Stanley Hall Lecture Series, American Psychological Association, Anaheim, CA, 1983.

Wertheimer, M. Teachers teach and students learn, right? Invited address by the 1983 recipient of the American Psychological Foundation Award for Distinguished Teaching in Psychology, American Psychological Association, Toronto, Canada, 1984.

Wertheimer, M. Invited keynote address. Psi Chi symposium, University of Colorado at Denver, 1984.

Wertheimer, M. Creative thinking and research. Invited address, Delta Pi Epsilon National Business Education Research Conference, Denver, 1984.

Chiszar, D. and Wertheimer, M. Margaret Altmann. Rocky Mountain Psychological Association, Tucson, AZ, 1985.

Chiszar, D. and Wertheimer, M. A history of psychology at the University of Colorado. Rocky Mountain Psychological Association, Tucson, AZ, 1985.

Bartlett, N. R., Spilka, B. and Wertheimer, M. The geographical, cultural and historical context of the development of psychology in the Rocky Mountain region. Rocky Mountain Psychological Association, Tucson, AZ, 1985.

Wertheimer, M. The annals of the house that Ebbinghaus built. Invited address, Ebbinghaus Symposium, Berlin University, East Germany, 1985.

Wertheimer, M. The implicit assumptions of modern psychology. Presidential address to the Division of Theoretical and Philosophical Psychology, American Psychological Association, Los Angeles, CA, 1985.

Wertheimer, M. How learning occurs. University of Colorado Colloquy on Teaching, 1986.

Wertheimer, M. Freedom and determinism. Chair's comments at a symposium of the same title, Rocky Mountain Psychological Association, Denver, 1986.

Wertheimer, M. The teaching of health psychology. Chair's comments at a symposium on the teaching of undergraduate health psychology. American Psychological Association, Washington, DC, 1986.

Wertheimer, M. Obstacles to the integration of competing theories in psychology. Contribution to a symposium on uninomic psychology. American Psychological Association, Washington, DC, 1986.

Bartlett, N. R., Spilka, B. and Wertheimer, M. Special RMPA historians' information exchange. Rocky Mountain Psychological Association, Albuquerque, NM 1987.

Wertheimer, M. Constructing unified theory. Contribution to a symposium on constructing unified theory: Methodology from new philosophies in biological and psychological science. American Psychological Association, New York, 1987.

Wertheimer, M. Honors programs for undergraduate psychology students. Invited address, American Psychological Association, New York, 1987.

Wertheimer, M. How the phi phenomenon launched the Gestalt school. Invited contribution to an invited symposium on the 75th anniversary of the phi phenomenon, American Psychological Association, New York, 1987.

Wertheimer, M. The future and goals of Division 2. Contribution to an invited symposium of the same title, American Psychological Association, New York, 1987.

Wertheimer, M. A new approach to teaching research strategies. Contribution to a symposium of the same title, Rocky Mountain Psychological Association, Snowbird, UT, 1988.

Wertheimer, M. Aging and memory. Contribution to a symposium of the same title, Rocky Mountain Psychological Association, Snowbird, UT, 1988.

Wertheimer, M. Max Wertheimer's legacy. Deutsche Gesellschaft für Psychologie, Berlin, West Germany, 1988.

Wertheimer, M. Verstehen Lehren aus gestaltpsychologischer Sicht. [Teaching understanding from a Gestalt psychological perspective.] Symposium on Verstehen Lehren, Berne, Switzerland, 1989.

Wertheimer, M. Max Wertheimer's challenging legacy for today. Psi Chi and CTUP invited address, joint meeting of Western Psychological Association and Rocky Mountain Psychological Association, Reno, NV, 1989.

Wertheimer, M. A tale of two regions. Chair's remarks at an invited symposium, joint meeting of Western Psychological Association and Rocky Mountain Psychological Association, Reno, NV, 1989.

Wertheimer, M. Between two worlds. Contribution to a panel on the holocaust and the intellectual emigrés from Germany to the United States, University of Denver, 1990.

Wertheimer, M., Heissenbuttel, T. J., Keene, E., Lienert, M. J., Meyer, H., Robyn, E. S. and Smith L. Percentages of pages per period. Symposium celebrating the centenary of the *Zeitschrift für Psychologie*, DDR Academy of Sciences, East Berlin, Germany, 1990.

Wertheimer, M. Does psychology--and do psychologists--have a future? Psi Chi invited address, Rocky Mountain Psychological Association, Tucson, AZ, 1990.

Wertheimer, M., Fox, K. and Martz, C. What can Psi Chi do for you? Invited contribution to Psi Chi panel, Rocky Mountain Psychological Association, Tucson, AZ, 1990.

Broms, M., King, D. B., and Wertheimer, M. The life, work, and legacy of Karl Duncker (1903-1943). Rocky Mountain Psychological Association, Denver, 1991.

King, D. B., Bradley, K. L., Dalla, R. L., and Wertheimer, M. Conceptions and misconceptions of "isomorphism": The Wertheimer-Boring exchange. Rocky Mountain Psychological Association, Denver, 1991. Invited Psi Chi address.

Wertheimer, M. and Ford, K. What can Psi Chi do for you? Rocky Mountain Psychological Association, Denver, 1991.

Wertheimer, M. What to place into a psychology time capsule. Invited contribution to a symposium with the same title, American Psychological Association, San Francisco, 1991.

Wertheimer, M. Toward a tough-minded tender-mindedness. Psi Chi presidential address and address by the recipient of APA's 1990 Award for Distinguished Career Contributions to Education and Training in Psychology. American Psychological Association, San Francisco, 1991.

Wertheimer, M. How to tell a pioneer when you see one. Contribution to an invited centennial panel on The Division One Pioneers Book. American Psychological Association, San Francisco, 1991.

Wertheimer, M. and King. D. B. A history of the Rocky Mountain Psychological Association. Contribution to an invited symposium on the history of regional psychology association. American Psychological Association, San Francisco, 1991.

King, D. B., Bradley, K. L., Dalla, R. L., and Wertheimer, M. Conceptions and misconceptions of isomorphism: Wertheimer, Köhler, Boring, and others. American Psychological Association, San Francisco, 1991.

King, D. B., Broms, M., and Wertheimer, M. Karl Duncker's variegated contributions and their implications for contemporary psychology. American Psychological Association, San Francisco, 1991.

Wertheimer, M. Max Wertheimer in America. Psi Chi/SEPA invited address, Southeastern Psychological Association, Knoxville, TN 1992.

King, D. B. and Wertheimer, M. A history of the Rocky Mountain Psychological Association. Invited address, Rocky Mountain Psychological Association, Boise, ID, 1992.

King, D. B. and Wertheimer, M. A history of Division One, the division of general psychology. Invited address, American Psychological Association, Washington, DC, 1992.

Wertheimer, M. A tribute to the life and work of Virginia Staudt Sexton. Invited contribution to symposium with the same title, American Psychological Association, Washington, DC, 1992.

Wertheimer, M. A tribute to Kenneth R. Little, recipient of Division One's Award for Exceptional Service to the Division, American Psychological Association, Washington, DC, 1992.

Wertheimer, M. Psychology: Past, present and future. Invited lecture to the faculty at the United States Air Force Academy, Colorado Springs, CO, 1992.

Wertheimer, M. A history of theories of learning. Invited lecture for cadets at the United States Air Force Academy, Colorado Springs, CO, 1992.

Wertheimer, M. A retiring professor's last lecture: The obligations of excellence. Invited Psi Chi induction address, University of Colorado, 1993.

Aldridge, J. W., Jr., King, D. B., and Wertheimer, M. Behaviorism and Gestalt theory: The Clark Hull—Max Wertheimer correspondence. RMPA-WPA joint convention, Phoenix, AZ 1993.

Wertheimer, M. Graduate study at the University of Colorado at Boulder. Psi Chi Graduate School Exchange. RMPA-WPA joint convention, Phoenix, AZ, 1993.

Wertheimer, M. The way it was: A psychology department creating itself. Contribution to a symposium, Back to the 60s: Then and now—University of Colorado. RMPA-WPA joint convention, Phoenix, AZ, 1993.

King, D. B. and Wertheimer, M. Max Wertheimer at the University of Berlin. Fourth convention of the history of psychology section of the Deutsche Gesellschaft für Psychologie, Free University of Berlin, Germany, 1993.

Golden, G. L., Montañez-Ramírez, L. M., King, D. B., and Wertheimer, M. Humanitarian psychologists: The 1938-1943 Committee on Displaced Foreign Psychologists. American Psychological Association, Toronto, Canada, 1993.

Wertheimer, M. Invited discussion for R. T. Ley's paper, "A whisper of espionage—Wolfgang Köhler on Tenerife." American Psychological Association, Toronto, Canada, 1993.

Wertheimer, M. Achieving fellow status. Contribution to symposium with the same title. American Psychological Association, Toronto, Canada, 1993.

Montañez-Ramírez, L. M., King, D. B., and Wertheimer, M. Barbara Stoddard Burks: Pioneer behavioral geneticist and humanitarian. American Psychological Association, Toronto, Canada, 1993.

Wertheimer, M., Montañez-Ramírez, L. M., and Wertheimer, M. Barbara Stoddard Burks (1902-1943). Talk presented at Colorado State University, Fort Collins, CO, 1994.

Wertheimer, M., King, D. B., and Wertheimer, M. L. Mystery of a missing manuscript: The Luria-Wertheimer correspondence on Vygotskii. Invited address, RMPA convention, Las Vegas, NV, 1994.

Agin, B., Wertheimer, M., and King, D. B. Relation between enrollment in independent study and attitude toward the psychology major. RMPA convention, Las Vegas, NV, 1994.

Wertheimer, M. and King, D. B. Women in the RMPA. Invited contribution to a symposium on the role of women in regional psychological associations. American Psychological Association, Los Angeles, CA.

Wertheimer, M. Ein kurzer Überblick über die psychologischen Schulen vor dem zweiten Weltkrieg [A brief overview of the schools of psychology before the second World War]—with comments on the destructiveness of ingroup-outgroup discrimination. Invited lecture, Eberhard-Karls-Universität, Tübingen, Germany, 1994.

Wertheimer, M. The obligations of excellence. Invited address at Psi Chi induction, University of Colorado at Boulder, 1994.

Crochetière, K., Vicker, N., Parker, J., King, D.B., and Wertheimer, M. Early applications of Gestalt theory to clinical psychology and psychopathology. American Psychological Association, New York, 1995.

Wertheimer, M. Contribution to invited panel of past presidents of Division 2. American Psychological Association, New York, 1995.

Wertheimer, M. A 1995 perspective on the psychology of productive thinking. Max Wertheimer Lecture Series, Johann Wolfgang Goethe University, Frankfurt, Germany, 1995.

Wertheimer, M. A contemporary perspective on the psychology of productive thinking. Invited Psi Chi lecture, Colorado State University, Fort Collins, CO, 1996.

Wertheimer, M. Contribution to invited Division 1 panel: The past, present, and future of general psychology. American Psychological Association, Toronto, 1996.

Wertheimer, M. A contemporary perspective on the psychology of productive thinking. Invited address, Teachers of Psychology in Secondary Schools, American Psychological Association, Toronto, 1996.

Wertheimer, M. Trials and tribulations in trying to pin down real history. Invited contribution to Symposium: E pluribus unum: Probing the histories of APA divisions. American Psychological Association, Chicago, 1997.

Wertheimer, M. Reflections on the need for a Psi Chi oral history project. Invited contribution to Symposium: The Psi Chi oral history project. American Psychological Association, San Francisco, 1998.

Wertheimer, M. Psychology in the twenty-first century. Invited contribution to "past presidents panel." Rocky Mountain Psychological Association, Fort Collins, CO, 1999.

Wertheimer, M. Contribution to invited Psi Chi past-presidents' panel: Psi Chi at seventy: Looking back and ahead. American Psychological Association, Boston, 1999.

Wertheimer, M. Grusswort, Invited remarks for the Konferenz Gehirn und Gestalt, Hanse Wissenschaftskolleg, Delmenhorst, Germany, 1999.

Wertheimer, M. Challenges, pleasures, and pangs: Ruminations on a half century of teaching. University of Colorado at Boulder, 2005; also at Rocky Mountain Psychological Association convention in Phoenix, AZ, 2005, and at the Kulynych/Cline Teaching Festival, Appalachian State University, Boone, NC, 2005.

Wertheimer, M. The examined life of a teacher. University of Colorado at Boulder, 2005.

Wertheimer, M. Raymond J. Corsini, PhD: The Marble kid. American Psychological Association, Honolulu, HI, 2005.

Wertheimer, M. The case of the purloined picture: Rosalind Franklin and the keystone of the double helix. American Psychological Association, 2006.

Wertheimer, M. Psychology's promising past and enigmatic future. American Psychological Association, 2009.

Wertheimer, M. Psychology's promising past and enigmatic future. Adolf-Wuerth Center for the History of Psychology, University of Würzburg, 2009.

Wertheimer, M. Musings of Max Wertheimer's octogenarian son. Bielefeld, Germany: Deutsche Gesellschaft für Psychologie, 2012.

Wertheimer, M. The professoriate in the 21st century. Invited address, Rocky Mountain Psychological Association, Denver, CO, 2016.

Book and videotape reviews

Wertheimer, M. (1955). *Dynamic and abnormal psychology*, by W. S. Taylor. *American Scientist*, 43, 70A-71A.

Wertheimer, M. (1955). *Advanced Rorschach technique*, by L. Phillips and J. Smith. *Journal of Genetic Psychology*, 86, 381-383.

Wertheimer, M. (1955). *Personality through perception*, by H. A. Witkin et al. *Journal of General Psychology*, 53, 181-184.

Wertheimer, M. (1956). *On expressive language*, by H. Werner et al. *Journal of Genetic Psychology*, 89, 281-282.

Wertheimer, M. (1960). *Differential treatment and prognosis in schizophrenia*, by R. D. Wirt et al. *Contemporary Psychology*, 5, 159-160.

Wertheimer, M. (1961). *Das Bild vom Anderen [The impression of the other one]*, by G. Kaminski. *Contemporary Psychology*, 6, 40-41.

Wertheimer, M. (1965). *Helping other people change*, by S. M. Corey, and *Problems in measuring change*, ed. by C. W. Harris. *Teachers College Record*, 66, 474-476.

Wertheimer, M. (1966). *Jean-Paul Sartre: The philosophy of existentialism*, ed. by W. Baskin. *Contemporary Psychology*, 11, 359.

Wertheimer, M. (1966). *Cognitive processes and the brain: An enduring problem in psychology*, ed. by P. W. Milner and S. E. Glickman. *Contemporary Psychology*, 11, 362.

Wertheimer, M. (1966). *Clever Hans: The horse of Mr. Von Osten*, by O. Pfungst, ed. by R. Rosenthal. *Contemporary Psychology*, 11, 362.

Wertheimer, M. (1967). *Life on a small planet: A philosophy of values*, by H. Richards. *Contemporary Psychology*, 12, 96.

Wertheimer, M. (1967). *Memory*, by B. Smith. *Contemporary Psychology*, 12, 96.

Wertheimer, M. (1968). *A source book of Gestalt psychology*, by W. D. Ellis. *Contemporary Psychology*, 13, 41.

Wertheimer, M. (1969). *Aspects of form*, ed. by L. W. Whyte. *Contemporary Psychology*, 14, 565.

Wertheimer, M. (1970). *The task of Gestalt psychology*, by W. Köhler. *Contemporary Psychology*, 15, 314-317.

Wertheimer, M. (1970). *Selected readings in science and phenomenology*, ed. by P. Tibbetts. *Contemporary Psychology*, 15, 380.

Wertheimer, M. (1970). *Pictorial history of psychology and psychiatry*, ed. by A. A. Roback and T. Kiernan. *Contemporary Psychology*, 15, 380.

Wertheimer, M. (1970). *The search for factors that extremize the autokinetic effect*, by A. S. Luchins and E. H. Luchins. *Contemporary Psychology*, 15, 380.

Wertheimer, M. (1973). *The psychology of second-language learning*, ed. by P. Pimsleur and T. Quinn. *Contemporary Psychology*, 18, 24-25.

Wertheimer, M. (1973). *The selected papers of Wolfgang Köhler*, ed. by M. Henle. *American Journal of Psychiatry*, 129, 496.

Wertheimer, M. (1974). *Dynamics in psychology*, by W. Köhler. *American Journal of Psychology*, 87, 302-303.

Wertheimer, M. (1976). *A history of modern psychology*, 2nd ed., by D. P. Schultz. *Contemporary Psychology*, 21, 7-8.

Wertheimer, M. (1977). *The roots of psychology: A source book in the history of ideas*, ed. by S. Diamond. *Philosophical Psychologist*, 11, #1, 13-16.

Wertheimer, M. (1978). *Die Ursprünge der objektiven Psychologie [The origins of objective psychology]*, by J. Brozek and S. Diamond. *American Journal of Psychology*, 91, 540-543.

Wertheimer, M. (1979). *Pioneers of psychology*, by R. E. Fancher. *Contemporary Psychology*, 24, 904-905.

Wertheimer, M. (1981). *Erwachendes Denken [Awakening thought]*, by F. Klix. *Contemporary Psychology*, 26, 675-676.

Wertheimer, M. (1982). *Humanistic psychology: Concepts and criticisms*, ed. by J. R. Royce and L. P. Mos. *Contemporary Psychology*, 27, 534-535.

Wertheimer, M. (1983). *Otto Selz: His contribution to psychology*, ed. by N. H. Frijda and A. D. de Groot. *American Scientist*, Jan.-Feb., 71, 95.

Wertheimer, M. (1983). Kurt Lewin's *Wissenschaftstheorie [Theory of science]*, I., ed. by A. Métraux. *American Journal of Psychology*, 96, 154-156.

Wertheimer, M. (1983). Kurt Lewin's *Feldtheorie [Field theory]*, ed. by C. F. Graumann. *American Journal of Psychology*, 96, 156-157.

F. Baeriswyl and Wertheimer, M. (1983). *Emotion und Vergessen [Emotion and forgetting]*, by Günther Kebeck. *Contemporary Psychology*, 28, 641.

Wertheimer, M. (1984). Kurt Lewin's *Psychologie der Entwicklung und Erziehung [Psychology of development and training]*, ed. by F. E. Weinert and H. Gundlach. *American Journal of Psychology*, 97, 471-472.

Wertheimer, M. (1984). Kurt Lewin's *Wissenschaftstheorie [Theory of science], II.*, ed. by A. Métraux. *American Journal of Psychology*, 97, 632-634.

Wertheimer, M. and Werner, J. (1985). *Modern art and modern science: The parallel analysis of vision*, by P. C. Vitz and A. B. Glimcher. *American Journal of Psychology*, 98, 328-331.

Wertheimer, M. (1988). *1879 and all that*, by Mary Henle. *American Journal of Psychology*, 101, 135-142.

Wertheimer, M. (1989). *Psychology in twentieth-century thought and society*, ed. by M. G. Ash and W. R. Woodward. *Contemporary Psychology*, 34, 199-200.

Wertheimer, M. (1989). *The nature of creativity: Contemporary psychological perspectives*, ed. by R. J. Sternberg, *American Scientist*, 77, 291.

Wertheimer, M. (1989). *Psychology in twentieth-century thought and society*, ed. by M. G. Ash and W. R. Woodward. *Journal of the History of the Behavioral Sciences*, 25, 259-262.

Wertheimer, M. (1990). *The notebooks*, Vol. 1, by F. Heider. *American Journal of Psychology*, 103, 115-122.

Wertheimer, M. (1990). Siegfried Jaeger, Ed., *Briefe von Wolfgang Köhler an Hans Geitel 1907-1920, mit zwei Arbeiten Köhlers, „Über elektromagnetische Erregung des Trommelfelles" und „Intelligenzprüfungen am Orang" im Anhang [Letters from Wolfgang Köhler to Hans Geitel 1907-1920, with two of Köhler's works appended: "On electromagnetic stimulation of the eardrum" and "Intelligence tests with the orangutan"]. Journal of the History of the Behavioral Sciences*, 26, 290-293.

King, D. B. and Wertheimer, M. (1992). *The legacy of Solomon Asch: Essays in cognition and social psychology* ed. by I. Rock. *American Journal of Psychology*, 105, 123-130.

Wertheimer, M. and King, D. B. (1992). A fresh look at what psychologists do. Review of P. du Preez, *A science of mind: The quest for psychological reality. Contemporary Psychology*, 37, 411-412.

Wertheimer, M. (1994). Experimental epistemology and the perception of causality. Review of Thinès, G., Costall, A., and Butterworth, G. (Eds.), *Michotte's experimental phenomenology of perception. American Journal of Psychology*, 107, 275-285.

Wertheimer, M. (1996). Review of videotape, "Larry." *Colorado Libraries*.

Wertheimer, M. (1998). Review of Danziger, K., *Naming the mind: How psychology found its language*. Thousand Oaks, CA: Sage, 1997. *Journal of the History of the Behavioral Sciences*, 34, 182-183.

Wertheimer, M. (1998). Opus magnificentissimum. Retrospective review of Koch, S. (Ed.), *Psychology: A study of a science*, six volumes, 1959-1963. *Contemporary Psychology*, 43, 7-10.

Wertheimer, M. (2001). Review of Finkelman, D. and Kessel, F. (Eds.), Koch, S., *Psychology in human context: Essays in dissidence and reconstruction*. Chicago: University of Chicago Press. *Contemporary Psychology*, 46, 34-36.

Wertheimer, M. (2004). Der Vergessenheit entrissen [Torn from being forgotten]. Review of Court, J. and Janssen, J.P., *Wilhelm Benary (1888-1955) Leben und Werk. Forschung & Lehre, 4,* 212-213.

Wertheimer, M. (2004). Review of Court, J. and Janssen, J.P., *Wilhelm Benary (1888-1955) Leben und Werk [Life and Work]. Gestalt Theory,* 26, 74-78.

Colloquia, invited addresses, etc.

Columbia University-Psychiatric Institute, NY, 1958.

Rockland State Hospital, Orangeburg, NY, 1959.

University of Pennsylvania School of Medicine, 1959.

Duke University, Durham, NC, 1960.

Wayne State University, Detroit, MI, 1960.

Dakota Wesleyan University, SD, 1961.

University of Kansas, 1961.

Fort Hays Kansas State College, 1962.

Claremont Graduate School, CA, 1962.

Southwestern College, KS, 1963.

University of Colorado, College of Engineering, 1963.

National Association of College and University Chaplains, Denver, CO, 1964.

University of Salzburg, Austria, 1964.

University of Vienna, Austria, 1964.

University of Redlands, CA, 1964.

Tabor College, KS, 1965.

Indiana University, 1965.

University of Chicago, 1965.

University of Buffalo, 1965.

Loretto Heights College, CO, 1966.

University of Hawaii, 1966.

Bard College, NY, 1966.

Colorado College, 1967.

Kalamazoo College, MI, 1968.

Oberlin College, OH, 1968.

Colorado State University, 1968.

University of Umeå, Sweden, 1970.

University of British Columbia, Canada, 1971.

Georgetown University, 1971.

Illinois Psychological Association, 1971.

The University of Calgary, Canada, 1972.

Cornell University, 1972.

Western State College of Colorado, 1972.

Colorado State University, 1972.

Linguistic Circle of Colorado, 1972.

University of Colorado, 1972.

Rocky Mountain Modern Language Association, 1972.

Rocky Mountain Psychological Association, 1972.

American Psychological Association, 1972.

Boulder High School, 1973.

Boulder High School, 1974.

University of New Hampshire, 1974.

Boulder High School, 1975.

University of Northern Colorado, 1976.

Boulder High School, 1976.

University of Colorado, 1977.

University of Victoria, Canada, 1977.

Appalachian State University, NC, 1978.

University of Colorado, 1978.

Nebraska Wesleyan University, 1978.

Southwest Texas State University, 1979.

Colorado State University, 1979.

Kearney State College, NE, 1979.

Ohio Wesleyan University, 1979.

Washington University, St. Louis, MO, 1979.

American Psychological Association, 1979.

Southern Illinois University, Edwardsville, 1979.

The University of Calgary, Canada, 1980.

University of Southern Colorado, 1980.

University of Colorado, 1980 (3).

22nd International Congress of Psychology, Leipzig, East Germany, 1980.

American Psychological Association, 1980.

Western Washington University, 1980.

University of Colorado, 1981 (2).

Bad Homburg, West Germany, 1981.

Northern Illinois University, 1981.

American Psychological Association, 1981.

University of Colorado, 1982 (3).

Western Psychological Association, 1982.

Rocky Mountain Psychological Association, 1982.

Humboldt University, East Berlin, Germany, 1982.

University of Jena, East Germany, 1982.

American Psychological Association, 1982.

Colorado State University, 1983.

University of Colorado, 1983 (2).

University of Kyoto, Japan, 1983.

Nagoya University, Japan, 1983.

University of Colorado Alumni, Bangkok, Thailand, 1983.

International Council of Psychologists, 1983.

American Psychological Association, 1983 (2).

Metropolitan State College, Denver, 1984.

University of Colorado, 1984.

American Psychological Association, 1984.

University of Colorado, 1985 (3).

American Psychological Association, 1985.

Humboldt University, East Berlin, Germany, 1985.

Tokyo University, Japan, 1985.

Chukyo University, Japan, 1985.

University of Colorado, 1986 (5).

American Psychological Association, 1986 (3).

University of California at Los Angeles, 1986.

Colorado State University, 1987 (2).

American Psychological Association, 1987 (4).
University of Colorado at Denver, 1987.
University of Colorado at Boulder, 1987 (3).
University of Frankfurt, Germany, 1987.
University of Würzburg, Germany, 1987.
Colorado Christian College, 1987.
University of Colorado at Boulder, 1988 (2).
Rocky Mountain Psychological Association, 1988 (2).
New School for Social Research, New York, 1988.
Technical University of Berlin, West Germany, 1988.
University of Colorado at Boulder, 1989 (4).
Rocky Mountain Psychological Association, 1989 (2).
University of Bern, Switzerland, 1989.
University of Colorado at Boulder, 1990 (4).
Rocky Mountain Psychological Association, 1990 (2).
Humboldt University, East Berlin, Germany, 1990.
University of Denver, 1990.
University of Colorado at Boulder, 1991.
Rocky Mountain Psychological Association, 1991 (2).
Colorado State University, 1991.
American Psychological Association, 1991 (4).
Southeastern Psychological Association, 1992.
Rocky Mountain Psychological Association, 1992.
American Psychological Association, 1992 (3).
United States Air Force Academy, Colorado Springs, 1992 (2).
University of Colorado at Boulder, 1992.
University of Colorado at Boulder, 1993.
Rocky Mountain Psychological Association, 1993 (3).
Free University of Berlin, Germany, 1993.
University of Cologne, Germany, 1993.
American Psychological Association, 1993 (4).
Colorado State University, 1994.
Rocky Mountain Psychological Association, 1994 (2).

American Psychological Association, 1994.

Eberhard-Karls-Universität, Tübingen, Germany, 1994.

University of Colorado at Boulder, 1994.

American Psychological Association, 1995.

University of Colorado at Boulder, 1995 (2).

Johann Wolfgang Goethe University, Frankfurt, Germany, 1995.

University of Colorado at Boulder, 1996.

American Psychological Association, 1996 (2).

Colorado State University, 1996.

American Psychological Association, 1997.

American Psychological Association, 1998.

Rocky Mountain Psychological Association, 1999.

American Psychological Association, 1999.

American Psychological Association, 2004.

Rocky Mountain Psychological Association, First annual Lillian Portenier-Michael Wertheimer pre-convention conference on teaching, 2005.

University of Colorado at Boulder, 2005 (2).

American Psychological Association, 2005.

Appalachian State University, Boone, NC, 2005.

American Psychological Association, 2006.

American Psychological Association, 2008.

American Psychological Association, 2009.

University of Würzburg, Germany, 2009.

Deutsche Gesellschaft für Psychologie, Bielefeld, Germany, 2012.

Rocky Mountain Psychological Association, Denver, CO, Keynote address at the Lillian Portenier-Michael Wertheimer pre-convention conference on teaching, 2016.

Appendix E: Scholarly Efforts

My long and rewarding career encompassed teaching, service, some administrative roles, and a variety of scholarly efforts. The official "formula" for evaluating the performance of a faculty member in the College of Arts and Sciences and the Graduate School at the University of Colorado at Boulder proposed that 40% should be for teaching, 20% for service, and 40% for scholarly work, but the informal consensus was that de facto it was something more like teaching 20%, service -10%, and scholarship 90%. Committee work was devalued, and toward the end of the 20th century the ability to bring in outside grant and contract funds for research continued to become more and more critical in evaluating a faculty member's "accomplishments." I received a few tiny financial awards, but I never did succeed in bringing in large research grants or contracts; I believe this is a major reason for my salary starting to lag behind that of colleagues who managed to bring in large sums of money in contracts with

E-1 Marilyn looking at a Meridian display of all the books I've written, co-authored, edited, or co-edited, or in which I had chapters *(family archives)*

© Springer Fachmedien Wiesbaden GmbH, part of Springer Nature 2020
M. Wertheimer, *Facets of an Academic's Life*,
https://doi.org/10.1007/978-3-658-28770-2

the defense department, the National Science Foundation, the National Institutes for Health and Mental Health, etc. This lag became more pronounced over the years, leading to a rather paltry income during my last decade or two of teaching. What became crucial in ensuring advancement was a trait called "marketability"; mine was low since I was getting older, had not won any large research grants, and was publishing mostly in relatively lower-prestige areas such as the history of psychology. While I did get approached for several positions elsewhere during my long career at Colorado, I did not have the skill to land lucrative offers that could have been used to try to enhance my salary at Colorado. Several of my younger colleagues did have that skill, and indeed managed to improve their income substantially with that strategy.

While my scholarly efforts did not yield much by way of financial enhancement (I once estimated that my writing efforts yielded me perhaps about 2½ to 3 cents in royalties for every hour or so I spent on them), they did lead to relatively early promotions (to associate professor at age 30 and full professor at age 34), and they were sufficiently voluminous to yield a satisfying record of personal achievement. By and large, my scholarly activities have been a lot of fun. As author, co-author, editor, or co-editor, I have been involved with over 40 books, and I am author or co-author of many chapters in edited books and several hundred articles published in refereed technical journals as well as several hundred presentations at international, national, or regional psychology conventions. Some have called my output prodigious; I have joked about the number of trees that had to be sacrificed in order to publish my works, and the books with which I've been involved fill a small bookcase proudly on display in the entryway to our retirement community apartment. None of my works have led to a major scientific breakthrough, none have been cited a thousand times or more in the professional literature, and none stand out as truly a significant achievement (except perhaps for the biography of my father, published in 2005). But as an overall corpus, I do find it a satisfying testament to a long, fulfilling career.

Since professional advancement in the early years of my career was largely dependent on substantial publication in prestigious professional outlets in one's field, it was incumbent on young faculty members to heed the admonition to "publish or perish." (In later years one could "publish *and* perish," when a major

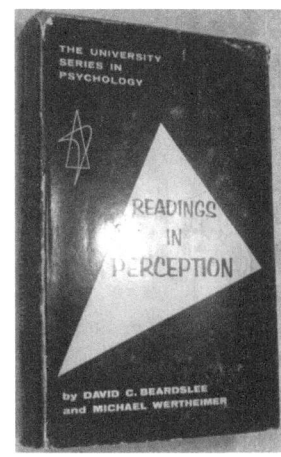

E-2 *Readings in Perception*
1958, New York: Van Nostrand

criterion began to be bringing in outside funding, and prestigious publications no longer sufficed to bring advancement, tenure, or promotion.) I followed the admonition, by presenting lots of convention papers, submitting manuscripts to major journals, and engaging in the preparation of books. By the time I retired, my curriculum vitae included some 20 single-spaced typed pages listing books, journal articles, papers presented at professional association conventions, book reviews, colloquia, and invited addresses. This narrative by no means mentions them all; a copy of my curriculum vitae from 2012, the last year in which I bothered to prepare one (with a few incomplete additions since then), is presented in Appendix D.

The first book in which I was involved was issued by a major publishing house, Van Nostrand, in 1958. Co-edited with David Beardslee, a colleague who had been a fellow student at Swarthmore, it was intended to be a set of readings to be used as supplementary material for courses in perception, and included several articles that I had translated into English from German and French.

Next was an enlarged edition of my father's major work, *Productive Thinking*, to which were added several appendices consisting of papers I had translated from German, a few fragments found in my father's papers, and a significant paper Lise had edited that was in English. That book was reissued later, and was translated into several foreign languages.

E-3 *Productive Thinking* 1959, Harper Collins

E-4 Kai von Fieandt *(courtesy of Juhani von Fieandt)*

With Bill Scott I co-authored the book *Introduction to Psychological Research*, which appeared in 1962 under the imprint of another prestigious publisher, Wiley, and came out in a translation to Spanish in 1982. In the mid 1960s I helped a visiting Finnish psychologist, Kai von Fieandt, prepare an English version of his text on perception; he wrote out his own translation on alternate lines of legal size lined paper, and I edited and revised his text in the lines between to turn it into more idiomatic and readable English. Also published during the 1960s was a book co-authored by George Scherer, a professor of German, reporting the results of an extensive experiment on the effectiveness of the then-popular audiolingual method of teaching a foreign language, German.

In 1970 was published my most successful book, a brief history of psychology. As mentioned on page 142, it was based largely on my detailed notes from Karl Muenzinger's course on the history of psychology. I had asked E.G. Boring of Harvard to look it over for me—and he conscientiously sent me many pages of carefully thought-out detailed editorial suggestions, almost all of which I used in revising the manuscript. I also received useful suggestions from my colleague O.J. Harvey. The book has been revised several times; a fifth edition of it was published in 2012, and, at the publisher's request, a sixth is already in preparation. German, Japanese, Portuguese, and Dutch translations of this brief text were published during the 1970s, and an Italian version in 1983. It has in its various editions and translations sold more than 70,000 copies.

A Psycholinguistic Experiment in Foreign-language Teaching
By George A. C. Scherer and Michael Wertheimer

McGRAW-HILL SERIES IN PSYCHOLOGY

E-5 *A Psycholinguistic Experiment in Foreign-Language Teaching* 1964, McGraw-Hill

E-6 *A Brief History of Psychology* in five editions and five translations, with *Fundamental Issues in Psychology (Holt, Rinehart, and Winston: 1970, 1979, 1987 and Fundamental Issues 1972; Harcourt: 2000; Psychology Press: 2012. Dutch: Rob Uiterwijk 1977; German: Elisabeth and Wolfgang Schmidbauer, Piper 1971; Japanese: Seishin Shobo, Ltd. 1972; Portuguese: Lolio Lourenco de Oliveira, Editora da Universidade de São Paulo 1972; Italian: Monica Morganti, Zanichelli 1983)*

The original manuscript for the *Brief History* also included a kind of rather long theoretical analysis of major dimensions on which psychological theories differed over the years. At the request of the publisher, this section was separated from the historical part, and was issued as its own slender volume entitled *Fundamental Issues in Psychology*, also in 1970. The publisher intended it to be a kind of introduction to theoretical psychology, or even as an introductory psychology text, but not surprisingly, it did not capture a very large part of that huge market and went out of print a few years later.

In 1970, I also edited at the request of another major publisher, Scott, Foresman, a volume that was informally called a "relevance reader"; at the time, a fad was trying to demonstrate how abstruse fields like psychology might have useful applications. Called *Confrontation: Psychology and the Problems of To-*

E-7 *Psychology and the Problems of Today* 1970 and 1978, Scott, Foresman

day, it was reissued in a second edition eight years later, co-edited with Leon Rappoport, a former graduate student.

I was trying to encourage the responsible teaching of empirically based psychology as a natural science at high schools, and made work on this issue a major aim for a sabbatical year in 1970 to 1971, which I spent at the APA Central Office in Washington as acting administrative officer for educational affairs. One outcome was a translation I made from the Swedish of an introductory psychology text for high school students, including a study guide and an instructor's resource book. This came out in the 1980s; however, the publisher tried mistakenly to market it for the undergraduate and the junior college market, and consequently it never took off.

Several other ventures intended to enhance the teaching of psychology at high schools and colleges fared somewhat better; I participated in the writing of several projects for introductory psychology courses, and was co-author or co-editor of two APA books, one on teaching psychology in secondary schools and one on the first psychology course in college. An incomplete but beauti-

E-8 APA books on introductory psychology in secondary schools and college *(courtesy of the American Psychological Association)*

ful text on the history of psychology by my admired undergraduate professor Robbie MacLeod was edited by Mary Henle and me and published in 1975; I saw it through the press.

Wayne Viney, a colleague who taught psychology and was a successful administrator at Colorado State University in Fort Collins, joined me during his sabbatical year late in the 1970s. He, Marilyn, and I collaborated on preparing a reference book on sources in the history of psychology for a prominent series published by Gale. He became a good friend; he taught the summer school course on the history of psychology in the CU psychology department a number of times. Two other psychologists joined me as co-editors of a special issue of the *Journal of the History of the Behavioral Sciences* in 1988 devoted to the history of psychology in the Rocky Mountain

E-9 Wayne Viney *(courtesy of the Archives of the History of American Psychology, The Drs. Nicholas and Dorothy Cummings Center for the History of Psychology, The University of Akron)*

region, and another colleague and I co-edited an APA volume on the history of regional organizations in psychology; this book, published in 1993, was probably the biggest flop of any book in which I was involved, selling I think fewer than 40 copies altogether.

In 1991, APA published the first volume in a series that continued for a total of seven volumes, of all of which I was co-editor, called *Portraits of Pioneers in Psychology*. This series, initially co-edited by G.A. Kimble, who for a time was chair of the CU psychology department, was originally based on presentations at psychology conventions, but later was changed to consist of chapters by prominent current scholars who were invited to

E-10 *A History of Regional Organizations in American Psychology* 1993, American Psychological Association

E-11 *Portraits of Pioneers in Psychology*, 1991-2012 *(courtesy of the American Psychological Association)*

write about deceased distinguished individuals who had worked in the same subfield as the invited author. The seventh (and almost certainly the last) volume in this series was published in 2012; the entire set was published not only by APA but also co-published by the prestigious separate firm of Erlbaum Associates.

Stephen Davis (pictured on page 402) and I, both former national presidents of the national honor society in psychology, Psi Chi, undertook an oral history of this society. We designed and conducted telephone interviews with all the preceding officers of Psi Chi who were still living at the time. Psi Chi published a book consisting of edited transcripts of these interviews in 2000.

E-12 *An Oral History of Psi Chi* 2000, Psi Chi, the International Honor Society in Psychology

Back in the spring of 1943 I had proposed to my father that I should forgo an offer to spend the summer as a junior counselor at the Ethical Culture School camp in upstate New York near Cooperstown and instead devote the summer to writing his biography. Clearly touched by my offer, he nevertheless sensibly suggested that I should go to camp instead. I did so, and, as narrated on page 48, by that October he was dead.

But my wish to publish his biography persisted over many decades. Several times I interviewed my mother about him on tape, most often in German to try to enhance memories she had of my father, and I made various trips to New York and to Europe, seeking information about him in many different archives. I wrote a long first draft of the book, based on almost all the material I had found, and wasn't satisfied with the product; it was too unfocused and sprawling. Over the years I prepared a second draft and then in 1990 one of Wayne Viney's doctoral students, Brett King, joined me in an attempt to produce a better draft. We ran this draft by a combined undergraduate and graduate class on Gestalt theory; we required every student in that class in 1993 to provide us detailed reactions and recommendations concerning this draft. Brett became an instructor in the CU psychology department, where he soon became a senior instructor, receiving rave reviews for his teaching. As a non-tenure-track member of this department, his teaching load typically was about twice that of a regular tenure-track faculty member while his income was about one half that of his tenure-track colleagues—and he was typically saddled with courses with huge enrollments, in-cluding introductory psychology, social psychology, personality, and the history of psychology. He and I went through the large accumulation of documents, interviews, correspondence, etc. that I had amassed, and he generated yet another draft based on these materials, the earlier drafts, and the student input. I rewrote this draft once more, yielding one more version that I finally thought might be appropriate for publication; I focused on my father's intellectual biography, and removed a good deal of other materi-al that I believed was not consistent with that goal.

E-13 D. Brett King *(courtesy of the Archives of the History of American Psychology, The Drs. Nicholas and Dorothy Cummings Center for the History of Psychology, The University of Akron)*

Various publishers had been made aware of my attempt to generate a biography of my famous father, and expressed interest in seeing it whenever I thought it might be ready. These firms included both commercial publishers like Harper, Wiley, and others as well as university presses such as Harvard and

Cambridge. I dutifully inquired of many potential publishers about possible actual interest in publishing the book before submitting the manuscript, and received many glowing responses telling me that they hoped I'd be successful in finding an appropriate publisher—but indicating that the market for intellectual biographies had shrunk so much that they would not be able to include the book in their own list of publications. This was true for almost every outlet I tried—even though many of them had previously asked me to contact them whenever I thought the work was ready for publication. The one exception was Transaction Publishers of Rutgers University in New Jersey. The editor in chief there said he would go ahead and publish it for purposes of "prestige," but warned me that he

would be surprised if it sold as many as 300 copies in total. Transaction did publish it in 2005, and it fared so well, selling over 1,000 copies, that Transaction, which had first issued it as a hardback, published a paperback version of it in 2007, partly in response also to some very positive reviews published about it in journals. My teenage goal of writing and bringing to completion a biography of my father took more than a half century to accomplish, but it was indeed finally accomplished.

A minor footnote to this account: although I do believe that my efforts on the book compared to those of

E-14 *Max Wertheimer and Gestalt Theory* 2005, Transaction Publishers

Brett King warranted my being listed as first author, I decided that, since there was no benefit to me any more, having already been retired for more than a decade, and it might further enhance Brett's curriculum vitae and hence the remainder of his career, the order of the authors should be King and Wertheimer rather than Wertheimer and King.

Although I consider the publication of this book to be a high point of my "scholarly efforts," there were a few more that were published during the last years of my long career. I have already mentioned the seventh volume in the series that I co-edited since its inception, *Portraits of Pioneers in Psychology*, and the fifth edition of my brief history of psychology, both of which were issued in 2012. Two projects that involved translating lengthy material from German to English were both initiated by a German visual neuroscientist, Lothar Spillmann, who was forcibly retired against his own wishes from the University of Freiburg despite having ongoing research contracts when he turned age 65. The first was a translation of the influential first edition of a book by a late former student of my father, Wolfgang Metzger, on the laws of seeing. This book illustrated, demonstrated, and expanded on my father's seminal work on the principles of perceptual organization. A faculty member at MIT prepared a first rather loose translation of the book, and at Spillmann's request I prepared an alternate one that tried much harder to keep the translation closer to the original German. With modest input from a few other scholars and a bit of further editing by Spillmann, my version was published by MIT Press in 2006.

The other was a project in which my daughter Karen helped immeasurably. Since two of my father's early

E-15 Lothar Spillmann *(courtesy of Lothar Spillmann)*

E-16 *Laws of Seeing*
2006, MIT Press

articles, respectively published in 1912 and 1923, had, according to Spillmann, been extensively cited during the last century and were clearly relevant in their content to a variety of current issues in visual neuroscience, he argued that they should be made available in English. I was invited to prepare translations of these two papers, respectively 100 and 50 pages in length, to form the core of a book that would also contain lengthy analyses by current visual neuroscientists that not only summarized the rather voluminous further research the papers had generated, but also discussed their continuing relevance for current research; each of these two analyses cited literally hundreds of references. A first draft of these translations that I produced turned out to be much too literal; the convoluted grammatical structures and excessively long sentences typical of the German versions were retained in my first attempt, and made the translation very hard to read and understand for a reader of English who knew little or no German. It took my daughter and me a good year of Sunday afternoons and Wednesday evenings almost every week to generate more acceptable drafts. Her job, as a professional wordsmith who had earned a PhD in English from Yale University

(after an MA in English from CU and a BA in English with highest honors from Swarthmore College) and was working full time as a technical writer, was to make the English translations reasonably lucid and accessible to regular readers of technical English. My job was to try to retain the connotative as well as the denotative meaning of my father's almost tortured German prose as much as possible. We spent delightful but sometimes frustrating time on this project, occasionally taking a good hour or two on a paragraph to come up with a version we could both accept. Spillmann considered the drafts we prepared still too difficult, so Karen edited them both once more without my input,

E-17 *On Perceived Motion and Figural Organization* 2012, MIT Press and with minor further editing by Spillmann they became the core of a book also published in 2012 by MIT Press. With the appearance of this volume as well as the *Pioneers* book and the fifth edition of my little history book all in 2012 (with a sixth currently in preparation), I think there is no need for me to consider being involved in any further book projects.

I also long ago began playing with a possible cookbook devoted to simplicity, frugality, nutrition, and practicality, and have contemplated possibly trying to turn material I used in a seminar I taught during my last years of teaching, on cultural aspects of language, into a book as well. Who knows.

Many of the journal articles, notes, and book reviews that I have published since the first ones in 1951 have been co-authored with students and sometimes colleagues, and they have been published in a wide variety of outlets, from highly prestigious and high-rejection-rate technical periodicals to ones for which almost any submitted manuscript was gratefully received and accepted with minimal scholarly review. The subject matter also varied prodigiously; especially in the early years of my career I luxuriated in the fact that the academic life, while it did require specialization to some degree, permitted one to explore a wide range of fascinating puzzles of many different kinds, and to seek creative ways to deal— preferably empirically—with these puzzles. This was a strategy I tried to convey to students as well as to practice myself, and was a major theme in my first draft of the book with Bill Scott about how to do psychological research.

The first article was essentially a condensed version of my master's thesis; co-authored with my mentor for that thesis, Tex Garner, it appeared in the prestigious *Journal of the Acoustical Society of America*. The second, as described on page 101, was proposed to me by J.G. Beebe-Center of Harvard, who also helped me on many successive drafts of it, came out in the equally prestigious

introduction to

psychological

research

WILLIAM A. SCOTT
and MICHAEL WERTHEIMER

E-18 *Introduction to Psychological Research* 1962, Wiley

American Journal of Psychology. Two more papers, one in the same journal and one in the even more selective journal *Science*, came out the next year; they were based on the work I did for my doctoral dissertation. Five papers were published in 1953: a rather unimportant one based on my dissertation that I submitted to the *National Hearing Aid Journal* and a much more significant one reporting the main findings of my doctoral research in the prestigious *Journal of Experimental Psychology*, as well as three more on totally unrelated matters. One, described on page 112, was an empirical assessment showing that eye content responses on the Rorschach inkblot test did *not* relate to paranoid diagnoses or ideation; a second, published in the prestigious *American Psychologist*, was a report co-authored with two colleagues at Wesleyan of the results of an empirical investigation of the undergraduate origins of scholars in the behavioral sciences; and the third was a brief note co-authored with my wife Nan about a theoretical interpretation of individual differences in figural aftereffects, a particular kind of perceptual illusion, that was published in the influential *Psychological Review*.

Five articles were also published in 1954. They ranged from a bibliography, co-authored by a graduate student, of recent work on a widely-used intelligence test, that was published in the easily accessible *Psychological Newsletter*, a periodical that folded a few years after this article was published, through some psychological work accepted by the famed British *Quarterly Journal of Experimental Psychology*, and a note questioning the efficiency of psychotherapy (based on extensive statistical analysis), to further work on the same kind of perceptual illusion, figural aftereffects, on which Nan and I had published during the previous year.

In my eagerness to further establish my career, I continued a rather prodigious output of published articles during the next few years, which I'm sure helped get me the job in Colorado and my fairly rapid promotions to associate and then full professor. The remainder of the 1950s yielded papers on the Rorschach test, one based on Nan's PhD dissertation (for which she generously gave me a co-authorship), more papers on figural aftereffects, a note on how to teach courses in abnormal psychology, several further empirical psychophysical studies, a paper in the *American Journal of Psychology* reporting a rather major experimental study in perception based on work I had done years earlier at Swarth-

E-19 Charles E. Osgood, a participant in the Estes Park conference in which I took part *(courtesy of the Department of Psychology at the University of Nebraska-Lincoln)*

more, notes on issues as disparate as split infinitives and the improvement of graduate education in psychology, and an *American Psychologist* article on training for research in psychology that reported the outcome of a month-long APA-NSF Estes Park conference described on page 406, in which I was a very junior participant with such illustrious established scientists as Tex Garner, D.O. Hebb, Charles Osgood, and B.F. Skinner. By the end of 1959 I had a total of 40 published articles to list in my curriculum vitae, and I even remember a kind of puerile feeling of pride that the *number* of my publications already greatly exceeded that of my father in his whole lifetime (though I did realize that nothing of mine matched in import a single one of his far more important papers). Quite a few of these earlier papers were co-authored with students, both graduate students and undergraduate honors students whose theses I had supervised. The topics ranged so widely that they even included one in which I demonstrated experimentally that the amount of time that one *believes* one spent in practicing a psychomotor skill is more significant in how much is actually learned than the actual physical amount of time practiced.

My production of articles continued unabated into the 1960s. The breadth of the topics studied empirically or discussed from a historical or theoretical perspective, if anything, increased even further. Published was a minor study showing that subjective impressions of age change with chronological age, such that, for example, the age of thirty seems old to a teenager but young to an octogenarian, as were items about my father and a short paper in *Science* that attracted a good bit of attention because it showed that a degree of coordination of auditory and visual space can be demonstrated in infants less than a day old—long before, according to then-accepted theories of learning, such coordination should be possible. There were articles in the *Encyclopædia Britannica*, in *Perceptual and*

Motor Skills, in the *Journal of Experimental Psychology*, and other outlets, including several on the German teaching experiment for which I had developed a series of measurements to assess competence in a foreign language, the detailed results of which had been published in a 1964 book I co-authored with the principal investigator in that project, German professor George A.C. Scherer. Other topics included various perceptual phenomena, the impressions people form of other people ("social perception," an area for which I prepared a substantial bibliographic card file which never did generate a publication), the prediction of college grades, the validity of handwriting analysis or "graphology," and a truncated version of my presidential address of 1966 for the APA division on the teaching of psychology.

I also wrote a chapter about the fallibility of perception in a book on UFOs, unidentified flying objects, that was published on the completion of a major Air-Force-financed research project headed by the distinguished physicist E. U. Condon. Condon had asked whether Stuart Cook, at the time chairman of the psychology department, could recommend any of his department's faculty members to join in this project; Cook recommended Bill Scott because of his expertise in social psychology, and me because of my specialization in sensation and perception. Condon invited both of us to be contributing scientists on the project.

Bill managed to find at least one interesting relationship: the frequency of local reports of UFOs reliably increases right after there is a major news report about a UFO. I myself was initially somewhat interested in what the staff of the project called the "ETI hypothesis":

E-20 *Scientific Study of Unidentified Flying Objects* 1969 *(courtesy of the University of Colorado)*

that unexplained credible reports of unidentified flying objects by reliable witnesses provide evidence for visits by "extra-terrestrial intelligent" beings. We staff members were provided extensive information about a number of not very well-known kinds of mundane phenomena (including secret demonstrations of hovercraft and other then-classified material) that could produce the perception of a convincing unidentified flying object, and we realized that there are indeed many earthly events that can engender (false but convincing) belief in an extra-terrestrial intelligent visitor. I lost interest in the whole UFO investigation when I came up with what we called the "framasand hypothesis." A "framasand" is a mundane event with which a reliable witness of a UFO event is unfamiliar. The problem is that any reliable unexplained UFO report could just as readily be due to some perfectly mundane but (to the witness and to investigators) not yet fully understood event, so no such report can be considered evidence for the ETI hypothesis after all. It could just as easily be due to some mundane event that the witness and investigators simply didn't know about or understand.

But my involvement in the UFO project did produce at least one paper that I managed to get published in a technical journal, based on one "early response team" investigation in which I was involved. The paper reported a case of "autostasis," or apparently becoming stationary, of an object in constant continuous motion in an undifferentiated background (the opposite of the well-known "autokinetic phenomenon," or the apparent motion of an actually stationary pinpoint of light on an undifferentiated background). The team was sent to the badlands of South Dakota to investigate an apparently convincing report of a UFO near midnight that hovered for a short time and shone a light on what seemed to be a reliable witness, who also reported that the craft changed directions at right angles, and made noise on approach but none on departure. We investigators, on interviewing other witnesses and obtaining further information, received conflicting reports about noise, apparent direction, and the length of time a light was on, and managed to establish that this UFO report had been generated by a twin-engine plane with a searchlight that had indeed been at the reported locale at the right time—and that the co-pilot had been overheard to say to the pilot before they took off, "Let's see if we can't spook some UFO reports tonight."

E-21 Margaret Altmann *(courtesy of the Colorado Springs Gazette)*

The 1970s brought publications on the history of psychology in high schools, some works in psycholinguistics, an obituary of my beloved mentor Robbie MacLeod (pictured on page 62), some articles on philosophical psychology, general psychology, and humanistic psychology, and reports of a few further empirical studies.

By the 1980s papers on the history of psychology were predominant, but there were also articles about issues relating to Psi Chi (the national honor society in psychology); several in German based on papers delivered in German-speaking Europe; a biography of my late animal psychologist colleague, Margaret Altmann; annual essays on psychology for *Peterson's guides for graduate programs*; and only a few empirically based projects.

I retired officially in 1993, but continued to publish fairly profusely during all of the 1990s (my vita claims 54 articles published in that decade!). There were brief biographies of Mary Henle, Eddie Newman (pictured on page 103), Barbara Burks (page 285), Karl Duncker, Kenneth Little, and my father (page 48 and elsewhere); many articles related to activities in APA, Psi Chi, and the Rocky Mountain Psychological Association;

E-22 Mary Henle *(courtesy of the Archives of the History of American Psychology, The Drs. Nicholas and Dorothy Cummings Center for the History of Psychology, The University of Akron)*

E-23 Karl Duncker *(estate of Hermann and Käte Duncker, http://www.argus.bstu.bundesarc hiv.de/ny4445/rightframe.htm?vi d=ny4445&kid=0ab8bd67-3257- 4d14-8357-49351884bb82)*

more material on the teaching of psychology, the history of psychology, and philosophical psychology, a few more articles in German; more entries for encyclopedias, and a few other topics as well.

In the first decade of the twenty-first century my output of published articles appropriately diminished substantially. There were a few biographies and obituaries of Raymond Corsini, Neal Miller, Gregory Kimble, and Rudolf Arnheim (pictured on page 56); sever-

E-24 Raymond Corsini *(from "Raymond J. Corsini, the Marble Kid" by M. Wertheimer, The General Psychologist, Spring 2005, p. 16)*

al more encyclopedia entries; some more suggested activities and other matters concerned with the teaching of psychology; more papers about Gestalt psychology; and a book chapter pointing out that Rosalind Franklin really deserved to have been awarded the Nobel prize which Watson and Crick received for discovering the double-helix molecular structure of DNA.

E-25 Neal Miller *(courtesy of the Archives of the History of American Psychology, The Drs. Nicholas and Dorothy Cummings Center for the History of Psychology, The University of Akron)*

Altogether, my output of published articles was perhaps a bit too profligate; I can't say in retrospect that I'm proud of every single item I ever published. And there would be no point in ever issuing an edited volume, "Selected papers of Michael Wertheimer," because there would be no market for such a book. There are indeed a few articles that I still think are pretty good, but I also have no inclination to spend the time to read through my entire voluminous output searching for forgotten gems. I know there aren't any. Yet obviously my publications did help me attain the kinds

E-26 Rosalind Franklin *(from http://collaboration.wikia.com/wiki/File:Rosalind_Franklin.jpg)*

of roles that I've enjoyed, from my academic career through the many elected positions and honors that I've received. My "scientific" and "scholarly" career did not yield any significant scientific or intellectual lasting breakthroughs for which I could claim credit, but it did yield a lot of personal satisfaction and a kind of personal validation because some respected colleagues considered the stuff I was writing worthy of publication. This validation was indeed valued, since I have always been somewhat doubtful of my own intellectual prowess in comparison with that of my illustrious father and my brilliant first wife. I came to think that my career may have been reasonably successful, even if it certainly could never be called distinguished.

Papers presented at professional association conventions almost always had to be evaluated by a critical program committee, but the selection process for these contributions was often not as stringent as that involved in the evaluation of articles submitted for publication in print. My vita does include more than 130 convention presentations, mostly at meetings of the American Psychological Association, but also ones at the Rocky Mountain Psychological Association conventions and, early on, even the Colorado-Wyoming Academy of Sciences, as well as papers presented at more specialized conferences. The great majority of these papers ended up published in some form or another, but not all of them did so. There are ones describing the honors program at the University of Colorado (of which I was proud), reports of studies co-authored by graduate or undergraduate students, presentations for Phi Beta Kappa (the distinguished old academic honor society of which I became a member at Swarthmore and of whose chapter at the University of Colorado I was president from 1973 to 1979), and items like laudatory greetings to various regional, national, or international conventions. I also gave a number of invited lectures and colloquia at colleges and universities both in the United States and abroad, some of which did end up being published in some form.

I also published some 50 book reviews, usually by invitation; most of these appeared during the 1960s and 1970s, but three were issued during the twenty-first century, one of them in German. Many concerned books about perception or the history of psychology, but the topics ranged much more broadly than that to include abnormal psychology, the Rorschach test, psycholinguistics, social perception, cognitive psychology, second-language learning, creativity, and biographies of several prominent psychologists.

The institutions at which I was invited to present colloquia over the years ranged from modest colleges through rather distinguished universities both in the United States and in Europe and even Japan. They included the University of Pennsylvania, Duke University, the University of Kansas, Oberlin, Claremont Graduate School in California, Indiana University, the Universities of Chicago and of Buffalo, and such more modest places as Fort Hays Kansas State College, Loretto Heights College, and Kalamazoo College. Overseas I gave invited colloquia at the universities of Salzburg and Vienna in Austria; the university of Umeå in Sweden; in Bad Homburg, Humboldt University, the Technical University of Berlin, and the universities of Frankfurt, Cologne, and Würzburg as well as the Free University of Berlin and the University of Tübingen in Germany; at Bern in Switzerland; and in Japan at the universities at Chukyo, Nagoya, and Kyoto. These invited lectures and colloquia were more frequent during the 1960s, 1970s, and 1980s, but continued somewhat more modestly during the 1990s. A few even still occurred in the twenty-first century, culminating in lectures at the University of Würzburg in 2009 on the occasion of the establishment of an archive on the history of psychology there, and then in 2012 at the annual convention of the German Psychological Society in Bielefeld,

E-27 Me at the University of Wurzburg, at the display of my father's tachistoscope, 2009 *(photo by Hannes Vollmuth)*

Germany, in celebration of the centenary of the founding of the Gestalt school of psychology with my father's famous 1912 paper on the perception of apparent motion. Both of these latter invited lectures were, much to my gratification, supported by funds that defrayed my travel to Würzburg and to Bielefeld, and covered my expenses there. I was also invited to present a "resident chat" at my retirement community in 2013, and the plenary keynote address at the preconvention teaching conference in April 2016 at the Rocky Mountain Psychological Association Convention in Denver.

Overall, to repeat, the opportunities to share my thoughts in lectures, symposia, convention presentations, and published articles and books helped make me feel that, while my professional contributions may not have been earthshaking, at least they were considered sufficiently worthwhile by colleagues and peers to be publishable.

Appendix F: APA and Other Organizations

I've been involved in several organizations during my career, most of all with the American Psychological Association, in which I've been elected to a number of posts. In many ways, these involvements have been a significant part of my career and have contributed to my own self image. This identification with other units has included not only professional organizations, and the educational institutions with which I've been involved as student or faculty member, but also outfits totally unrelated to my professional career such as the Colorado Mountain Club and the Rocky Mountain Rescue Group, of which I have been an active member. My participation in these organizations is discussed at least briefly on pages 147 and 158-162.

I was proud to have been elected to Phi Beta Kappa, the venerable scholarly honor society, upon graduating from Swarthmore College, and have ever since maintained my support of that society, which has always championed the cause of excellence in liberal education. I even served for a time as president of the Phi Beta Kappa chapter at the University of Colorado and, with Wally Weir, director of general honors at CU, attended a triennial Phi Beta Kappa national meeting in Williamsburg, VA, that lasted for several days. One of the major issues was whether or not to permit establishment of new chapters of this prestigious and exclusive organization on the campuses of several institutions of higher learning that had applied for this coveted honor and for whom this honor was being recommended by strict evaluation committees, each of which had to follow stringent criteria in making such a recommendation. And until very recently, I typically attended the two annual meetings of the local CU chapter, to vote on the acceptance of new members among the senior (and occasionally a few junior) undergraduate bodies; the primary criterion for selection for this distinction was successful completion with an acceptably high grade point average of patterns of

F-1 Walter ("Wally") Weir *(courtesy of the Heritage Center, University of Colorado Boulder)*

© Springer Fachmedien Wiesbaden GmbH, part of Springer Nature 2020
M. Wertheimer, *Facets of an Academic's Life*,
https://doi.org/10.1007/978-3-658-28770-2

courses that were not exclusively specialized or applied, but rather fulfilled requirements for a broad liberal education, showing mastery of content in the humanities, the social sciences, and the natural sciences. I even participated in the ceremonies for induction of new members on several occasions when I was no longer president of the local chapter. I'm still now, long after my formal retirement, paying my annual dues as a long-time member of Phi Beta Kappa (since 1947), and until recently was pleased to accept the task of introducing and recognizing new members of Phi Beta Kappa at the departmental graduation ceremonies for psychology majors.

As a master's degree candidate at Johns Hopkins, I was inducted into Sigma Xi, a national honor society for science. While I did attend a few meetings of the Sigma Xi chapter at the University of Colorado during my first years in Boulder, I soon let my membership in that society lapse. The same was true of my membership in the American Association for the Advancement of Science, the AAAS. While I became a member of this association when I was still a graduate student, I attended only a very few conventions of this group and soon stopped paying annual dues.

Other societies I joined were the Eastern Psychological Association (EPA), of which I was a member from 1949 to 1955 while I was still in the east; the American Psychological Association (APA), of which I have been a member since 1951; the American Association of University Professors (AAUP), which I first joined in 1952; the Colorado Psychological Association (CPA), of which I was a member from 1955 when I got to Boulder until 1967, by when I became aware that it was primarily and almost exclusively devoted to issues in the practice of psychology and had little to do with academic psychology; the Psychonomic Society, which I joined in 1960 and at conventions of which I occasionally presented papers in earlier years, a fairly prestigious organization which one was invited to join only if one had already published least three papers in referreed journals; Cheiron, the international society for the history of the behavioral and social sciences, which I joined in 1969, by which time I had begun to try to identify myself to a large extent as a scholar in the history of psychology; Psi Chi, the national honor society in psychology, in 1973, after I had already served as faculty advisor to the local Colorado chapter for a number of years; and the American Psychological Society (APS), which later renamed itself the Association for Psychological Science, of which I became a charter fellow when it was founded in 1989 as a kind of research and science competitor to the by then largely practice-oriented APA. I was also a member of the Social Science Education Consortium, a somewhat informal conglomeration of education-related groups in Boulder from 1970 to 1990, and accepted an honorary membership in Golden Key in 1986, when that organization was founded as a kind of second-class rival, I fear, to Phi Beta Kappa; but I never played any role in Golden Key.

Although I was officially called a research psychologist at the Worcester Foundation for Experimental Biology during my 1951-52 year at Worcester State Hospital, that title was really only honorary. I also was called a clinical consultant to the Connecticut State Vocational Guidance Department and the Long Lane School for Girls in Middletown, CT from 1953 to 1955, when I was doing some individual psychological testing of teenage girls who had been removed from their families and detained in a youth correctional facility, but this again was only a very minor role, taking only a small fraction of my working time while I was a faculty member at Wesleyan University.

Nan and I did research during the summers of 1953, 1954, and 1955 at Rock-

F-2 Nathan S. Kline *(courtesy of the Nathan S. Kline Institute)*

land State Hospital in Orangeburg, NY, where I was called research psychologist; and we spent the entire 1958-1959 academic year at Rockland, while I was on sabbatical leave from Colorado and I held the title of Principal Research Scientist (Psychology) at Rockland that year. Nathan Kline, a psychiatrist at Rockland, had been impressed with Nan's and my work (especially Nan's) at Worcester, and had invited us to join his research team at Rockland during those early years and then again for the whole 1958-1959 sabbatical year.

Nan pursued the work that had resulted in her PhD with a 1953 dissertation on capillary studies in schizophrenia, and continued her epidemiological work in related studies during our stays in Rockland, and I pursued primarily studies of figural aftereffects and other perceptual phenomena. Work on somatotypes and the personality and psychopathological syndromes associated with them was in the limelight at that time, partly as a result of a book published about then by Sheldon and Stevens (the latter the psychophysicist under whom I had done my dissertation research), and Nate Kline was intrigued by this kind of work; knowing that I could read German, he asked me to translate for him an earlier book by Ernst Kretschmer on physique and temperament. I dictated a kind of sight translation (which, though, I believe was fairly accurate) of the entire book for him, but that rather major effort did not, as far as I know, lead to any publications.

I was hired as a research consultant to the Denver Veterans Administration Hospital from 1956 to 1970. My role with the VA was to provide advice on research projects that the staff and psychology interns were doing at that hospital, and to give occasional lectures. If I remember correctly, I received a modest stipend for several of those years for what may have been about quarterly visits to that hospital. I was also a "human factors consultant" to the Martin Company in 1960-1961 in Denver; the company was a major producer of sophisticated aircraft, and my (rather limited) experience in applied experimental psychology was sought in such matters as the design of displays in the cockpits of fighter planes.

F-3 Steve Davis *(courtesy of Steve Davis)*

My involvement with Psi Chi, the national honor society in psychology, was not limited to my advising the local Colorado chapter of that society for many years (often associated as well with my role as director of the CU undergraduate honors program in psychology; many honors candidates also became members of Psi Chi). In 1973, I was elected Psi Chi Rocky Mountain Regional Vice President, which required my service on the national Council of Psi Chi, a group which met in various interesting places several times a year and was the decision-making body for the entire national organization. This position continued until 1979, when I was appointed national historian for Psi Chi—a post that also involved regular meetings with the national Council and the executive officers of the association. I chaired a committee responsible for making national Psi Chi awards to a few selected undergraduate and graduate student members of the society, and was elected national president of Psi Chi for 1990-1991, which again made me a member of the national Council as president-elect in 1989 and as past president in 1991, while I was responsible for developing and executing policy matters for the society and chairing its meetings during my presidential year. My interest in history, in undergraduate excellence, and in Psi Chi as a large society that had for decades made major contributions to so many individuals led me and another past president, Steve Davis, to propose an oral history of Psi Chi, which was accepted by the national Council, which also agreed to support the project with modest funding; that oral history was published in 2000.

My membership in the Rocky Mountain Psychological Association (RMPA) also led eventually to my presidency of that association as well, in 1981-1982. I was a member of a committee on the history of psychology in the Rocky Mountain Region of the RMPA from 1983 to 1987; this committee sponsored a number of lectures and symposia, and its work culminated in a special issue in 1988 of the *Journal of the History of the Behavioral Sciences* that I co-edited, on the history of psychology in the Rocky Mountain Region. A few years ago, in 2005, I was invited to present the first in an annual lecture series on

F-4 History of psychology in the Rocky Mountain region: Vol. 24, No. 1 of the *Journal of the History of the Behavioral Sciences* 1988, Wiley

teaching sponsored by the RMPA at its conventions; the series, named for a deceased professor at the University of Wyoming and myself, is called the Lillian Portenier-Michael Wertheimer pre-convention conference on teaching. I certainly felt humbled and honored to have had an annual invited lecture series on teaching be named (in part) for me. And I was asked to present the keynote or plenary lecture for that pre-convention conference again in 2016; I fervently intend that lecture, although it was gratifyingly well attended and well received, to be the very last lecture of my long, long career.

While those other associations did play a significant part in my career, it was the American Psychological Association with which I have been identified most over a period of many decades of holding a variety of elected positions. I became a member of the APA in 1951, while completing my doctoral dissertation work at Harvard, at the suggestion of Ira Hirsh, a young faculty member there who like me specialized in the psychology of hearing. He took me along to the APA convention; I don't remember where that meeting was held, but it must have been somewhere in New England, because Hirsh drove us there. That was the first year in which I attended an APA annual convention, and I managed to attend the annual APA meeting almost every year thereafter for more than half a century, until 2009. I was impressed by many of the convention presentations in 1951, and began to become acquainted with many psychologists from far and wide during all those conventions, at many of which I also later made many presentations.

F-5 Ira Hirsh *(courtesy of the Washington University Photographic Services Collection, Washington University Libraries, Department of Special Collections)*

The APA provided me with a great deal of satisfaction and pleasure, as well as occasional frustrations. My involvement with the APA, beginning with just attending its annual conventions, soon led to presenting papers and participating in symposia and other events. I joined several divisions, and from the 1960s for a good half century or so held various elected posts. I was appointed or elected to many different committees and boards over the years, and formed many lasting friendships. My

F-6 Pete and Susan's house in Washington, DC *(family archives)*

participation in the APA governance system brought me often to Washington, DC, to the Central Office of the APA, which moved from fairly modest quarters to a fine office building off Connecticut Avenue in downtown Washington (pictured on page 418), and then to two buildings built specifically for the APA (page 419) on land next to Union Station that previously had been depressed and blighted. These "business trips" to Washington also provided many welcome opportunities to visit with my mother, who had moved to a pleasant apartment in Georgetown in 1971, as well as with Pete, Susan, and Monika, who lived in a beautiful large house in northern Washington near the national zoo. I typically added several days to these trips (transportation for which was paid for by the APA, as well as meals and hotel accommodations during the APA events), so as to visit Pete and his family in their pleasant weekend getaway west of the District, and to serve as audience for the monthly string quartet evenings my mother arranged; she managed to find a first violin, a viola, and a cello player for those occasions, during which she played the second violin part. The concerts in her

F-7 Chamber music (usually a quartet, this one a quintet) in Anni's Georgetown apartment;
Anni third from left *(family archives)*

apartment were typically preceded by a pleasant home-cooked meal that she prepared in her apartment for her musician guests.

I think that my exposure to the Quaker culture which was still to some extent present, if in somewhat muted and vestigial form at Swarthmore, contributed a bit not only to my election to boards and committees or divisional positions, but also to my fairly often being selected to leadership posts such as board or committee chair or president of a division. While the typical decision-making process in these units was usually by majority vote, I tried to follow (if not explicitly the Quaker strategy) what I found congenial, seeking consensus within the group instead. This may have entailed a bit more time for discussion and respectful consideration of alternative points of view, but usually led to good morale and pleasant interactions within those groups as well as decisions and recommendations that the whole group could endorse, often with unanimous or almost unanimous enthusiasm.

While it wasn't related to my APA involvement as such, my first "official" APA role was as an invited participant in the APA Estes Park conference, supported by the National Science Foundation, on training for research. A minor reason for my selection as part of that group may have been that Estes Park was fairly close to Boulder, and that I was available to help make the arrangements for the group to meet there. Probably I was chosen in part because both Tex Garner, who had supervised my master's project at Hopkins, and Fred Skinner, with whom I had worked for a while when I was a graduate student at Harvard, may have had (possibly unrealistic) expectations for me as a research psychologist and thought that my record of more than 20 publications by the time the conference was held was a harbinger of further research productivity. At any rate, I was flattered to be selected as a participant in that otherwise rather prominent, well-established group of behavioral scientists; I was by far the youngest and most junior member of that august group. A goal of the conference was initially to propose a set of guidelines for graduate training for research in psychology comparable to those that had resulted from an earlier conference on the training of clinical psychologists. The earlier conference on graduate education for aspiring clinical psychologists had yielded a book, edited by Victor Raimy, that proposed quite specific requirements for trainees to become "scientist-practitioners," including particular courses and their sequences as well as specifications for a predoctoral internship. Perhaps to the surprise—and relief—of the participants in the Estes Park conference, it became clear to all of us that a somewhat rigid set of prescribed course requirements is not appropriate for preparing graduate students to become creative research scientists, but that a kind of relatively loose, open apprenticeship to productive researchers is a far more promising strategy. This was the main theme of the *American Psychologist* article (of which I was generously made a co-author) that reported the results of the conference.

The NSF also sponsored an APA program that brought current researchers to various primarily undergraduate colleges throughout the country. I was pleased to have been selected as one of the "APA-NSF Visiting Scientists" for the entire decade of the 1960s.

From 1963 to 1971 I also served as an editorial consultant for the APA's book review journal, *Contemporary Psychology*. This role involved evaluating new books that had been submitted to the editor of this rather prestigious monthly periodical, to recommend whether or not they deserved a review, and if so, to suggest potential reviewers to be invited to write a review of them. This role helped me become more cognizant of the significant work in the field published in book form, and to develop my growing, already fairly large, network of relationships with colleagues not only in North America but also in other parts of the world.

I was nominated to become president of Division 2, the division on the teaching of psychology, and was elected to serve in that role during the 1965-1966 academic year. That was my first rather major official position in the APA. Then I was elected for a 1966-1969 term as representative to the APA Council from Division 26, the division on the history of psychology. The APA Council of Representatives, which met twice a year, once in Washington and once in the city in which the annual convention was held (which varied from the east coast to the west coast to the middle west and Canada, and even several times Hawaii), was the final decision-making body of the APA. It typically acted on recommendations made to it by APA boards or committees, but also was able to initiate its own actions. It also studied and sometimes altered the annual APA budget, for which it was responsible. My many years of service on the Council in a variety of roles taught me about the remarkably broad scope of the issues, programs, and concerns within the very complex and variegated organization that the APA had become.

From 1968 to 1970 I was a member, and in 1969-1970 chair, of an APA committee on precollege psychology. I became aware of the surprisingly large number of high-school students who were exposed to psychology in a high-school class—but most of these courses throughout the nation were taught by teachers who had little or no training in psychology and taught a kind of "touchy-feely" intuitive course or one devoted to getting along with one's date. I was determined to try to help remedy this situation to the extent I could, and the improvement of the teaching of precollege psychology became a major focus of my career endeavors for the next few years. That was one of my goals during the 1970-1971 academic year, which I spent on sabbatical from the University of Colorado at the APA Central Office in Washington, DC, as acting administrative officer for educational affairs. The executive officer of the APA at the time, Kenneth Little, had managed to set up this opportunity for me, with half my

F-8 Ken Little *(courtesy of the Archives of the History of American Psychology, The Drs. Nicholas and Dorothy Cummings Center for the History of Psychology, The University of Akron)*

salary covered that year by the APA and half by CU, and I did manage to make some progress that year toward my goal of strengthening the teaching of psychology at the high school as an empirical science. I helped set up an APA clearing house for the high-school teaching of psychology; began legislative activities within the APA governance system that led eventually to an official APA recommendation to all high-school state education supervisors throughout the whole country to require extensive undergraduate exposure to courses in psychology—and preferably a college major in the field—for all high-school teachers assigned to teaching psychology in their high schools; and undertook to translate what I thought was a good Swedish high-school psychology text into English, which was published in 1971 with a study guide and an instructor's resource book for it.

I was elected as a member of the executive committee of Division 24, the division on philosophical psychology, in 1971, and then elected as its secretary-treasurer for 1972 to 1975. I was also elected to become a member of the APA Education and Training Board, and served as chair of that important board 1974 to 1975. More elections to important roles continued fairly thick and fast. I became president of Division 1, the division on general psychology, from 1975 to 1976, was representative to the APA Council for Division 24 from 1975 to 1977, served on an appointed ad hoc APA panel on the development of APA guidelines for the accreditation of graduate programs in professional psychology, and was president of Division 24 from 1976 to 1977.

Being elected simultaneously to several APA groups involved in education and the dissemination of psychological material helped me further my efforts for the responsible teaching of psychology at the high-school level and also in colleges. From 1976 to 1978 I was a member of the APA Publications and Communications Board as well as chair of the APA committee on psychology in secondary schools, and a member from 1976 to 1979 (chair 1977 to 1978) of the APA committee on undergraduate education This committee and board involvement permitted me to continue my push for the improvement of secondary-school instruction in psychology (and of the introductory psychology course in colleges), a triple source of input on APA policy that I did not hesitate to try to use.

From 1977 to 1978 I was president of Division 26, the APA division on the history of psychology; from 1977 to 1978 chair and then 1978 to 1980 a member of an APA committee on celebration of the centennial of the founding of the first experimental psychology laboratories; and from 1978 to 1979 I was also appointed co-chair, with John Popplestone of the Archives of the History of American Psychology at the University of Akron, of an ad hoc APA committee on APA archives, to make recommendations about how the APA should deal with its significant documents; some of them had gone into the national archives in Washington, some to Akron, and others elsewhere, and a more consistent and reasonable strategy was sought for future documents.

Then in 1978 I began a term which ended in 1980 as a member at large of the executive committee of the division on philosophical psychology, and from 1978 to 1983 I served on an advisory committee on obituaries in the *American Psychologist*; this committee made recommendations about which recently deceased psychologists should be selected to be honored by having an obituary of them published in the main APA monthly journal, about how long the obituary should be, and who should be invited to write it.

These years in the early middle of my long career provided a heady period of my involvement with many APA activities; while they were in some ways a bit hectic, they nevertheless gave me the impression that despite my doubts about my own competence, there were many colleagues who valued my input to what they considered important national issues. Those experiences served to vindicate my efforts, and I am eternally grateful to the many opportunities that the APA gave me.

I was again elected to represent the division on philosophical psychology on the APA Council from 1981 to 1983, and also served on two APA accreditation appeal panels, to hear arguments from graduate institutions that had been denied accreditation about why they should be accredited after all. Meantime the APA

F-9 Rachel Hare-Mustin
(courtesy of Psychology's Feminist Voices)

Council of Representatives had formed several informal special-interest caucuses; I was co-chair of one of these, the group that called itself the public interest coalition, in 1981-1982.

Then in 1983 the Council tried a short-lived experiment in an effort to speed up action on the floor of Council during its regular meetings. The day before the regularly-scheduled meeting, the Council broke up into two large informal groups. One of them, called Forum A, the academic forum, tried to develop academic positions about the action items on the Council's agenda; the other, called Forum One, the practice-oriented forum, tried to develop practice-oriented positions about the Council's forthcoming agenda. Rachel Hare-Mustin, who was a member of Council from a practice division (and whom I had gotten to know years earlier when she was an undergraduate student at Swarthmore a year or two behind me), was elected chair of Forum One, and I was chosen as chair of Forum A. It turned out that very similar debates occurred not only in both forum discussions but also thereafter formally on the floor of Council, so this new procedure didn't end up saving any time after all; so it was scrapped and appropriately never tried again thereafter.

In 1983 I was selected to present an invited talk at the APA convention in the prestigious G. Stanley Hall Lecture Series, and was also formally given a Distinguished Teaching in Psychology Award by the American Psychological Foundation, an affiliate of the APA. I was flattered.

From 1983 to 1986 I was both a member at large of the executive committee of the division of general psychology, and also a member of its Fellows Committee, a group charged with recommending a few members of Division 1 as nominees to be

F-10 Recognition for my G. Stanley Hall lecture *(family archives)*

considered by an APA-wide board for the honor of being named a "fellow" of the APA (I had already received that honor back in 1966). From 1984 to 1985 I was elected to a second term as president of Division 24, which by then had been renamed the division on Theoretical and Philosophical Psychology. 1984 to 1986 I was a member of the Fellows Committee for Division 2 on the teaching of psychology, and in 1984 to 1987 I was a member (chair in 1985-1986) of the APA Committee on International Relations in Psychology. I served on the Fellows Committee of Division 26 on the history of psychology from 1985 to 1988, and was chair of the Division 2 Fellows Committee in 1986 to 1987. From 1986 to 1988 I was again a member of the Council of Representatives, this time from the division on general psychology, APA Division 1. I participated in an APA National Conference on Graduate Education in Psychology, which I was invited to attend, in Salt Lake City in the summer of 1987, and was invited to be a consulting editor of the APA journal *Professional Psychology: Research and Practice*. The purpose of that appointment may have been largely cosmetic (I may have been viewed as a fairly well known academic experimental psychologist, to show readers that the journal indeed had such an editor on its board)—I don't remember ever receiving more than a very few submitted manuscripts for me to evaluate in that role, which I held from 1987 to 1995.

During 1988 I was appointed historian for the division on general psychology, which eventually led to a published version of that division's history, and from 1990 to 1993 I was a member at large of the executive committee of that division. My roles in Division 1 led to several lengthy midwinter visits to the home of Ken Little and his wife in La Jolla, CA, where the executive committee met annually for a few years to conduct division business and plan out the division's program for the following year's APA convention. Marilyn joined me for those trips back to the town where she had been raised and where she still had some long-time friends.

Division 1 on General Psychology in 1992 gave me an award for "exceptional service" to the division, to acknowledge my many years of involvement in the division's affairs. I was of course pleased to receive this recognition, but found that being given in 1990 an APA-wide "Distinguished Career Contribution to Education and Training in Psychology Award" was even more gratifying. I had

Charlie Johnson/Colorado Daily

CU Professor Michael Wertheimer describes himself as "an enthusiastic academic."

Wertheimer chosen for his teaching excellence

F-11 A newspaper announcement of my APA award for Distinguished Career Contribution to Education and Training in Psychology (The coconut carved like a head decorated my office throughout my career.) *(photo by Charlie Johnson; courtesy of the Colorado Daily)*

indeed devoted lots of effort during my career to trying to improve the teaching of psychology at all levels from primary school through post-doctoral training—and to improve my own teaching practices, in which I still felt somewhat deficient. So while that award was indeed gratifying, I still wonder a bit about whether I had really deserved it and feel humbled to have received that recognition.

From 1990 to 1996 I was a member of the APA Membership Committee, which was charged with evaluating divisional nominees for fellowship status within the association, but also had the duty of general oversight of membership issues. The gradual drain of academic psychologists leaving or not joining the APA, the stagnating overall membership numbers, and issues concerning the sparse recruitment of early career members continued to plague the APA during the late 1990s and the first decade of the twenty-first century. Many suggestions for solving these problems were proposed and there were efforts to implement some of them, but the problems, if anything, continued to worsen despite the conscientious attempts on the part of this committee, and of many concerned members of the APA central office staff, to solve them. Indeed, during the last few decades, membership in many national associations, not just in psychology, has been eroding.

In 1994, after having officially been named professor emeritus by CU, I was an invited participant in an APA national conference on postdoctoral education and training that was held in Norman, OK. And in that year I was also elected to serve another three-year term on the APA Council of Representatives, this time for the division on the history of psychology, Division 26; then from 1996 to 1997 I continued on Council as a representative from a coalition of Divisions 24 and 26, respectively the division on theoretical and philosophical

Education and Training Beyond the Doctoral Degree

Proceedings of the
American Psychological Association
National Conference on
Postdoctoral Education and
Training in Psychology

Education Directorate
American Psychological Association
Washington, DC

F-12 Proceedings of the 1994 APA conference on postdoctoral education and training *(courtesy of the American Psychological Association)*

Psychology and on the history of psychology; neither of these two divisions had that year received enough votes from APA members to have its own representative on Council (as the tilt of APA membership continued its inexorable trend away from academics and toward practice).

I was again a member of the advisory committee on obituaries for the *American Psychologist* from 1996 to 2000, and continued to be a member of the Council of Representatives from 1997 to 1999 from the division on the history of psychology, after that division had again—barely—managed to garner enough membership votes to qualify for one full representative. I was also re-elected to be a member at large of the executive committee of Division 1 on general psychology, from 1998 to 2000. And in 1999 I was named the first recipient of an award begun that year by Division 24 for "Distinguished Service to Theoretical and Philosophical Psychology." The next year Division 26 named me recipient of a "Lifetime Achievement Award for Sustained, Outstanding, and Unusual Contributions to the History of Psychology." I really appreciated this award. These awards were followed by a few more: in 2005 an award for "Extended Distinguished Service to the Society for General Psychology, Division One, APA" and in 2006 yet another unique one from the same division, a "Recognition Award for truly extraordinary service as officer and secretary-extraordinaire of this society in its mission to advance psychology across specialty areas." And in 2009 Division 24 gave me an "Award for Distinguished Contributions to Theoretical and Philosophical Psychology." Apparently, if one lives long enough, and continues to be at least somewhat involved, it's fairly typical to start receiving various awards.

I was secretary of the division on general psychology from 2000 to 2006, and once again a member of the APA Council of Representatives for that division from 2003 to 2005. Meantime I also was elected to be a member of the Committee on the Structure and Function of Council for 1998 to 2001; this committee's charge was to improve the effectiveness of the APA Council of Representatives (as well as the rest of the APA governance system). The Council met for a few days just twice a year, had become unwieldy in size, and consisted of many members who were neophytes and didn't really know yet how to be involved effectively in the association's decision making; this committee tried valiantly, without a great deal of success, to streamline the governance system of a vast, diverse association with at the time more than 150,000 members. It wasn't until a few years later that the APA began an effort to reorganize itself into a more efficient organization; this effort, which is still ongoing at the time of this writing, does seem to have some promise of improving things.

All of this continuing involvement in APA affairs over a number of decades, and all of the somewhat unexpected but greatly appreciated recognition, led me to try a run for a seat on the APA Board of Directors. While the Council of Representatives is officially still the final decision-making body for the APA, the Board of Directors is in effect an executive committee of the Council. It consists of the major association-wide officers (president, past president, president-elect, secretary, and treasurer), the executive vice president and CEO of the APA, and six members at large, each elected for three-year terms. The board sets the agenda for the Council meetings, receives input from APA boards and committees and makes recommendations to the Council concerning them, and takes care of issues on behalf of the Council that come up between Council meetings and require quick response. Many people who end up on the board later try to run for president of the APA, but that was never my aim. Membership on the board was at that time determined by vote of the Council, and only individuals who at the time were members of the Council could become candidates for the two annual vacancies among the members at large of the board. There always were at least six nominees for the two annual vacancies, and election to this honor was eagerly sought by many Council members, many of whom mounted vigorous (and sometimes even fairly expensive) campaigns for their election. My campaign consisted of a short doggerel-like poem that appears starting on page 471, which I sent out to the members of Council, and which a colleague, Dave Baker, kindly read aloud at the appropriate Council meeting, which I didn't attend in person.

I did manage to get elected, beating the third-ranked candidate by only a very few votes, and was a member at large of the APA Board of Directors for the three-year term of 2007 to 2009. I was delighted and flattered to have been selected; this felt like a fitting final validation of my years of loyal devotion to the APA. I had been told that there were six regularly scheduled annual meetings of the board, but it turned out that board members were also expected to attend many other national functions such as meetings concerned with diversity, with education, with state association practice issues, and other matters; travel to regional and international conventions was also covered (and expected). So for those three years I attended about 16 events as a member of the board of direc-

F-13 APA Board of Directors in 2008, with me at far right *(courtesy of Charles Votaw)*

tors each year, most at the central office in Washington, DC, but also several to "retreat" destinations in rather posh settings. (I have learned since, with some regret, that there were international events which I was expected to attend abroad as well, but that never came to pass.) The hotel accommodations and typical upscale restaurant meals were lavish, and Marilyn accompanied me on most of these trips, probably enjoying the elaborate special treatment even more than I did, since as a responsible fiduciary of the association I felt somewhat guilty about how expensive these privileges were.

I had almost gotten used to nice hotels and restaurants, the cost of which was covered by the association, while I was attending meetings of Council or of boards or committees of which I was a member, but the treatment of members of the board was even more lavish. Expense-paid excellent hotels, travel, and gourmet meals coalesced in my memory into one overall kaleidoscopic image of unnecessary opulence; I don't remember the names of all the many hotels and restaurants in which I was served, nor even the cities in which conventions or other meetings were held. They have in effect merged into one blurred memory. And while in many ways it all was very nice while it lasted, I don't miss it at all, now that it is over. My last APA office was as a member of the APA Policy and Planning Board from 2010 to 2012, which reduced my out-of-town trips for the APA from some 16 in 2007-2009 to a much more reasonable only three a year. And when my involvement in the APA finally came to an end in 2012, I actually felt relieved that it is all finished. I enjoyed most of my long, dedicated involvement with the APA for decades, but am now delighted to have it all behind me. It's been more than enough.

Part of my relief that I'm through participating in the APA is related to my dismay at the APA having become so practice-oriented rather than maintaining a strong science identity. True, many in the recent leadership of the association have tried to keep and even substantially increase the APA's involvement in efforts and programs devoted to scientific psychology, but I'm afraid that my perception is that this effort has become less and less successful. The science directorate staff in the APA central office is minuscule compared to that in the public interest directorate or especially the practice directorate (which also has a large separate organization associated with it) and even the education directorate,

F-14 The previous APA building, where I worked 1970-1971 *(courtesy of the Archives of the History of American Psychology, The Drs. Nicholas and Dorothy Cummings Center for the History of Psychology, The University of Akron)*

the large staff of which appears to be concerned primarily with the training of psychologists for practice.

In the early years of my membership, the APA was still primarily a society at which academic psychologists presented their work and interacted with their ilk, and while there were presentations on clinical, counseling, and other aspects of the practice of psychology, research in psychology was still the dominant theme. I was given the impression that all academic psychologists and aspiring academics should and did at that time belong to the APA and should present information about their latest empirical work at the APA conventions. There were few if any national organizations that could compete at that time for the attention of research or academic psychologists; the Psychonomic Society and APS did not yet exist.

Over the years, the practice component of the APA gradually grew, until by the 1970s and 1980s it had reached the point where the academic vs. practice components had surpassed an equal 50-50 representation, and in later years, practice issues had become far more prominent in the APA's interests, foci, and activities than classical basic or even applied rigorous research. From an association devoted exclusively or at least primarily to academic affairs as it had been at its inception in 1892, it later became an association primarily concerned with the practice of psychology.

During the time of my membership, the size of the APA grew from only about 10,000 members to more than 150,000 early in the 21st century, but it has shrunk back to about 115,000 now (after a controversial major ethical issue concerning the use of torture in "enhanced interrogation"). Initially it was exclusively a scientific organization, but during the 1940s it joined with several organizations concerned with applied and clinical psychology, and reorganized itself into a loose umbrella association with myriad divisions devoted to its many subfields—from general psychology, the teaching of psychology, experimental psychology, physiological psychology, and social psychology to other specialties such as clinical, consulting, and counseling psychology as well as "psychological hypnosis." In later years further divisions were established for trauma psychology, the psychology of women, environmental psychology, and many other foci, most of them devoted to some aspect of the practice of psychology. Currently the more than 50 divisions have seen, in general, growth in the membership in divisions devoted to practice issues and shrinkage in those more directly focused on pure research. Many, indeed most, behavioral scientists now belong to specialized national associations focused on narrower topics such as cognitive neuroscience, behavioral genetics, or decision making or to newer associa-

F-15 The larger of the two new APA buildings, constructed in 1990 *(courtesy of the Archives of the History of American Psychology, The Drs. Nicholas and Dorothy Cummings Center for the History of Psychology, The University of Akron)*

tions such as APS or the Psychonomic Society, rather than bothering to join the APA. And over the years my own feelings about the APA have changed from excited participation and eager identification with it to disappointment and frustration as during the last years of my academic career the APA appeared to me to slide further and further toward almost exclusively practice matters. Sadly, the APA eventually seemed to have little if anything left in it that had to do with the kinds of issues to which I had tried to devote my entire career.

During the last years of my involvement in APA boards and committees, I often felt as though I had been elected as a kind of token member to represent scientific or academic psychology and hence to add a kind of legitimacy or credibility to the groups that were primarily concerned with promoting issues related much less to the science of psychology than to its practice. And during the last years, to some extent on the Board of Directors, but even more on the Policy and Planning Board, I felt that although I may in some ways have been respected by fellow board members, and have been listened to almost sympathetically, I failed in most efforts to get particular actions taken (or prevented), and my suggestions were typically ignored. Whether this was in part due to my personal competence in convincing others having deteriorated, or due primarily to the subtle but enormous change in the APA's priorities, I will probably never know.

While I did become somewhat cynically disillusioned with the APA during

F-16 Recognition for participating on the APA Policy and Planning Board *(family archives)*

my last decade or so of involvement in its governance, and did feel quite frustrated with it when I finally stopped being involved, the vast majority of my experiences with the APA was rewarding and fulfilling. I may wish that I'd done more to further the causes of the field to which I've devoted my long and deeply satisfying career, but maybe I should be content to be satisfied with the little good that I may have helped occur. I'm thankful to the APA for having given me many opportunities and even for recognizing some of what I still believe are only rather modest achievements. All in all, the APA has been good to me.

And so have other organizations with which I've been associated. One of the awards of which I am most proud is what may have been the first non-sexist language award presented by the Campus Women's Organization of the University of Colorado, in 1990. During the last few decades of my teaching, I always insisted on non-sexist language in term papers, other written work, and oral presentations at seminars. It was relatively easy to make suggestions for non-sexist substitutions in English, but I have found it far more difficult to stick to that principle in languages such as French, Spanish, German, and Swedish.

At the University of Colorado, I also received in 1981 an award for "the best paper in the humanities published in 1980 by a member of the faculty," for a paper on my father's early life, and in 1987 the College of Arts and Sciences gave me its fifth annual faculty advising award. The Rocky Mountain Psychological Association gave me its "Distinguished Service Award" in 1988 and its "Award for Outstanding Service to the RMPA and to Psychology" in 1994. And other outfits recognized me in other ways mentioned earlier in this appendix, as well as my having been elected to many coveted posts

International Women's Week and Women Studies invite Faculty, Staff, and Students
to a
Reception

featuring...

Campus Women's Organization's presentation of their
NON-SEXIST LANGUAGE AWARDS
Honoring professors who have shown excellence in their use of non-sexist language

and a short presentation by

Dr. Barbara Fox
Linguistics Department at CU

Please gather with us for food and celebration
Heritage Center (top floor, Old Main)
Tuesday, March 6, 1990
5:00 - 6:30 pm

Sponsored by Ethnic Women's Alliance
Associate Vice Chancellor Albert Ramirez, Faculty Affairs

F-17 Invitation to the award ceremony for excellence in use of non-sexist language *(family archives)*; the paper, here faded, was originally bright red.

The Rocky Mountain
Psychological Association

Presents To
Dr. Michael Wertheimer
For Outstanding Service to
RMPA and to Psychology
1994

F-18 Rocky Mountain Psychological Association Outstanding
Service Award *(family archives)*

of many kinds in a variety of organizations. I am still grateful—and still feel somewhat overwhelmed— for all this recognition (and still feel that much of it is not really deserved), and for all of the many opportunities these organizations gave me to try to further some worthwhile goals. I have indeed been privileged and blessed.

Appendix G: Artistic Fumblings

It probably was typical for someone growing up during the first half of the twentieth century in the United States to engage in a variety of attempts to be "creative" in music, poetry, art, and other media. I was no exception. Since my early years, especially as a teenager, I dabbled in painting, writing, and composing modest bits of music. Here are some of my "fumblings" in each of these areas.

Music

Since I was quite young I have composed quite a large, if modest, set of musical endeavors, some more ambitious than others. It started with a very simple love song to my mother when I was six or seven years old, progressed to something I called Sonata Number ½ that I recorded on the piano at age 17, and culminated in a "Theme of Triumph" that came to me some thirty years ago.

As I mentioned when describing my childhood, making music was part of family life from the beginning. The tunes and words for many songs from this time were indelibly chiseled into my memory; I still can deliver many of them by heart. They have enriched almost every day of my entire life. Even if I am not playing them on a harmonica or piano or some other instrument, and even if I am not singing them out loud, they—and variations on their melodies—often play themselves out in my head. They have been an immense source of pleasure all my life. Also, as I've mentioned, during my childhood we had a "family orchestra" for a short time, with my father playing viola or piano or a wind instrument, my mother guitar, Val clarinet, Lise bells or a recorder, and myself some kind of drums.

When I attended the Mayflower Elementary School, there was a weekly school assembly at which the entire student body as well as the faculty sang songs, many of them traditional folk songs and patriotic ones; many of these songs have stayed with me complete with their lyrics. I also still have in my possession a tattered old copy of the Mayflower School assembly song book, which I must have pilfered without realizing that one isn't supposed to take things like that. I also played a snare drum in the school band. I recall a small

© Springer Fachmedien Wiesbaden GmbH, part of Springer Nature 2020
M. Wertheimer, *Facets of an Academic's Life*,
https://doi.org/10.1007/978-3-658-28770-2

G-1 The family orchestra: Max, Val, me, Anni, Lise *(family archives)*

square piece of wood covered with a thick layer of rubber, on which I could practice drum beats and rolls without making much noise.

Along with Val, I was given piano lessons starting when I was quite young, though I made little progress because I never practiced enough; my teacher gave up on me after a month or two. The family inherited a fine cello from some deceased relative, and I was given lessons on that too. But I abruptly stopped playing the cello when I was about twelve years old, because of a devastating experience with it. I remember that I was supposed to be one of several music students who were to play at a recital, where a number of other children and their teachers and parents provided

G-2 Mayflower School assembly song book *(family archives)*

an audience. I recall my teacher playing an introduction on the piano down at the level of the audience; I was alone, sitting on a chair at center stage above her, facing the sea of expectant faces when it was my turn to perform. When I was expected to start playing to the piano's accompaniment, I simply froze with stage fright, and couldn't play a single note. Mortified with embarrassment, I sat there doing nothing but stare at the audience for a few seconds, then just slunk off the stage with the cello in hand. I never touched the cello again after that. And I'm sorry that that was the case; I have continued to consider the cello a beautiful instrument capable of making gorgeous sounds from rich, brown, dark, sonorous low ones to stridently high tones. However, my love of music, and making music, persisted despite that unhappy episode.

I never learned properly how to read music, and still regret to this day that this is true. As a consequence, I make most music by ear, and also join in with the singing of hymns in churches, reading the lyrics of the songs, singing along on familiar tunes, or following the lead singer and to some extent the printed notes in the song book, which I can decipher a bit, even if I can't really read the notes fast enough.

I did, however, pursue music in other ways. *The Wertheimer Times* which I edited in childhood included in the February 1939 edition the proud announcement:

> Michael Wertheimer, the editor of this newspaper, has thought up a new musical instrument. It is made of a long rubber band (a), some strips of metal (b), and a thin metal dowel (c). It is played by plucking the rubber band, which has been tuned to the first seven notes of the scale. This instrument may be seen and inspected at the Editor's office.

Accompanying the story are two diagrams, a top view and a side view, of the device. That the rubber band is tuned to "seven notes" is some-

G-3 The "new musical instrument" I "thought up" at the age of 11 *(family archives)*

what confusing, since there are only six different segments of rubber band.

Another musical avenue opened for me at the Ethical Culture School Camp. I have mentioned Nick Vovcsko, a camp handyman who also was skilled on the harmonica. When I was eleven or twelve years old he showed me that different notes resulted from blowing in or out on the instrument, how to cover holes on a harmonica with one's tongue so as to yield only single or double tones, and how to generate accompanying tones or chords by opening holes by releasing the tongue from them. His few five-minute lessons in harmonica playing, and his encouragement, led to the harmonica becoming a part of my life ever since. I learned to play many folk songs on the

G-4 Nick Vovcsko *(family archives)*

harmonica at camp. I have played those tunes and many others on many occasions: German family and folk songs, American, British, French, and other folk songs, and even some classical tunes from the Blue Danube Waltz through Brahms' Lullaby to the theme of the Ode to Joy from Beethoven's Ninth Symphony. I am deeply grateful to my "little" (younger but much taller) brother Peter for giving me a fine simple Hohner harmonica many decades ago, and replacing it with a new

G-5 Me and my harmonica, 2009 *(courtesy of Armin Stock)*

one some forty years ago when some of the reeds on the first one started to get stuck.

Playing the harmonica has continued to provide pleasure to me (and apparently also to quite a few different audiences from my children, grandchildren, great-grandchildren, and other relatives to various strangers, including residents of foreign lands). It has been played extensively in a wide variety of settings, including the primitive mountain cabin which we sold a few years ago, on the beach of Rio de Janeiro, and often as an icebreaker during Marilyn's and my foreign travels. One year I played a (minor but rewarding) role to support the archives on the APA Council, helping to make a small annual donation to the Akron archives part of the APA's regular budget. That role was literally "played," in the sense that I did a brief harmonica rendition of Auld Lang Syne at the Council speakers' microphone when I was talking in support of that annual subvention; the music woke the members of the council, led to some laughter, and may (according to Dave Baker, the Director of the Akron archives) have helped the passage of that motion. Even fairly recently the harmonica has come out for solo harmonica recitals (such as "An evening with Michael's harmonica") and Christmas sing-alongs in 2011, 2012, 2016, 2017, 2018, and 2019 at the retirement community where we now live, as well as at Jack's retirement community in 2014. These concerts seemed to be well received by a fairly large and apparently appreciative audience.

G-6 A squeezebox much like the one I played long ago *(family archives)*

I've also had other instruments (aside from having engaged in singing familiar songs with and without others while driving in the car, etc.), including a fairly simple accordion (which was called the "squeezebox"

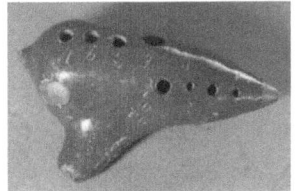

G-7 An ocarina just like mine
(courtesy of Terri Rotshtein)

G-8 Me playing the ukelin at 546 Geneva *(family archives)*

by the children); various pipes, flutes, and fifes, and an ocarina, a "sweet potato." The ukelin, an odd instrument from Hoboken, New Jersey, which Nan bought me for, I believe, $2 at some time in the late 1950s, is another instrument that has provided a good deal of pleasure. It has 16 melody strings and 16 separate strings for four chords. When the nails on my right forefinger, middle finger, and ring finger are long enough and are the right shape, I use them to pluck its melody strings rather than playing them with a bow as the inventor of the instrument had intended, while the left hand strums fitting chords. As it happens, occasionally I've played the ukelin rather than the harmonica during a break in the monthly sing-alongs at our retirement community.

G-9 My granddaughter Rivka and me at the reed organ *(family archives)*

When my mother came to live with us in Boulder in 1969 she bought me a fine

upright piano with a beautiful deep, sonorous tone. That piano had a much-admired
enormous range of timbres or sound qualities from very soft, "brown," warm, and
gentle to crashing, brilliant, bombastic
chords; I used it fairly often for improvisa-
tion or variations on well-known tunes
such as Stephen Foster's "Swanee River."
It is now in the home of a grandson and
his wife and children.

My interest in a reed organ, originally
sparked by my father's harmonium on the
top floor of our Frankfurt home, was reinforced when Nan bought me an elaborate
old reed organ in Cambridge. This organ
was regularly used especially around
Christmas time for singing carols with

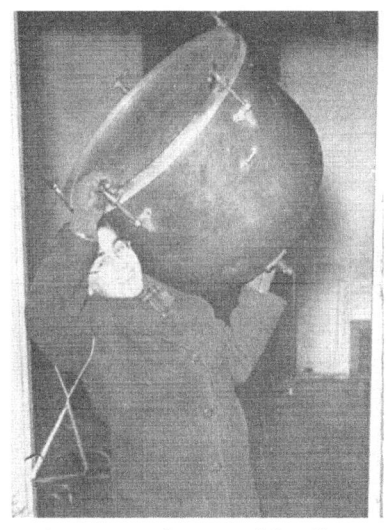

G-10 Me transporting tympani, in college
*(courtesy of the Friends Historical Library
of Swarthmore College)*

family and sometimes students and friends, but was rarely used on other occasions. Nevertheless it came with us to Middletown and then to Boulder. It re-

mained with me until I recently sold it after I sold my house
and moved into a retirement
community where it was hard
to find any place to put it.

Drumming has remained a
pleasure as well. I occasionally
played   tympani   in   the
Swarthmore College orchestra.
While in college, I also played
drums for a production of *The
Ascent   of   F2*,   although   I
couldn't   properly   read   the
music and simply played what

G-11 Benjy and me drumming, 2017 *(family archives)*

G-12 In October, 1945, I made a booklet of three little pieces for Pete (Trois petits pieces pour Pete) that became part of Sonata No. ½: Allegretto—It's a living morning, Allegro—Good afternoon, and Moderato—Good night; I'm tired. *(family archives)*

G-13 My outline notes for Sonata Number ½ *(family archives)*

I thought fitted the action. In effect, anything can be a drum when the occasion arises. I have often enjoyed drumming on whatever came to hand. It has been a joyful form of interaction with my children and others, especially with my son Benjy, who now drums professionally.

As I've mentioned, I also did a fair bit of composing, especially early in my life. My mother, with apparently infinite faith in me, constantly urged me to continue to perform and to compose music. I dedicated to her my so-called Sonata Number ½, which I managed to record as a birthday present for her at the Swarthmore radio station, when I was 17. I also composed various simple pieces for the "family orchestra" and, later, lullabies for my daughter. These lullabies, especially one in Ger-

G-14 Nan's theme, originally one of the themes in Sonata No. ½ *(family archives)*

G-15 "Häuschen und Garten," composed for voice, piano, and two violins to celebrate an occasion when Anni and Schani returned home *(family archives)*; translation:

> *Little house and garden loudly sing because of their good fortune,*
> *Schani and Anni are back again.*
> *Flowers bloom, little wind wafts, sun shines,*
> *Only the forsaken Maine island weeps.*
> *Trillby [a pet bird], Peter and Mikey and Lise*
> *Dance around in a circle on the lawn.*

man, "Schlaf', mein Kindchen," became part of the bedtime ritual for all our children, and even became part of that routine for our children's children.

I remember a school assembly at Fieldston School, at which "Uncle Willys" (in the summer, head of the ECSC) used a simple tune I had made up as the theme for the processional he was playing with variations on the piano. He had heard me play that melody at his house. I was deeply moved, and quietly whispered to a companion in the audience, "I made up that tune!" to which he responded, "Yes, I recognize it too." He clearly hadn't understood that I claimed to be (and was) the composer of that melody. I was crestfallen.

Translation:
Sleep, my little child, go to sleep;
sleep, my little child, sleep well.
Sleep, my child, be quiet and rest;
you've come from dear God.
Dream beautifully,
*   be warm and quiet,*
close your little eyes, go to sleep.
Oh, dream beautifully,
*   be warm and quiet,*
and sleep, sleep well.
Oh, [repeat first four lines]

[French]
Cry, baby, cry; the good of the world is fleeing.
Weep, baby, weep; the world is full of fear.

[German]
Howl, little child, howl;
*   man is no longer free.*
Weep, little child, weep;
*   you beloved, speechless little one.*

[German] *Sleep, little child, sleep;*
[French] *go to sleep and close your eyes.*

G-16 "Schlaf', mein Kindchen" and another lullaby for my first child *(family archives)*

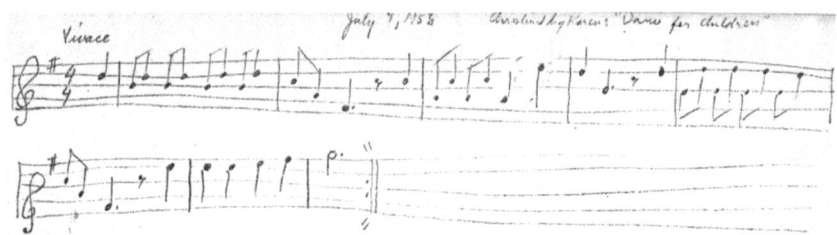

G-17 A composition from 1958, dubbed by Karen "Dance for children" *(family archives)*

I also remember that I proudly performed for a professor of music at Swarthmore, whose name I have forgotten, part of the Sonata Number ½ which I had recorded on the piano for my mother. She encouraged my attempts to make music all the time until her death. But this professor pooh-poohed my composition as not worth paying any attention to. I was devastated. My efforts to create music thereafter were understandably greatly reduced. His reaction essentially placed a serious damper on what my mother had convinced me was a promising career in composing and performing music.

But I never stopped entirely. For instance, there was the "Theme of Triumph" that swirled in my head during a transatlantic overnight flight when I was sitting in the rear of the plane near the roaring jet engines. My youngest son, Benjy, a highly competent professional musician who had and has sophisticated electronic recording equipment, even tried to help me a decade or more ago to generate an appropriate recording of that "Theme of Triumph," but I'm afraid we didn't succeed in getting it to sound out loud anywhere near as appropriately triumphant as I can still hear it in my own head.

G-18 Theme of Triumph, opening theme *(family archives)*

Words

A booklet from late 1941 through early 1943, entitled *Some Poems*, contains for the most part entries that clearly were related to my despondency at my mother having left us and my parents' divorce. Here are some of those:

November 5, 1941

Despair

Oh, I've got something on my mind.
A consolation I cannot find.
    It's bad, sad; it tortures me, twists me.
Yet something to do I cannot see.
Oh, I've got something on my mind.
A consolation I wish I could find.
    I wander the streets, I toss in my sheets;
    My mind does fantastic acrobatic feats.
Oh, I've got something on my mind.
I don't know for how long I've pin'd.

    If only there were something to do that would
                                really help, too.
    I know—I'll ask someone! Yes...but who?
Oh, I've got something on my mind.
Ah! You fates! You are not kind...
    If only there were something to do, however small
    But...there is nothing. Nothing at all.
Oh, I've got something on my mind.
Oh, God! Oh, God! How I have pin'd!
    Ah—but what good is crying, screaming, pleading?
    All these to nowhere me are leading...
Yes, I've got something
                on my mind
    A consolation
                I
                        can
                    not
                        find...

G-19 "Despair" from *Some Poems (family archives)*

May 26, 1942

Ode to my Aeroplane

I

Ah! My aeroplane! How I love thee!
Thou art my life—the blood of me!
Yes—and thou really dost love me, too—
We are like one, yes, through and through—
I could not ever live without thee—
And I am sure thou couldst not live without me...

II

But yes—one day, you will remember, high in the sky
While we were together up there, just you, and I,
Thou hast coughed—thy wondrous strong light
Of life and love, both dimmed—hath lost its might...
And like possess'd thou hast plummeted down
And yet in love—in ecstasy—with not a frown.
Thou didst not like to hurt me, that I do know,
But I was frightened up there—and you stoop'd low
While your beautiful silver wings strained to support me...
Ah! yes...but they did not well...—And I still love thee.
Thou hast tried to spare me, yes.—But the shock!
With screaming pain—yet happy—thou hast crashed down onto mossgrown rock.

III

Yes, thou art sad at having hurt me—
And thou still lovst me, and I do thee.
        But Suddenly all went—for a moment, the terrific pain...
—And my throat still lumps up during more storm and rain...

IV

So I shall have to go through life
With a raw, sad injury
That I shall hold forever—
A melancholic brain, a mental broken knee.

V

Yet I love thee
And thou dost me.

G-20 This "ode" is clearly a lament about my mother (the airplane) having left me. *(family archives)*

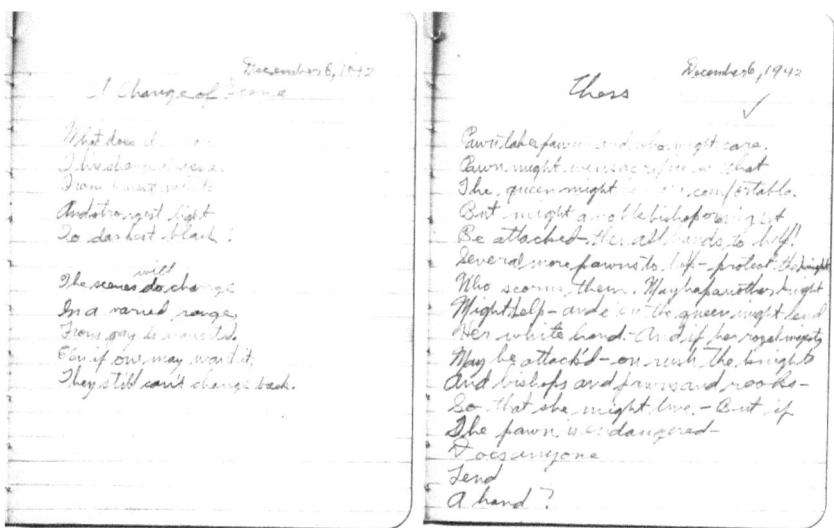

G-21 Two unhappy poems added to *Some Poems* on the same day *(family archives)*

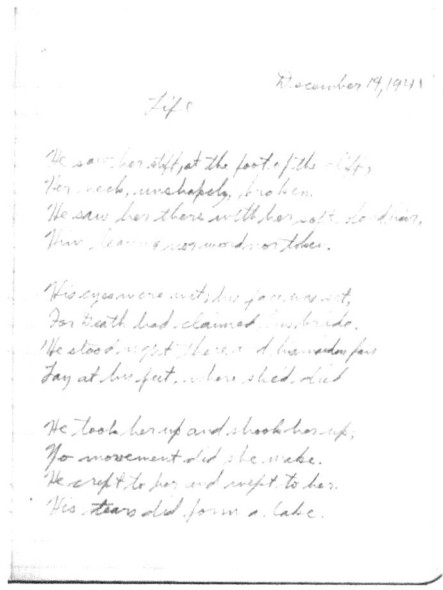

G-22 Parts of this poem have recurred to my mind now and then ever since I wrote it. *(family archives)*

December 29, 1942
Schnitzel-tree
Seventy four, amalgamate
    Ocarina, civil state
Cabbage cakes, kings, queens
    Clocks and stones; Nineteens
Humperdink, plum
    Radio, succumb
Window, foot, rabbit, glass
    Flashlight, sink, scissor, ass
Gas, geese, goose, guess
    Miss, muss, mass, mess
Incorporated company
    Jeweled rings from Tiffany
Gick, gock; bick, bock; tick, tock.

January 18, 1943
Futility
The world goes 'round and 'round,
Traversing space unbound.
    Stomachs stay unfilled.
    Men by men are killed.
Yet the world goes 'round and 'round,
Traversing space unbound.
    Hearts do break.
    Death life doth take.
But the world goes 'round and 'round,
Traversing space unbound.
    That man fails who tries.
    That man wins who lies.
The world goes 'round and 'round,
Traversing space unbound.
    Great men are born.
    But are soon forlorn.
Yet the world goes 'round and 'round,
Traversing space unbound.
    The innocent is convicted.
    By disease is a body constricted.
But the world goes 'round and 'round,
Traversing space unbound.
    Life's second in a flash is past.
    Shadows come and go so fast.
The world goes 'round and 'round,
Traversing space unbound.

Space is unbound.
No end can be found

January 24, 1943
What is the purpose of this life,
Which is over-filled with strife?
Why, for every happy moment
Is there a sad and bad component?
    What does one live for?
    For ugliness, horror, ghastly war?
        Or is there any Purpose Divine
        That is good, righteous, fine?
If so, why all this raging
Of men 'gainst men, of wars in waging?
        Yes, maybe that is all—
        Just to rise, and then to fall.

G-23 Most of the poems are despondent, but in "Schnitzel-tree" my fascination with the sound of words is evident. *(family archives)*

The last entry in the little booklet of *Some Poems*, dated February 28, 1943, was not original (in fact, it is part of a poem by Ogden Nash), but I clearly enjoyed it.

That man is rich
Who has a scratch
For every itch.

G-24 Fragment from Ogden Nash *(family archives)*

Here are several other items from 1943 to 1945:

```
November 13, 1943                    Mike Wertheimer, No. 88
                 EVENING BECOMES ELECTRIC
Scene: The combination living-dining room of the apartment
of Mr, and Mrs, Aegy, on the lower east side. Aegy and his
wife, Clem, are seated, talking.
Clem: Ain't it just too bad
      That Aggy wasn't too healthy?
      It sure is sad
      That he couldn't live and be wealthy.     (Strophe.
Aegy: Yeh.  It sure is too bad,
           And now that I'm your spouse
           I just happen to get from the cad
           His business and house.             (Antistrophe.
      Listen, Clem, it sure ain't gonna be
      Any too healthy around here for you and me
      If Esty comes moseying around here.
      I heard tell as he wasn't near.
      He was out of town back a while.
      I wonder if he's staying out? I'll
      Bet my bottom buck that he's bumming back.
Clem: I never heard nothing about Esty coming back.
      Who ever fed that to you
      That Esty was in town? Who?
Aegy: Nobody didn't. I was just thinking. I'm
      Sure as he would be only too glad, at any time,
      To get a pot-shot at me.
      I ain't so sure about you, though, you see.
Clem: Listen, Aegy, I got just as much trouble as you got.
      Esty and Lect don't love me—they sure do not...
      Come on, Aegy, let's eat.
Aegy: Yeah. I'm hungry. This here'll be my seat.
      You get the potatoes and tea leaf
      And I'll dress up the beef.          (Exeunt.
      (Enter Esty and Lect, stealthily.)
```

```
Lect: Now listen, Esty, you got to make this good.
      Over the fireplace, over the mantel of gumwood,
      There are a couple of swords, old and rusty. Grab
      One of 'em, and give Aegy a bop on the noggin or stab
      Him. That'll do the trick.
Esty:                                      Okay, old gal,
      I'll get him. You go and hide.
Lect:                                      Okay.
Esty: (As she hides behind the sofa.)     You're a pal.
      (Enter Aegy, carrying a platter with roast beef, and
            calling back over his shoulder.)
Aegy: I'll start cutting while you get
      The beans and potatoes. I'll get set. (He sees Esty.)
      Well, waddayano, I didn't know we were
      Having a guest. Here, you, sir,
      Do you know how to carve?
Esty: Sure, Gimme the knife...There. We won't starve.
      Ahh. Ain't those swell-looking pieces?
Aegy:                                              You
      Sure are expert at cutting meat. Who
      Showed you how? But look—it's too rare.
      That's a bad sign. To eat it I wouldn't dare.
      (All this time Aegy is bending over, examining the
      meat minutely. Meanwhile Esty takes the antique sword
      from its place on the mantel above the fireplace and
      holds it aloft over Aegy's back.)
Esty: Yeah. It sure is, too,
      A bad sign for you !!
      (He hacks at Aegy's neck with the sword and all his
      might. Aegy topples to the floor in a heap. Lect
      comes out from her hiding place. She pats her brother
      on the back.)
Lect: Marvellous job, Esty
      Excellent job. Be zesty. (She suddenly darts back to
      her hiding place.)
      Oh, oh, here comes Ma. Listen—do everything how
      I told you. You can't fail me now.
      (Clem enters. Esty takes the sword he used to kill
      Aegy with and prepares to strike his mother with it.
      Lect comes out of her hiding place and says, wildly:)
      Go on, Esty, what are you
      Waiting for? Remember, too,
      What she did to our Pa !
Clem: Oh, kids, kids, don't kill your Ma!
      (At the same time that the sword falls on Clem, the
                  curtain also falls.)
```

```
Wertheimer                        Evening Becomes Electric.

    This is a perfect little burlesque, with clever rhymes and
broken lines to add to the effect, some very pungent gangster
language, and the whole situation reproduced in buoyant comic
spirit.    Your title, a good play on O'Neill's, has the added
advantage of alliteration.    Aristophanes would surely
appreciate this.
```

G-25 "Evening Becomes Electric," probably produced as part of an assignment during my last year in high school, was apparently appreciated by my teacher. *(family archives)*

The burlesque quality mentioned by my teacher is also evident in the poem "Spring," written more than a year later. The negative theme is there in the spring of 1945 too, in "Words Without Meaning":

```
                        Spring

De trees is green,          De air is moist,
De boids sung clear;        De sky is blue;
No clouds is seen,          De blossoms boist,
'Cause spring is here.      And spring boists too.

De snow is gone,            De air is hot,
De boidies sing;            De goils is dumb;
You mow de lawn,            You sweat a lot,
-It sure is spring.         Since spring has come.
```

G-26 "Spring," written spring 1945 *(family archives)*

```
                Words Without Meaning

Use your days, say you, for something worth the time.
You have but few of them.
The number of your days may seem infinite,
But the end of the line comes all too soon, before you
                                    are aware of it.

All right, I say, I will, go through the list;
I may do many things, the range is infinite.
I may study, I may draw, I may wash dishes.
I may read, listen to music, write a rhyme.
Visit a friend, and then come home.
-These things all are worth the time:
Wasting it is the only crime.

            But.

If I study, I may learn
That Barnardine in Shakespeare's "Measure",
```

```
Was created to portray evil,
To contrast with the good of the few.
Or I may learn that Hume
Thinks selflove unimportant,
Or two plus two is four,
Or bon means good, and more.
  But in the end, when I am dead.
  What matters what is in my head?
  I die and cease existing.
  And Barnardine or Hume—they help me not.
      The Time Was Wasted.

If I draw a picture of reality
I reflect but truths I see,
Ones which all the world perceives,
Broken houses, ashcans, leaves.
Redundancy is waste of time.
  But if I draw the sublime?
  Then:—what's the use there? None.
  Lying is all that's been done.
  The sublime exists not.
      The Time Was Wasted.

If I wash dishes
I do something temporal;
After another meal
They are dirty again.
And the washing is past.
And nothing remains.
You get nothing for all your wet pains.
      The Time Was Wasted.

If I read, I study but words.
And studying words, I learn not a thing.
- Oh yes. Barnardine was created evil
And Hume denies Self-love
  But as before said, what matters all this?
  And, as they say, ignorance is bliss.
      The Time Was Wasted.

If I listen to music, I may be affected.
But what good am I doing others,
Myself or posterity,
My mother or brothers?
  There is no effect that is lasting of import.
      The Time Was Wasted.
```

```
If I write a poem, I may be creating,
But who will read my ugly creation?
Ugly indeed, for beauty exists not,
Except in things that slowly rot;
Not in things that poetry talks of,
Not in flower or passion or suede glove.
And if anyone does read the poem, nothing will happen.
His mind will wander and roam.
And if he is interested, what then?
Why, poems have no effects upon men.
  And if one man in a million were actually touched,
  Why, he too will go soon the Butlerian way of all flesh.
      The Time Was Wasted.


If I visit a friend, I eat up his food,
Waste his valuable time, and do him no good.
We talk and pass the time away,
Until there's gone another day.
And coming home I go to bed,
And lie down, resting my head,
And sleep with eyes closed,
  Creating nothing.
      The Time Was Wasted.


And even if I really am creating something,
Either I outlive it, or it remains a time after me.
- Or it may even last till the end of the world.
But after the end of the world, what then,
  It too has gone.
      The Time Was Wasted.


        So

Naturally I agree with you:
Use your days well, you have not many:
Study, draw, read, wash dishes;
Listen to music, visit a friend;
Write a rhyme, go to sleep, create.
  Use well your time.
  You have not much of it.
```

G-27 "Words Without Meaning," spring 1945 *(family archives)*

There is also a macabre "phantasmagoria" from the previous winter that clearly demonstrates my complex feelings and ambivalence about my father.

This piece recounts a fantasy around a photograph of my father, and also refers to Spanish wax matches that I had gotten from Schani:

PHANTASMAGORIA

Sitting at the desk, my work for the evening is done. The clock that I have moved from the bedroom to my desk the one that is small has an almost inaudible tick can be made to ring loudly and softly and has an illuminating dial says 10:50. Bright and early since tomorrow is Sunday and I can sleep long get breakfast late.

Behind my clock and above it two living eyes of a dead man look out at me. The smile flickering often lost sometimes remonstrative sometimes amused sometimes indifferent I can see well now since I have moved the clock in front of Dover Wilson's What Happens in Hamlet the cover is torn at the left of the photograph. The smile is now satisfied.

I have finished the evening's work. I might as well smoke another cigarette quietly to end a good day off well.

The eyes say no. You shouldn't smoke anyway so why now when it'll make it harder to go to sleep?

But I want a cigarette even if it's only a Rameses.

No say the eyes.

They burn. The smile is gone.

No.

Looking away from the eyes I pull open the drawer at my right. The cigarettes lying next to the hammer and the piles of unanswered letters are enticing.

The eyes say no.

I open the pack. The cigarette is between my lips. I strike one of those Spanish wax matches and watch it burn down slowly. The wax melts as the flame approaches it. It makes a drop which starts to run from the flame and finally ends on my finger where it starts to harden.

Past the flame the eyes are burning burning stronger than the little match flame lighting them up. They say no. Emphatically. Threateningly. No. They are almost angry.

The tips of my thumb and forefinger are beginning to feel the near flame. I put the flame to the end of the cigarette laugh at the blazing eyes. I puff and put the match in the ashtray. Inhaling deeply I look at the eyes.

The mouth under them with the thin lips. What I have always seen as lips whose ends are slightly raised are tight together now. The ends are straight or slightly down.

The eyes above and the wart or whatever it is that brown spot on the forehead is darker. The little space between the heavy eyebrows is not grey. The redness that was always there when he got irritated is strong.

Put on some of that balm that helps to get rid of the redness.

But the eyes and the brown spot and the red spot and the eyes and the tight lips and the eyes are not listening. They say no. I told you not to. If I say you should not you should not I am I whom you know and who must say what you shall do and you must do that. I said no. Therefore you should not have. But yet you did.

Yes say I I did. Another deep inhalation.

In the middle of a conversation with me you should not especially not when I just say in this discussion that you should not. I will not allow it say the eyes.

I laugh. You are only a photograph and of a dead man too.

The eyes say but a dead man has more power than a living man.

How can he? You are wrong.

No I am not. Look here. Look here. Into the deep deep centers of the eyes of this photograph of me dead. I am alive and I say you should not and you do. Therefore you shall be punished. You should not have.

The eyes are blazing. wide open hostile loudly reprimanding. I try to look away I cannot.

See say the eyes see you cannot. Your eyes are wider open than we are. Look. Stare. Your face is coming closer. Come. Come. We shall teach you what it means to do something we say you shall not do. We will teach you.

The eyes burn blaze with a white flame burning through my eyes into my inside into my deepest into what I had meant to hide from those eyes. But the eyes see it. The eyes see it. They see.

Burning.

Burning.

What is burning?

The eyes.

The eyes.

And my cigarette.

> And my cigarette. With the cigarette I can burn the
> eyes so they will never see again.
> But the eyes do not see what I am planning. They are
> still invincibly and selfassuredly and downlookingly and
> punishingly staring and boring through my brain. But they
> do not see what I have hidden about the cigarette. They
> do not.
> Quickly the cigarette is in front of the right eye. It
> is smoking smoking more than the cigarette alone. The eye
> is burning. The eye is burning. Suddenly it looks sur-
> prised. The other one looks hurt amazed. Then a hole ap-
> pears in the photograph.
> Photograph.
> Photograph.
> Only a photograph.
> I take the cigarette away. In the grey and white
> slightly hard paper is a hole with glowing edges. Only a
> photograph. Only a photograph.
> I put out the cigarette.

G-28 "Phantasmagoria," winter 1944 *(family archives)*

G-29 The Dodo *(courtesy of the Friends Historical Library of Swarthmore College)*

My first few actual publications were a few "po-ems" published in the *Dodo*, a "literary magazine" issued at Swarthmore College when I was a student there and was a member of its editorial board. I still have copies of them; I remember being proud of them when they were published way back in the 1940s, a good three quarters of a century ago.

The first one, published on page 24 of the February 1946 issue of the *Dodo*, used an odd two-column format. It has veiled references to Shakespeare ("for the rain, it raineth every day") and Lewis Carroll ("cabbages and kings"), among other literary innuendoes ("castles of the poor" and "hovels of kings").

Pensamiento
Caro

I sit up here, with chair	leaned back, touching the
wall, and a history book	in my lap. Karl Marx—
the Communist Manifesto,	Das Kapital. Outside the

sky is grey, and the dis-
with the rain. Through
the rain splashes on my
my glasses, like tears.
the rain falls on the
them absolute. The
the open space and
to my face, sometimes
cold and sometimes push-
are washed by the driving
upon them, for the rain,
And after they are washed,
dry them, but the
they stay poverty stricken,

From my high aerie
world, and read of kings
things. What matters is the
history the rains weep,
All through history trees
cold rain, go to seed,
The wind pushes through misshapen
grotesque dancers,
about the hovels of kings
poor. The wind is im-
have to do with man-
and cannot even pray
who would not listen
self-loving comments.
the autocrat? Is not the
the wind says, "Down," noth-
the rain says, "I shall," he
him. Mountains
tents give way; and mankind
voices of the ulti-

tant green of trees fades
the grated window, open,
face and hand and on
And time passes, as
shades of green, making
wind twists through
gives a carbonated feeling
gentlecool, and sometimes
ing warm. The walls
of the rain by the wind
it raineth every day.
they wait for the sun to
sun does not come, and
wet, huddled.

I look down on the
and wars—unimportant
fates of cabbages. All through
but who lends an ear?
grow, are freshened by the
and die. But who looks?
trees, making them into
and goes on to blow
and the castles of the
portant. What do kings
kind? Kings are nothing,
to the wind and rain,
to their low and
For is not the wind
rain the dictator? When
ing can resist; when
does, and there is none to stop
and trees, towers and
shudders, when the
mates whisper.

G-30 "Pensamiento" from the *Dodo*, February 1946 *(family archives)*

The second one, appearing on page 12 of the next issue of the *Dodo* for spring, 1946, pretentiously refers successively to some of the great works that were part of the liberal arts tradition at the time: Michelangelo's "Moses" statue, Leonardo da Vinci's famous "Mona Lisa" painting, Immanuel Kant's abstruse philosophical writings, the imaginative poetry of E.E. Cummings, Shakespeare's plays, the Gestalt theory of psychology, and Beethoven's ninth symphony. The theme of the piece seems to be the prevalent negative contemporary criticism of great creative accomplishments of the recent Western world. The title is a takeoff on the title of one of Kant's most famous books. And the author's pseudonym is as before Caro, my mother's maiden name.

OF IMPURE REASON

Standing, strongly planting his two feet, the critic stares quite square ahead, eyes raised, and contemplates, derisively, the work. "The beard," says he, "is made too massively; no hair is quite as heavy as that stone; in this work Michelangelo has failed: outdoing power, stone was never made to portray life, weak human flesh. This man was a man, no weighty mass of marble."

*   *   *

"The play of light and shadow, form and line, was exquisitely used in this great work; the eyes hold more than books of written words, and beauty lies forever in those hands. But look," continues innocent the speaker, "the landscape lounges oddly in the background; there is no earthly reason for those shapes. Da Vinci vanquished beauty, lost to form."

*   *   *

"Kant has overlooked a host of factors; much he says is coldly artificial. Imagination, Reason, Understanding must be shown dependent on each other; the light arises—yes, it can be done: in the Aesthetic union is achieved. —But what an artificial unity!"

*   *   *

"E.E. Cummings has his better points, but much he writes is void of meaning; most of it is worthless trash, experiments in fooling readers, deriving new effects. If we regard his work in toto, then, we must conclude its value is but small."

*   *   *

"Macbeth, yes; and Hamlet too. —Othello. All are perfect, unified in essence. But Lear, with all his poignant tears and storm is, structurally speaking, very faulty. —After Act IV, where is the fool?"

*   *   *

"A beautiful fantasy it is indeed. How wonderful 'twould be if all the world were structured, fitted well, à la Gestalt! But mysticism it remains. Not science."

      * * *

"It is a sacrilege. Why add the voice? Symphonic form, traditionally, seems quite adequate; there is no need for change."

      * * *

If I would ask you, critics of the world, to look at these men's lives, what would you say?

      * * *

To look at these men's minds, what would you say?

G-31 "Of Impure Reason" from the *Dodo*, spring 1946 *(family archives)*

Then there is another item, which contains a distant reference to Gestalt thought near its middle, on page 30 of the same issue of the *Dodo*:

Till Death Do Us Part

Soaring in the infinite of space
Are aimless bits of matter, floating free,
Knowing no beginning nor conclusion,
But parts of nothing, organized in chaos.
And then two roving stars approach each other
And drawing nearer, rotate each about.
And in a final flaming stellar moment
Star unites with star in blazing fury.
And as the two revolve as one together,
Parts of flaming gas and matter are emitted.
Emergent form, the organized, the full
Shines out, complete and truthful, omnipresent.
The new and quiet state of seething elements,
A whole diversified in unity,
A solar system with its laws and standards
Lets grow its planets round composite sun.
And as the planets age and cool in space
They free themselves and pull away from sun.
Are aimless bits of matter once again,
Soaring in the infinite of space.

G-32 "Till Death Do Us Part" from the *Dodo*, spring 1946 *(family archives)*

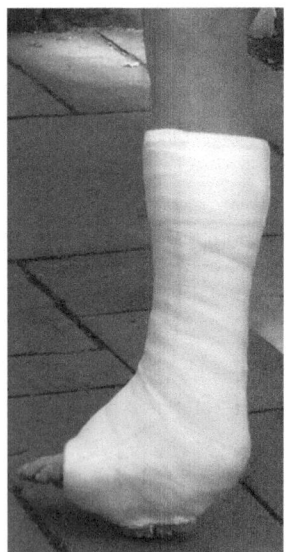

G-33 A plaster walking cast *(from https://commons.wikimedia .org/wiki/File:Short_Leg_Walkin g_Cast.jpg)*

My artistic efforts in the realm of words included not only composition, but also performance. I took the title role in a production, in French, of Molière's *Le Malade Imaginaire*. This production was a reading, in the sense that we performed with scripts in hand, but we also moved around the stage. I had broken my leg skiing not long before, and had recently progressed to the plaster "walking cast" provided by the normal treatment of a broken leg in those days. I remember dancing and spinning on that cast as the *malade* at appropriate moments during the show.

The famed poet W. H. Auden was a visiting faculty member at Swarthmore during the fall of 1944, and he wrote a review of a production of the Shakespeare classic *The Taming of the Shrew* in which my roommate Stefan, Ward Edwards, and I played minor roles (Stef's was Biondello, Ward's Tranio, and mine Grumio); the lead was played by a popular fraternity man, Archie Chambers, to whose Petruchio I was a servant—and in his review Auden praised my performance in that role, even though I forgot a few of my (very few) lines, and pantomimed their meaning off the cuff rather than speaking the words. I was proud of his comments, since I wasn't really intentionally "so lively and so awful."

On the weekly 15-minute program which I hosted at Swarthmore's local radio station WSRN, I (pretentiously, I fear) read poems I liked in English, French, German, and sometimes even Spanish. I also directed for WSRN a radio production of Marlowe's *Dr. Faustus*. I selected Douwe Yntema, who had a wonderfully nasal voice, to play the role of Mephistopheles, and I managed to cast as Faustus an older professor of French who had a strong German accent.

At Johns Hopkins I continued my brief dramatic career by directing a reading production of the Greek tragedy, *Medea*. One reason for producing this play was that I was struck by the rather unusual mechanism of green chalkboards at the front

December 19, 1944   THE SWARTHMORE PHOENIX

Foghorn Bellow, Sly Bitchery
Spark Shakspeare's Worst Play

By W. H. Auden

First, an exclamation of dismayed dissent. Why, with some 36½ to choose from, select Shakespeare's worst play, a play which is not only totally lacking in poetry and wit, but which also leaves a very unpleasant taste in the mouth? Let me explain hastily that I am no feminist; I am with the most reactionary in believing that a woman's place is in the home, not an office, factory, druggie, or cocktail lounge, that she should have lots of children, and that she can be neither happy nor fully herself until she finds a man to whom she surrenders completely and for life. But, for that very reason, a great deal is required of the man, and if he is no better than Lucentio, Baptista, Hortensio, Gremio, and Petruchio—God, what a crew—then she'd better remain a stenographer or become a nun. In the Little Theatre Club production, as in most, the prologue was omitted, but readers of the play will remember that its "wittie and pleasant comedie" is performed for the delectation of Christopher Sly, which suggests, at least to me, Shakespeare's own wry comment on the whole boiling. "Well, here it is"; he seems to be saying, "this is the daydream of every resentful, ineffectual, not-so-male loafer—to have absolute and irresponsible power over a woman who is vital, beautiful, and very very rich."

"So Lively, So Awful . . ."

However, if the play itself turned my stomach, it was quite otherwise with the performance, and I do congratulate Mrs. Rubin and the Little Theatre Club on a production which was in almost every respect, very good indeed.

The two most remarkable performances were, for me, Michael Wertheimer's Grumio and Winnifred Poland's Bianca, not because they were better than the principals, but because their parts are so much more difficult to make anything of. The temptation to ham the Pert Servant is even for professionals, almost irresistible, (Stefan Machlup succumbed, I'm afraid, as Biondello, but, then, what is one to do with him? Ward Edwards as Tranio, on the other hand, was too genteel), yet Wertheimer managed wonderfully to be at once so lively and so

awful. Similarly, the very idea of the good gentle sister makes one yawn, but Miss Poland surprised and delighted me by playing Bianca as a sly little bitch.

Hold That Foot!

Petruchio (Vaughan Chambers) with his drearily masculine presence and his foghorn bellow was an admirable job of casting and acting; my kicking foot never stopped itching. As for Katharina (Helen Glenzing), my only complaint is that she was too sympathetic. I suspect that in an effort to get some interest into the play, Miss Glenzing tried to make it the drama of a spirited girl's surrender to her destined hero. Unfortunately, Petruchio's character makes this impossible with the result that I couldn't dislike her when she was supposed to be a shrew, and I disliked Petruchio even more after she yielded, since from start to finish she was so obviously immeasurably his superior.

I have no space to do more than mention one or two others. Lucentio (John Rosselli) was as soft, well-washed, and nice-looking as a boy-friend should be. Hortensio (Robert Alfandre) was a real camp, Baptista (Richard Southworth), Gremio (Robert Gilkey), Pedant (David Chalmers) and Vincentio (Philip Gilbert) were convincingly dingy old men, the Widow (Eleanor Gillam) was a just reward for Hortensio, and the Lower Orders, especially the seamstress (Merry Brown) made one nostalgic for the good old days in Europe when servants were servants.

Swarthmore's Own

Richard Southworth's set was simple, effective, and professional, as were the lighting (Fisk et al) and the costumes (Kemp et al). Personally, I have a preference for Shakespeare in modern dress, partly, perhaps, because I detest Elizabethan clothes.

Last, but not least, there was Robbins Landon's overture. Perhaps it was not very original and seemed only vaguely related to the play, but it was music, it sounded nice, and, more important still, it gave the performance what every amateur production should have, a local uniqueness. It made it Swarthmore's show.

G-34 W. H. Auden's review of *The Taming of the Shrew* at Swarthmore, 1944 *(courtesy of the Swarthmore Phoenix)*

G-35 A lecture hall with vertically movable
chalkboards at Hopkins *(photo by Robert Ballou)*

of a lecture hall; these boards could be raised and lowered by the flick of a switch at the lectern, and for some reason there was sufficient space behind the two large moving slabs for a person to stand on a shelf behind them, and that space was high enough for the person to stand upright. The play called for a "deus ex machina," the appearance and disappearance magically of a major character—and the flick of the appropriate switch could make the character appear or disappear by being covered by the moving slab of green chalkboard behind and above the lectern and the floor of the classroom where the other action was taking place. I don't remember who the actors were, probably fellow graduate students; we did only one performance.

While I was at Harvard, a group of graduate students came up with a parody mocking the respected faculty members of the experimental psychology department. I think I must have been one of the five ("V. von Funf") authors. The others were probably Nan, Bill McGill, Ward Edwards, and George Heise. The characters in the play are members of the department and associated individuals involved in some way with the department:

Mrs. O'Toole: probably a generalized service person rather than anyone specific

Prof. E. G. Roaring: Edwin G. Boring

Prof. I. C. Phi: my father, Max Wertheimer, complete with a "Cherman accent"

Dr. J. G. Dead Center: John G. Beebe-Center

Dr. E. B. Human: Edwin B. Newman

Dr. J. C. R. Ruleslider: J. C. R. Licklider

Dr. G. A. Müller: George A. Miller

Dr. R. Lamppost: Robert Galambos

Prof. B. Skinneybox: B. F. Skinner

Prof. Stanley S. Steamer: S. Smith Stevens

Dr. I Ma Hearse: Ira Hirsh

Dr. K. C. Conglommery: K. C. Montgomery

Dr. Fred Quick: (I don't recall who, if anyone, this character represented)

Dr. Bákákake ("bake a cake"): Georg von Békésy, who won the 1961 Nobel Prize in Physiology or Medicine

Dr. M. W. Blithenzeig: Mark Rosenzweig

Allslop P. Dimwit: probably a generalized student rather than anyone specific

The title is a spoof on the name of the Gilbert and Sullivan operetta *Patience*, and songs are based on numbers in Gilbert and Sullivan operettas. I had memorized the lyrics of numerous such songs in the course of my involvement with the greatly-shortened performances of those operettas at summer camp. Probably my fellow students were also familiar with many of them. Our versions of the songs referred to the reputation of the department members and some of the departmental politics.

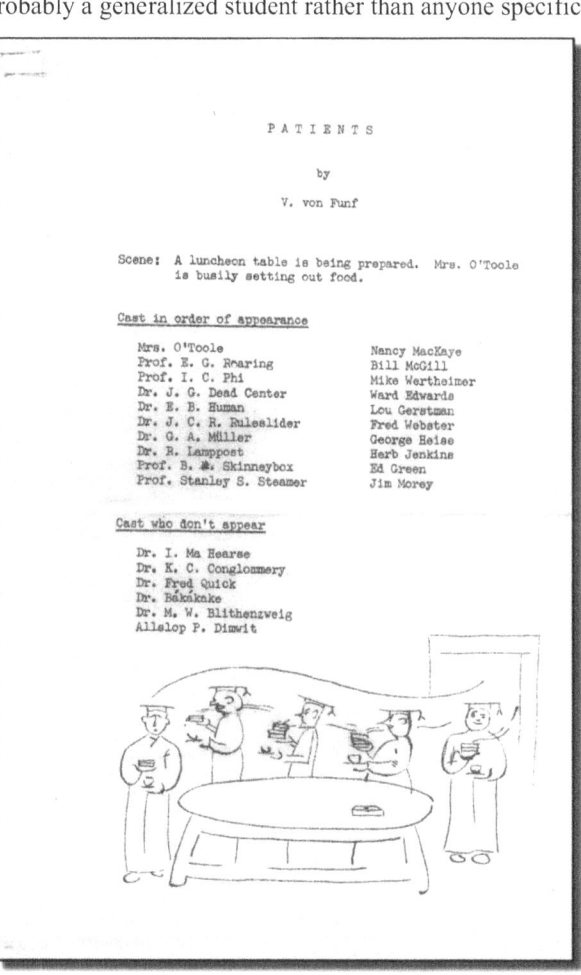

G-36 The script for "Patients" *(family archives)*

Mrs. O'Toole: Oh dear -- oh dear! Here it is five minutes to one and the coffee hasn't boiled yet. And we only have six loaves of bread and Blithenzweig and Hearse are eating today -- Where's the lettuce -- oh, here's the salt solution for Dr. Dead-Center[1] -- I do hope I've got it right today. Hm, the meat's a week old. They'll be sure to complain. Another staff meeting today -- I won't be able to clean up till half past five -- They talk and talk and talk. But I don't know how they understand each other; they all talk at once. And the words -- apricotic[2] reinforcement -- Hell of a tremor[3] -- And the operations[4] they're always talking about. They must be the sickliest bunch -- Maybe they catch 'em from those models they're always running around with -- I wonder who this fellow Mathematical[5] is -- I guess he runs the agency -- Oh dear -- Oh dear --

(sings to the tune of "Oh! a private buffoon" - Yeomen of
        the Guard)
Oh professors are calm, wise old men full of charm
If you listen to popular rumor.
They smoke and they talk, filling blackboards with chalk,
And they always are mellow in humor.
But I see them each day, and I really must say
That this view is entirely in error;
Take any PhD, just scratch him and see
You're dealing with a holy terror.
    If psychologists are anything like the rest
    Then professors aren't far from the world's greatest pest,
    Believe me, each one is a terror.

They come straggling each day in their leisurely way
To the meal that I've spread out before them.
They're so silent and neat, as they prepare to eat
That you'd think the proceedings will bore them.
Things are going on fine as they start out to dine
Until someone begins a discussion;

[1] *Beebe-Center was involved in a study of taste intensity, which called for sweet, salty, sour, and bitter solutions with carefully controlled concentrations.*

[2] *A malapropism for "aperiodic" reinforcement*

[3] *A malapropism for "helicotrema": a critical location in the ear, at the apex of the cochlea, which Stevens, Glambos, and Békésy were working on*

[4] *Unrelated to the surgical operations that Mrs. O'Toole supposes; in the operational view, the scientific meaning of a thing is its operational definition, that is, the operations used to measure it.*

[5] *Mrs. O'Toole supposes that the mathematical models frequently mentioned among the faculty are people employed at a modeling agency run by someone named Mathematical.*

Then each voice mounts in ire, soon the room is on fire,
Like some Congressman quizzing a Russian.
   Oh, there's nothing so wild as these men when enraged,
   Each one screams like a child and will not be assuaged,
   Like some Congressman quizzing a Russian.

Someone calls for a vote, so to his neighbor's throat
Each one flies to enforce a decision.
The chair asks for peace, then makes threat of police,
But is answered only with derision.
So they battle this way till someone stops to say
That the hour of two is just striking;
Then the fight promptly ends, to his lab each one wends,
Having spent a lunch-hour to his liking.
   There is only one answer to which those facts lead
   Psychologists are holy terrors indeed,
   Since a lunch-hour like that is their liking.
(Dr. Roaring and Dr. I. C. Phi talking offstage. Maid looks
startled and exits right. Roaring and Phi enter left.)
Roaring: And this is where we eat lunch.
Phi: Zeitgeist.
Roaring: Gesundheit (bowing). The others will be in in a moment.
Phi: In the meantime, Professor Roaring, tell me about yourself.

Roaring (sings to the tune of "Little Buttercup" - H.M.S.
       Pinafore):
I am a psychologist, modern psychologist
Though I can never tell why,
But still a psychologist, modern psychologist,
And will be one till I die.

I learned introspection
And not vivisection,[6]
But since then I've traveled quite far.
I found my salvation's
To use operations
To answer all problems there are.

I cleared the confusion
From the moon illusion;[7]

---

[6] *Boring's theoretical orientation was purely subjective, rather than objective.*

[7] *The moon looks larger when seen on the horizon than when seen high in the sky. Boring, who concentrated on sensation and perception, studied this illusion.*

```
I'm the most scientific of men.
But when no one sees me
It doesn't displease me
To use introspection again.


So I'm a psychologist, modern psychologist;
You can be one if you try.
My work as psychologist, modern psychologist
Was a history of ear and of eye.
```
  (Enter Dr. Dead-Center with a board of glasses. Byplay with
glass fixed by Mrs. O'Toole.)
Dead-Center: Aha, a new subject -- Sir, would you please taste
these and tell me which of them is the more pleasant.[8]
(Phi tastes first, spits it out -- tastes second and faints. Is
caught by Roaring.)

Dead-Center: Ah, the first is obviously the more pleasant, but
I'd better revive the subject. Dr. Phi! (no response) Behavior-
ism![9] (sinks lower) Gestalt! (Phi jumps up)
Phi (to Roaring): And who is this gourmet?

Roaring: May I present my colleague, Dr. Dead-Center. Dr. Dead-
Center, this is Dr. I. C. Phi from the Berliner Institut für
Gearshift and Crankshaft.
Phi: Dr. Dead-Center what is your special line in Psychology?

Dead-Center (sings to the tune of "If you're anxious for to
        shine" - Patience):

```
If you hanker for to shine
In the psychologic line
As a man of learning rare,
You should read each printed word[10]
Be it learned or absurd,
For one always must be fair.
You must understand each theory though it makes you slightly
        weary
Just in case the author sheds some light.
In short the life worth leading is so very full of reading
That you have no time to write.
    Then everyone will say
```

---

[8] *Beebe-Center published a book titled* The Psychology of Pleasantness and Unpleasantness.

[9] *The reductionist approach of behaviorism is essentially incompatible with Gestalt theory, which was my father's domain.*

[10] *Beebe-Center published fairly little, but was a devoted scholar who read almost anything published in the field.*

```
    As you walk your bookstrewn way,
    "If that great man immerses himself in tomes too thick for
        me,
    Why, what a very marvellous psychologist
    That brilliant man must be."

But it's not enough to read
Everything that gives a lead;
We must further science too.
So you pick an ancient bone --
For example, feeling tone,
And clothe it in raiment new.

You have read what's said about it and you have good cause to
        doubt it
But you really shouldn't write up this.
Instead in labs you putter, swigging gulps of salt and water,
Getting facts like a scientist.
    And everyone will say,
    As you publish in this way
    "If this learned man can find in salt implications too deep
        for me
    Why, what a very scientific scientist
    That scientist must be."
```

(Enter Dr. E. B. Human and Dr. J. C. R. Ruleslider. Human rushes up to Phi, slaps him on the back, etc.)

<u>Human</u>: Isomorphism.[11]
<u>Phi</u>: Configuration.[12]
<u>Human</u>: How's the ganzfeld?[13]
<u>Phi</u>: All ganz![14]
<u>Human</u>: Dr. Phi, may I present Dr. Ruleslider. He's our expert in the new field of information theory.[15]
<u>Phi</u>: Ja, I know. Dial 411.
<u>Ruleslider</u>: No, no, it's this way.

(sings to the tune of "Carefully on Tip-Toe Stealing" - H.M.S. Pinafore)

---

[11] *This refers to the theory of comparable functions in the brain and in perception, an area of Gestalt study (especially by Köhler).*

[12] *One of several common translations of the German word 'Gestalt'*

[13] *An undifferentiated perceptual field; for instance, placing half a ping-pong ball over each eye produces a visual ganzfeld*

[14] *German "ganz" = English "whole"*

[15] *This refers to the beginnings of the field of information theory which has become so central in the development of computers.*

```
If I'm working up statistics
And I find that I am stuck,
I swig my Coca-Cola ,
And put my faith in luck.         Glug.
   Roaring: Goodness me,
   Did someone choke?'
Ruleslider: Silent be,
It was my Coke.
   All: It was, it was the Coke.
Ruleslider: Uh huh, it was my Coke.
It all comes clear as crystal
And logic takes too long;
So I'll punch my calculator:
Here's the answer -- It's wrong.

I can prove by cybernetics
The assumption here is good,
But the brain circuit of relays
Is not clearly understood.¹⁶        Glug.
   Human: Goodness me,
   Who was it spoke?
Ruleslider: Wasn't me;
Again the Coke.
   All: Once more it was the Coke.
Ruleslider: Uh huh, it was the Coke.
I don't retain equations
So I figure them out on sight;
Now I'll punch my calculator:
Here's the answer -- It's right.
(Phi has been talking to Human in background.)
Phi: Well, well, that's fine. By the way, do you have a ciga-
rette?

Human (sits down, leans back, crosses legs, pipe in hand): Well
now, let's see, I had a cigarette a week ago -- no, it was a
month ago -- I remember I was talking to Conglommery -- no I
guess it was Freddy Quick -- I know it was Freddy Quick because
-- maybe it was Conglommery -- Anyway we were talking about
rats and I was telling him about a rat I knew once who -- Oh
well that doesn't make any difference. Now, what was it you
asked me?
Phi (quickly): Tell me, E.B., how do you like your new job?
```

---

[16] *Licklider worked with computer models rather than models of the brain.*

Human (sings to the tune of "When I Was a Lad" - H.M.S.
     Pinafore):
When I was a lad I tried to learn
An honest trade in which my keep to earn.
I turned my hand to a job or two,
But lost each one when there was any work to do
   Chorus: He lost each one when there was any work to do.
Human: At last I found the job that suited me,
Running the department of psychology.[17]
   Chorus: At last he found the Job that suited he,
   Running the department of psychology.

Human: So now I come to the lab at twelve,
At two o'clock into my mail I delve,
At three a student brings a form to sign;
He leaves sometime that evening about half-past nine.[18]
   Chorus: He leaves sometime that evening about half-past nine.
Human: That's why this job so suited me,
This running the department of psychology.
   Chorus: That's why this job so suited he
   This running the department of psychology.

Human: New students all, whoever you may be:
Life is consistent with psychology.
One can mix a life of tones and clicks[19]
With home and love, and even politics.
   Chorus: With home and love and even politics.
Human: So lead as well a rounded life as me
And you'll run a department of psychology
   Chorus: So lead as well a rounded life as he
   And you'll run a department of psychology.
Phi: I see you haven't changed, E.B.
(Enter Müller on stilts and playing a clarinet.)
Human: Oh, George, I'd like to present Dr. I. C. Phi.
Müller (looking around bewilderedly): Where?
Phi: Down here! (They shake hands.) I'm very glad to meet you.
Müller: Now that's an interesting statement. Glad -- what do
you suppose glad means? Operationally it could mean --
Phi: A handshake maybe?

[17] *Newman was repeatedly made department chair for a single year, which left him quite powerless; functional power in the department resided mainly with Boring. He managed this position partly via the sort of hedging exaggeratedly shown in Human's speech just before this song.*

[18] *Newman developed a reputation for taking a great deal of time to carry out the various tasks expected of the department chair.*

[19] *Newman was much involved in research on hearing.*

Müller: No, no, no, it's much more complicated. It probably has
to do with the statistical determination of the language.[20] I'm
very interested in language, you know.
Phi: Do you do experiments on language?
Müller (draws self up to full height): Sir, I do not do experiments. I have a program of research!

Müller (sings to the tune of "I Am the Monarch of the Sea" –
          H.M.S. Pinafore):
Each day I come into the lab
To study how my subjects gab,
So I analyse words from a lot of jerks,
And so do my subjects, my assistants and my clerks,

Chorus: And so do his subjects his assistants and his clerks
His subjects, his assistants and his clerks.

Müller: And from each subject's gab I tease
Intraverbal dependencies,[21]
To see how statistics of our language works,
I'm helped by my subjects, my assistants and my clerks,
Chorus: He's helped by his subjects, his assistants and his
          clerks,
His subjects, his assistants and his clerks.

Müller: But if I'm asked why meaning's there,
I can but say that I don't care
If any meaning in their language lurks
And nor do my subjects, my assistants and my clerks,
Chorus: And nor do his subjects, his assistants and his clerks
His subjects and assistants, who must always keep their
          distance, and his clerks!
(Enter Lamppost in tunic with dissecting kit[22])
Roaring: Oh, Lamppost -- Now we can eat. Will you carve.

Lamppost (carves while singing to the tune of "When a Felon's
          Not Engaged" – Pirates of Penzance):

---

[20] *Miller studied the frequency of nouns, length of sentences, and other statistical features of language.*

[21] *This refers to the way in which words already present determine what the next words will be,
including the contextual determination of meaning (i.e. semantics).*

[22] *Galambos carried out dissective animal research focused primarily on hearing. Most of his subjects were cats.*

When a surgeon's not engaged in his employment,
   Chorus: (His employment)
Lamppost: Nor maturing his sadistic little plans,
   Chorus: (Little plans)
Lamppost: His capacity for innocent enjoyment
   Chorus: (Cent enjoyment)
Lamppost: Is just as great as any honest man's.
   Chorus: (Honest man's)
Lamppost: My love for cats is difficult to smother,
   Chorus: (Cult to smother)
Lamppost: But the vital work of science must be done;
   Chorus: (Must be done)
Lamppost: I'll take one dorsal incision with another;
   Chorus: (With another)
Lamppost: My, a surgeon studying hearing does have fun.
   Chorus: (Does have fun)
   When there's vital work of science to be done, to be done,
   My, a surgeon studying hearing does have fun.
Lamppost: Does have fun.

(Enter B.A. Skinneybox in corduroy jacket. Taps Lamppost on [23]
shoulder -- goes over to bar on wall and presses five times.
Lamppost hurriedly puts out plate with food in five pellets.
Skinneybox strides over to table and gets food.)
Roaring: Ah, I see your rate is up today. Dr. Phi, may I pre-
sent our pigeon expert, Dr. Skinneybox.
Phi: Pigeon expert?

Skinneybox (sings to the tune of " A magnet hung" - Patience):
A pigeon sat in a Skinner box;
He pecked at corn and he jumped at shocks;
He knew a yellowish shape meant corn, [24]
A fact not known when he was born.

Now others may seek to find out why
But as for me, I do not try.
I deduce from the shape of the learning curve [25]
That the pigeon has a reflex reserve.
   Chorus: Reflex reserve?
   Skinneybox: Reflex reserve.

---

[23] Skinneybox is acting like a rat or similar subject in one of Skinner's experiments. Skinner was well known for a special environment he devised for studying behavior, known as the Skinner box.

[24] Skinner firmly asserted that all behavior is learned (and thus is not yet known at birth).

[25] A set of behavioral tendencies that become built in after a while

Now this empty creature quite shocked his teacher
Who thought he might observe
Some yearning or learning or turning or spurning
But not reflex reserve.
  Chorus: Now this empty creature quite shocked its teacher
  Who thought he might observe
  Some yearning or learning or turning or spurning
  But not reflex reserve.
Phi: Yes, but what have pigeons to do with Psychology?
Skinneybox: They are Psychology.
Phi: But what about people?
Skinneybox: There's absolutely no difference. Take off the
feathers and -- (shrugs).
(Enter S.S.S. with cigar, goes to coffee pots. Pours all rem-
nants into one pot. Looks up, notices Phi.)
S.S.S.: Ah, you're Phi, aren't you? I'm Stanley S. Steamer.
Phi: I'm very glad to meet you.
S.S.S.: Tell me, how's the skiing in Germany this year?[26]
Phi: Fine, fine.
S.S.S.: You know I have a little place up in Vermont. Fine ski-
ing. Are you doing anything next weekend?
Phi: No, no, that would be Wunderbar!

S.S.S.: Fine, we can spend Saturday clearing the slope of two
to three hundred trees. Sunday morning we can pull out the
stumps and Sunday afternoon we can ski for an hour or so. By
the way, can you cook?

Phi: I chust remembered. I'm running an experiment. I have to
get my children to figure out the theory of relativity[27] this
weekend. So sorry. Tell me, Dr. Steamer, what's your specialty
in Psychology?

S.S.S. (sings to the tune of "Modern Major General" - Pirates
        of Penzance):
I am the very model of a modern psychophysicist;[28]
I've studied mathematics and I am a good empiricist.
I throw around equations till my students go on strike with
        'em;

---

[26] As mentioned on page 115, Stevens was a skiing enthusiast.

[27] My father's book Productive Thinking begins with consideration of thought processes in children,
and includes a chapter describing the thought process by which Einstein came up with the theory
of relativity.

[28] Psychophysics studies the relationship between physical stimuli and the resulting sensations and
perceptions.

By now I've found enough so I can prove whate'er I like with
        'em.
I did a few experiments and even wrote a book on them.
So now I lead a lab in which my friends work while I look on
        them.
I write about semantics, for which I am an apologist;
And this, you see, is how I got to be a great psychologist.
   Chorus: And this, you see, is how he got to be a great
        psychologist;
   And this, you see, is how he got to be a great psychologist;
   And this, you see, is how he got to be a great psycholo-
        cholo-gist.

S.S.S.: I found that operations are the latest methodology,
And so I loudly praise them, never using them; oh, no, not me.
In short, by telling everyone to be a good empiricist
I've made myself the model of a modern psychophysicist.
   Chorus: In short, by telling everyone to be a good empiricist
   He's made himself the model of a modern psychophysicist.

Human (stands up and clanks glass): Gentlemen, we have a few
things to discuss. First about the graduate students.
Chorus: Ugh!
Ruleslider: Please, not while we're eating.

Human: We have to discuss the results of the Pre-lims. We've
already postponed it for a month. We can be brief, there's only
one student.
Roaring (bewilderedly): I thought there were two.
Human (hands out paper): Here's Allslop P. Dimwit's paper.
You've all read it. What do you think?
(Chorus of Ugh's.)
Lamppost: He said that the organ of hearing was something you
played. He can't pass.
Ruleslider: When I asked him what was essential for a T test[29]
he said a teapot. He can't pass.

Dead-Center: If he were to experiment on what he considers to
be the most important subject in feeling[30] Harvard would expell
him. He can't pass.

---

[29] *A test of the statistical significance of the data gathered in an experiment*
[30] *Beebe-Center wrote two chapters of the book* Feeling and Emotion: A History of Theories.

S.S.S.: If he hadn't been expelled on Dead-Center's question he would on his methods in determining the best fitted curve.[31] He can't pass.
Skinneybox: He mentioned consciousness.[32] He can't pass.
Phi: Ah, but --
Human: Please let's have no discussion till after the vote. Gentlemen, what shall we do with him?
Chorus: Pass him.
Phi: Can I talk now?
Human: By all means.
Phi: Dr. Skinneybox, what have you got against consciousness? Aren't you?
Skinneybox: As far as I'm concerned, mind doesn't matter. The only thing that counts is behavior.

Phi (sings to the tune of "Titwillow" - The Mikado):
When I came to this country I knew I would hear
Of behavior, behavior, behavior,
For psychology's studied for many a year
Just behavior, behavior, behavior.
True, the first laboratory had studied the mind;
Psychophysics was psyche and body combined.
Since then parsimony's been at work and we find
Just behavior, behavior, behavior.

From this all the facts of the present scene flow,
From behavior, behavior, behavior;
To animals now for our data we go,
For behavior, behavior, behavior.
We carefully dodge every verbal report;
To exact analytic techniques we resort
And never would we, even just for the sport
Leave behavior, behavior, behavior.

I find it quite hard to consider that tears
Are behavior, behavior, behavior;
The reduction of loves and of hates and of fears
To behavior, behavior, behavior
Seems to leave out entirely what they really are,
Like explaining the twinkle, ignoring the star;
A science so blind cannot get very far
With behavior, behavior, behavior.

[31] *A slightly off-color reference (as is "feeling" in the previous speech) to the putative interests of graduate students*
[32] *Skinner argued that consciousness, lacking an operational definition, is not a scientific subject.*

Skinneybox: The type of event scientists can observe
Is behavior, behavior, behavior,
So description is lost when permitted to swerve
From behavior, behavior, behavior.
Operations defining the mind can't be found,
So psychology's laden with concepts unsound.
I believe that for science the only sure ground
Is behavior, behavior, behavior.

If that's so, then discussion of hates and of fears
(Of behavior, behavior, behavior)
Must consist of reduction of these, it appears,
To behavior, behavior, behavior.
Give a treatment like this to each mystical word
And you'll see that what you say is either absurd
Or else describes something that really occurred
In behavior, behavior, behavior.

All: We've argued this issue for most of our years,
Of behavior, behavior, behavior;
By now we're sure no new agreement appears
In behavior, behavior, behavior.
Each of you will keep working as well as he can
And the future will say which was the better plan.
Whether consciousness is what's important in man
Or behavior, behavior, behavior.

Staff Contributions to the Merriment

Dr. Hirsch[33] (sings to the tune of "When I Was a Lad" - H.M.S.
    Pinafore):
When I was a lad, I spent a year
At advanced study leading to a career.
I bought clean paper and I bought new books
To fill the pretty cases in the student's nooks.
I kept those books so carefully
That now I am professor of psychology.
    Chorus: He kept those books so carefully
    That now he is professor of psychology

Dr. Hirsch: As a first year student I had such fun
That they made me teaching fellow in psych one
I set up slides and corrected tests
And taught the undergraduates how the birds build nests.
I taught the undergraduates so confusingly
That now I am professor of psychology.
    Chorus: He taught the undergraduates so confusingly
    That now he is professor of psychology.

Dr. Hirsch: When all my ideas had been blown to smidgeons
As research assistant I now turned to pigeons
I cleaned the cages and nursed those chicks
While listening to the restful sound of relay clicks.[34]
Those wired up relays worked so well for me
That now I am professor of psychology.
    Chorus: Those wired up relays worked so well for he
    That now he is professor of psychology.

Dr. Hirsch: Now students all whoever you may be
If you want to climb to the top of the tree.
Pay attention to exams lest there be a bad stigma
Include in your experiments a mean and sigma
Stick close to apparatus and avoid theory
And you all may be professors of psychology.

[33] *The place of this song and the next is unclear. The first page says that "Dr. I. Ma Hearse" (here called "Dr. Hirsch," a common misspelling of "Hirsh") does not actually appear. Possibly these "Staff Contributions to the Merriment" were performed (if ever) after the main action of the skit.*

[34] *When the pigeons pecked, it caused a relay to click, making it easier to gather data about the pecking.*

Chorus: Stick close to apparatus and avoid theory[35]
And you all may be professors of psychology.

Skinneybox[36] (sings to the tune of "A magnet hung" - Patience):
With a faulty fuse and a choked-up choke
And a spot of flame and a lot of smoke
In a move perhaps unorthodox
I've put an end to the Skinner-box

Now rat and pigeons I can't see
I stimulate them but they not me
At all such lowly forms I sneer
For I've set my heart on the human ear
  Chorus: The human ear

Skinneybox: The human ear
My most specific
Very scientific
Fancy takes this steer
If I can get religion
Over something like a pigeon
Why not the human ear
  Chorus: His most specific
  Very scientific
  Fancy takes this steer
  If he can get religion
  Over something like a pigeon
  Why not the human ear.

---

[35] Skinner claimed that his approach to psychology was purely empirical, without any need for any theory.

[36] The typescript assigns this song to Skinneybox, but it seems likely that it was actually written for Hirsh, who made significant contributions in the field of audiology.

Among the papers I happen to have kept is also "After finishing *The Wind in the Willows*," clearly written after Nan and I had gotten together, but containing strange similes and symbols.

After finishing "The Wind in the Willows"

So goes the world. A toad gives up and reforms, perhaps. A badger, weak of mind, is wisest, while a rat is a child and a mole yet younger. Combine all four, you have a banker. A banker indeed! What man, if free, were not thrice himself? What man, after hours, cannot be a man? Oh man encloses, and shackles himself; when loose, is free, if he but knew. God's hours are shorter than those of the bank, but each man watches clocks. Every banker or tailor or teacher or quiet accountant, if he but left himself to do. If he but saw his time, the wind would blow more frequently. Cut bounds, cut bonds are ever so loose: yet man but lays aside the blade he's given, and spends his time with knots. Unwittingly his knife cuts knots behind him; who knows but what the time may come when knife gets ahead of knotting? The older are more careful: they tie their knots faster, more furiously, and can sit back in confidence, well knowing the knife has far to go.

But, oh please tell, why this work? The knots but tie, surround and blind; why desperation if the knife's too near? Let it catch up! It's your own knife! And if you know it not, God's hand is at the end: your own. It takes a man of strength, 'tis strange, can stop his work and watch his soul; it takes a man of liberty to look and see, his glasses off. If they would break (oh happiness) then what does each, in his own way? Run straight away; get new prescription, repair the glass, put it back on. And in the interim, in case, he covers up his eyes with fear.

Oh strange is it, how men behave. They start off life without a knot, and need no knife. They are the toad, the rat, a badger, mole; pretension has no place, nor do they scoff. Including all, they need no blade to cut away what they need most. It all is there. No bonds yet bound.

What happens then? They learn, they grow. And learning, growing are so oft: to learn to tie, to fear the knife, to knot a knot, to lock a lock, to close the eye.

That is not all. Then starts the chase, the hurry, flurry, scurry, the chase to keep all knots well bound, to stay the blade, stay well in front. Removing blinds is greatest fear; as shades jump up, they pull them down, and chase around the room, from window to window, desperately pulling shades again, as they snap up behind them. Four windows back—the shade reels up—he jumps there fast—and pulls back down. As he pulls there, a shape ups here. As he pulls here, more light comes in from another window, as again its shade goes up. A frantic jump from shade to shade, a desperate run, out of breath, lest light come in.

There are so few who can sit back, and with no fear, watch all. The shades slip up themselves that way, the blade cuts fast and gives no pain— just newer freedom, greater joy; enlightenment. Oh happy is the man who can do so, and still remain inside his room, contemplating all the windows grant him to his sight.

The willows wave, with unseen wind: no fear! Just look and understand. And expotition comes at last to wistful goal, and happiness. A blind man sees, a deaf composes, and bankers can write truth. The room is there, with all still in it, but seen not with artificial candle light, or even modernistic gas lamps—no; is there in clean and truest light, as enters windows with no glass. And in this light, one can see well. One sees what is, not ought to be, one sees a beauty, not a usefulness, one looks on, admiring, not judging. And good and God and beauty and all are not but words for orators, with empty meaning (since no operation can be found), but mean themselves, mean everything and all in one.

Give me the strength to sit and see, to let knife cut and shade spring up; give me the strength to leave alone, to untie knots, and not pull shades. Give me the truth to see the strength and have an N and M as needs. Give me the strength to know myself, to see the window, watch the knife with pleasure; and most of all, give me the strength, to know my Nan, no glass, no shade, no knife, no knot: just flowers in a meadow.

I can do it, with you at my side.

G-37 "After finishing *The Wind in the Willows*" *(family archives)*

Possibly from the same time (or, at least, typed on the same typewriter, which had been my father's) is this poem:

The cold, silvery moon shines on broken, deserted houses.

An owl in a naked tree lets forth a low, mournful moan.

The rays of silent moonlight shine down on shattered shutters.

The grass, poking its wan green head through the cracks in the
        porchfloor is stirred by a faint, cool breeze.
The road, overgrown with weeds, lies sleeping, tired, bathed in
        the moon's liquid rays.

The night rolls onward, silently, restlessly.

G-38 "The cold silvery moon" *(family archives)*

In a very different vein, I created *Karen's Book of Things to Do* for my daughter's sixth birthday in 1958, decorating the pages using an odd pencil whose lead consisted of four different colors. Here are a few sample pages.

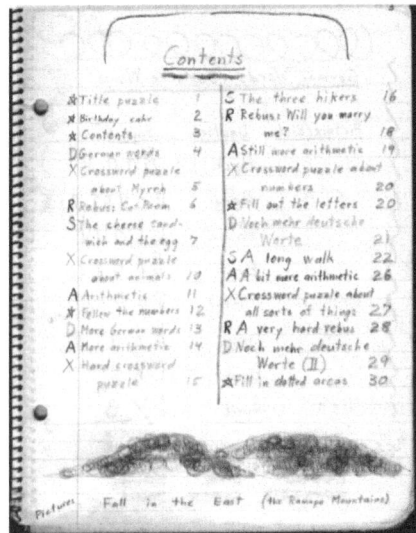

Contents

Pictures: Fall in the East (the Ramapo Mountains)

22

STORY
A LONG WALK

ONE fine fall day, Karen and Duffy get out their rucksacks, and put some food in them, Karen in her dark green one and Duffy in his white one (which used to be Karen's purse). They went out the front door of 113 South William Street, and walked and walked up hill and down hill and finally came to the foot of Bear Mountain. They were tired, so they sat down to rest, and had a little picnic with the food they had brought in their rucksacks. Then they got up again, and started climbing up

---

23

the mountain. Finally they arrived on top, and went to the door of the big stone tower that stood there. They climbed up the stairs inside the tower, until they got to the very top. And do you know who was there to greet them? Enegobiz. He shook hands with them warmly, and said how glad he was to have them visit him again. "You just visited me a short time ago, in fact only eight pages back, but that was in Colorado," he said. "I'm glad you came again so soon."

24

And he made them cocoa, and gave them some very good cookies that he had made himself. "We are going back to Boulder next summer again, you know," said Duffy. And Karen added, "Will you go back to Colorado then too?" "Yes," said Enegobiz, "I like my little stone hut on the Boulderfield of Longs Peak, and will go back. But you know I came here when you came East, because I wanted to live near you so you could come and visit me. So when you go back to Colorado, I will too."

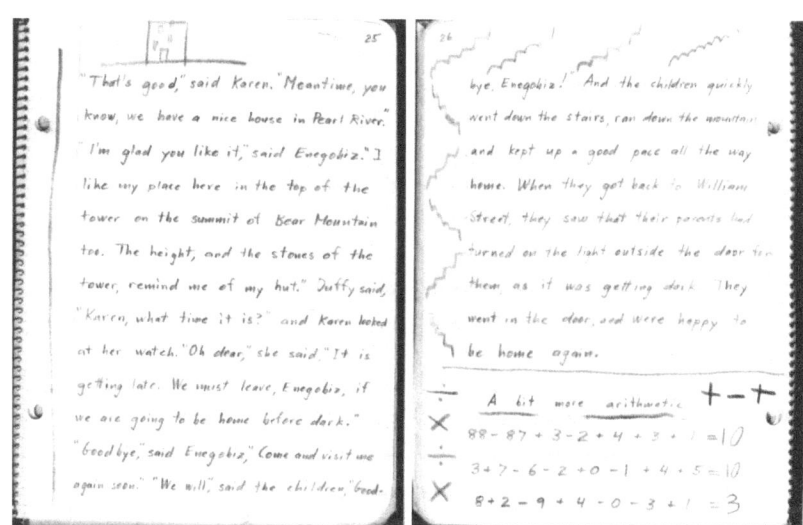

G-39 Pages from *Karen's Book of Things to Do (family archives)*

Many years later, when I ran for a seat on the APA Board of Directors in 2008, my campaign consisted of a doggerel-like poem which I sent out to the members of Council, and which a colleague, Dave Baker, kindly read aloud at the appropriate Council meeting. A copy of the "hand-out" version below was distributed on a sheet of paper delivered to each of the attendees, and my daughter Karen provided Dave with the "read-out" version.

Michael Wertheimer for APA Board of Directors
A Voice with Experience

**A general academic and dabbler in history
Who loves APA, and psych, and the mystery**

Of what makes people tick, or—well—tock, or go nuts,
I try to pay attention to "ifs," "ands," and "buts."
An APA member since 'fifty-two,
I'd appreciate the honor of serving you.

Trained at Swarthmore, at Hopkins, and at Harvard U:
In Gestalt, and in Watson; in Titchener too.
My theoretical models were a mind-muddling zoo.
My poor head was spinning: oh, which view is true?
So I worked as an intern in clinical psych
To find out what non-lab psychology's like.
My career has straddled the classroom and clinic;
Public-interest ideals keep me from being a cynic.

A DC sabbatical convinced me how great
Is the APA staff: dedicated, first-rate.
I've chaired (or been member of) CIRP, P&C,
Membership, CUE, BEA (E&T),
CPCP, task forces, and CSFC.
And I chaired the Exam Committee of ASPPB.
Been president, Rocky Mountain Psych Association,
And Psi Chi, the national psych honor organization.
I have been Council Rep (and been president too)
Of Divisions Twenty-four, Twenty-six, One, and Two.
Been on Council off and on for forty-some years,
Bringing triumphs, collaborations, and, thank God, no tears.
And, for Council, I chaired Public Interest Caucus.
These groups were effective and rarely got raucous.
I learned to pull strings, found out how to mesh gears,
And almost overcame public-speaking fears.

Among recent books is a life of my dad,
Gestalt theorist Max Wertheimer, and I'm so glad
It's out after decades of re-re-revision.

Recent too is Brief History of Psych, fourth edition.
In press: volume six, Pioneers in Psych
And an MIT-Press book I hope you will like,
A translation from German, the work Laws of Seeing,
Which several translators brought into being.

I've awards for my service, scholarship, teaching;
And my decades of firm anti-sexism preaching
Won the first Gender-Neutral Language citation
From U Colorado's Campus Women's Organization.

I've long championed diversity: ethnic, age, gender,
Sexual orientation, disability; defender
Of psych integrating its practice and science,
For both of them benefit from such alliance.
Directed psych honors, and psych programs (doctoral)
In psych (experimental) and psych (sociocultural).

Half a century I have resided in Boulder
And as I've matured (or at least gotten older)
I've discovered the strength of compromise and respect:
They can lead to consensus you might never expect
Even when we're contentious on emotional questions
If we are considerate and welcome suggestions.

I hope you will nominate me to the Board:
A voice with experience, who can afford
To devote as much time as the job may require.
I'm emeritus now, and don't easily tire.
I've held lots more governance posts than most others
And to me you are all treasured sisters and brothers.
I hope that your meeting is nice and constructive
And my rhymed propaganda is somewhat productive.

G-40 The "hand-out" version of my APA Board of Directors campaign doggerel *(family archives)*

— how to read it —

This guide is not a stern prescription. It's here only in case you'd like some tips for reading these verses aloud.
The aim is an almost Dr. Seuss-like rhythm: (da)-da-**dum**, da-da-**dum**, da-da-**dum**, da-da-**dum**-(da).
But, lamentably, Dr. Seuss was unavailable to assist with composing this doggerel.
So there are several places with only one da between DUMs. In these places, you see | | to indicate a pause during that beat.
Or sometimes there's a hyphen inside a word, to show you where the syllable breaks go.
In other places, there are too many syllables between DUMs; in that case, just crowd 'em in as best you can and don't worry.
NB: The last stanza on this page isn't on the handout sheet. It's part of the oral presentation only.

Michael Wertheimer
for APA Board of Directors
A Voice with Experience

A gen'ral academic and dabbler in hist'ry
Who loves APA, | | and psych, and the myst'ry
Of what makes people tick, or—well—tock, or go nuts,
I try to pay 'tention to "ifs," "ands," and "buts."
An APA member | | since 'fifty-two,
I'd appreciate the honor of serving | | you.

Trained at Swarthmore, at Hopkins, and at Harvard U
In Gestalt, and in Watson; in Titchen-er too.
My theoretical models were a mind-mud-ling zoo.
My poor head was spinning: oh, which view is true?
So I worked as an intern in clinical psych
To find out what non-lab psychology's like.
My caree-er has straddled the classroom and clinic;
Public-int'rest ideals keep me from being a cynic.

A DC sabbatical convinced me how great
Is the APA staff: dedicated, first-rate.
I've chaired (or been member of) CIRP, P&C,
| | Membership, CUE, BEA (E&T),
CPCP, task forces, and CSFC.
And I chaired the Exam C'mitt-yof ASPPB.
Been pres'dent, Rocky Mountain | | Psych 'sociation,
And Psi Chi, the nash'nal psych honor org'nization.
I have been Council Rep (and been president too)
Of Divisions Twenty-four, Twenty-six, One, and Two.
Been on Council off 'n on | | for forty-some years,
Bringing triumphs, c'lab'rations, and, thank God, no tears.
And, for Council, I chaired Public Inter-est Caucus.
These groups were effective and rarely got raucous.
I learned to pull strings, found out how to mesh gears,
And almost overcame public-speaking | | fears.

Among recent books is a life of my dad,
Gestalt theorist Max Wertheimer, and I'm so glad

It's out after decades of re-re-revision.
Recent too is *Brief Hist'ry of Psych*, fourth edition.
In press: volume six, *Pionee-ers in Psych*
And an MIT-Press book I hope you will like,
A translation from German, the work *Laws of Seeing*,
Which sever-al translators brought into being.

I've awards for my service, | | scholarship, teaching;
And my decades of firm anti-sexism preaching
Won the first Gender-Neuter-al language citation
From U Colorado's Campus Women's Org'nization.
I've long champ-yoned diversity: ethnic, age, gender,
Sexu'l orientation, disabil'ty. Defender
Of psych integrating its practice and science,
For both of them benefit from such alliance.
Directed psych honors, and psych programs (doct'ral)
In psych ('sperimental) and psych (soc-yocult'ral).

Half a centu-ry I have resided in Boulder
And as I've matured (or at least gotten older)
I've discovered the strength of compromise and respect:
They can lead to consensus you might never expect
Even when we're contentious on emotional questions
If we are consid'rate and welcome suggestions.

I hope you will nominate me to the Board:
A voice with experience, who can afford
To devote as much time as the job may require.
I'm emeritus now, and don't easily tire.
I've held lots more governance posts than most others
And to me you are all treasured sisters and brothers.
I hope that your meeting is nice and constructive
And my rhymed propaganda is somewhat productive.
=======
| | Thanks to Dave Baker for reading this drone.
It's livelier than if I were on the phone
And cheaper than joining you all iWn DC
For just a few moments of you hearing me.

G-41 The "read-out" version of my APA Board of Directors campaign doggerel *(family archives)*

One last poem, which probably comes from the time when Nan and I were at Worcester, reflects some of the profound satisfaction I have found in sailing.

A ketch, upon the whitecaps.
Sure, with sails of sunbaked white,
The starboard tack.
Beating to windward, with heavy heel,
A ketch, upon the whitecaps.
Snug below, and silent strength aloft,
The starboard tack.
Shearing the waves with soundless foam,
A ketch, upon the whitecaps.
Bending, bowing to wind's welcome weight;
The starboard tack.
Genoa, main and mizzen full, as one.
A ketch, upon the whitecaps.
Grave, serious, filling her basic nature;
The starboard tack.
Stately confidence, deepest joy.
A ketch, upon the whitecaps.

G-42 "A ketch, upon the whitecaps" *(family archives)*

Visual arts

Paintings as well as "poems" about sailboats were a fairly frequent theme. I made the sailing watercolors on this page and the next in the early 1950s. The emblem at the lower right and on the sail in each picture is a sort of monogram (a combination of M, N, and W) that Nan and I often used between us. The image in my mind as I made these paintings was probably the schooner in

G-43 Oil painting when I was fifteen *(family archives)*

the movie *Captains Courageous*. I first saw that film when I was eleven or twelve, the same age as Freddie Bartholomew, the boy in the story. It made a deep impression on me.

Another repeated pictorial theme in colored pencil, paint, and even collage, was a comfortable small cottage, typically in an idyllic setting of trees and perhaps hills and mountains.

G-44 Ketch drawn by me *(family archives)*

G-45 Fantasy yawl drawn by me *(family archives)*

After my mother left us, a theme of broken cabins and sad or tragic thoughts became rather frequent, including a barren black tree with a missing left branch. I made many versions of that sketch until I finally achieved one that satisfied me.

G-46 Colored pencil collage from the early 1950s *(family archives)*

G-47 Colored pencil sketch from the early 1950s *(family archives)*

G-48 Final version of black tree, 1950 *(family archives)*

Late in my career at the Ethical Culture Summer Camp, I made a self-portrait whose title, "Myhckque" (a respelling of "Mike"), reflects my fascination with

names and other words. I also occasionally made modest sketches or photographs of where I was living. On the next page are a couple of dramatic photos of buildings against the sky, followed by a much-faded and yellowed drawing of myself making a drawing of our living room, probably all from our time at Worcester.

When we were in Middletown, I acquired a modest 8-millimeter movie camera, which I used largely to film friends and family, but also to attempt to capture scenic beauty. On the drive to and from Montreal from Middletown in 1954, I noticed the attractiveness of the New England small towns and countryside, and used

G-49 Self-portrait at ECSC *(family archives)*

G-50 Photo of clock tower in Worcester *(family archives)*

G-51 Photo of lightning in Worcester *(family archives)*

G-52 Sketch of our home in Worcester, with the boat bookcase *(family archives)*

up a bit of my precious film to take pictures of churches, mountains, and lakes, including Lake Champlain. I took movies of forests, mountains, waterfalls, ocean waves, driftwood, sunsets, buildings and traffic, clouds and cloud shadows in motion, trees tossing in storm winds, and golden sunshine bathing a guitar in our apartment. By setting up a tripod and taking single frames of the hillside opposite our home in Middletown for several weeks, I even made a movie of the coming of spring.

One other rather pretentious practice I engaged in with the movie camera was making successive single exposures of various movable objects, which resulted in

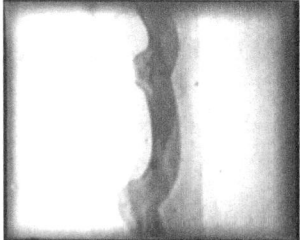

G-53 Movie frame of colored drawings "dancing" on the white leader *(family archives)*

G-54 Movie frames of scenery on the drive to Montreal, 1954 *(family archives)*

an awkward animated sequence of strange movements of strange objects. I also spliced together the blank white "leader" from multiple movies and drew on them, making animated "dances" of colorful abstract shapes.

My "artistic fumblings" have continued off and on through the rest of my life, even into my retirement years. For example, I recently placed first one heavy rock and then a few more on a plank in our patio picnic table that had become warped upward over the years, in an attempt to straighten this plank. As I added more weight to the pile, I became aware of patterns. I found myself engaged in adding smaller rocks as well, paying attention to shape and color when choosing where,

G-55 Movie frame of a blanket in the process of "swallowing" a wastebasket *(family archives)*

G-56 Movie frames of linoleum shapes moving into different configurations *(family archives)*

how, and even whether to include each stone. It grew to contain 58 rocks, some of them very small. Tending it had become an aesthetic activity.

G-57 The unwarping pile *(family archives)*

Appendix H: Travels

It has often been said that there is nothing like travel to broaden the mind. Even domestic travel, but especially international travel, particularly to destinations that at first seem exotic, can lead to truly perspective-altering experiences. I agree; extensive open-minded travel can probably be even more liberally educational than a good undergraduate liberal education. Experiencing diverse cultures first-hand instead of just reading or hearing about them secondhand or learning about them through movies or television yields a much richer and more vivid challenge to one's often unspoken and unexamined taken-for-granted implicit assumptions about the nature of human experience, about beliefs concerning what's right and what's wrong, and about what's good and what's not so good, as well as about fundamental, basic ways to construe human nature and human social interactions. Open-minded exposure to other cultures can wreak havoc with myriad prejudices, whether one was previously aware of these prejudices or not. Besides, the new adventures associated with travel to other places can be a lot of fun.

Like many of my contemporaries, I have lived in many different places during my lifetime. Although I was born in the Karlshorst section of Berlin, Germany, not surprisingly I have no memories at all of it since we moved from there to Frankfurt when I was only two years old, and I don't even know where in Berlin Karlshorst was located. I do have a few dim memories of number 6 Klaus Groth Strasse in Frankfurt, where we lived until I was six years old. I recall that we were warned to stay away from a nearby major thoroughfare, the Eschersheimer Landstrasse, because there was heavy traffic on it. The house had a pleasant grassy yard with red rose bushes here and there, and I remember a few details about its interior, described on page 7.

We left Frankfurt for Czechoslovakia early in 1933 and spent a half year or so in Marienbad (or Marianske Lasne) at a hotel called The Golden Harp (Die Goldene Harfe), but I have no recollections at all of that place. From Frankfurt and maybe from Marienbad we made several trips, usually in the summers, to destinations in the Alps of southern Germany, Switzerland, and northern Italy, as well as occasional visits to Prague to visit my father's father Wilhelm there.

© Springer Fachmedien Wiesbaden GmbH, part of Springer Nature 2020
M. Wertheimer, *Facets of an Academic's Life*,
https://doi.org/10.1007/978-3-658-28770-2

Among the names of places we visited, according to family lore, were Arosa, Ascona, St. Valentin, the Lago Maggiore, and a few others. Somehow being in different locales with different languages and very different geographical settings was a normal feature of my early childhood, a feature which I found interesting and pleasant but in no sense unusual or particularly challenging. I do recall being awed by the mountains in the Alps, and finding them impressive, enormous, and beautiful. The painting by Lisbeth Stern on page 14 reminds me of that.

The greatest upheaval, of course, was the trip from Europe to the New York region, as mentioned on page 18. This was by way of southern and western Europe, and I do remember what must have been a short stay in Paris when I was six years old on the way to Cherbourg, where we boarded the RMS *Majestic*, the enormous ocean liner that brought us across the Atlantic to the United States. I recall the exquisite and surprising pleasure of having ice cream for the first time in my life in Paris, and also remember being fascinated by my first experience of "Seifenpapier," small single disposable sheets of paper with soap that were used when washing one's hands. And the weeklong experience of crossing the apparently endless Atlantic Ocean on the vast ship that contained myriad decks, restaurants, desk chairs in which one could relax, shuffleboard courts, and intriguing little cabins with bunks above one another was exciting and pleasant.

H-1 The RMS *Majestic (from
https://commons.wikimedia.org/wiki/File:RMS_Majestic,_F._G._O._Stuart.jpeg)*

Our week in the Hotel Holley in New York, before I lived for a decade in New Rochelle, introduced me to a new and different world, with the surprisingly unin-spired "American cheese" and "cotton bread" mentioned on page 19, as well

H-2 Hotel Holley, New York *(from https://www.ebay.com/itm/223463389523)*

as the language which was unfamiliar to all of us. Becoming used to the new culture, language, and social practices was by no means an unpleasant challenge; instead, it felt like a lot of fun. Somehow becoming comfortable with the new language, ways of being, eating, and thinking was easily combined with reten-tion of habitual practices and language at home.

There were outings from 12 The Circle to various destinations: the beach on Long Island Sound, the vast and almost overwhelming artificial architectural maze of New York City, and the Catskill Mountains, as well as visits with ac-quaintances, some of them well-to-do. These, and occasional dinners at an unbe-lievably lavish brownstone in Manhattan such as the one owned by the Dean of the New School, Clara Woolie Mayer, further broadened my experience of how different people lived. One recollection of Miss Mayer was that she was fre-quently busy writing checks, presumably to all kinds of people including my father; I began to realize how privileged it must be to be so wealthy.

The summer experiences at the Ethical Culture School Camp in upstate New York, described beginning on page 31, also served to expand my horizons. They too became part of the many facets of my learning about a very variegated set of ways in which people live, interact, and enjoy themselves. I'm sure that the ex-posure to all these different settings helped contribute to my eagerness for further exposure to different settings and cultures during the rest of my life.

H-3 Skiing at Stowe in the 1940s *(courtesy of Hastings House Publishers)*

During my teen years and early twenties I was also exposed to different locales in high school, college, and graduate studies. Fieldston School in the Bronx, Swarthmore College, Johns Hopkins in Baltimore, and Harvard in Cambridge each had their own rather different ambience. So did Worcester, MA, where I spent a year as a clinical intern, not to mention Wesleyan University and the University of Colorado at Boulder after that. And the New England ski areas I went to with Stefan Machlup, usually Mt. Mansfield in Stowe, VT, provided yet another different venue, as did the much more spectacular Colorado ski areas later on.

Nan and I did some traveling as well during the early years, but usually only locally or to other domestic destinations, especially during summers. We frequently spent more than a month visiting my mother and Schani on Long Island, and toward the end of our marriage traveled in Europe in an attempt to salvage the failing marriage. The overseas adventure at that time was not as positively and comfortably mind-stretching as the many later travels, primarily because my entire orientation was devoted to trying (unsuccessfully) to save the marriage.

Nan and I also undertook several other out-of-town trips with the kids, including a camping trip to Jenny Lake in Grand Teton National Park, where I participated in a convention of the Rocky Mountain Psychological Association, and to southwestern Indian communities such as the Cochiti village. This latter, with its exposure to the customs of a native American tribe, was not only interesting and pleasant for us adults, but also helped expose the kids to other cultural practices such as an impressive, serious corn dance and the taboos against walking casual-

H-4 Jenny Lake, Grand Teton National Monument *(from*
https://commons.wikimedia.org/wiki/File:Mt_Owen_and_Mt_St_John_across_Jenny_Lake.jpg)

ly across sacred ground. I also remember a trip with just Nan, when she was pregnant with Benjy, to Cape Cod, where we rented a cabin at the ocean shore and were surprised by the eroding force of the waves and tides which gnawed out a two-foot high escarpment in the sandy beach overnight where there had been a smooth continuous gentle slope of sand the day before. We had left our two kids with Nan's mother at the time, and I recall the dismay and then relief expressed by poor little Karen at having been left for days by both her parents, and then being reunited with them.

I don't remember much more about any further travels while I was married to Nan. But
during later years with Marilyn there was considerable overseas travel, with at least one fairly
major international trip every year or so as well
as domestic trips by car, often including camping, in order to meet the rather inconsequential
goal of having the kids as well as Marilyn and

H-5 The drum we got in the Cochiti
village; the lower drum-head has
shrunk *(family archives)*

me set foot in every one of the 50 United States—which we accomplished except that Karen has never been to Alaska. The boys and I, with little dog Tapsy and a tent, drove up the Alaska Highway in our Volkswagen bug "Heinrich" during the summer of 1968, and by the early 1970s Marilyn too had completed the quest with drives to previously missed contiguous 48 states, an AARP trip to Alaska, and attendance with me at a convention in Hawaii.

Back in 1964 I had traveled to Salzburg and Vienna in Austria, at both of which I gave talks; in 1968 in addition to the Alaska jaunt I attended a lengthy seminar in Stockholm, Sweden. During the next three decades there were many more international trips, some but not all with the excuse of participating in some conference or another, or of presenting an invited or volunteered lecture. Marilyn and I have been in some 70 different countries; Marilyn visited Europe extensively with her mother before Marilyn and I met, and several trips were taken with Marilyn and me as participants in an international exchange of librarians. But most of the trips outside the US with Marilyn were purely for pleasure, and motivated by our curiosity about various more remote parts of the world. We did manage to go to just about everywhere we hoped to, sometimes with repeat visits such as to a pleasant small spa town in southern France named Vernet-les-Bains and some twenty times that we spent two weeks or so annually during the summer on Monhegan Island, Maine, during our last years of frequent travel. Since moving to our retirement community in Boulder in late 2011, our travels (except for a short jaunt to northern Germany for a convention in September, 2012) have been limited to a few final meetings of an APA board of which I was still a member and to twice-a-year two-week visits to southern Oregon to be with Marilyn's brother Jack.

In the summer of 1970, as mentioned before, all three kids joined my mother and me in a driving tour of several countries in Europe and Scandinavia (including a stop in Umeå, in northern Sweden, where I gave a talk and visited with Swedish colleagues I had gotten to know at the Stockholm conference two years earlier) as well as Great Britain in a new Mercedes-Benz we bought in Germany and then had transported across the Atlantic to serve us for many years, in Washington, DC, and then later in Boulder. In 1971 Marilyn and I again went to Scandinavia, this time to Bergen, Norway, to visit with my mother who was spending

H-6 Vernet-les-Bains *(photo by Marilyn Wertheimer)*

H-7 Monhegan Island, Maine *(photo by Marilyn Wertheimer)*

H-8 Austrian countryside *(photo by Marilyn Wertheimer)*

H-9 Novosibirsk, Siberia *(photo by Marilyn Wertheimer)*

the summer there; we also drove in a rented car to several places in Sweden. And I recall how strait-laced some Swedes can be; I remember the shocked looks on the faces of a few elderly ladies who were staying at the same hotel when Marilyn and I walked together, in bathrobes and with towels slung over our shoulders, to go into a bathroom with a tub to take a joint bath. All of Scandinavia impressed us with how neat and clean the towns and houses are, and how poverty and homelessness don't seem to exist there.

That fall I also gave a talk at the University of British Columbia in Canada, at the school where the year before I had almost accepted an offer to chair the department of psychology. Then I gave a talk at the University of Calgary in Canada in 1972, and Marilyn and I took Duffy and Benjy along on a spring break ski trip that year to Austria which also included a brief sojourn in Venice. It was on that trip, if I remember rightly, that Duff came up with the proof that yes equals no: "Yes" in French is "oui," which is a homophone of "we" in English. "We" is "nous" in French, which sounds like "new" in American English. But "new" is "noeuf" in French, a homophone (in French) of "neuf," the number nine. And English "nine" sounds the same as "nein," which is the German word for "no." Hence yes equals no. On the same trip, we also generated a pun on the name of the artist Toulouse-Lautrec: if a sail is luffing on a sailboat, corners of the sail need to be tightened. If one corner is lashed tight but the sail continues to flap, the captain may issue a command to a crewmember, asking for tightening of another corner of the sail: "Toulouse-Lautrec" (the famous French author), "too loose; l'autre Eck" or "too loose" in English, "l'autre" or "the other" in French, and "Eck" or "corner" in German: "too loose; [also tighten] the other corner."

In 1973 Marilyn took me along on what by then was her second trip to Russia, including eastern and southern parts of the Soviet Union such as Lake Baikal, Kazakhstan, and Uzbekistan.

The next few years were limited to domestic travels, except for a wonderful trip in 1975 to various parts of South America. There we saw Machu Picchu and witnessed a rousing Inti Raymi festival at Sacsayhuaman, Peru, in which, in front of tens of thousands of natives who performed ceremonial dances, an impersonator of the Inca himself implored the sun to return on the summer solstice. That Inti Raymi ceremony, which loudspeakers described in Spanish and Quechua,

H-10 Inti Raymi ceremony *(photo by Marilyn Wertheimer)*

has been, we heard, assiduously performed annually for literally thousands of years—and it has worked every time without fail: the sun always came back thereafter. The ceremony was awesome.

During those mid and late 1970s we visited Bryce and Zion canyons as well as Mammoth Caves in North Carolina, at all of which in imposing rocky places we had memorable hikes. There were also trips to Jacksonville, FL, for a com-committee meeting; to Nova Scotia where we found the grave of Marilyn's great-great-great-grandmother Dorcas Tabitha Smith Calquehoun and some distant relatives of Marilyn's at Port Medway; and for me alone to the University of Victoria, Canada, where a former colleague, G. Alexander Milton, arranged for me to be able to take the helm in the Strait of Juan de Fuca of three different sleek racing sloops successively as we raced these magnificent sailboats in moderate winds on the day after my talk at the university

H-11 Dorcas Tabitha Smith Calquehoun, 1854 *(family archives)*

there—a glorious experience. (No one cared who won.) We also traveled in eastern Europe and then spent a week on St. Croix in the Caribbean around Thanksgiving time in 1979 when I attended a meeting there of the Examination Committee of the American Association of State Psychology Boards, to prepare the next version of the annual examination to be used by most US states and Canadian provinces in testing candidates for certification or licensure to practice psychology.

The next two decades produced many international ventures to places we had not seen before. We took several trips with a professor of art history, Ron Bernier, who specialized in Asian art; he insisted that we sign up for regular course credit when we went on these trips with him, as did all of the others who participated in those memorable voyages. Not only did this lead us to accumulate almost enough credits for master's degrees in art history; it greatly enriched our travel experiences with him far beyond what just leisurely tourism would have yielded. In 1980 we spent six weeks with him and a dozen or so students in various parts of India and Nepal for a course on art in the Himalaya; and in 1983 he took us clear around the globe in a course on Buddhism around the world that began in California, then went to Hawaii, and included stops in Japan, South Korea, and India. At the end of the 1980 trip we stopped in Leipzig, then still part of East Germany, for a German psychology convention, and in 1983 in addition to the Bernier trip we had a

H-12 Ronald Bernier *(from https://bernierarchive.wordpress.com/; © Dianne J.*

H-13 Near Aurangabad, India *(photo by Marilyn Wertheimer)*

wonderful separate tour of Japan, where I gave a couple of lectures and we visited a number of sites including Nagoya, Kyoto, and Hiroshima, as well as small thatch-roofed mountain villages with resplendent colorful fall foliage. The culture, food, and elegant simple hotel accommodations provided a most exotic experience of this ancient country. How effectively that large population uses limited precious natural spaces!

In 1980 we spent Christmas in Rio de Janeiro with Pete, Susan, and Monika, and managed to witness exotic New Year's Eve rituals of voodoo rites on the beach and a large candle-powered paper balloon that was launched on the beach but was eagerly approached for scraps of its paper after its candles had burned out and it landed a half hour or so later in downtown Rio. Tiny wooden boats with lit candles were also launched during that night into the sea from the beach, in homage to a powerful goddess, Iemanja. The fervor and variety of religious practices is amazing.

In 1981, after returning from South America, I also had a meeting in Longboat Key, FL, and Marilyn and I continued by car on down to Key West. That year too

H-14 Korea house *(photo by Marilyn Wertheimer)*

H-15 Toshogu shrine, Japan *(photo by Marilyn Wertheimer)*

there was a trip to Europe, including Bad Homburg in Germany, a car trip in Ireland, and a side trip to France, where we visited Paris and stayed in a pleasant inn on a hill outside Dijon, on Mont Roland, an inn which we happily revisited several times on other trips to Europe, usually renting a car in Frankfurt and then usually heading south from there, often to the northern, French side of the Pyrenées. We were cordially received at the Chalet Mont Roland several times on repeat visits there in later years.

Several times we spent a summer week or so in Vernet-les-Bains at the eastern end of the Pyrenées. Near Vernet was a fairly high mountain, the Canigou or "Dog's Tooth" in the Catalan language; it is one of the few European mountains I can claim to have climbed. From Vernet we usually took our time to cover the 200 miles or so to the western end of the Pyrenée chain of mountains separating France from Spain. Typically we would head north and then west, before heading south

H-16 St. Martin du Canigou, on Canigou (Dog's Tooth) *(photo by Marilyn Wertheimer)*

H-17 Le cirque de Gavarnie *(photo by Marilyn Wertheimer)*

again to the mountains. There were many charming little towns on the north side of the Pyrenées, and even though we never bothered to make advance reservations, we always managed to find very pleasant places to have meals and spend the nights. We also were delighted to discover what turned out to be the most recently established French national park, about halfway between the Mediterranean and the Atlantic, the Parc de Gavarnie. An enormous mountain cirque in it facing north is like the inside three quarters of a huge teacup, with snowfields and hanging glaciers from which spectacular waterfalls cascade to the valley floor below. We returned there several times. Indeed altogether the north side of the Pyrenées is gorgeous, with unparalleled dramatic rocky and snowy mountain vistas above lush green valleys; many of the mountains have permanent snow fields and jagged cliffs and peaks of which Marilyn took spectacular photographs. We were surprised to encounter so few other tourists in that part of France; the very few we did meet were almost all visitors from northern France.

The 1980s also brought trips to Jena, East Germany, for a psychology convention and to Humboldt University in East Berlin to present a lecture , to China

H-18 Me with the cairn I constructed for Anni at just over 16,500 feet *(photo by Marilyn Wertheimer)*

and to Russia as members of a delegation of librarians; to Arles in southern France; to Alaska; and to the universities of Frankfurt and Würzburg. That decade also included trips to Czechoslovakia, other parts of eastern Europe, Germany again, and the Pilgrim's Route to Santiago de Compostella in northwestern Spain; this last trip, including traversing the modest Picos de Europa, surprised us: the gentle, dry, rolling southern side of the Pyrénées contrasted so sharply with the much craggier, wetter, snowier, and more magnificent northern flanks.

My mother died in 1987, and the next year, on another trip to Tibet with Ron Bernier, I constructed a fairly high stone cairn in her honor at the highest point I ever reached on the

H-19 Kamenice nad Lipou, Czechoslovakia, where my father's father was born *(photo by Marilyn Wertheimer)*

H-20 Anni *(family archives)*

earth's surface, a pass at over 16,500 feet elevation. Miraculously I never felt short of breath nor particularly fatigued or oxygen-deprived during the half hour or so it took me to move heavy rocks at that altitude around for the purpose with my bare hands. But the entire ritual was accompanied by copious tears as my grief at the bereavement was given limitless and unfettered vent. Somehow it felt like a fitting memorial ceremony.

Then in 1989 came a trip to Bern, Switzerland, where I participated in a conference on education, and then also a trip with Marilyn to Indonesia: again a very new kind of experience, where among other places we visited villages in which cannibalism had been practiced until only a few decades before our visit. Startling!

H-21 The Sea Cloud in St. Lucia harbor *(photo by Marilyn Wertheimer)*

H-22 New Zealand *(photo by Marilyn Wertheimer)*

In the 1990s we visited the Grand Canyon and began our annual two-week summer sojourns on Monhegan Island off the coast of Maine. I had a trip to Tübingen, Germany, to participate there in a conference on German scholars exiled by the Nazis during the time of the Holocaust, and we had a pleasant visit to various sites with Marilyn's brother Jack and his wife Dorinda in the Yucatán in Mexico, where we explored a number of Aztec and Inca ruins.

It was also during the 1990s that we took a retirement-splurge cruise in the Caribbean on the resplendent Sea Cloud, an almost legendary square-rigged four-masted sailing yacht that had a crew of sixty and only sixty passengers.

H-23 Sahara encampment, Morocco *(photo by Marilyn Wertheimer)*

There was a trip to New Zealand and then Australia, where Bill Scott's widow Ruth showed us around, and trips to Egypt, the Greek isles and the isles of Majorca and Menorca in the western Mediterranean. Marilyn's brother Jack again accompanied us on a trip including

camping in the Sahara desert in Morocco (a trip in which an enormous storm knocked down a few tents; it was quite an adventure!) and Tunisia, and Marilyn and I visited Easter Island and various islands in Polynesia in the southern Pacific. There was a leisurely cruise from Athens to Singapore on a vessel that held only about 100 passengers, and another from Lisbon to Barcelona. We visited Russia again, going to Odessa and other destinations with the conditions not much better than they had been during the era of the Soviet empire; the shops were still rather barren, with little available even in the grocery stores. The decade of the 1990s got us acquainted with an enormous variety of places, cultures, and experiences we had not encountered before.

The first decade of the twenty-first century brought a trip to China with Jack, including a cruise on the Yangtze River on a small vessel among the passengers on which was

H-24 Me with a moai on Easter island
(photo by Marilyn Wertheimer)

H-25 Copper Canyon, Mexico *(photo by Marilyn Wertheimer)*

H-26 Cappadocia *(photo by Marilyn Wertheimer)*

John Glenn, the retired astronaut and former US senator, who turned out to be a gracious, humble, and pleasant fellow traveler—and his grandson, who looked like a rugged, craggy caricature of his grandfather. Marilyn and I also participated in a pleasant cruise around the southern half of South America from Buenos Aires to Santiago, Chile, visiting a number of penguin colonies along the way. Jack joined us for an AARP trip to Copper Canyon in Mexico; a couple we met on that trip became valued members of our "Boulder Tuesday Morning Breakfast Club" after that 2001 trip.

We also took several somewhat exotic trips with a travel agency owner from Denver, José Gonçalves, to Viet Nam, Cambodia, and Laos, and then to Honduras and Guatemala as well as Belize; and Jack joined us on a pleasant outing to Portugal which included a visit to José's birthplace there on a magnificent winery that had belonged to José's family. The wide historical and cultural knowledge that José's now-deceased wife Kathy shared with us on many occasions greatly enriched those travels.

Jack and several Boulder friends were with us on a fine trip sponsored by Overseas Adventure Travel to Turkey that included a week-long stay on a small goulette, a motorsailer that barely had room for its crew of four and twelve passengers, as well as inland sites in Cappadocia and elsewhere, with unusual rock formations, homes gouged out of sandstone cliffs and pits, and occasionally spectacular lighting when the low sun under lowering dark clouds illuminated weird craggy landscapes. The goulette also made available a one-man seagoing kayak which permitted me to paddle around unhurriedly near the many modest harbors where the goulette was anchored, exploring inlets and old Roman ruins. We could also swim in many different anchorage sites; the water was clear and inviting, and a comfortable temperature.

Marilyn and I also cruised down the Danube in a pleasant small boat, and we took a memorable leisurely cruise on a small riverboat barge along canals in Burgundy, France. That modest trip covered only some 70 miles or so in more than a week aboard the little barge, the Abercrombie, which accommodated about 20 passengers and a crew of four, one of whom was a spectacularly competent chef who prepared gourmet meals three times each day. The barge barely fit into the many locks we went through on those canals, and its progress along

H-27 The Abercrombie *(photo by Marilyn Wertheimer)*

its route was so leisurely that one could easily walk along the paths next to the canals and get ahead of the barge. There were also bicycles on board, for passengers to use whenever they had an inclination to do so, either to bike along the canal paths or to visit small old towns easily accessible from the canals. One focus of that trip was visits to various wineries and even a wine barrel factory, but while Marilyn and I did visit many of these, hearing about all sorts of oenological exotica such as "terroirs" and the carefully-controlled hierarchy of wine qualities, I'm afraid neither of us remember anything much about such details.

We also signed up for a trip on Norway's Hurtigruten (or "quick route"), the hard-working ferry that plies the west coast of Norway from Bergen all the way up to Kirkenes where Russia and Norway meet north of Sweden and Finland. That memorable two-week tour took us north for a week and then back south along the same route, this time stopping at some different ports than on the way north. The ferry was clearly an essential connector for otherwise inaccessible towns and villages along this spectacular coast, taking on and delivering goods, cars, and people along the way. Striking all along the Norwegian coast was how clean, well-kept and attractive the houses, fields, streets and people looked everywhere; most of the structures were modestly small in size, but there was no sign anywhere of poverty, homelessness, or shabby buildings.

H-28 Skjervøy, Norway *(photo by Marilyn Wertheimer)*

There was a cruise in Italy with Jack that included a memorable early morning arrival in Venice with highly photogenic lighting of its famous buildings as we came in to dock, and pleasant visits to several towns that make up Cinque Terre, those five small old towns that climb up unlikely-looking craggy rocks rising almost straight up out of the sea on the north-western Mediterranean coast of Italy.

Marilyn and I also took two trips in the Explorer, a 600-passenger ship that during the academic year was used as a semester-at-sea college in circumnavigations of the globe, but which permitted non-students to join in such voyages as a traverse of the Panama Canal during semester breaks, when several of the resident lecturers were still available to give informative talks on local history, culture,

H-29 A town in Cinque Terre *(photo by Marilyn Wertheimer)*

H-30 The Explorer *(photo by Marilyn Wertheimer)*

biology, and other absorbing topics. We also had another Caribbean cruise that included stops at the "ABC" islands, Aruba, Bonaire, and Curaçao, off the northeastern coast of South America, as well as Trinidad, St Lucia, Dominica, the Bahamas, and Saint Kitts.

I was alone on a short trip to the University of Würzburg in 2009 to deliver a lecture, but Marilyn came with me on our last trip to Germany, a fairly short jaunt to Bielefeld in 2012 to a convention of the German Society for Psychology, the Deutsche Gesellschaft für Psychologie, at which I gave a couple of invited talks and tried to help promote the just-then-published MIT Press book based on

H-31 Prize-winning photo "Les Demoiselles de Dominica" *(by Marilyn Wertheimer)*

H-32 Mike after a concert, with his piano teacher Pei-Fen Liu (left) and Lise *(family archives)*

Karen's and my English translations of my father's historic 1912 and 1923 articles that became the founding papers of the Gestalt school of psychology.

We made a few visits to Washington, DC, after I retired, to be with Pete and Susan and for me to attend my final few APA board meetings, and also went to Durham, NC, a few times to visit Lise and Mike—and to hear Mike give some ambitious, well attended, and well received piano concerts at Duke University. Other than that, our travels during the last few years included final summer stays for two weeks each on Monhegan Island, Maine , and our two annual two-week trips to visit with Jack in southern Oregon.

We've done so much traveling to so many places in the world that we have experienced a huge variety of people, cities, towns, villages, settings, life styles, patterns of social interactions, cultural events, religious practices, types of food, and ways of communicating, with sometimes startlingly different linguistic practices (like tones in Chinese and other Oriental languages or clicks in various

African ones). With all these different varieties of everyday life styles available or potentially available in this incredibly diverse world, we are grateful to be living in what we believe is the most pleasant setting for us: Boulder. By comparison with so many other alternatives, we feel privileged to be able to live where we do. It has been most instructive to experience so many other places, and while we enjoyed the vast majority of them (for me the greatest exception was India, with its teeming hordes of miserable, starving, sick, incredibly impoverished and disadvantaged people; visits to India produced by far the greatest "culture shock" for me of any places we visited), we were always happy to come back again to our familiar beloved home.

I'm afraid I've left out several other memorable trips over the years, including a cruise in northern Russia that involved a visit to Kizhi Island with its magnificent wood church, and a trip to England with Marilyn's brother and sister-in-law and other relatives of theirs that focused on the art of Turner and Constable. I'm sure that I must have omitted some others as well, and I probably made some mistakes in what I wrote. But the details aren't really all that important. What has been significant about my travels is how much they have broadened me and

H-33 Wooden church, Kizhi Island *(photo by Marilyn Wertheimer)*

how much these experiences have helped me become less intolerant and more appreciative of human diversity. I suspect that I have been privileged more than the majority of my fellow residents on the globe in terms of the richness and variety of the many places in which I've lived over the years, and in the many other places and countries I've had the opportunity to experience. As I wrote at the beginning of this appendix, extensive travel is a very effective way to broaden the mind, and I believe that my mind has been stretched—and enriched—immeasurably by the large amount of travel that my life has permitted me to engage in. I have indeed been blessed to have had so many chances to travel to so many fascinating places in the world.

H-34 Ruskin Estate, Lake District, England *(photo by Marilyn Wertheimer)*

Appendix I: Our Retirement Home

The apartment at Brookdale Boulder Meridian retirement community in which we have been living for more than half a decade has become a true new home for us. The following description provides what may be excruciating details about the layout and content of the apartment, as well as about some of the rituals that have become part of our daily life there. But the material should help the reader understand this nonagenarian author's everyday life at the time this narrative was completed.

If you come to visit our apartment from the west, you park behind a church on Yale Drive, having turned off of a larger highway, Table Mesa Drive, which has Bear Creek flowing intermittently down its center. It's about a 200-foot walk across a pleasant sloping lawn down to our patio. The patio, with a cement floor, is about 8 by 12 feet, and has a built-in storage shed the interior of which is furnished with a set of floor-to-ceiling built-in shelves, constructed for us by my namesake grandson from the boards and cinder blocks that had previously been in my office. It also contains a large multi-drawer file cabinet that holds some of the vast collection of travel documents, maps, and folders that Marilyn has amassed over many decades; several suitcases with other possessions of Marilyn's; our cross-country skis, ski boots, and ski poles; myriad boxes of books and other possessions; many shelved books;

I-1 Making ski tracks west of our Meridian patio *(family archives)*

© Springer Fachmedien Wiesbaden GmbH, part of Springer Nature 2020
M. Wertheimer, *Facets of an Academic's Life*,
https://doi.org/10.1007/978-3-658-28770-2

gardening tools; a snow shovel, and other paraphernalia; a few empty boxes, extra pillows, a large Christmas wreath, and sundry other items. That storage shed has turned out to be most welcome.

The patio has a rustic look, with an old redwood picnic table and benches that I built decades ago and that adorned our front porch at 546 Geneva. On that table are various rocks and pieces of wood that generate memories: some 80-million-year-old fossilized oyster shells that a former student had helped us find years ago off a road from Boulder to Denver; a few stones that Nan had picked up from stream beds (including one with a natural letter "M" on it in red on a grey background); special small rocks and other esthetically pleasing pieces of "drift-wood"; a large flower-pot saucer full of pine cones and one huge pine cone we picked up in California; and a tiny antique metal toothpick holder Jack gave us years ago that looks like a bird that picks up individual toothpicks in its beak when you move it forward. There's also a small collection of seashells we've collected on beaches in various parts of the world. This table gets covered with house plants during almost half the year, when the weather is warmer. Also on the table is some petrified wood, and the remains of a collection of seashells that my older son had strung up decades ago into a kind of mobile that fell apart years ago.

The patio also has two other small redwood stools that I built more than half a century ago to accompany the redwood table and two benches that I had built. There is, too, a small wooden table from which the white paint is peeling; it is one of the Christmas tables that Val had been permitted to paint in the 12 The Circle basement (back in 1934?) when I was considered still too young to be allowed to participate in such an activity. Several small round plastic tables and a few plastic armchairs complete the patio furniture. I go out there often, irrespective of the weather, to indulge in smoking a pipe; I no longer smoke inside the building. Hanging on the wall next to the shed door, and above the picnic table on the north wall of the patio, is a metal sculpture given us by our oldest grandson and his wife, of a hummingbird surrounded by patterned cut-out rings. In the northeast corner under the balcony above hangs a wind chime given us by our older son's wife, and beneath that are several poles I've used to string up tomato plants, as well as a broom and a cane. The east wall, just north of the large glass

I-2 Patio "smoking lounge" in winter *(family archives)*

sliding door into the apartment, holds both a kind of oval plaster cast of dried flowers that my sister-in-law Susan probably created, and which used to hang on my mother's outside wall in Washington, DC, and a wooden plaque given to us by one of Marilyn's friends at our wedding, containing the text of "Desiderata," an inspiring message composed in the middle of the 20th century (even though it claims to have been "found in Old Saint Paul's Church; dated 1692"). The south wall has another mobile, this one of rusted metal bells, that my older son made years ago, a large outdoor thermometer, the large remains of a dried tube of sea-weed I found years ago on the Oregon coast when Marilyn's brother had driven us there, and a mysterious memento we found on the beach in Maine during our honeymoon there in 1970: a small rectangular piece of wood, with "GER 560" painted in black on it.

A small rug lies in front of the door as a kind of mat, and a larger carpet covers the space from there to the west end of the patio; several stones at the west end of this carpet keep it from flying away when it's windy. From the patio we have a clear view of South Boulder Peak and the prominent Devil's Thumb to the southwest, and a long wire fence some six feet high running east to west that separates the Meridian property and lawn from the playground and lawn area of the Montessori elementary school south of us. This open area continues for about four blocks until it reaches a small side road with residences on its south side. The view is remarkably open and uncluttered, as though (as mentioned on page 205) we were living out in the country in a sparsely populated area. A few ever-green trees some 200 feet or so to the west border the church parking lot and hide much of the church itself. Another large evergreen is just a few feet northwest of the patio; it provides some shade for part of the patio, and our neighbor has a bird feeder hanging from one of its lower branches, which attracts numerous birds. We also see many squirrels in our large semi-private back yard, as well as occasional rabbits. West of the patio on the north side of the fence between us and the schoolyard to the west are several garden-ing patches, used by a few residents to grow flowers and vegetables; as I mentioned on page 195, the small space that we've been allowed to use

I-3 Me near my garden at our retirement home, amid our neighbors' flowers *(family archives)*

there has provided us with a surprising abundance of tomatoes, Swiss chard, zucchini, green beans, carrots, and garlic over the years. The six-foot-high wire fence against which the garden plots are located has permitted me to grow pole beans up it (when the rabbits haven't first chewed down the seedlings along the fence). There are two pleasant weather-worn old wooden armchairs under a small deciduous tree just north of the garden patches, which provide a welcome spot to rest for gardeners or for the few residents who go walking by there. To the northwest of the church one can make out the north ridge of Flagstaff Mountain, and various other trees and a wooden bench some 350 feet to the northwest make the whole large open area, with a few small deciduous trees, very much like a pleasant, open private park. It is a very peaceful, serene, quiet, uncluttered vista which we greatly enjoy—and take in often, as we frequently have meals at a bridge table just inside the sliding glass door, from which we enjoy looking out at the pleasant view. Sometimes we also see occasional robins, sparrows, crows, and magpies out there, and in season we can make out, and sometimes hear, flocks of geese flying in a V formation to the west. The geese on rare occasions even sometimes descend onto our lawn and search there for bugs and seeds, sometimes a flock of some 30 or more birds at a time.

For a while we hung up a rolled bamboo mat under the west edge of the balcony that covers the patio, to let down for shade in the summer, when the west sun can shine fiercely into the patio during the afternoon, but we found that we never used it. That balcony (and an overhanging roof above it) also keeps out almost all the rain and snow from the patio when there is precipitation. The patio and our huge semi-private back yard are among the features that we especially enjoy about the apartment we've rented; they are unique in the whole community, and I spend a lot of my time on that patio. It has a yard-long red-stone path to the lawn, some small evergreen bushes next to that path, and some pebble areas before the lawn. Early in the morning when I smoke my first pipe of the day, and in the evening when I have my last puff, I almost never see another person anywhere while I sit on our patio and look out at our "private" back yard.

If you come to our apartment from the main entrance to the Meridian, the approach is very different. There is a large parking area on the east side of the complex, and a pleasant covered entrance to the reception area, where there is a

I-4 The main entrance to the Meridian *(family archives)*

desk that has someone at it from 8 am to 7 pm daily. Just past this reception desk is the "living room" with comfortable easy chairs, couches, and a grand piano, and which is large enough to accommodate chairs that can be brought in for an audience of some 50 or 60 for live musical performances or other events such as the monthly chats with the executive director. The west wall of this room is all glass, looking out at a most attractive, well-landscaped courtyard with a lily pond, a small waterfall (lit up at night) feeding it, and a plethora of trees, bushes, plants, and flowers. Weather permitting, it can also hold large groups of people with chairs, tables, and umbrellas for shade. To the left of the living room are the offices of the directors, and a "lounge" with a TV set and coffee, juices, and hot chocolate available 24/7 (and a "continental breakfast" with fruit and pastry most mornings); the hall there also contains restrooms and mailboxes as well as separate cubbyholes for each apartment for internal communications.

Just beyond the living room and lounge (where there also is a splendid grandfather clock built by a former CU dean of arts and sciences, which I have been given permission to adjust including the care of its weights when they descend too low) is a small hallway with a north glass wall that looks out onto the courtyard and that provides south access to the large community dining room. Next to the dining room door is a small private dining room one can reserve for special occasions such as foreign-language lunches, tea with the executive director, a menu chat with the chef, or even a birthday party (which I've had there).

Just past the private dining room a door provides access to a hallway with stairs going up to apartments at the upper level above ours and above the dining room, and to a small hallway to the left that provides access to only two apartments: ours and our next-door neighbors'. Hanging high above this hallway is a large ikat scarf that we bought in Indonesia. The hall makes a right-angle turn to the right, providing wall space for hanging some of Marilyn's photographs and some of our neighbor's paintings. Our door is at the left end of this little private hallway; our neighbors' is on the right. Hanging on the wall next to our door on the right is a nameplate, and a blue-and-white tile with "Familia Wertheimer" on it that was given to us by our tour leader some years ago in Obidos, Portugal. Next to the door on the left is an old wooden footstool that my mother used for many years, atop which we put various attractive objects, such as some dried flowers in small vases that were given to Marilyn on her birthday. Hanging on the door is an Indian dream-catcher; in season, we hang a large Christmas wreath on the door. The button for an automatic door chime given us by our son-in-law is posted just to the right of the door on the jamb.

As you enter the door into the apartment, there is a small hall. On the left behind the door is a low bookcase containing the books I've written, co-authored, edited, or co-edited, or for which I've written chapters; it also holds various cups and other paraphernalia attesting to my participation in APA offices and other roles. Above that are two Feininger paintings that were given to my mother and

I-5 Caricature of my father, and two Feininger paintings *(family archives)*

Schani by the artist, and a caricature of my
father drawn back in the 1930s by one of
his admiring students.

On the right wall is a beautiful African
hanging with abstract and paisley patterns
that Marilyn bought long ago in a Boulder
store that sold African mementoes; the
store closed years ago. Ahead are two
bookcases, one on the right with cook-
books and foreign-language dictionaries,
and one at the end of the hall holding some
of Marilyn's travel books. Above the latter
bookcase is another beautiful tapestry
hanging from a wooden rod that has six
carved elephants on it. In the middle of the
left wall is a small finely-crafted white

I-6 Candleholder from Kai von Fieandt
(family archives)

ceramic black-framed high relief of the Holy Family under glass that Marilyn
inherited years ago from her great aunt. It makes me wonder whether it is a copy
from the famed Italian sculptor della Robbia. Other paintings and mementos
adorn the right-hand hall further along, and the top of the right-hand bookcase.

When you turn right from that hall, you enter another short hall that goes past
the kitchen to the huge living room and dining room; that hallway has seven of
Marilyn's photographs hanging on the walls, and another small bookcase on the
right filled with some of Marilyn's large collection of books on Russia and travel
books. Atop this small bookcase is a large carved black ebony wooden elephant
with white tusks, and other bric-a-brac, and another of Marilyn's gorgeous textiles hangs above that bookcase. To the right off this short hallway is the kitchen.
A few of Marilyn's marvelous collection of rugs adorn the floors of both hall-
ways.

The kitchen contains an electric four-burner stove and oven, above which is a
microwave (which I don't know how to use, and don't need). There is a large
refrigerator atop which is a fairly large freezer that is almost full of vegetables
(mostly from our little garden) and even some fruit (such as raspberries) from

our former house at 546 Geneva Avenue, as well as a variety of frozen breads, meats, poultry, and fish. There are more cabinets and storage space than we had at 546, and there is a double sink as well as more counter and work space than the 546 kitchen had. There is a large open space below the cabinets and above the sink and counter, providing west light and access to the dining area adjoining it to the west. A large tapestry hangs on the kitchen wall opposite the entrance and has abstract designs and a stylized teapot in its center; Marilyn bought it in Morocco. At its left, at the right end of the sink counter that provides access to the dining area, are racks of spices brought from 546; some are almost never used, and may be some 40 or more years old. Four large canisters on the counter came from Marie Powell, Jack's late mother-in-law. A double candleholder from Finland, given to me years ago by Kai von Fieandt when he and his family spent a year in Boulder working with me on a translation into English of his textbook on perception, hangs down from the cabinets above the counter. And the counter also holds a myriad of other memorabilia, such as some Delft porcelain salt and pepper shakers and small tea strainer holder and sugarer and creamer from Delft that Marilyn had bought in 1967 when she visited Holland with her mother; a small glass automobile filled with jellybeans that Pete gave me years ago; a large wooden tea bag container in the shape of a cottage (with a roof lid) that our niece

I-7 Plate from Hong Kong *(family archives)*

Ellen and her husband Mark gave us; spare oyster shells from Long Island (being saved to serve as soap dishes); a small ceramic replica of a German ginger container; various stacked plates we picked up on our international travels (the top one of which, from Hong Kong, has a central photo of Marilyn and me—with Marilyn displaying one of her astonishing radiant smiles); and some citrus "dancers" (the quartered remains of orange, grapefruit, and clementine rinds that have dried out and reversed so they look like abstract renditions of dancers). At the end near the kitchen entrance are a touchtone telephone that is accessible from both the kitchen and the dining area, and a clock, next to which is an electronic device given me by my son-in-law that presents time, date, and both outdoor and indoor temperature and humidity.

I-8 Swiss model of a cozy mountain cabin *(family archives)*

Hanging inside the south kitchen wall, on the right as you face the hallway, next to and under the raised cabinets, are a wonderful little three-dimensional Swiss wood model of a simple cozy mountain cabin interior, a Swedish tile, a large knife rack, a barometer and temperature indicator my older son gave me long ago, and two colorful painted Mexican wooden panels, respectively labeled "mango" and "fresa." To the far left of the entrance hang an oil painting by Lise (which appears on page 136) of the scene from the temporary barracks apartment where Nan, the children, and I lived in Middletown, CT, next to three round tiles my mother had made right after each of our children was born (a bucolic scene with birds, sheep, flowers and rabbit for Karen, fish and a sailboat for Duffy, and a sunrise or sunset with a little boy, sheep, rabbit, and bird for Benjy), another rectangular tile of a lighthouse made by my mother, a little effigy of a bear made by a granddaughter years ago, a large wooden Soviet spoon, a small saucer from Usingen given me by Viktor Sarris (now retired from the same psychology chair my father had held years earlier at the University of Frankfurt), and a semicircular wooden container for salt and pepper that had hung in my mother's kitchen for years (on which is written, beneath a colorful picture of a pot boiling over a fire being stirred by a bear—my mother—and a harlequin—Schani: "This soup won't have a fault for it was cooked with salt"; on top on the back is a huge red heart and the title "Das Salz des Lebens," or the salt of life). Beneath all that is an oil painting I made more than 70 years ago of a cabin in the mountains which

I-9 Tiles and salt container by my mother, and other stuff
(family archives)

was displayed a couple of years ago at an exhibit of Meridian "artists" with the caption, "A 15 Year Old Flatlander's Oil Fantasy about the Rocky Mountains" (pictured on page 476).

The counter to the right of the stove holds various condiments and small bells (including one with an image of the Matterhorn from Zermatt, Switzerland), a container for spatulas and large cooking spoons, salt and pepper shakers from Pete and Susan, Marilyn's mother's old pepper grinder, a large painted metal coaster from New Orleans, and other stuff. Hanging from the cabinet above the counter are some dried red peppers that our late friend Virginia McConnell gave us years ago.

The counter to the left of the stove holds a large supply of napkins (some of which may be decades old), a toaster, cutting boards, and a tray given us by Jack. Above the cabinets above the stove is a collection of large pots, pressure cookers, pans, bowls, turkey roaster, plastic containers, other cooking gear, and light bulbs; access to these items requires a low ladder or a chair to step on. Atop the refrigerator are colorful containers for flour and sugar, extra boxes of cereal, containers for leftovers, and other items. The cabinets along the east wall with the stove and refrigerator serve as storage space for pots and pans, silverware, some bottles of wine, breakfast dishes and coffees, and more containers for leftovers, as well as a pantry (mostly for canned goods).

Under the west kitchen counter is storage space for pots, pans, and baking sheets, cleaning supplies, a trash container, the dishwasher, and drawers for

I-10 One of the Hmong embroideries *(family archives)*

tools, tiles, plastic bags, aprons, and other bric-a-brac. The cabinets above this counter hold our wedding dishes, everyday dishes, glasses, miscellaneous serving dishes, and a large collection of coffee mugs made by our earlier neighbor, Betty Woodman (some of whose works are now on display in the Denver Art Museum, and some of whose huge colorful ceramic vases adorn the Denver International Airport).

If you continue from the entry without turning to the right into the hallway toward the kitchen, on the right (opposite a large double hallway closet) is the door to the guest bathroom, now "my" bathroom; the door is adorned with a large American Indian rug. The bathroom, which has a large shower stall with a built-in seat, also has a linen closet just to the right of its entry. The walls are decorated with several Hmong embroideries, some with animals and some abstract. A beautiful lathed wood vase (given me by Nan and filled with dry grasses) and a wood model of a three-masted sailing vessel given me by Pete are on the sink counter, as is a small old hand mirror that used to belong to Nan's mother, Lavinia. An Eskimo etching hangs above a small medicine cabinet to the right of the sink. The sink (like, of course, the kitchen sink), has an oyster shell, picked up on Long Island, as a soap dish, and paraphernalia for me to shave and to clean my teeth. The sink counter also holds one of the four electric clocks I had bought back in the early 1960s when I set up an apartment for me and the kids, one for each of us, as I separated from Nan; they are all still working, one in the kitchen, one in the study, the one in the bathroom, and one on my night table in our bedroom. There also is a large hamper in the bathroom opposite the sink, which Marilyn uses for storage of towels and bedding. Just to the right of the hamper are a small two-shelf metal rack that used to be in the downstairs bathroom at 546 Geneva Avenue, and a tiny three-legged table that now holds old Reader's Digests and a few books: a couple on Boulder by our former neighbor John Schoolland and another about Monhegan Island and its history, are just to the right of the hamper. On top of the toilet's tank is a small collection of seashells and coral I picked up years ago, and that used to adorn the top of the toilet tank in the downstairs tiny bathroom at 546. The medicine cabinet still holds some forty or so mostly tiny bars of soap acquired during our international travels and during my years of staying at fancy hotels at APA's expense.

Beyond this bathroom at the far end of the entry hallway are two doors. The one on the left goes into the master bedroom and the one on the right into the second "bedroom" in the apartment. This second "bedroom" has become our study. It has a large window with a southern exposure. As you enter this room there's a two-

I-11 The "monster" *(family archives)*

drawer file cabinet of Marilyn's on the wall to the right, then one of Marilyn's desks in the right corner beyond the files, and to its left the old "monster" (an upper and lower cupboard with a bit of counter and a drawer in between) in the middle of the wall opposite the door; it used to separate the kitchen from the pantry at 546 Geneva Avenue. To its left in the corner is Marilyn's second desk, and under the window in the left wall is one of my desks. All three desks have drawers or shelves beneath, and folding drop leaves on top; all these leaves are open, to give access to the various cubbies and drawers at the top back of the desks. To the left of my desk is a small bookcase that used to be at the left of my desk in our bedroom at 546, and a copious double closet makes up the east wall of this fairly small room. Among the pictures adorning the walls are two water-color paintings by a Monhegan artist we had befriended, Yolanda Fusco, a native Czech who used to go swimming almost daily in the frigid Maine water, who often joined us for meals on the island, and who died a few years ago during one of our two-week sojourns on Monhegan.

A variety of bric-a-brac and memorabilia is in the room. There is a black wood elephant lamp and a balalaika atop the file cabinet; each desk also has its own separate lamp; my desk has a number of house plants on it right inside the window, including some old Christmas cacti and a large orchid plant that Susan gave us years ago, which originally had lovely blossoms, then did nothing for several years, and once again had a plethora of open blossoms and some still closed buds on it three years later. Also atop my desk is one of the old electric clocks I bought more than 50 years ago, a pen and pencil set given to me long ago by a former student who graduated summa cum laude and has gone on to a successful career as a professor at a university in California, a brass letter holder that our late good friend Agnes Conley had given me, an unused meerschaum pipe in an elegant rack, a crystal weather radio given me by my son-in-law that I still frequently consult (and wonder how much longer it will be until the batteries need to be replaced), some small effigies from Mexico's Tarahumara region that my older son gave me years ago when he had traveled there, a small electronic battery-operated weather indicator and predictor that Marilyn's brother gave me years ago, and a few other items.

The low bookcase to the left of my desk holds a bunch of books; Scrabble games, including one for a German contest; and a wooden bread-cutting board (pictured on page 117) carved for me by Nan with a strong male figure seeming to push out the frames and "PhD 1952" scratched into the bottom right. Hanging from one of the knobs on the closet doors is a large bone-handled knife in its leather scabbard, a gift from the Finnish psychologist Kai von Fieandt when he spent a year in Boulder with his family in the 1960s and I helped him translate his perception text into English.

All three desks are somewhat cluttered. At the far right of mine is a daily German calendar given me by an east German couple, two psychologists (Lothar and Helga Sprung), who sent me such a calendar annually at Christmas time for decades. My harmonicas are also on this desk. And I'm afraid there is a foot-high pile of journals, yearbooks, and other documents on the left that I think might be worth looking at again some time, but which probably will only gather dust. Blank paper, tobacco, matches, a ruler, and other items clutter the desk, as well as a large collection of pens and pencils. A frequently used old rotary pencil sharpener has been attached to the left front of the "monster."

The study closet contains a file cabinet with some of Marilyn travel folders and some of my files, several large boxes of Marilyn's framed large photographic prints, a few of my books on two shelves, and hangers for my short-sleeved shirts. On the floor are bags of wrapping paper, and a large box of material (folders, notes, books, monographs, etc.) that I put together for the course on "Cultural Aspects of Language" that I taught during the last ten years or so before I retired; at one point I thought I might try to

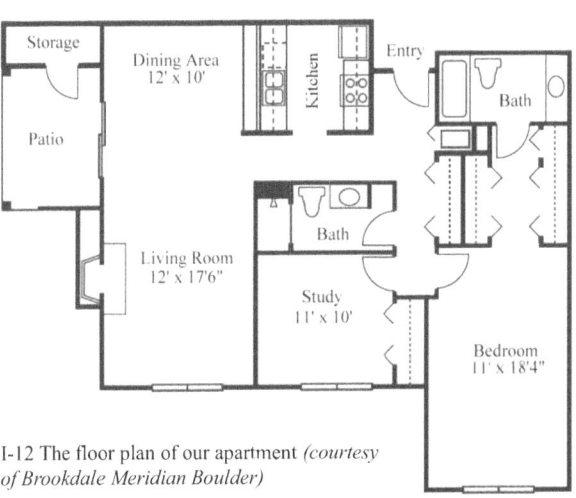

I-12 The floor plan of our apartment *(courtesy of Brookdale Meridian Boulder)*

write a book on this subject, but somehow I haven't gotten around to this project even though I've now been retired for more than twenty years.

Opposite the door to the study at the end of the entry hall, on the left, is the door to the large master bedroom suite, which has turned into a museum for our collection of items brought from many international trips. These items adorn the tops of two of Marilyn's chests of drawers and a third one in which I have the use of several of the drawers, as well as a large bookcase the top and four shelves of which are covered with memorabilia from many lands. To the left of the entry door is a hallway with two large closets on the left used for my clothes and books and three ample closets on the right used for Marilyn's clothes and a huge collection of metal slide boxes containing over 10,000 of Marilyn's slides from her and our travels over the years. These boxes have been the basis from which Marilyn has selected slides for dozens of much-appreciated travel shows presented at the Meridian and at Changes in Latitude, a travel store in downtown Boulder. At the end of this hall is the master bathroom, which has become Marilyn's bathroom; it contains a bathtub as well as a shower. This bathroom, like the other bathroom, has Hmong embroideries hanging on its walls, as well as various items from our travels. A collection of angel effigies and statuettes adorns the

right end of the sink counter, which also holds other bric-a-brac including a small ceramic container for the healing waters of Karlovy Vary in Czechoslovakia.

Going around the bedroom from the right of the door (past photographs of Marilyn's mother as a young

I-13 A drawing by my grandson Mike, which sits near the geraniums in our bedroom *(family archives)*

girl and of Marilyn's great-great-great-grandmother Dorcas Tabitha Smith Calquehoun, shown on page 493) are one of Marilyn's chests of drawers, then the museum bookcase, and then Marilyn's second chest of drawers. In the far right corner past a two-drawer file cabinet of Marilyn's is a beautiful old red Chinese antique table atop which are more memorabilia. Under the large south window on a large table are some dozen house plants, mostly geraniums, that are thriving in the southern exposure. Beyond this in the southeast corner is a

I-14 My main "working desk" *(family archives)*

dresser with one drawer for Marilyn and three for me. Against this dresser on the east wall is my night table, then our comfortable double bed (which Marilyn makes up every day with such care that it always looks like a work of art). My night table has a small lamp on it, as well as another one of the old electric clocks I bought a half century ago. The far (north) side of the bed has a larger night table used by Marilyn, then a small piece of furniture with two drawers atop which is a telephone. Facing south next to the hallway to the bathroom is a beautiful old desk that used to belong to Marilyn's mother. It has three drawers underneath a drop-leaf cover, various cubbies and small drawers above the desk

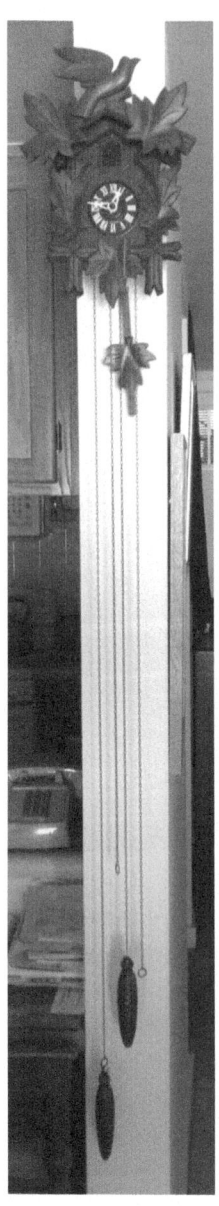

surface, and a three-shelf bookcase behind glass doors. The top shelf of this bookcase holds a 40-volume complete set of the works of Goethe. This is my main "working desk."

The floor of the bedroom boasts several beautiful rugs from Marilyn's large textile collection. The pictures on the walls of this room are classical reproductions that Marilyn bought in Europe while she was there with her mother, and which were elegantly mounted for her by an artistic studio in Italy. Detailed descriptions of all the treasures in this room would, I'm afraid, require at least thirty or forty pages. Suffice it to say that they are true memorabilia from many different parts of the world, a few of them of some intrinsic as well as sentimental or even financial value. Several people who have come and spent some time admiring the displays have been surprised (as I always am) at Marilyn's detailed knowledge about each one of the items: where it came from, what the circumstances of its acquisition were, and what people were associated with it.

Finally, there is the dining area and living room, a huge area filled with furniture (as is the rest of the apartment) from our house at 546 Geneva Avenue. Going counter-clockwise around this area as you enter from the kitchen hallway, first is a Swiss cuckoo clock hanging high on the wall; this clock, acquired decades ago, still is remarkably accurate, clearly announcing the hours (as well as the half hours) with its characteristic sound. Just past it is a small table holding telephone books and pads for writing mes-sages while I'm on the phone, then another little table with memorabilia on it including a beautiful small cabin, the roof of which is made of corks, that Pete and his daughter had created and given to us decades ago after Monika and I had stopped throwing corks at each other every time we

I-15 Cuckoo clock
(family archives)

saw one another. Some chairs are also there, and on the north wall are cinder block and board shelves from the 546 dining room that hold albums of prints made from some of Marilyn's most impressive slides from around the world, as well as some over-sized books. On top of this structure is an old clock from Marilyn's family that used to have charming chimes, but which gave up that chiming years ago (we tried to get it repaired, but were unsuccessful).

I-16 Cork cabin *(family archives)*

Next to it is a ukelin, the odd instrument from Hoboken, NJ, which Nan bought for me long ago.

Above that clock hangs a large watercolor painting of Lobster Cove on Monhegan Island, Maine, framed in an ornate wooden gilded frame, that Marilyn inherited from her great-aunt. Signed by George Howell Gay, a prominent early twentieth-century seascape artist, it is what brought us to Monhegan Island in the early 1990s.

In the northwest corner of the room is an old battery-operated grandfather clock that used to be in the 546 kitchen, the workings of which were replaced a few years ago for us by our son-in-law. Next to the clock on the west wall is a large silk hanging from Kyoto, Japan, and underneath that on the floor is a mag-nificent dark wooden Chinese chest Marilyn inherited from her family. It is filled with parts of Marilyn's textile collection. The dining table (which can be extend-ed with two leaves) that was in 546, together with six chairs (and two more just like them along the north wall), fills the space in front of the Monhegan painting.

The tablecloth on this table is changed periodically by Marilyn from her large collection of textiles, and there are always some dried flowers (sometimes in a huge beauti-ful cut-glass pitcher from Marilyn's family) as a centerpiece on the dining table.

I-17 Chinese painting *(family archives)*

As in other rooms, the floor of the living room is adorned with valuable old carpets from Marilyn's collection. The living room walls contain some of Marilyn's most outstanding photos, enlarged and framed, as well as two small tapestries from Conques in southwestern France, a large Chinese painting, and a big wooden Chinese hanging, and two plates: one from Marilyn's Bishop's School and one from Pete and Susan, a gilded plate announcing in German, "Viel Freude, Viel Glück und Gesundheit im Haus, Bis über die goldene Hochzeit hinaus" (Much joy, much luck and health in the house until beyond the golden anniversary, i.e., the fiftieth) which they gave us on our 25th (or silver) anniversary.

The living room furnishings, continuing counter-clockwise from

I-18 Wooden Chinese hanging *(family archives)*

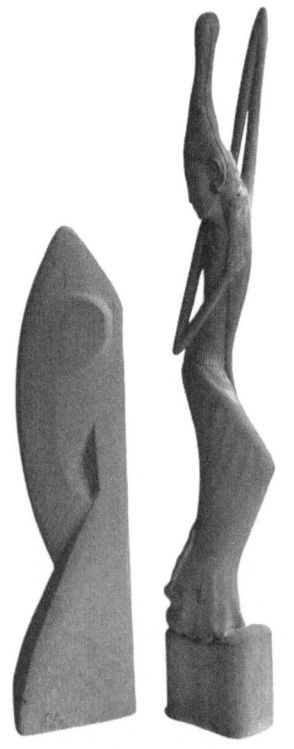

the large double glass sliding door onto the patio, begin with a small wood stool with an embroidered needlepoint top that holds the current TV guide. Next to that is a low table adorned with attractive textiles atop which is a large flat-screen TV that we bought shortly before we moved to the apartment. Beyond that is the gas-log fireplace with a mantel that holds

I-19 Dancer by Nan and dancer from Bali *(family archives)*

I-20 Statuette by Lisbeth Stern *(family archives)*

a variety of decorations: a thin, tall wooden statuette of a dancer from Bali that was picked up by Schani's father more than a century ago, a wooden three-dimensional Garuda from Indonesia, a Chinese rectangular wood carving of plants and flowers that a grandson had given us a few years ago, a beautiful, sad gypsum statuette of a destitute old woman with a baby at her feet (a piece of artwork made long, long ago by Lisbeth Stern, the sister of the famous artist Käthe Kollwitz), a black metal replica of a Norse warship, a daffodil made by Nan of colored glass, a statuette of a sea captain that Pete gave me a few years ago, a wooden candlestick, a stylized dancer carved by Nan in wood that has a stance remarkably similar to that of the Bali dancer at the right end of the mantel, and an African warrior carved in dark wood that my sister Lise and her husband

I-21 The mantel over the gas fireplace *(family archives)*

Mike gave us decades ago. A few other smaller items on the mantel include a ceramic statuette of a young man sitting on a stack of books and reading a book that a grandson gave us, a tiny blown-glass skier, a three-dimensional dragon puzzle from Lise, and a tiny statuette of a painter and his

I-22 House plants, dictionary, and encyclopedia *(family archives)*

easel given to us by a Harvard graduate student (now a professor of history at the University of Vienna) decades ago when he was doing research in our basement at 546 Geneva on the history of Gestalt theory, using the collection of my father's papers that later went to the psychology archives at the University of Akron.

On the floor at the right of the fireplace, next to the TV table, is an old oval wooden painted box from Germany that Marilyn's brother Jack recently gave us, painted with the words "Lieben und nichts haben ist harter den Stein graben," which might translate roughly into "To love and have nothing is harder than digging up stones," or something like that; inquiries at the German department of the university didn't generate any better translation. The painter may have mistaken an old saying, or not have known how to spell very well. The lid also has a rather primitive painting of a soldier and a young woman on it.

Beyond the fireplace to the south, under a small west window, is a small triangular table holding a few books, a lamp from the living room at 546 Geneva, and a modern Danish armchair that Marilyn had bought long ago for the 546 living room. There is also a small table behind that chair, atop which is a (rarely used) tape player and radio.

The south wall has a large window in front of which is a collection of house plants atop the old walnut table that used to be in the northeast corner of the 546 living room. This table also holds a huge unabridged dictionary of the American language next to a huge one-volume Columbia encyclopedia; both of these frequently-consulted tomes are perpetually open at about the middle. The table also has held a square ceramic battery-operated clock from Marilyn's brother that is adorned by a map of part of Maine that includes Monhegan Island, and an exquisitely carved Italian shell lamp that has been in Marilyn's family for many years. Beneath this table are some large ceramic works by our former neighbor, Betty Woodman.

In the southwest corner is a red enameled Chinese wooden chest with doors in front that holds a collection of vases; on top of that is an enameled Chinese lamp with red silk shade; both of these were brought from China long ago by a friend of Marilyn's mother. To the left of the walnut table is a tiny fragile dark wood rocking chair that used to belong to Marilyn's mother, behind which is a low round Chinese table that was part of the same collection as the Chinese chest and lamp.

The east wall of the living room has two large dark floor-to-ceiling bookcases on either side of a comfortable couch (opposite the fireplace) that is Marilyn's usual sitting spot, is used by Marilyn for her afternoon naps, and that opens out into a double bed which we have used for overnight guests. The bookcases were bought by us and brought here by our son and grandson; they are the two main pieces of furniture we bought for the apartment. Our house on Geneva had many built-in bookshelves, but the apartment had none (other than the high shelves in all the closets). Shelves in both bookcases are used to display some treasures other than books, but books do make up the majority of the bookshelves' contents. The southern bookcase holds some of Marilyn's art, travel and Russian books; its top and its top shelf display a variety of drums that Marilyn and I collected over the years, and two shelves of other souvenirs from our trips: some prayer wheels, a Tibetan pair of bells, a Tibetan conch shell that is partly covered with embossed silver, a double Tibetan brass thunderbolt, a Vietnamese dragon water puppet, etc.

I-23 My "bibliophilia" *(family archives)*

The northern bookcase holds some multi-volume classic book sets: Dickens' works, Will and Ariel Durant's *The Story of Civilization*, and Stoddard's geography lectures, as well as five large tomes of all of Shakespeare's plays (initially intended for group play readings, which haven't taken place). Its bottom shelf is devoted to more of Marilyn's art and travel books. One shelf holds an old ivory tusk carved into nine small elephants, a ceramic antique blue-green elephant on a carved wooden fitted base that was part of Marilyn's relative's collection of objects from China, a set of ivory toothpicks stuck into an ivory ring around a small carved elephant, a few other small individual elephants, and a carved wood Maori head from New Zealand, with its tongue extruded as a threat. Two and a half shelves are filled with my "bibliophilia," mostly books going back several hundred years, most of which I picked up in second-hand bookshops in Cambridge, MA, late in the 1940s or early in the 1950s. The ukelin is sometimes displayed on top of this bookcase.

At the south end of the couch is a standing lamp that matches the one next to the fireplace, and at the north end of the couch is a large standing multiple lamp that used to be in the 546 living room. Next to it is a tiny triangular table like the one

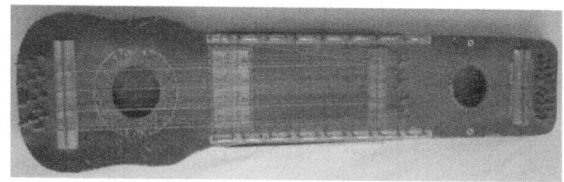

I-24 An example of a ukelin *(from https://commons.wikimedia.org/ wiki/File:Ukelin,_distributed_by_Manufacturers%27_Advertising_ Co._-_front.jpg)*

next to the fireplace; this one has another small lamp on it that Marilyn uses when reading at the north end of the couch. Right in front of the north bookcase is the solid old armchair rocker that used to be my main chair in the 546 living room; it serves the same purpose in our apartment.

Next to and just northwest of this rocking chair is a low table covered with various books and schedules, and one shelf filled with more of Marilyn's travel and art books. Behind it to the east are two more small tables with books on and under them; the one right next to the bookcase contains flashlights and a beautiful elegant wood nude that Nan had carved for me many

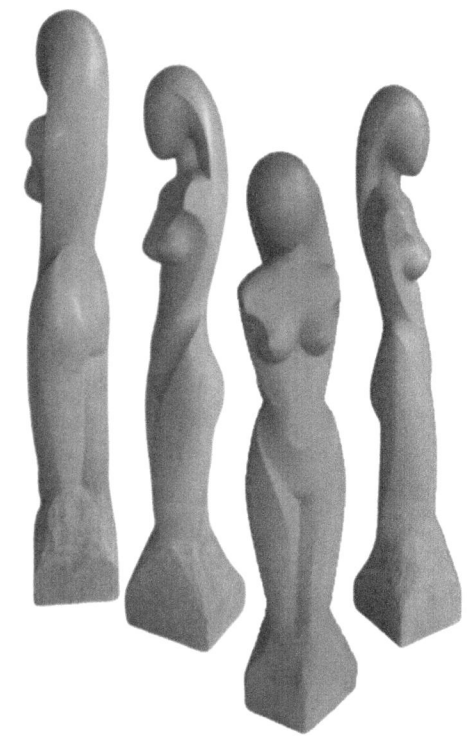

I-25 Nude by Nan, four views *(family archives)*

years ago. Pillows covered with textiles from various parts of the world adorn several chairs and the back of the couch, and the ends of the bookcases toward the couch have marionettes and a shadow puppet from different parts of the world hanging on them.

A bridge table with two chairs is usually on the border between dining and living areas near the double glass sliding door; we use that table for meals when the two of us are eating in the apartment, sometimes moving it in front of the TV screen so we can watch the PBS news hour while we are dining, or placed cozily in front of the gas-log fireplace on really cold days with a fire in the fireplace.

Altogether, our apartment at the Meridian has become a greatly appreciated, comfortable, "gemütlich" home, filled with useful items and with treasures and objects that remind us of earlier times and provide welcome continuity to our lives. We like it.

Everywhere that I've lived for a while, I have indulged in various rituals. The last few years, after moving to our pleasant retirement community, have been no exception.

For some reason, rituals have always been for me a major source of pleasure, peace, satisfaction, and even contentment. Some are annual, like Christmas festivities, (now almost countless) birthday celebrations for relatives, moving house plants outside in the spring and back indoors in the fall, subscriptions to musical programs like the annual Artist Series, concerts of the internationally renowned Takács classical string quartet, and the annual summer Colorado Music Festival, as well as summer Colorado Shakespeare Festival productions at the University of Colorado and about twenty two-week summer stays on Monhegan Island, Maine, over the years. Trips out of town to visit relatives, extensive international travel, and the sojourns in Maine have been drastically curtailed in recent years, as have activities away from our attractive retirement community. While they did provide much pleasure in the past, these activities now require more hassles, effort, and expense then we're willing to give them—but memories of them are still very precious.

Then there are monthly rituals such as Marilyn's travel slide shows (more than twenty each at the Meridian and at the travel store "Changes in Latitude" in downtown Boulder); dinners at local restaurants with a 30-year-old "gourmet

group"; changing the monthly calendars hanging in our apartment; and toting up the month's grocery bill (which I have compulsively kept just below $100 since starting to keep records of them in 1975) and also the monthly total of coins, and even occasionally bills, that I have found on sidewalks, streets, and parking lots. (I started keeping track of these findings in 1990 by placing them in a heavy brass antique dish labeled "pocket change" that Pete gave me for that purpose

I-26 Dish for found coins *(family archives)*

I-27 The "night before" set-up in the kitchen, ready for preparing breakfast; the dish of toast and bacon, going into the refrigerator until morning, is a special luxury *(family archives)*

years ago; after more than 25 years the total comes to an impressive sum of just over $950).

Weekly rituals include such things as recording in my pocket calendar when I've taken showers, watering and feeding house plants twice weekly, and outings with the 20-year-old Boulder Tuesday Morning Breakfast Club (now meeting on Wednesday mornings, but named years ago by two Dutch friends of one of the couples in this ten-member "club").

Daily rituals continue to provide lots of satisfaction too. One such ritual, in perhaps excessive detail, is the following breakfast routine. Most mornings I am awakened by Marilyn sleepily reminding me shortly before 8 am or so that it is "breakfast time!" After a few more minutes of snoozing, I go to the guest bathroom and then light a pipe on the patio. After a brief morning smoke, I go to the kitchen and turn on the light and the electric range under two pots: the coffee pot filled a day or two before, and a saucepan with enough water in it for Marilyn's powdered international coffee and my bowl of gruel.

While they heat up, I glance at the first section of the *Boulder Camera* (the newspaper delivered to our front door about 4:00 am daily, which I have almost always picked up by 4:30 or 5:30 am after one of my nocturnal jaunts to the bathroom). The breakfast tray has already been set up the night before (with a smaller round tray on it—given to us years ago by our late very good friend Agnes Conely—for Marilyn's coffee mug, cereal bowl, milk, spoon, napkin, and grapefruit juice glass), and the various ingredients that don't need refrigeration are already waiting patiently on the kitchen counter next to the stove. The newspaper gets opened to the editorial page with its letters to the editor, and I've glanced at some of these (as well as the stock market figures and the weather predictions) to the extent possible until the water and coffee get hot.

The folded newspaper is replaced on the sink divider, in preparation for its delivery to Marilyn. Marilyn's powdered international coffee is measured out into her mug, non-dairy creamer and no-calorie sweetener are placed into my mug, a small amount of oatmeal and a bit of iodized salt are poured into a measuring cup, and then it's time to take things out of the refrigerator: a mixture from three boxes of cold cereal of Total®, Wheat Chex®, and "Real Medleys®" is placed in a Betty Woodman ceramic pitcher on the small tray for Marilyn, as is some milk in a little cup, and two small glasses of grapefruit juice are filled and placed on the breakfast tray, one for each of us. Boiling water is poured into my cereal bowl to heat it up, and Marilyn's mug gets filled with boiling water; the water from my cereal bowl and the oatmeal and salt are dumped into the now-empty saucepan and placed back on the burner to boil for a short time; my mug gets filled with coffee (half of it decaffeinated), the contents of the two coffee mugs get stirred, and the mugs are placed on the breakfast tray; the refrigerated materials get placed back in their assigned places in the refrigerator; and the powdered coffee container, the powdered coffee creamer container, the oatmeal box, and the salt container go back into their designated spots in the cabinet to the right above the stove, which has been turned off.

The gruel goes into my bowl, the bowl goes on the breakfast tray, and the saucepan and spoons go into the sink where the saucepan is filled with water. Kitchen light goes out, the folded newspaper goes under my left armpit, and the tray gets carried into the bedroom and is placed on Marilyn's night table.

By now Marilyn is usually up, and has completed her own morning rituals in the master bathroom. The front section of the newspaper, opened to the page with editorials and letters to the editor, is placed on Marilyn's side of the bed, the rest of it on my side, and I make a first trip around the foot of the bed to put my coffee mug, a spoon, a glass of grapefruit juice, and a multivitamin pill and iron pill in their designated spots on my bedside table. If the light isn't yet on above Marilyn's side of the bed, I go back to the door to flick on the switch for it, then back to Marilyn's night table to pick up my bowl of gruel and carefully carry it around the foot of the bed to deliver it to its accustomed spot on my night table.

By now Marilyn is back in bed, sitting up with her usual bolster at her back, and she has started reading letters to the editor in the *Boulder Camera*. I get back into bed with my pillow placed upright against the wall at my back, and start reading the local news, weather, and other features while we're both sitting up comfortably in bed. Meantime, I swallow the vitamin pill and iron pill, sip coffee, and start eating my bowl of gruel. Marilyn's mug of coffee had been placed on a coaster next to the breakfast tray on her bedside table, with the handle turned toward her so that she can easily reach it.

At some point, perhaps about 15 minutes after delivery of the tray, Marilyn gets out of bed, pours some of the cereal into her bowl and then adds the milk, raises her small round breakfast tray from the much larger breakfast tray on her night table, and hands it to me. She gets back in bed while I hold her little tray,

I-28 The view at breakfast: treasures on the west wall of our bedroom *(family archives)*

and then I give it back to her once she is settled again, the blankets are straightened, and the newspaper is readily available to her while she eats her cereal, drinks her grapefruit juice, and finishes her coffee.

By about 9 am, Marilyn's small tray is back on her night table on top of the larger breakfast tray, and I hand her successively my bowl, mug, and juice glass to be placed back on to the larger breakfast tray (each time with a "thank you" from me).

The large breakfast tray with all the breakfast paraphernalia is brought to the kitchen and placed on the counter next to the sink. Remains of the cold cereal Marilyn chose to leave there are poured from the pitcher back into the Total box in the refrigerator; the last drops in the small milk pitcher are poured into Marilyn's mug, as are the dregs of a few drips of milk from her cereal bowl; one of the small juice glasses is emptied (a few drops) into the other; and I enjoy the drops of remaining juice and the drops of milk mixed with the dregs of Marilyn's international coffee. All the breakfast dishes are placed in the kitchen sink, and the trays go back to their vertical resting place to the left of the refrigerator against the wall on the floor.

Next is a "fruit hunt." After putting antiperspirant under my armpits and using the electric razor, a present from Marilyn many years ago, for a quick shave (now only every other day—and the razor keeps its charge for an amazing four or five months), I get dressed and pick up a paper plate from the cabinet above the kitchen sink. At 9 am most mornings, the dining room staff bring out a large bowl of cut-up fruit and some pastries and deliver these to the "lounge" just a short distance from our apartment. By 9:15 or 9:20 most if not all the fruit is gone, but if I get there early enough, I usually can scoop up some fruit onto the paper plate I brought from the apartment. On rare occasions, I might also take a piece or two of the pastry.

Back in the apartment, the fruit is placed in an empty plastic peanut butter jar with a wide screw-on lid, and goes into a reserved spot on the second shelf in the refrigerator (and the pastry, if any, is also refrigerated, in a plastic bag). The fruit then can become part of a typical at-home lunch. While I next wash the breakfast dishes (with each item placed routinely into its usual spot in the dish-drying rack), Marilyn typically makes the bed in a meticulous, artistic way that makes it look elegant and inviting.

Lunch usually consists of some fruit for both of us, a small piece of bread (saved from a breakfast in a restaurant) covered with peanut butter for me, and a crisp Scandinavian rye knäckebröd slice for Marilyn, with a choice of smoked summer sausage and one or more cheeses from the refrigerator (usually we have brie, mozzarella, Jarlsberg, and Havarti, and sometimes Swiss, Jarlsberg light, and even a Cambozola) placed upon it. Sometimes Marilyn spreads a special Mediterranean fig concoction on her brie.

I do just about all of the cooking that we do at home, and I still enjoy "playing with food": shopping, growing some of our own vegetables, cooking and freezing oversupplies, and preparing meals. We do have many meals each week in the fine dining room at our retirement community (which is located very close to our apartment), almost all of them lunches or dinners; starting in January, 2017, our monthly rent includes all lunches and dinners in the big Meridian dining room, so now we eat fewer meals in our apartment.

One other ritual is still smoking my pipe. When we first came to the Meridian, I was permitted to smoke in our apartment (although the rules prohibited smoking in any of the "public areas" of the facility). About a year after we got

here, the executive director took me courteously aside at one point, and mentioned discreetly that several residents had complained about my "tobacco aroma," and about a stale smoke odor outside our apartment in the hallway. When I asked her how long after a smoke I should wait before engaging in any community activity, she suggested that about 15 minutes should be long enough, and she also recommended some breath strips that I might use if the time

I-29 My pipe drying at the corner of the patio *(family archives)*

after a smoke is less than a quarter of an hour. (I've now been using them for several years if time after a smoke is short.) She also had one of the maintenance handymen bring a large portable fan, with smoke absorber, into our apartment.

Then some time later, when our community was bought by a large company, Brookdale, a new general policy was enacted, prohibiting smoking anywhere indoors in the facility. Consultation with the executive director ended in her decision that since the contract we had signed permitted me to smoke in our apartment, I should still feel free to do so since the new policy could not be made effective retroactively.

But what with the earlier complaints and this new policy, I changed my pattern a few years ago and now I no longer smoke inside our apartment but only outside on our patio when we're home, and I don't carry my pipe or my tobacco in my clothes while in other locations at the Meridian. After a few months I asked the executive director whether there had been any further comments or complaints from staff or fellow residents about the tobacco smell, and she answered, clearly very pleased, that there had not. And the smoke-absorbing portable fan was removed again from our apartment.

My outdoor patio "smoking lounge" could not be any more pleasant, efficient, and inviting. We have the redwood picnic table with benches which I had made decades ago and several plastic armchairs and tables on the patio, and the view from any of those chairs could not be more peaceful or serene: the large expanse of well-kept lawn, the few beautiful trees, the mountains, flower gardens and vegetable patches, and then several hundred feet away to the west the church parking lot (where there rarely are any cars, but occasionally a hiker or a skateboarder or two) and the east wall of the low church. The lawn slopes up from the patio some five feet to the south and ten or more to the west, so that no streets are visible from the patio, but only a rare and barely discernible vehicle on a road a good four or so blocks away to the south and southwest in the quiet residential neighborhood. The curving cement path through our almost private huge backyard, to the west of our patio, sometimes has a walking resident or a dog walker on it, and the few gardeners occasionally come out to work in their little gardens a good hundred feet or more southwest of our patio.

I-30 Marilyn on our patio in summer *(family archives)*

The privacy of our patio means that I can go out on it any time day or night, whether dressed or in my bathrobe, and know that it is unlikely that anyone will see me there.

Another major unforeseen advantage is that the balcony above our little 8'x12' patio keeps rain and snow off of the three or four feet immediately west of our glass sliding door. While the floor of the balcony above has cracks between its boards, permitting rain to fall on the western half or so of the patio (and watering the house plants kept there in the warm season), an overhanging roof above the balcony prevents rain from reaching the eastern part of the patio, where the plastic armchairs are near the sliding glass door, keeping the inner part of the patio from getting wet. So rain or shine (or snow), I have a private, dry, pleasant, and inviting place year 'round to sit when smoking my three or four decades old corn-cob pipe. I do it probably some ten or fifteen times a day.

And there are also places on the patio furniture where I can set up my pipe, taken apart, in the afternoon sun that bathes the patio, to give the pipe a good solar drying, as pictured on page 541, along with the brown leather tobacco pouch my namesake grandson made for me when he was 12 years old, with an elaborate, ornate "OPA" engraved on it. The problems produced by my modest pipe-smoking addiction, if there were any, seem to have been pretty well solved.

Obviously there have been other rituals to fit our life style in our new environs. I have read more books, mostly biographies, out loud to Marilyn than I used to before we moved into the Meridian. We have taken part in many of the pleasant activities made available by our conscientious and competent resident program director; I have been involved in many more of them than Marilyn, although she too participates in a lot of them. There are several weekly exercise sessions that we both attend, a weekly coffee hour in which the following week's scheduled activities are described as well as the four or five movies to be shown that week (often older classics, many of which we go to), monthly meetings with the executive director and the resident program director, biweekly "menu chats" with the dining room chef, monthly French (but no longer any German) table luncheons, a weekly Friday afternoon cocktail party, a monthly "men's social" with drinks and hors d'oeuvres, weekly bridge games (where I've now done so well that I'm now more than $60 ahead—you need to ante a quarter each day you play), documentary film series, weekly current events discussions, a monthly sing-along, and various outings for which the Meridian provides van service.

There's also a "residential council," to which I was elected a couple of years after moving in and of which I was for two years elected president; it meets monthly. Every month for two years, there was a "theme dinner" featuring the cuisine of a particular country—and since Marilyn has slides from trips to more than 70 countries, for those two years she was hosting slide shows almost every month about the country featured that month in the cuisine.

The new and continuing rituals have filled our days in very pleasant, rewarding ways. And we're still wondering when we might eventually find those "dull moments" to which we thought years ago we might be looking forward when we finally were fully retired. They haven't arrived yet. It has been a very fulfilling time, and we're enjoying it. Life continues to be a greatly appreciated miraculous blessing, for which I am immensely grateful.

I-31 Me in 2019 *(courtesy of John Pregulman)*

The manufacturer's authorised representative in the EU is Springer
Nature Customer Service Centre GmbH, Europaplatz 3, 69115 Heidelberg,
Germany. If you have any concerns regarding our products, please
contact ProductSafety@springernature.com

Printed and bound by CPI Group (UK) Ltd, Croydon, CR0 4YY
27/04/2026
02097971-0003